Ocean Law and Policy of the People's Republic of China

Yongming Jin

Ocean Law and Policy of the People's Republic of China

知识产权出版社
全国百佳图书出版单位

Springer

Yongming Jin
School of International Affairs and Public Administration
Ocean University of China
Qingdao, Shandong, China

Translated by
Qi Xu
Law School/Intellectual Property College
Jinan University
Guangzhou, China

ISBN 978-981-95-3165-3 ISBN 978-981-95-3166-0 (eBook)
https://doi.org/10.1007/978-981-95-3166-0

Jointly published with Intellectual Property Publishing House
The print edition is not for sale in China (Mainland). Customers from China (Mainland) please order the print book from: Intellectual Property Publishing House.

ISBN of the Co-publisher's edition: 978-751-30-6845-1
Translation from the Chinese Simplified language edition: "新中国的海洋政策与法律制度" by Yongming Jin, © Intellectual Property Publishing House Co., Ltd. 2020. Published by Intellectual Property Publishing House Co., Ltd.. All Rights Reserved.

This Springer imprint is published by the registered company Springer Nature Singapore Pte Ltd.
The registered company address is: 152 Beach Road, #21-01/04 Gateway East, Singapore 189721, Singapore

Foreword

On the 70th anniversary of the founding of New China, a systematic review of the theory and practice of China's ocean policy and legal system is important in accelerating China's efforts to build a strong maritime state and safeguard its national sovereignty, security, and development interests.

The construction and improvement of New China's ocean policy and legal system is an obligation as a party to the United Nations Convention on the Law of the Sea (UNCLOS) and a requirement to integrate international ocean rules into domestic law. Bringing domestic law in line with the principles and systems of international laws and adhering to the demand by the international community for the rule of law at the international level is necessary to realize the goal of "governing the sea in accordance with the law" and contribute to building a strong maritime nation.

China has adopted a transformative approach in incorporating the international rules of the sea into domestic law, that is, by incorporating the principles and institutions of the international law of the sea into domestic laws by legislation, which has become an integral part of domestic law, constitutes China's legal system for the oceans and seas.

At the same time, in the process of incorporating international maritime rules into domestic law, China should base legislation on the principles and institutions of the international law of the sea, particularly those regulated by the UNCLOS, which represents the foundation of modern law of the sea. To this end, this article first describes China's policies and institutions in the field of oceans and seas by providing an overview of the development of the UNCLOS system, its basic features, and important principles. Second, it summarizes China's achievements and challenges in the practice of the oceans and seas, especially in the area of legislation. Third, it identifies the major challenges faced by China in accelerating the construction of a strong maritime country. Finally, it analyzes China's further participation in international maritime rule-making and proposes a number of countermeasures to improve China's maritime legal system.

Qing Dao, China Yongming Jin

About the Author

Yongming Jin, born in September 1966 in Shaoxing, Zhejiang Province, is a doctor of jurisprudence and a postdoctoral fellow in theoretical economics. His current research interests are the international law of the sea.

Currently, he is a Distinguished Professor for Fanrong Scholars Program and doctoral supervisor at the School of International Affairs and Public Administration, and a senior researcher at the Institute of Ocean Development, all at the Ocean University of China.

Previously, he was a researcher at the Institute of Law of the Shanghai Academy of Social Sciences. He has been a visiting scholar at Hiroshima University, Kyoto Sangyo University, the Sasakawa Peace Foundation of Japan, Waseda University, and the University of Tokyo.

His representative monographs are as follows: *Theoretical Studies on China's Law of the Sea* (first edition, 2014; updated edition, 2016);*Current Review of Ocean Issues* (1st–2nd series) (Chinese edition, 2015, 2018; English edition, 2017, 2019); *Research on China's Strategy for a Stronger Ocean State in the New Era* (2018); and *New China's Ocean Policies and Legal System* (2020).

About the Translator

Qi Xu is currently an associate professor at the Law School of Jinan University. He serves as the assistant to the dean of the law school and director of the law department. He was awarded the doctorate degree from the University of Groningen in the Netherlands.

His scholarly pursuits primarily concentrate on international law, law of the sea, and ocean governance. He has published some articles in leading international journals such as the Chinese Journal of International Law, Ocean Development & International Law, Marine Policy, and Ocean & Coastal Management, among others.

Contents

Abbreviations

AIIB	Asian Infrastructure Investment Bank
ARP	Armed Police Force
ASEAN	Association of Southeast Asian Nations
BBNJ	Biodiversity of Areas Beyond National Jurisdiction
BRI	Belt and Road Initiative
CCFA	Central Commission for Foreign Affairs
CCG	China Coast Guard
CIIE	China International Import Expo
CLCS	Commission on the Limits of the Continental Shelf
CMS	China Marine Surveillance
COC	Code of Conduct in the South China Sea
CPC	Communist Party of China
DOC	Declaration on the Conduct of Parties in the South China Sea
DOD	Department of Defense
ECS	East China Sea
EEZ	Exclusive Economic Zone
EU	European Union
FON	Freedom of Navigation
FONP	Freedom of Navigation Program
GAC	General Administration of Customs of the People's Republic of China
GDP	Gross Domestic Product
GMP	Gross Marine Product
ICJ	International Court of Justice
IMO	International Maritime Organization
ISA	International Seabed Authority
ITLOS	International Tribunal for the Law of the Sea
MARA	Ministry of Agriculture and Rural Development of the People's Republic of China

MEE	Ministry of Ecology and Environment of the People's Republic of China
MEP	Ministry of Environmental Protection of the People's Republic of China
MFA	Ministry of Foreign Affairs of the People's Republic of China
MIIT	Ministry of Industry and Information Technology of the People's Republic of China
MLR	Ministry of Land and Resources of the People's Republic of China
MND	Ministry of National Defense of the People's Republic of China
MNR	Ministry of Natural Resources of the People's Republic of China
MOA	Ministry of Agriculture of the People's Republic of China
MOFCOM	Ministry of Commerce of the People's Republic of China
MOHURD	Ministry of Housing and Urban-Rural Development of the People's Republic of China
MOST	Ministry of Science and Technology of the People's Republic of China
MOT	Ministry of Transport of the People's Republic of China
MPS	Ministry of Public Security of the People's Republic of China
MWR	Ministry of Water Resources of the People's Republic of China
NASG	National Administration of Surveying, Mapping and Geoinformation
NCHA	National Cultural Heritage Administration
NDRC	National Development and Reform Commission
NFGA	National Forestry and Grassland Administration
NOC	National Ocean Committee
NPC	National People's Congress
NTA	National Tourism Administration
PAP	Chinese People's Armed Police Force
PLAN	Chinese People's Liberation Army Navy
PRC	People's Republic of China
SCIO	State Council Information Office of China
SCS	South China Sea
SOA	State Oceanic Administration
SRTA	Silk Road Think Tank Association
UK	United Kingdom
UN	United Nations
UNCLOS/Convention	United Nations Convention on the Law of the Sea
UNGA	United Nations General Assembly
UNSC	United Nations Security Council

US/U.S.	United States
USS	United States Ship
USSR	Union of Soviet Socialist Republics
VCLT	Vienna Convention on the Law of Treaties

Chapter 1
Formation and Development of International Ocean Rules

On the occasion of the 70th anniversary of the founding of New China, reviewing the legislative and development process of the United Nations (UN) in the field of oceans has certain reference and enlightening significance for us to correctly understand and comprehend the maritime order and system, and deal with current maritime disputes.

The main contribution of the UN in the field of the sea lies in the organization and codification of the laws of the sea, symbolized by the formulation of the Geneva Convention on the Law of the Sea and the UNCLOS, which, in a narrow sense, constitute the modern international law of the sea. In particular, the formulation and implementation of the UNCLOS have played an irreplaceable and significant role in establishing a legal order for the sea; facilitating international traffic, and promoting the peaceful use of the sea, the equitable and effective use of marine resources, the conservation of marine living resources; and the study, protection, and preservation of the marine environment.[1] In view of the importance of the UNCLOS, it has been dubbed the "Constitution for the Oceans" and has become a universal legal document that comprehensively regulates the oceans. However, with the implementation of the UNCLOS, especially the increasing demand for ocean space and resources by countries, the development of marine technology, and the emergence of some unforeseen and ambiguous normative issues in the UNCLOS, new challenges have been posed to the law of the sea system, and the need for continuous enrichment and improvement has emerged.

[1] See the Preamble to the UNCLOS.

Y. Jin, *Ocean Law and Policy of the People's Republic of China*,
https://doi.org/10.1007/978-981-95-3166-0_1

1.1 History and Achievements of the UN in the Codification of the Law of the Sea

Under the UN Charter, the General Assembly, a principal organ of the UN, is mandated to "initiate studies and make recommendations for the purpose of encouraging the progressive development of international law and its codification".[2] Therefore, developing and codifying the international law of the sea falls within the mandate of the General Assembly.[3]

Codifying the law of the sea means the international development of the principles, rules, regulations, and institutions related to the sea into conventions (treaties) according to their nature and type, such that states may take measures in accordance with the procedure for entering the treaties in international law into force. The purpose is to determine the legal regime governing various maritime regions and regulate the rights and obligations of states regarding the usage and exploitation of the sea.[4]

The law of the sea has been codified by the UN primarily through discussions and deliberations at conferences and concluding treaties. In this context, the four important conferences are the Hague Conference on the Codification of International Law, convened by the League of Nations in 1930, and the three conferences on the law of the sea convened under the auspices of the UN.

---

[2] See Article 7(1) and Article 13(1) of the UN Charter.

[3] In 1947, the UN General Assembly decided to establish the International Law Commission (ILC) with a specific mandate to "initiate studies and make recommendations for the purpose of encouraging the progressive development of international law and its codification". The ILC may codify such matters as it deems appropriate, the resulting draft treaties may be submitted to the UN General Assembly (UNGA). The UNGA may organize a United Nations diplomatic conference or consider the draft treaty if it deems the draft appropriate. The ILC has achieved some success in codification. Examples include Four Geneva Conventions on the Law of the Sea in 1958, the Convention on the Reduction of Statelessness and the Vienna Convention on Diplomatic Relations in 1961, the Vienna Convention on Consular Relations in 1963, the Vienna Convention on the Law of Treaties and the Convention on Special Diplomatic Missions in 1969, the Convention on the Prevention and Punishment of Crimes Against Internationally Protected Persons, including Diplomatic Agents in 1973, the Vienna Convention on Succession of States in Respect of Treaties in 1978, the Vienna Convention on Succession of States in Respect of Treaties in 1983, the Convention on the Law of Treaties in 1972, the Vienna Convention on Succession of States in respect of Treaties in 1978, the Vienna Convention on Succession of States in respect of State Property, Archives and Debts in 1983, the Vienna Convention on the Law of Treaties between States and International Organizations or between International Organizations in 1986, and the Statute of the International Criminal Court in 1998.

[4] See Min, Wei, 1987. *The law of the sea*. Beijing: Law Press. p. 12.

1.1.1 Hague Conference on the Codification of International Law

The Conference on the Codification of International Law convened by the League of Nations was held at Hague from March 13 to April 12, 1930. The territorial sea was one of the three major issues discussed at the Conference. Although little was achieved in terms of the codification of the law of the sea due to the states' divergent views on the breadth of the territorial sea and the establishment of the contiguous zone, it was the first large-scale conference in the history of international law, including the law of the sea, in which governments participated. The draft "Legal Status of the Territorial Sea" proposed by the participants laid the initial foundation for the subsequent codification of the law of the sea.[5]

1.1.2 First UN Conference on the Law of the Sea

The First UN Conference on the Law of the Sea was convened in Geneva between February 24 and April 27, 1958. The outcome of the conference was four conventions (the Convention on the Territorial Sea and the Contiguous Zone, the Convention on the High Seas, the Convention on Fishing and the Conservation of the Living Resources of the High Seas, and the Convention on the Continental Shelf, or the "Geneva Conventions on the Law of the Sea") and an Optional Protocol of Signature concerning the Compulsory Settlement of Disputes arising from these conventions.[6] These comprise the body of the 1958 Geneva Convention on the Law of the Sea.

However, because many Asian and African countries had not yet gained independence at the time and, thus, were unable to participate, the Geneva Conventions on the Law of the Sea failed to faithfully reflect the interests of most developing countries, and certain provisions favored the few major maritime countries. For example, Article 1 of the Convention on the Continental Shelf uses two criteria to define the continental shelf: a depth of 200 m or, beyond that limit, to where the depth of the superjacent waters admits of the exploitation of the natural resources of the said areas (i.e., the criterion of exploitability). With regard to this criterion, the extent to which the continental shelf can be extended is not only open to different interpretations but also depends on the technological capabilities of the coastal state. Such provisions

---

[5] See Min, Wei, 1987. *The law of the sea.* Beijing: Law Press. pp. 13–15; Zhonghai, Zhou. 1987. *International law of the sea.* Beijing: China University of Political Science and Law Press. p. 2, 6.

[6] The dates of entry into force of the four Geneva Conventions on the Law of the Sea and their Protocols are as follows: the Convention on the High Seas and the Optional Protocol of Signature concerning the Compulsory Settlement of Disputes: September 30, 1962; the Convention on the Continental Shelf: June 10, 1964; the Convention on the Territorial Sea and the Contiguous Zone: September 10, 1964; and the Convention on Fishing and the Conservation of the Living Resources of the High Seas: March 20, 1966. See Min, Wei. 1987. *Law of the sea.* Beijing: Law Press. p. 17.

clearly favor a few major maritime countries to the detriment of developing countries. The greatest shortcoming of the Geneva Conventions on the Law of the Sea is the failure of the states to reach an agreement on the breadth of the territorial sea.

1.1.3 Second UN Conference on the Law of the Sea

The second UN conference was convened in Geneva from March 17 to April 17, 1960, with the aim of resolving the issues of the breadth of the territorial sea and the limits of fishing zones. However, as there were major differences among states regarding these matters, the meeting ended inconclusively. As the interval between this meeting and the first UN Conference on the Law of the Sea was too short, and the meeting itself was very brief, it was not possible to coordinate the views of states and reach an agreement.

1.1.4 Third UN Conference on the Law of the Sea

In order to resolve the outstanding issues in the previous two meetings, especially the modification of the exploitable standards for territorial sea width and continental shelf, and in view of the development of marine resource exploration and development technology, developed countries are increasingly exploiting seabed resources. Therefore, developing countries represented by Malta have proposed the establishment of an international seabed system, accelerating the convening of the third United Nations Conference on the Law of the Sea.[7]

The Third UN Conference on the Law of the Sea opened in New York on December 3, 1973, and lasted for nine years until its signing on December 10, 1982, with a total of 11 sessions and 16 meetings. The outcome of the conference was the formulation of the UNCLOS (which entered into force on November 16, 1994). Hereinafter referred to as "the Convention." It consists of a preamble, 17 parts containing 320

[7] On August 17, 1967, Ambassador Pardo of Malta, with an explanatory memorandum, requested for the inclusion of a supplementary item in the agenda of the 22nd session of the UNGA, that is, "Declarations and treaties concerning the reservation exclusively for peaceful purposes of the sea-bed and the ocean floor and the subsoil thereof, underlying the high seas beyond the limits of present national jurisdiction and the use of their resources in the interests of mankind." In response, the General Assembly adopted Resolution 2340 (December 18, 1967), establishing the Ad Hoc Committee to Study the Peaceful Uses of the Sea-bed and the Ocean Floor Beyond the Limits of National Jurisdiction, comprising 35 member States, and initiated a study on the international seabed regime. At the 25th session of the UNGA in 1970, Resolution 2750 was adopted. The resolution comprises three parts, namely, Resolution 2750A, Resolution 2750B, and Resolution 2750C. Resolution 2750C convened the Third United Nations Conference on the Law of the Sea in 1973 to conduct a comprehensive study of various aspects of the law of the sea. See Yongming, Jin. 2006. *Studies on the international seabed regime*. Beijing: Xinhua Publishing House. pp. 7–23.

articles, and 9 annexes totaling 446 articles. These constitute the basic elements of the Convention system.[8]

With regard to the relationship between the UNCLOS system and the Geneva Convention on the Law of the Sea, Article 311(1) of the Convention provides that, "This Convention shall prevail, as between States Parties, over the Geneva Conventions on the Law of the Sea of 29 April 1958."

1.2 Basic Characteristics and Perfection of the System of the Convention

As noted above, the Convention is a universal legal instrument that comprehensively regulates the sea. One of the hallmarks of its universality is the significant number of states that have ratified the Convention, which currently stands at 168, including the European Union (EU).[9] The Convention's universality is determined by its content and character.

1.2.1 Basic Characteristics of the Convention

The Convention is characterized by the following six features: First, it establishes the maximum extent of the breadth of the territorial sea, as exemplified by Article 3, which states that states may establish the territorial sea at a maximum of 12 nautical miles.

Second, the scope of maritime areas was refined according to their status, namely, internal waters, the territorial sea, the contiguous zone, archipelagic waters, the exclusive economic zone (EEZ)/continental shelf, the high seas, and the international seabed area. This definition changed the traditional dualistic view of the high seas as being outside the territorial sea.[10]

Third, the criteria or scope of the continental shelf regime was modified, and Commission on the Limits of the Continental Shelf (CLCS) was created. As mentioned above, Article 1 of the Convention on the Continental Shelf establishes the criterion of exploitability at 200-m water depth. In turn, pursuant to Article 76(1), the Convention adopts the natural prolongation standard or the distance standard of 200 nautical miles for the continental shelf, greatly expanding the jurisdiction

---

[8] For example, Article 318 of the UNCLOS provides that "The Annexes form an integral part of this Convention and, unless expressly provided otherwise, a reference to this Convention or to one of its Parts includes a reference to the Annexes relating thereto."

[9] See UNCLOS. UN. http://www.un.org/depts/los/reference_files/status2018.pdf, accessed January 21, 2019.

[10] For example, Article 1 of the Convention on the High Seas provides that the term "high seas" means "all parts of the sea that are not included in the territorial sea or in the internal waters of a State."

of coastal states over the continental shelf. Simultaneously, the Convention made provisions to limit the extent of coastal states' continental shelf, namely, the outer limits of the continental shelf. Its content is manifested in three aspects: first, restrictions on the limit distance; second, restrictions on the limit-setting procedure; and third, restrictions on the exploitation of non-living resources.[11] Furthermore, to effectively comply with the outer continental shelf regime, the Convention established the CLCS.[12]

Fourth, the EEZ regime was established with four main elements. (1) Regarding the scope of the exclusive economic zone, according to Articles 55 and 57 of the Convention, the EEZ is an area beyond and adjacent to the territorial sea, which should not extend beyond 200 nautical miles from the baseline from which the breadth of the territorial sea is measured. (2) Regarding the delimitation of the exclusive economic zone, this is mainly stipulated in Article 74 of the Convention. From its content, it can be seen that the delimitation of the EEZ does not mention the principle of equidistance or median line, nor does it mention the principle of equity, but only emphasizes the importance of relevant countries delimiting the boundary according to the agreement and the result of the delimitation being fair. (3) Regarding the rights of states in the EEZ, it includes two aspects: one is the rights of the coastal state in the EEZ; the other is the rights of other states in the EEZ.[13] (4) A preparatory stipulation on conflicts regarding the attribution of rights and jurisdiction in the EEZ lies in, for example, Article 59 of the Convention.

Fifth, a regime for the international seabed area was created, and a specialized body was established. The Convention established a regime for the international seabed area (the Area) based on the principle of "the common heritage of mankind." For example, Article 136 of the Convention provides that the Area and its resources are the common heritage of mankind. The establishment of the legal status of the principle of the common heritage of mankind in the Area is an outcome of the struggle against the application of the principles of *terra nullius*, the property of the community, and the freedom of the high seas. It is also the outcome or product of the extensive solidarity and cooperation of the third world, especially the Group of 77, at the Third UN Conference on the Law of the Sea.

It should further be noted that the Convention established the International Seabed Authority (ISA) as the body regulating activities in the Area. For example, Article 157(1) provides that the Authority is the organization through which states shall, in accordance with this paragraph, organize and control activities in the Area, particularly to administer its resources. At the same time, the Convention established a parallel system of exploitation of the resources of the international seabed, namely, Article 153(2).

---

[11] See UNCLOS Article 76(2)-(8), UNCLOS Annex II (CLCS), and UNCLOS Article 82.

[12] For example, Article 1 of Annex II to the UNCLOS provides that "in accordance with the provisions of article 76, a Commission on the Limits of the Continental Shelf beyond 200 nautical miles shall be established in conformity with the following articles." For the competence of the Commission on the Limits of the Continental Shelf, see Article 3 of Annex II.

[13] See UNCLOS Articles 56 and 58.

Sixth, a dispute settlement system was created, and the International Tribunal for the Law of the Sea (ITLOS) was established. To settle maritime disputes, the Convention not only provides for methods of dispute settlement but also establishes a procedure and institution for the settlement of disputes—the ITLOS. This overcomes the shortcomings of the Geneva Conventions on the Law of the Sea, which do not provide a dispute settlement mechanism but only do so in the annexed protocols.[14] The specifics are established in Part XV (Settlement of Disputes) and Annexes VI (Statute of the International Tribunal for the Law of the Sea) and VII (Arbitration) of the Convention.

1.2.2 Development and Improvement of the Convention System

In addition to the above-mentioned characteristics, the Convention also has some shortcomings. For example, the attribution of residual rights in the EEZ is unclear. The concept of the regime of islands, especially its legal elements, is vague. The principle of delimitation of the EEZ and the continental shelf lacks operability. The system of resource exploitation in the international seabed area takes too much care of a few large industrial countries. These issues give rise to confrontation and disagreement among the states; thus, there is still a need to revise and perfect the Convention. Nevertheless, it must be acknowledged that the code is a comprehensive regulation of maritime issues that must be complied with by all states.

Furthermore, following the establishment of the Convention and rectifying its shortcomings, including improving the norms governing deep-sea prospecting and fulfilling the Convention's requirement of universality, the United Nations General Assembly (UNGA) adopted the Agreement Relating to the Implementation of Part XI of the United Nations (which entered into force on July 28, 1996, referred to as the Part XI Implementing Agreement) on July 28, 1994, which has been ratified by 150 states to date. At the same time, to address the problem of overfishing on the high seas, the UNGA adopted the Agreement for the Implementation of the Provisions of the United Nations Convention on the Law of the Sea of 10 December 1982 Relating to the Conservation and Management of Straddling Fish Stocks and Highly Migratory Fish Stocks on August 4, 1995 (which entered into force on December 11, 2001, referred to as the "Straddling Fish Stocks Implementing Agreement"), which has been ratified by 89 states to date.[15] This further completes the body of the Convention.

---

[14] The Optional Protocol of Signature concerning the Compulsory Settlement of Disputes is not an integral part of the Geneva Conventions on the Law of the Sea, as Article 5 provides that, "This Protocol shall remain open for signature by all States who become Parties to any Convention on the Law of the Sea adopted by the United Nations Conference on the Law of the Sea and is subject to ratification, where necessary, according to the constitutional requirements of the signatory States."

[15] See UNCLOS. UN. http://www.un.org/depts/los/reference_files/status2018.pdf, accessed January 21, 2019.

The relationship between the Convention and the two implementing agreements can be divided into two aspects. Regarding the relationship between the Convention (Part XI) and the Part XI Implementing Agreement, Article 2 of the Part XI Implementing Agreement provides that "The provisions of this Agreement and Part XI shall be interpreted and applied together as a single instrument. In the event of any inconsistency between this Agreement and Part XI, the provisions of this Agreement shall prevail." Thus, the Part XI Implementing Agreement modifies the provisions of Part XI of the Convention and gives precedence to the Convention.

Second, regarding the relationship between the Convention and the Straddling Fish Stocks Implementation Agreement, Article 4 of the Straddling Fish Stocks Implementation Agreement provides that "Nothing in this Agreement shall prejudice the rights, jurisdiction, and duties of States under the Convention. This Agreement shall be interpreted and applied in the context of and in a manner consistent with the Convention." According to Article 2, "The objective of this Agreement is to ensure the long-term conservation and sustainable use of straddling fish stocks and highly migratory fish stocks through effective implementation of the relevant provisions of the Convention." As such, the Straddling Fish Stocks Implementation Agreement is complementary to the regime assisting in the implementation of the norms of the Convention.[16]

In conclusion, the Convention, which was adopted in 1982 and entered into force in 1994, has become an international treaty that comprehensively regulates ocean issues and is universally obeyed. However, despite certain developments and improvements, the Convention continues to face some challenges.

1.3 Basic Contents and Important Principles of the System of the Convention

1.3.1 Basic Contents of the Convention System

From the development process of the Convention system, its content and institutional construction can be summarized as follows:

First, the elements of a foundational/general and principled nature are reflected in the Preamble and Part I (Preamble: Use of Terms and Scope of Application), Part XVI (General Provisions), Part XVII (Final Provisions), Annex I (Highly Migratory Species), and Annex IX (Participation by International Organizations). Second, the regimes governing the various maritime areas (including waters and continental shelf, etc.) are embodied in Part II (Territorial Sea and Contiguous Zone), Part V (EEZ), Part VI (Continental Shelf) and Annex II (Commission on the

[16] On the separability of treaty provisions and the implied termination or suspension of the operation of a treaty by virtue of a subsequent treaty, see Articles 44 and 59 of the Vienna Convention on the Law of Treaties (VCLT).

Limits of the Continental Shelf), Part VII (High Seas), Part XI (The Area), Annex III (Basic Conditions of Prospecting, Exploration and Exploitation), Annex IV (Statute of the Enterprise), Part XI Implementing Agreement and the Straddling Fish Stocks Implementing Agreement.

Third, the functional regimes of the sea include Part III (Straits Used for International Navigation), Part XII (Protection and Preservation of the Marine Environment), Part XIII (Marine Scientific Research), and Part XIV (Development and Transfer of Marine Technology).

Fourth, the special regimes of the sea include Part IV (Archipelagic States), Part VIII (Regime of Islands), Part IX (Enclosed or Semi-Enclosed Seas), and Part X (Rights of Access of Landlocked States to and from the Sea and Freedom of Transit).

Fifth, the dispute settlement system for the sea contains Part XV (Settlement of Disputes), Annex V (Conciliation), Annex VI (Statute of the International Tribunal for the Law of the Sea), Annex VII (Arbitration), and Annex VIII (Special Arbitration).

As is the case with the stages of development of the Convention, the results of the theoretical and practical development of the three main organizational bodies of the Convention (the CLCS, the ISA, and the ITLOS) also constitute important parts of the Convention system.[17]

1.3.2 Some Basic Principles of the Convention System

According to the Preamble to the Convention, the Convention's purpose is to establish a legal order for the sea that promotes the peaceful use of the sea, the equitable and efficient utilization of its resources, and the protection of its living resources and the marine environment, with due regard for the sovereignty of all states. In the author's view, the following principles underlie the Convention system.

(1) Principle that the land dominates the sea. Although the concept of the land's dominion over the sea is not directly regulated or defined, there are numerous articles embodying this principle, for instance, including Articles 3, 5, 13, 33(2), 47, 48, 57, 76(1) and (5), and 121 (2)–(3). It is generally accepted that this principle began in the North Sea Continental Shelf case in 1969) and was confirmed in the Aegean Sea Continental Shelf case in 1978 and the Black Sea case of 2009. In the North Sea Continental Shelf case, the International Court of Justice (ICJ) stated that the rights of coastal states to the continental shelf are legally subordinate to and directly derived from the territorial sovereignty of the continental shelf of adjacent coastal

[17] For the development and challenges of the three major organizational bodies created by the UNCLOS, see Yongming, Jin, 2015. On development and challenge of the law of the sea. *Southeast Asian Affairs* 3 (3): 1–10. For the functions and systems of the three major organizational bodies created by the UNCLOS, see Yongming, Jin, 2011. A study of the organizational characteristics of the United Nations Convention on the Law of the Sea. *Oriental Law* 1, 22–34.

states; the continental shelf is a legal concept of applying "the principle that the land dominates the sea."[18] In the Aegean Sea Continental Shelf case, the Court noted that, in international law, the coastal state possesses the prerogative to explore and exploit resources located on the continental shelf. This reflects the coastal state's exclusive sovereignty over the land. In essence, the rights of the coastal state regarding the continental shelf are the extension of its territorial sovereignty and serve as an inherent appendage.[19]

(2) The principle of freedom of the high seas, in particular, freedom of navigation and overflight. The content of the freedom of the high seas, encompassing freedom of navigation and overflight, has evolved from four forms in the 1958 Geneva Convention on the Law of the Sea system to six freedoms within the Convention system.[20] From their content, their differences and characteristics are mainly reflected in the following three aspects.

First, there have been changes in the content and types of freedoms of the high seas. As noted above, the freedom of the high seas has evolved from four freedoms to six, for example, Article 2 of the Convention on the High Seas and Article 87 of the Convention.

Second, states are subject to certain limitations in the exercise of the four freedoms specified in the Convention, reflecting the development of the Convention from a "dualistic" (outside the territorial sea, i.e., the high seas) to a "pluralistic" (the territorial sea, archipelagic waters, the EEZ/continental shelf, and the high seas) maritime area and the diversification of interests to be protected.[21] For example, under Article 56(1) of the Convention, the coastal state has exclusive jurisdiction over the construction and utilization of artificial islands, installations and structures, and marine scientific research in the EEZ and its jurisdiction is exclusive (Articles 60(2), and 246(2), of the Convention).[22]

---

[18] See ICJ Reports, 1969, p. 51, para. 96.

[19] See ICJ Reports, 1978, pp. 3–83. See also [Japanese] Ozaki, Shigeyoshii. 1996. The Aegean Sea continental shelf case, in *Judgments and opinions of the International Court of Justice (Volume II) (1964–1993)*, eds. Ribot Hatano, Shigeyoshi Ozaki. Tokyo: Kokusai Shoin. p. 129, p. 146.

[20] For example, Article 2 of the Convention on the High Seas and Article 87 of the UNCLOS.

[21] For example, Article 1 of the Convention on the High Seas and Article 86 of the UNCLOS.

[22] In the case of marine scientific research, Article 240 of the UNCLOS sets out not only the content but also the principles, while Article 246(2) reflects an indirect definition of marine scientific research. Article 5 of the Convention on the Continental Shelf, however, divides marine scientific research into two categories according to its nature: first, basic marine research for scientific purposes only, that is, pure marine scientific research; and second, practical marine scientific research for the economic purposes of exploring and exploiting the resources of the continental shelf. The two types of marine scientific research have different requirements. In the case of pure marine scientific research, the principle of the freedom of the high seas is required for research to be conducted with the aim of publicizing the results, whereas in the case of practical marine scientific research, the consent of the coastal state should be obtained. In addition, the coastal state should not normally refuse to provide consent for purely scientific research of the physical or biological characteristics of the continental shelf, whereas the coastal state has a wide margin of discretion as to whether or not to provide consent for an application to conduct practical marine scientific research. See [Japanese] Yamamoto, Soji. 2000. A comparative study of domestic legal systems in relation to

Third, in the Convention on the High Seas and the UNCLOS, states should exercise the freedom of the high seas with "due regard" for the interests of other states.[23] For example, Articles 1 and 2 of the Convention on the Continental Shelf concerning the extent of the continental shelf and the coastal state's exercise of sovereign rights to explore and exploit natural resources break not only the dualistic structure of the high seas beyond the territorial sea but also the traditional absolutism of the freedom of the seas.

This is particularly evident in the Convention, for example, in the regimes of the EEZ and the international seabed area created within the Convention. In other words, the principle of freedom on the high seas has gone through a phase of "laissez-faire" (absolute freedom) to "due regard" (relative freedom), which has been influenced by the judgments of the ICJ.[24] Thus, "due regard" requires all states, when exercising their freedom of the high seas, to be aware of and consider the interests of other states and avoid activities that interfere with other states' exercise of the freedom of the high seas. Therefore, states must refrain from any acts that adversely affect the use of the high seas by other states.[25]

The history of the law of the sea is one of balancing the rights and interests of coastal and user states and the freedom of the high seas, especially the freedom of navigation and overflight. In other words, the history of the law of the sea is the history of mutual opposition and adjustment between the jurisdiction claimed by coastal states and the freedom of the seas claimed by others, and of the interests of coastal states and the general interests of the international community.[26]

(3) Principle of distance. The Convention provides various legal regimes for delimiting maritime spaces and areas, the main principles of which are the principles of land dominance over the sea and distance. The principle of distance plays a supplementary role to that of land dominance over the sea. At the same time, the principle of distance can be changed by modifying the relevant treaties. The maritime spaces and

---

marine scientific research in the exclusive economic zone and on the continental shelf. in *Report on a survey of domestic legal systems of various countries in response to marine scientific research in the exclusive economic zone and on the continental shelf*, ed. Japan Institute of International Studies. Tokyo: Japan Institute of International Studies. pp. 2–3.

[23] The provisions of the UNCLOS that deal with the elements of "due regard," including "reasonable regard" and "particular regard," are Articles 27(4), 56(2), 58(3), 87(2), 147–149.

[24] For example, the ICJ, in its 1974 judgment in the Fisheries Jurisdiction case, noted that the development of the international law of the sea, with the increase in the scope of fisheries activities, had resulted in the replacement of what had once been laissez-faire measures on the high seas in respect of living marine resources by the adoption of the obligation to recognize the rights of others and to take appropriate measures for the preservation of all persons in need. See [Japanese] Sakamoto, Shigeki. 2015. The impact of the expansion of the functions of regional fisheries management bodies on the development of international law: From fisheries regulation to ocean management, in *The practice of international law*, eds. Shunji Yanai, Shinya Murase. Tokyo: Shinzansha Publishing. p. 459.

[25] See Sohn, Louis B., et al. 2014. *The law of the sea in a nutshell (2nd ed.)*, (trans. Fu Kuen Chen, et al). Shanghai: Shanghai Jiao Tong University Press. p. 17.

[26] See [Japanese] Mizukami, Chiyuki. 2014. The formation of the freedom of the sea (1), *Hiroshima Law Journal* 28(1): 1–2.

areas defined in the Convention, primarily through the application of the principle of distance, are the territorial sea, the contiguous zone, the EEZ, and the continental shelf, including the outer continental shelf.[27]

In the author's view, there are three modalities involved in determining the extent of maritime spaces and areas by the Convention's member states: first, maritime areas requiring proclamation or declaration by states, such as the territorial sea, archipelagic waters, and the EEZ; second, areas that do not require a state to proclaim or declare boundaries, for example, the continental shelf within 200 nautical miles[28]; and third, areas subject to declarations of limits, recommendations, and monitoring by the relevant international bodies, for example, the continental shelf beyond 200 nautical miles. The limits of the continental shelf beyond 200 nautical miles relate to the recommendations of the CLCS. In addition, the ISA is authorized to supervise and determine mining areas for exploring and exploiting the international seabed under the Area regime (parallel exploitation regime).[29]

(4) Principle of equity. In the Convention, Articles 59, 74(1), 83(1), 82(4), and 140(2) engage with the "principle of equity." They cover three major aspects: First, Article 59 deals with disputes over unvested rights in the EEZ, especially disputes over security issues unrelated to the legislative purpose of the EEZ. For example, the question of military activities in the EEZ needs to be resolved on an equitable basis considering relevant circumstances. This issue needs to be determined by the theoretical and national practice development of the Convention system in the future. Second, Articles 74 and 83, which deal with the "equitable settlement" of the delimitation of the EEZ and the continental shelf, have been developed in international judicial practice, and a delimitation paradigm (i.e., the "three-stage delimitation method") has been established to achieve an equitable result.[30] Third, the question of "equitable sharing" and "equitable distribution" by the Authority of the benefits or finances of the non-living resources of the continental shelf beyond 200 nautical miles, which is dealt with in Articles 82 and 140, is an important issue for the ISA in the future.

(5) Principle of the common heritage of mankind. As noted above, the Area regime based on the principle of the common heritage of mankind has been established in Part XI of the Convention. For example, Article 136 provides that the Area and its resources are the common heritage of mankind. The establishment of the principle of the common heritage of mankind in the Convention not only reflects its essential requirement for maintaining and implementing the Area maritime order to achieve common management, development, and benefits, but also becomes an important

[27] For example, Articles 3, 33(2), 57, 76(1) and (4)-(5) of the UNCLOS.

[28] Article 77(3) of the UNCLOS provides that "The rights of the coastal State over the continental shelf do not depend on occupation, effective or notional, or on any express proclamation."

[29] For example, Articles 76(8) and 153 of the UNCLOS.

[30] The "three-stage delimitation method" consists of, first, drawing a provisional equidistance or median line; second, considering the relevant circumstances and exploring the need to adjust the provisional equidistance or median line to achieve an equitable result; and, finally, calibrating the ratio of the length of the coastline to the area of the allocated maritime space to determine whether it leads to an inequitable result to rectify it. See ICJ Reports, 2009, pp.101–103, paras.115–122.

principle of "non-derogate." Therefore, strengthening comprehensive management of the oceans, including managing and allocating behaviors and interests within the Area through the establishment of the ISA, has significant theoretical innovation and practical significance.[31]

In addition to the various principles, the Convention has elements such as the principles of the peaceful uses of the sea, flag state jurisdiction and universal jurisdiction, cooperation, and peaceful settlement of disputes. These elements will not be discussed here.

1.4 Developments and Challenges Since the Entry into Force of the Convention

As the Convention is the result of compromise and coordination, it is inevitable that it will have multiple problems and shortcomings.[32] In particular, the organizations established by the Convention (the CLCS, the ISA, and the ITLOS), while having evolved since the Convention entered into force, have encountered a number of problems and challenges that had not yet been considered.

1.4.1 Developments and Challenges Relating to the CLCS

It is generally believed that the CLCS, established in 1997, is a specialized body responsible for implementing the unified interpretation of the provisions of the Convention on the outer limits of the continental shelf as the main basis for all contracting parties to delineate the outer limits of the continental shelf. The method of dealing with the provisions of the Convention on the outer limits of the continental shelf is quite complex and has high scientific and technical issues.[33] Concurrently, the outer limits of the continental shelf established by a coastal state on the basis of the recommendations of the CLCS are definitive and binding.[34]

[31] For example, Articles 154, 311(6), 155, 156, 157(1), 140(2) of the UNCLOS.

[32] On the holistic content of the UNCLOS, see Duo, Ding. 2018. Exploration of the holistic problem of the United Nations Convention on the Law of the Sea under the threshold of treaty interpretation—Another comment on the arbitration case in the South China Sea of the Philippines, in *South China Sea commentary (Vol. II)*, ed. Wu Shicun, 65–77. Beijing: World Affairs Press.

[33] See Kuen Chen, Fu. 2003. *Legal issues of ocean management*, New Taipei City: Wensheng Book Store, p. 218.

[34] For example, Article 76(8) of the UNCLOS provides that "Information on the limits of the continental shelf beyond 200 nautical miles from the baselines from which the breadth of the territorial sea is measured shall be submitted by the coastal State to the Commission on the Limits of the Continental Shelf set up under Annex II on the basis of equitable geographical representation. The Commission shall make recommendations to coastal States on matters related to the establishment

To accomplish the aforementioned mandate, the CLCS meticulously governs and perpetually enhances the operations of the regime, encompassing the formulation of the Modus Operandi (February 1997), the Rules of Procedure (September 1998), the Scientific and Technical Guidelines (May 13, 1999), the Internal Code of Conduct (September 2005), and the Revised Rules of Procedure (April 17, 2008), thereby providing the prerequisites for initiating the deliberation of the submissions concerning the outer boundaries of the continental shelf.

Pursuant to Article 4 of Annex II to the Convention, a coastal state that has established the outer limits of its continental shelf beyond 200 nautical miles in accordance with Article 76 shall, within 10 years of the entry into force of the Convention for that state, submit detailed scientific and technical information to the Commission. However, due to the complexity and difficulty involved in making a submission, the eleventh Meeting of States to the Convention (2001) adopted a resolution extending the time limit for submissions; that is, the statutory 10-year time limit for submissions could be calculated from May 13, 1999, for all states that had formally ratified or acceded to the Convention prior to that date. Thus, since the first submission on the outer limits of the continental shelf of a state was made to the CLCS by the Russian Federation on December 20, 2001, as of May 13, 2009, the CLCS had received 50 national submissions.[35]

Despite the resolution on delaying the time for making submissions at the 11th Meeting of States to the Convention, submitting survey data and providing information on the continental shelf continued to be very burdensome for many developing states; thus, at the 18th Meeting of State Parties to the Convention (2008), a further resolution was adopted to ease the conditions—as long as the submission by May 13, 2009, preliminary information contained the outstanding data, the corresponding obligation would be considered fulfilled. In other words, states using the deferred application system are considered to have met their obligations by submitting preliminary information indicating the limits of the continental shelf beyond 200 nautical miles to the Secretary-General, along with an indication of the status of preparations and plans regarding the date of the application.[36]

To date, 81 submissions have been made to the CLCS, 26 of which have provided recommendations,[37] and 54 states have submitted preliminary information to the

---

of the outer limits of their continental shelf. The limits of the shelf established by a coastal State on the basis of these recommendations shall be final and binding."

[35] See Submissions, through the Secretary-General of the United Nations, to the Commission on the Limits of the Continental Shelf, pursuant to article 76, paragraph 8, of the United Nations Convention on the Law of the Sea of 10 December 1982. UN. https://www.un.org/Depts/los/clcs_new/commission_submissions.htm, accessed May 14, 2009.

[36] Decision regarding the workload of the Commission on the Continental Shelf and the ability of States, particularly developing States, to fulfill the Decision regarding the workload of the Commission on the Continental Shelf and the ability of States, particularly developing States, to fulfill the requirements of article 4 of annex II to the United Nations Convention on the Law of the Sea, as well as the decision contained in SPLOS/72, SPLOS/183.

[37] See Submissions, through the Secretary-General of the United Nations, to the Commission on the Limits of the Continental Shelf, pursuant to article 76, paragraph 8, of the United Nations

CLCS.[38] From the content and pattern of the outer continental shelf delimitation cases submitted by these countries, it can be seen that they have both individual delimitation cases and joint delimitation cases; there are both partial delimitation cases and overall delimitation cases. Concurrently, the CLCS only reviews the submitted information and data and has formed a practice of not reviewing disputed areas and making recommendations.[39] Based on its quantity, it can also be discerned that the workload of the CLCS in scrutinizing the delineation of the outer continental shelf remains substantial, and the assignment is still extremely challenging.[40]

Simultaneously, there is uncertainty regarding whether a coastal state establishes an outer continental shelf on the basis of the recommendations of the CLCS and how the limits of such outer continental shelves are to be assessed, as the Convention provides for no procedures for such a review. Furthermore, there are no procedural provisions in the Convention on how to deal with the delineation of the outer continental shelf by a coastal state that exceeds the limits recommended by the CLCS.[41] These are among the challenges confronting the CLCS.

1.4.2 Developments and Challenges Relating to the ISA

In accordance with Resolution 1 (Preparatory Commission for the International Seabed Authority and for the International Tribunal for the Law of the Sea) of Annex I to the Final Act of the Convention, the Preparatory Commission for the ISA, as

Convention on the Law of the Sea of 10 December 1982. UN. https://www.un.org/Depts/los/clcs_new/commission_submissions.htm, accessed January 21, 2019.

[38] See Submissions, through the Secretary-General of the United Nations, to the Commission on the Limits of the Continental Shelf, pursuant to article 76, paragraph 8, of the United Nations Convention on the Law of the Sea of 10 December 1982. UN. https://www.un.org/Depts/los/clcs_new/commission_submissions.htm, accessed January 21, 2019.

[39] For the submission of the outer continental shelf made by a coastal state and the recommendations of the CLCS, see Jianjun, Gao(translation) and Haiwen, Zhang (revision). 2014. *Delineation of the outer limits of the continental shelf beyond 200 nautical miles—Executive summary of the submission and summary of the recommendations of the Commission on The Limits Of The Continental Shelf*. Beijing: Ocean Press.

[40] During the 1978 preparatory discussions in the Third United Nations Conference on the Law of the Sea, it was anticipated that 33 states would be involved in the outer continental shelf, whereas in the 2009 study, 70 states were involved in the outer continental shelf, and nearly 80% of those states were developing countries. Due to the complexity and difficulty of the issue of the outer continental shelf, a trust fund was established in 2001, financed at the discretion of the states, to defray the cost of participation for the Commission on the Limits of the Continental Shelf and ensure the implementation of the outer continental shelf regime. See [Japanese] Sato, Kuni. 2013. The United Nations Convention on the Law of the Sea and Japan: Commemorating the 30th anniversary of the opening for signature and focusing on the development of two novel systems. *Journal of International Law and Diplomacy* 112(2): 89–91.

[41] See [Japanese] Koga, Mamoru. 2013. Activities and functions of the Commission on the Limits of the Continental Shelf: Developments of the law of the sea by international institutions, *Journal of International Law and Diplomacy* 112(2): 46–47.

the institution for implementing the regime for exploring and exploiting the Area resources, was established. Its main work during 1983–1994 was reflected in two aspects: first, it resolved the registration issues of seven pioneer investors, marked by the Arusha Declaration reached in 1986, which resolved the understanding reached by four pioneer investors from France, Japan, the former Soviet Union, and India on resolving overlapping application areas and allocating mining areas. Second, it passed a statement on the implementation of Resolution 2 in Annex I (Governing Preparatory Investment in Pioneer Activities Relating to Polymettallic Nodules). Based on the Arusha Declaration, the Preparatory Committee passed the Declaration on the Implementation of Resolution 2 after repeated and tense consultations in 1986. Its biggest feature is that it stipulates the time and procedures for applying for registration, promotes the registration system of pioneer investors, and is conducive to the implementation of the Area resources development system within the framework of the Convention.[42]

New developments in the ISA's regime are reflected in the following: First, at its sixth session in July 2000, it adopted the Regulations on Prospecting and Exploration for Polymetallic Nodules in the Area. Second, at its May 2010 session, the Assembly adopted the Regulations on Prospecting and Exploration for Polymetallic Sulphides in the Area. Third, the Regulations on Prospecting and Exploration for Cobalt-rich Ferromanganese Crusts in the Area were adopted in 2012. These three stipulations are distinct provisions derived from the occurrence conditions and distribution of numerous mineral resources, coupled with the conceivable effect of exploration operations on the environment and the demand for technical conditions. It can be argued that the formulation of these regulations offers a framework of systematic processes and guidelines for the exploration and exploitation activities of resources within the Area, rendering the activities within the Area more precise and refined. At the nineteenth session of the ISA in 2013, amendments to the Regulations on Prospecting and Exploration for Polymetallic Nodules in the Area were considered for adoption.[43]

In addition, on May 11, 2010, the ISA requested the Seabed Disputes Chamber of the ITLOS, to render an advisory opinion on the responsibilities and obligations of states sponsoring persons and entities with respect to activities in the Area.[44] The Seabed Disputes Chamber issued an advisory opinion on February 1, 2011, that sponsoring states shall take a precautionary approach and ensure that contractors fulfill their obligations of environmental impact assessment and the protection and

[42] See Yongming, Jin. 2011. *Monographs on ocean issues (Vol. 1)*. Beijing: Ocean Press. pp. 220–222.

[43] See Research Group of the China Institute For Marine Affairs of the State Oceanic Administration. 2014. *China's ocean development report(2014)*. Beijing: Ocean Press. pp. 21–24.

[44] For example, Article 191 of the UNCLOS provides that "The Seabed Disputes Chamber shall give advisory opinions at the request of the Assembly or the Council on legal questions arising within the scope of their activities. Such opinions shall be given as a matter of urgency."

preservation of the environment.[45] This was the first case in which the ISA utilized the Convention's advisory opinion regime.

In view of the fact that the first contracts for exploration for polymetallic nodules awarded by the ISA will expire in 2016. According to the terms of the contracts, these contracts will enter the stage of commercial development. How to evaluate their work plans and extend these contracts, how to formulate regulations for the development of these resources, and how to allocate the proceeds of resources in the Area are major issues facing the ISA. Moreover, other resources, such as biological genetic resources, have been found in the Area. How to formulate relevant regulations and how to coordinate the relationship with the Convention on Biological Diversity are also challenges facing the ISA.

1.4.3 Issues and Challenges of the ITLOS

Regarding the Convention's system for the settlement of maritime disputes, under the relevant provisions of the Convention, states are required to settle their disputes peacefully, respecting the peaceful means of settlement of disputes of their own choosing as provided for in the agreements of states, and, in accordance with the principle of the sovereign equality of states, they are granted the right to choose the means of dispute settlement.[46] For disputes concerning the interpretation or application of the Convention, any state may, at the time of signing, ratifying, or acceding to the Convention, or at any time thereafter, be free to choose in writing one or more methods, that is, to rely on the ITLOS, the ICJ, the Arbitral Tribunal and the Special Arbitral Tribunal. If the parties to the dispute have not accepted the same procedure for the settlement of the dispute, the dispute may be submitted only to arbitration as provided for in Annex VII to the Convention unless the parties have agreed otherwise. At the same time, states have the right to make a written declaration of nonacceptance of the compulsory jurisdiction of a court or tribunal of their choice regarding one or more of the categories of disputes enumerated in Article 298.[47]

Since its establishment in 1996, the ITLOS has not only developed the Statute of the International Tribunal for the Law of the Sea based on the Statute of the International Court of Justice but has received 25 cases so far.[48] Some of these have been cases of prompt release and provisional measures for vessels/crews, requests for advisory opinions by the Authority (2010–2011), maritime delimitation (2009–2012), and requests for advisory opinions (2009–2012). These changes not only

[45] Responsibilities and Obligations of States Sponsoring Persons and Entities with Respect to Activities in the Area (Request for Advisory Opinion (Request for Advisory Opinion submitted to the Seabed Disputes Chamber) (Case No. 17), Advisory Opinion of February 1, 2011, The Seabed Disputes Chamber of International Tribunal for the Law of the Sea. https://www.itlos.org/fileadmin/itlos/documents/cases/case_no_17/17_adv_op_010211_en.pdf, accessed April 27, 2015.

[46] For example, see Articles 279, 280, and 282 of the UNCLOS.

[47] See Articles 287 and 298 of the UNCLOS.

[48] See https://www.itlos.org/en/main/cases/list-of-cases/, accessed January 21, 2019.

reflect the advantages of the ITLOS in terms of speedy trials but also the diversification of the types of cases it reviews, indicating the growing importance of the ITLOS.[49]

To date, 53 states have made declarations of their choice of procedure in accordance with Article 287 of the Convention, and 38 states, including China, have submitted written declarations excluding the optional exceptions in Part XV of the Convention in accordance with Article 298.[50] For example, on August 25, 2006, China submitted a written declaration in accordance with Article 298 of the Convention to the Secretary-General, regarding disputes concerning maritime delimitation, territorial sovereignty, military activities, and law enforcement activities covered by the Convention. The Government of the People's Republic of China does not accept any of the procedures provided for in Section 2 of Part XV of the Convention with respect to all the categories of disputes referred to in paragraph 1 (a) (b) and (c) of Article 298 of the Convention.

Regarding the compulsory arbitration case initiated by the Philippines on the South China Sea (SCS) issue, the court or arbitral tribunal should not only consider whether the preconditions for the Philippines to initiate arbitration are met but also whether the matters raised are disputes over the interpretation or application of the Convention. It should also consider whether the matters raised by the Philippines are matters that China has excluded, including issues of admissibility and jurisdiction. If an award is made, enforceability and effects should also be considered.[51] Therefore, the ITLOS or the arbitral tribunal, faces severe challenges in how to handle this case to ensure its authority, independence, and rationality. The international community will pay serious attention to this, mainly focusing on whether the arbitral tribunal has admissibility and jurisdiction over the issues raised by the Philippines.[52]

---

[49] See Research Group of the Institute of Marine Development Strategy of the State Oceanic Administration. 2014. *China ocean development research report*. Beijing: Ocean Press. pp. 24–26.

[50] See Settlement of disputes mechanism. Division for Ocean Affairs and the Law of the Sea. http://www.un.org/depts/los/settlement_of_disputes/choice_procedure.htm, accessed January 21, 2019.

[51] The Ministry of Foreign Affairs is authorized to publish the content of the position paper by the Chinese Government on the issue of jurisdiction over the South China Sea Arbitration initiated by the Philippines, see Interpretation of the position paper issued by the Chinese government on the jurisdiction issue regarding the South China Sea Arbitration case initiated by the Philippines. Xinhua News Agency. http://www.gov.cn/xinwen/2014-12/07/content_2787666.htm, accessed December 8, 2014.

[52] For more on content on whether the arbitral tribunal has admissibility and jurisdiction, see Shengti, Gau. 2015. The Sino-Philippine Arbitration on South China Sea disputes: Admissibility and jurisdiction issues, *China Oceans Law Review* 1: 64–165.

1.4.4 *Issues and Challenges Concerning the Regime of Islands*

Since the Government of Japan's submission to the CLCS on November 12, 2008, regarding the outer continental shelf, including the claim of the rock of Oki-no-Tori (Oki-no Tori-shima) as a basepoint, a confrontation over the regime of islands has become apparent.[53] Japan's submission on the outer continental shelf, which claims the presence of an EEZ and continental shelf based on the rock of Oki-no-Tori (Oki-no Tori-shima), is a measure taken by Japan's one-sided understanding of the meaning of the regime of islands and has naturally met with opposition from countries such as China and the Republic of Korea.[54] Eventually, the CLCS did not make recommendations on the limits of Japan's outer continental shelf in relation to the rock of Oki-no-Tori (Oki-no Tori-shima) on April 19, 2012.[55]

Indeed, in terms of the structure of the provisions on the regime of islands, Article 121(1)-(3) of the Convention all concern the regime of islands. Specifically, paragraph 1 alludes to a comprehensive conception of islands, as elucidated by the Convention. Its deficiency lies in its exclusive delineation of the notion of islands anchored in natural attributes, and the determination of whether an island possesses a benefit from an EEZ and continental shelf becomes challenging due to this incomplete island concept that neglects other pertinent attributes such as societal and economic factors. Paragraph 2 articulates a narrow-scoped clause for islands, i.e., islands possessing equal legal standing as land territories may secure correlative maritime rights. Paragraph 3 pertains to rocks, which is not directly predicated on the notion of rocks but rather rooted in the standpoint of rock effectiveness. In other words, rocks capable of sustaining human habitation or their own economic life can, like islands, claim the EEZ and the continental shelf. Therefore, there are two types of rocks: those that can claim the EEZ and the continental shelf and those that cannot. The overall understanding of Article 121, paragraph 3, is a constraint on paragraph 2, that is,

---

[53] For the content of Japan's outer continental shelf submission, see Yongming, Jin. 2009. The contents of Japan's submission on the extended continental shelf and China's position, *China Oceans Law Review* 1: 28–39.

[54] The Permanent Mission of China to the UN submitted a written statement to the Secretary-General on February 6, 2009, in response to Japan's submission concerning the rock of Oki-no-Tori, see https://www.un.org/depts/los/clcs_new/submissions_files/jpn08/chn_6feb09_e.pdf, accessed March 12, 2009. The Republic of Korea submitted a written statement with the same content as the Chinese Government's statement on February 27, 2009, in response to the issue, see https://www.un.org/depts/los/clcs_new/submissions_files/jpn08/kor_27feb09.pdf, accessed March 12, 2009.

[55] The CLCS made recommendations only regarding the 31 square kilometers within the outer continental shelf of 740,000 square kilometers claimed by Japan. No recommendation was made regarding the portion relating to the rock of Oki-no-Tori that was objected to by China and the Republic of Korea, and the CLCS did not consider this area due to the divergent views. This, however, does not represent a rejection of the recommendations, but merely a decision made as a reservation, that is, there is a possibility that recommendations may be made in the future. See [Japanese] Koga, Mamoru. 2013. Activities and functions of the Commission on the Limits of the Continental Shelf: Developments in the law of the sea by international institutions, *Journal of International Law and Diplomacy* 112(2): 42.

not all rocks can claim the EEZ and continental shelf in the same way as the islands in paragraph 2. From Article 121, paragraph 3, it can be seen that rock reefs are a kind of island other than a narrow island, and from a broad island point of view, such rocks should also meet the island requirements.

As can be seen, Articles 121(1) to (3) have different characteristics. The provisions on the natural attributes (islands in the broader sense), social and economic attributes (islands in the narrower sense), and those without social and economic islands within the broader definition of islands (rocks) together constitute the entirety of the regime of islands. Therefore, Article 121 cannot be singularly interpreted and applied but should be understood in light of the three paragraphs of the article as a whole. Its legislative purpose is that the three paragraphs of Article 121 are provisions on the regime of islands, which is a holistic norm; however, rocks are only a special type of island, which should also meet the elements of islands.

Thus, islands, including rocks, must meet specific legal requirements to claim the interests of the EEZ and continental shelf. These requirements focus on aspects such as natural, social, and economic attributes. From the provisions of Article 121, the stipulations for determining the legal elements of islands and rocks do not appear to be specific enough; that is, the definitions of the legal requirements determining islands and rocks are not clear, resulting in opposing views and practices.

In the absence of any modifications of the Convention's regime of islands or a unified consensus among the international community, the legal elements of rocks within the regime of islands should be carefully interpreted to avoid an expansive ruling that may jeopardize the regimes of the high seas and international seabed area.[56] Such an approach is not only consistent with the original intent and purpose of the Convention but is also in line with Article 300, which requires that states fulfill their obligations in good faith and avoid abusing their rights. The strict interpretation of rocks is reflected in the following aspects: first, in terms of natural attributes, rocks are a particular type of island; they must be naturally formed land areas that emphasize the natural attributes of the constituent materials and the formation process. Second, in terms of social attributes, rocks must be capable of sustaining human habitation for a considerable period of time. Third, in terms of economic attributes, the resources needed by the rocks to sustain their own economic life should be limited to those produced by themselves and not imported resources from within or beyond their territorial waters, as that would suggest an expansion or abuse of rights. Concurrently, the exploitation of the resources of the rocks must be consistent with the principles of economic development and protection of the marine environment. Some countries, in order to make the rocks conform to the requirements of "economic life," will certainly try to develop the resources of the rocks without paying attention to the general principles of economic development and polluting the marine environment,

[56] It is clear from the provisions of the regime for amending the UNCLOS that amendments need consensus, and that even if there are proposals to amend UNCLOS using a simplified procedure, it would be quite difficult to substantively amend and to improve the UNCLOS. See Articles 312 and 313 of the UNCLOS.

in violation of the obligations of the contracting parties to protect and preserve the marine environment.[57]

1.4.5 Issues and Challenges Relating to Residual Rights

In the Convention, the controversy over military activities (surveying, espionage and reconnaissance, and joint military exercises) in the EEZ is the prominent issue of undefined residual rights. The confrontation between China and the U.S. over the issue of free use and prior consent regarding military activities in the EEZ is an example.

As the Convention does not clearly regulate military activities, even when analyzed from the perspective of peaceful uses of the oceans and marine scientific research, there are distinct perceptions, leading to different and opposing approaches. In other words, the framework of the Convention cannot resolve the issue of military activities.[58] In view of the highly sensitive nature and practical necessity of military activities, they should only be decided according to Article 58(3) of the Convention in light of the principle and legislative purpose of Article 59.[59]

If China and the U.S. cannot resolve the issue within the Convention's framework, it can only be resolved through bilateral consultations, including the conclusion of relevant agreements. Thus, China and the U.S. should abide by the Memorandum of Understanding on Notification of Major Military Activities and Confidence-Building Measures Mechanism (October–November 2014) and the Memorandum of Understanding Regarding the Rules of Behavior for Safety of Air and Maritime Encounters (November 2014) concluded by their militaries to regulate their maritime and air security actions. This will ensure their activities in the EEZ are regulated and orderly

[57] For an analysis of the legal elements of islands and rocks, see Yongming, Jin. 2010. An analysis of the legal elements of islands and rocks—From the perspective of the Okinotori issue, *Political Science and Law* 12: 99–106.

[58] For the dispute between China and the United States over military activities in the EEZ, see Yongming, Jin. 2011. A dissection of disputes between China and the United States over military activities in exclusive economic zone by the law of the sea, *Pacific Journal* 19(11): pp. 74–81.

[59] Article 58(3) of the UNCLOS provides that, "In exercising their rights and performing their duties under this Convention in the exclusive economic zone, States shall have due regard to the rights and duties of the coastal State and shall comply with the laws and regulations adopted by the coastal State in accordance with the provisions of this Convention and other rules of international law in so far as they are not incompatible with this Part." Article 59 of the UNCLOS provides that, "In cases where this Convention does not attribute rights or jurisdiction to the coastal State or to other States within the exclusive economic zone, and a conflict arises between the interests of the coastal State and any other State or States, the conflict should be resolved on the basis of equity and in the light of all the relevant circumstances, taking into account the respective importance of the interests involved to the parties as well as to the international community as a whole."

and safeguard the freedom of navigation and security of the oceans.[60] In fact, the U.S. policy of freedom of navigation, including in the SCS, has a long history, with representative policy documents such as Presidential Proclamation No. 2667, Policy of the United States with respect to the Natural Resources of the Subsoil and Sea Bed of the Continental Shelf (the Truman Proclamation for short, September 28, 1945), and the US Policy on Spratly Islands and South China Sea on May 10, 1995, the Statement on the South China Sea on August 3, 2012, and Limits in the Seas: China's Maritime Claims in the South China Sea issued by the U.S. Department of State on December 5, 2014.[61]

Additional efforts can be made to improve the Convention's regime by establishing new norms, such as implementing agreements on the issue of military activities in the EEZ. The content in this regard can make use of the preexisting accomplishments of the international community. For example, the Ocean Policy Research Foundation from Japan formulated the Guidelines for Navigation and Overflight in the Exclusive Economic Zone in September 2005 and the Principles for Building Confidence and Security in the Exclusive Economic Zones of the Asia–Pacific in October 2003 to promote new consultations and agreements on military activities in the EEZ and contribute to further improving the Convention's regime.[62] The development of a coordinated document on military activities in the EEZ under the Convention is a major challenge for the international community.

---

[60] For the Memorandum of Understanding on Notification of Major Military Activities and Confidence-Building Measures Mechanism, see https://dod.defense.gov/Portals/1/Documents/pubs/141112_MemorandumOfUnderstandingOnNotification.pdf, accessed February 10, 2015. For the Memorandum of Understanding Regarding the Rules of Behavior for Safety of Air and Maritime Encounters, see https://dod.defense.gov/Portals/1/Documents/pubs/141112_MemorandumOfUnderstandingRegardingRules.pdf, accessed February 10, 2015.

[61] For example, the Truman Proclamation states that "The character as high seas of the waters above the continental shelf and the right to their free and unimpeded navigation are in no way thus affected." See Department of International Law of Peking University Law School, ed. 1974. *Law of the sea materials compilation*. Beijing: People's Publishing House. pp. 386-387. For the US Policy on Spratly Islands and South China Sea, see Shicun, Wu. 2001. *Compilation of literature on the South China Sea*. Haikou: Hainan Publishing House. pp. 377–378. For the Statement on the South China Sea, see http://www.state.gov/r/pa/prs/ps/2012/08/196022.htm, accessed August 8, 2012. United States Department of State, Limits in the Seas: China's maritime claims in the South China Sea, https://www.state.gov/wp-content/uploads/2019/10/LIS-143.pdf, accessed January 8, 2015.

[62] See Japan Ocean Policy Research Foundation. 2006. *Ocean white paper: Japan's trends, world trends*. Tokyo: Japan Ocean Policy Research Foundation. pp. 195-197. Ocean Policy Research Foundation. 2013. *Principles for Building Confidence and Security in the Exclusive Economics Zones of the Asia-Pacific*. Tokyo: Japan Ocean Policy Research Foundation. pp. 1–12.

1.4.6 Issues and Challenges the Convention Does not Predict or Explicitly Regulate

With regard to the delimitation of maritime areas, in particular the EEZ and the continental shelf, as mentioned above, the Convention only provides for achieving an equitable solution in Articles 74 and 83 but does not specify the method or criteria for delimitation. Furthermore, the purpose of an equitable settlement can only be developed and established through the international community, in particular, the international judicial practice. So far, such practice has entailed developing a paradigm for an equitable solution, which involves making a comprehensive judgment that considers the specific circumstances of different maritime areas. This includes the following aspects: first, the delimitation of a provisional equidistance or median line; second, considering the relevant circumstances to achieve an equitable result and exploring the necessity of adjusting the provisional equidistance or median line; and third, verifying the ratio of the respective coastal lengths and the ratio between the relevant maritime area of each state and determining whether this produces an inequitable result to make corrections.[63]

Discussions on the protection of marine biodiversity have become increasingly active following the Convention. However, the issue of marine biodiversity was not fully recognized during the deliberations of the Convention. Even in the Convention, there is no term for marine biodiversity,[64] and there is no provision for methods that are considered useful for the preservation of marine biodiversity, such as marine protected areas. At the same time, the Convention on Biological Diversity was adopted in June 1992. How to coordinate and supplement the relationship between the two treaties is also a challenge to the Convention for the Preservation of Marine Biodiversity and Sustainable Development, which are common concerns of the international community.[65]

Regarding the issue of marine genetic resources arising in the high seas, including the international seabed area, what kind of international law should be applied to their investigation, exploitation, and research activities has also become the focus of the international community. The focus of the dispute is whether the principle of the common heritage of mankind, which is the basis of the international seabed area system, should be applied, or the principle of freedom of marine scientific research on the high seas should be applied.

---

[63] See [Japanese] Tanaka, Norio. 2013. A Study of the UN Convention on the Law of the Sea: At the standpoint of 30th Anniversary of the Adoption of UNCLOS, *Journal of International Law and Diplomacy* 112(2): 17. See also Mariko Kawano. 2013. International courts and tribunals and the development of the rules and methods concerning maritime delimitation, *Journal of International Law Diplomacy* 112(3): 14.

[64] For example, Article 194(5) of the UNCLOS provides that measures in accordance with Part 12 shall include necessary measures to protect and preserve rare or fragile ecosystems, as well as the habitat of depleted, threatened, or endangered species and other forms of marine life.

[65] See [Japanese] Tanaka, Norio. 2013. A Study of the UN Convention on the Law of the Sea: At the standpoint of 30th Anniversary of the Adoption of UNCLOS, *Journal of International Law and Diplomacy* 112(2): 20–21.

In conclusion, to preserve the conservation and sustainable use of marine biodiversity, including marine genes, the specific elements that should be considered include how to distribute benefits, how to develop rules for the management of areas, including marine protected areas and environmental impact assessment systems, as well as capacity-building and the transfer of marine technology.[66] These are all issues that the Convention cannot avoid and should improve.

[66] See [Japanese] Sato, Kuni. 2013. The United Nations Convention on the Law of the Sea and Japan: Its 30th anniversary and the evolution of two innovative regimes. *Journal of International Law and Diplomacy* 112(2): 89–91.

Chapter 2
Achievements of New China in Ocean Policy and Legal System

After 70 years of development, and especially during the 40 years of reform and opening-up, China has made great achievements in its legal system and ocean policies, providing institutional guarantees for the development of China's maritime endeavors. Thus, it is necessary to systematically sort out New China's achievements and contributions to the construction of its marine policy and legal system.

2.1 Achievements of New China in the Ocean Legal System

The author categorizes China's development in the field of the law of the sea since the founding of New China 70 years ago into the following four stages.

2.1.1 The Embryonic Stage of the Rule of Law for Oceans (1949–1978)

The main maritime laws and regulations formulated by New China at this stage, including the Interim Regulations on the Administration of Seaports in 1954, the Order on the Engine Trawl Fishery Prohibited Areas in the Bohai Sea, Yellow Sea and East China Sea in 1955, the General Rules for Joint Inspection of Import and Export Vessels in 1958, the Rules for the Administration of Foreign Non-Military Ships Passing Through the Qiongzhou Strait in 1964, the Interim Provisions for the Prevention of Pollution of Coastal Waters in 1974, and the Detailed Rules for the Implementation of the Frontier Health and Quarantine Law of the People's Republic of China in 1977.

China's marine legislation at this stage was not only limited in quantity and had a low legislative level, with no law in the strict sense of the term. The most important

Y. Jin, *Ocean Law and Policy of the People's Republic of China*,
https://doi.org/10.1007/978-981-95-3166-0_2

of these is the Declaration of the Government of the People's Republic of China on the Territorial Sea in 1958. It only declared the width of the territorial sea and some basic principles, was a legislative declaration without any specific provisions, and did not announce the basepoints of the territorial sea baselines. Nevertheless, it is still of great historical significance for the maintenance of China's national defense and security and maritime rights and interests because it declared, for the first time, that the breadth of China's territorial sea is 12 nautical miles.[1]

2.1.2 *The Development Phase of the Rule of Law for the Oceans (1979–1990)*

After the reform and opening-up, the ocean legislation of New China has greatly improved at this stage. Not only has the number of ocean laws and regulations increased greatly, but also the level of legislation has also improved. This is mainly reflected in the following aspects:

(1) The utilization of marine resources. In 1979, the Interim Regulations on Fisheries Management and the Measures for the Administration of Foreign Engineering Vessels, Crews, and Accompanying Personnel Engaged in Offshore Oil Exploration in China's Coastal Areas were formulated. In 1980, the Opinions on the Delimitation of Prohibited Fishing Zone Lines for Motorized Bottom Trawlers in the South China Sea and Fujian Coastal Areas were formulated, and the Rules for the Supervision and Administration of Fishing Ports (Provisional) were put into effect. The Interim Provisions on the Conservation of Aquatic Resources in the East and Yellow Seas, the Regulations of the People's Republic of China on Exploitation of On-shore Petroleum Resources in Cooperation with Foreign Enterprises, and the Fisheries Law were enacted in 1981, 1982, and 1986, respectively.

(2) Navigation safety. Legislation in this area includes the Provisional Regulations on Radio Health Quarantine for Internationally Navigating Ships and Regulations on the Administration of Foreign Ships in 1979, and the Maritime Traffic Safety Law in 1983. The Maritime Traffic Safety Law applies to all vessels, facilities, personnel, and owners and operators of ships and facilities sailing, berthing, and operating in China's coastal waters. The Chinese Port Supervision Agency is the competent authority for unified supervision and management of traffic safety in coastal waters. At the same time, the Law stipulates management measures and systems for ship inspection and registration, personnel on

[1] Article 1 of the Declaration of the Government of the PRC on the Territorial Sea states that the breadth of the territorial sea of the PRC is 12 nautical miles. This provision applies to all territories of the PRC, including the Chinese mainland and its offshore islands, Taiwan and the various affiliated islands, the Penghu Qundao, the Dongsha Qundao, the Xisha Qundao, the Zhongsha Qundao, the Nansha Qundao and other islands belonging to China.

ships and facilities, navigation, berthing and operation, safety and security, transportation of dangerous goods, rescue in case of marine accidents, salvage and removal, and investigation and handling of traffic accidents, as well as the legal responsibilities that must be assumed for violations of the Law.[2]

(3) Marine environmental protection. The main legislative acts contain the Marine Environmental Protection Law in 1982, the Regulations on the Prevention of Vessel—induced Sea Pollution and the Regulations on the Administration of Environmental Protection in the Exploration and Development of Offshore Petroleum in 1983, the Regulations on Control over Dumping of Wastes in the Ocean in 1985, the Administrative Regulation on the Prevention of Environmental Pollution by Ship Breaking in 1989, the Administrative Regulation on the Prevention and Treatment of the Pollution and Damage to the Marine Environment by Land-based Pollutants and Administrative Regulation on the Prevention and Treatment of the Pollution and Damage to the Marine Environment by Marine Engineering Construction Projects in 1990. All these have formed the legal system for the protection of the marine environment in China.

2.1.3 *Formative Phase of the Rule of Law for the Oceans (1991–2009)*

New China's marine legislation in this period was characterized by the fact that, with the entry into force of the UNCLOS (November 16, 1994) and the Decision of the Standing Committee of the National People's Congress of China on the Ratification of the UNCLOS (May 15, 1996) and its entry into force in China on June 7, 1996, China formulated and revised a large number of relevant maritime laws and regulations according to international customs, the norms of the UNCLOS and other maritime regimes, thus establishing the basic framework of China's ocean legal system, that is, the law of the sea system of New China has basically taken shape. It mainly entails the following:

(1) The formulation of a basic legal system for the sea. In 1992, China enacted the Law of the People's Republic of China on the Territorial Sea and the Contiguous Zone, and in 1998, the Law of the People's Republic of China on the Exclusive Economic Zone and the Continental Shelf. These laws established China's territorial sea system, the width of the contiguous zone, and the EEZ and the continental shelf, as well as their specific delimitation principles, forming the basic framework of China's legal system for the oceans and providing a basis for formulating other specific legal norms.

(2) Improving the basic legal system for the sea. To provide a concrete effect to the scope of China's territorial sea, as stipulated in its Territorial Sea and Contiguous Zone Act, and improve the law on the territorial sea, in accordance with the relevant provisions of the Territorial Sea and Contiguous Zone Act, the Declaration

[2] Articles 9–10, 26, 42–43 and 44–47 of the Maritime Traffic Safety Law.

of the Government of the People's Republic of China on the Baselines of the Territorial Sea was issued on May 15, 1996, which proclaimed the baselines of part of China's territorial sea on the Chinese mainland and of the Xisha Qundao. The baselines of the above-mentioned areas of the territorial sea of the mainland and the Xisha Qundao are straight lines between adjacent points. The Declaration further stipulates that the Chinese Government shall declare the baselines of the rest of China's territorial sea.

(3) Other sectoral legal regimes for the sea. This is manifested in the following areas:

First, concerning the use of maritime areas, on October 27, 2001, China adopted and promulgated the Law on the Administration of Sea Areas. This provided the necessary legal means for the establishment of China's system for the use of sea areas to standardize the order of sea area use, protect the legitimate rights and interests of sea users, and promote comprehensive management of the oceans. This legislation was a major step forward in China's management of sea areas and served as the basis for establishing China's legal system for the use of sea areas. Its purpose is to strengthen the management of sea area use, safeguard the legitimate rights and interests of China's sea area ownership and sea area use rights holders, and promote the rational development and sustainable use of sea areas.

Second, regarding the fisheries resources management, the Fisheries Law, adopted on January 20, 1986, was amended twice, on October 31, 2000, and on August 28, 2004. The purpose of these amendments was to strengthen the protection, enhancement, exploitation, and rational utilization of fisheries; develop artificial aquaculture; safeguard the lawful rights and interests of fisheries producers; and promote the development of fisheries production in response to the socialist construction and the needs of the people. According to Article 2 of the Fisheries Law, "All productive activities of fisheries, such as aquaculture and catching or harvesting of aquatic animals and plants, in the inland waters, tidal flats, territorial waters and exclusive economic zones of the People's Republic of China and in all other sea areas under the jurisdiction of the PRC shall be conducted in accordance with this Law."

Third, in terms of the protection of the marine environment, in order to protect and improve the marine environment, conserve marine resources, prevent damage from pollution, maintain ecological balance, safeguard health, and promote sustainable economic and social development, the Marine Environmental Protection Law was adopted and promulgated by the Standing Committee of the National People's Congress (NPC) on August 23, 1982. It was further amended three times on December 25, 1999, December 28, 2013, and November 7, 2016. In addition, in order to implement the relevant contents of the Marine Environmental Protection Law, the State Council of the PRC (SC) issued the Decision on Amending the Administrative Regulations on the Prevention and Treatment of the Pollution and Damage to the Marine Environment by Marine Engineering Construction Projects on September 25, 2007. It further formulated the Administrative Regulations on the Prevention and Treatment of the Pollution and Damage to the Marine Environment by Marine Engineering Construction Projects, as well as other ancillary norms.

Fourth, with regard to the marine scientific research, Article 4 of the Provisions on the Administrative Provisions on Foreign-Related Marine Scientific Research (adopted on June 18, 1996, and came into force on October 1, 1996) stipulates that, in the internal and territorial seas of the PRC, foreign parties (i.e., international organizations and foreign organizations and individuals) shall conduct marine scientific research in cooperation with China. Furthermore, in other maritime areas under the jurisdiction of the PRC, foreign parties may conduct marine scientific research individually or in cooperation with China. Such activities must be subject to the approval of the state administrative department for ocean Affairs, or reported to the SC for approval by the national ocean administrative department and in compliance with the relevant laws and regulations of the PRC. Article 5 stipulates the date on which a written application shall be accepted, the organization to which the application will be submitted, and the time within which a decision on the application should be made.

Fifth, regarding the protection of islands, the Islands Protection Law of the People's Republic of China was adopted on December 26, 2009, and came into force on March 1, 2010. The purpose of the law is to "protect the ecosystems of islands and their surrounding waters, rationally develop and exploit the natural resources of islands, protect the oceanic rights and interests of the state, and promote sustainable economic and social development (Article 1)." "The term 'island protection' as mentioned in this Law refers to the protection of the ecosystems of islands and their surrounding waters, protection of natural resources of uninhabited islands and protection of special purpose islands (Article 2)." "The state shall apply the principle of "scientific planning, giving priority to protection, rational development and sustainable utilization" to islands (Article 3)." In accordance with Article 22, "The state shall protect the military facilities established on islands, and it shall be prohibited to damage or endanger such military facilities. The state shall protect the public facilities legally established on islands for navigation assistance or guidance, surveying, meteorological observation, marine monitoring, seismic monitoring, etc., and it shall be prohibited to damage, move without authorization or impede the normal use of such facilities." In the case of uninhabited islands, according to Article 28, "The status quo of an uninhabited island shall be maintained if the use of it has not been approved; and such activities as quarrying, excavating sea sand, felling trees, production, construction and tourism shall be prohibited." "Where the development and utilization of an uninhabited island involves the utilization of any special purpose island, or really needs any sea filling to connect islands or connect the island with continent or any serious change of the natural terrain or landform of the island, it shall be subject to the examination and approval of the SC (Article 30)." The state shall apply special protection to the islands where the territorial sea base points are located, islands for the purpose of national defense, islands within the marine natural reserves, and other islands for special purposes or with special conservation value (Article 36)." These elements comprise the core of protecting the islands in China.

(4) Implementation of international maritime rules. In addition to ratifying the UNCLOS, decided at the 19th meeting of the Standing Committee of the

Eighth NPC on May 15, 1996, China has supplemented and improved other legal measures according to the trends in the development of the international community and China's marine situation. The main rules are as follows:

First, on August 25, 2006, China submitted a written declaration to the UN Secretary-General in accordance with Article 298 of the UNCLOS regarding disputes over maritime delimitation, territorial sovereignty, military activities, and so forth. The Government of the People's Republic of China does not accept any of the procedures provided for in Section 2 of Part XV of the Convention with respect to all the categories of disputes referred to in paragraph 1 (a) (b) and (c) of Article 298 of the Convention, In other words, the aforementioned disputes between China and other countries over maritime issues are not subject to adjudication or arbitration and will be resolved by the states concerned through bilateral political consultations. Therefore, maritime disputes between countries are resolved through political means.

Second, on May 11, 2009, the Permanent Mission of China to the UN submitted the Preliminary Information Indicative of the Outer Limits of the Continental Shelf Beyond 200 Nautical Miles of the People's Republic of China (Preliminary Information) to the UN Secretary-General, delineating the outer limits of the continental shelf beyond 200 nautical miles in part of China's East China Sea (ECS). According to the Preliminary Information, the outer limits of ECS's continental shelf beyond 200 nautical miles does not exceed the outer envelope of 60 nautical miles from the Foot of the Slope or 350 nautical miles from the baselines from which the breadth of the territorial sea is measured. China's submission of Preliminary Information indicates that China has fulfilled its obligations under the UNCLOS and the requirements of the Conference of the Parties to the UNCLOS.

Third, the Permanent Mission of China to the UN submitted a written statement regarding Japan's rock of Oki-no-Tori (Oki-no Tori-shima) to the UN Secretary-General on February 6, 2009. It pointed out that Oki-no-Tori (Oki-no Tori-shima) is a rock, not an island, and that it is not possible to use it as a basepoint from which the continental shelf or the outer continental shelf can be claimed. The CLCS does not have the authority to consider information relating to the outer continental shelf with the rock of Oki-no-Tori (Oki-no Tori-shima) as a basepoint.[3]

Fourth, in response to the joint submission made by Malaysia and Vietnam on the outer continental shelf (May 6, 2009) and the separate submission made by Vietnam on the outer continental shelf (May 7, 2009), the Permanent Mission of China to the UN submitted a note verbale (No. CML/17/2009) to the UN Secretary-General on May 7, 2009, stating that China has indisputable sovereignty over the islands in the SCS and the adjacent waters, and enjoys sovereign rights and jurisdiction over the relevant waters as well as the seabed and subsoil thereof. The above position is consistently held by the Chinese Government, and is widely known by the international community. In response to the note verbale submitted on April 4, 2011, by the Ministry of Foreign Affairs of the Philippines to the Chinese Embassy in the Philippines claiming that "the Republic of the Philippines has sovereignty and

[3] See https://www.un.org/depts/los/clcs_new/submissions_files/jpn08/chn_6feb09_e.pdf, accessed October 18, 2018.

jurisdiction over the Kalayan Islands," the Permanent Mission of China to the UN addressed a further note verbale to the UN Secretary-General on April 14, 2011 (No. CML/8/2011). It emphasized that "China has indisputable sovereignty over the islands in the South China Sea and their adjacent waters, and enjoys sovereign rights and jurisdiction over the relevant waters as well as the seabed and subsoil thereof; China's sovereignty and relevant rights and jurisdiction in the South China Sea are supported by abundant historical and legal evidence."[4] These positions and views were reaffirmed in the July 12, 2016, Statement of China on Territorial Sovereignty and Maritime Rights and Interests in the South China Sea.[5]

Fifth, to control the SCS issue, the Declaration on the Conduct of Parties in the South China Sea (DOC) was signed between China and the Association of South-east Asian Nations (ASEAN) on November 4, 2002, the Guidelines for the Implementation of the Declaration on the Conduct of Parties in the South China Sea were concluded on July 20, 2011, and the Joint Statement of the Foreign Ministers of China and ASEAN on the Comprehensive and Effective Implementation of the Declaration on the Conduct of Parties in the South China Sea was issued on July 25, 2016."[6] Meanwhile, in August 2013, China and ASEAN began consultations and negotiations on formulating the Code of Conduct in the South China Sea (COC). These measures and documents have greatly stabilized the situation in the SCS and produced positive results.

In addition, China and Vietnam signed the Agreement between the PRC and the Socialist Republic of Vietnam on the delimitation of the territorial seas, the exclusive economic zones and continental shelves in Beibu Bay on December 25, 2000, and the Agreement between the Government of the PRC and the Government of the Socialist Republic of Vietnam on Fisheries Cooperation in Beibu Bay (effective June 30, 2004). Meanwhile, China and Japan signed the Agreement between the Government of the People's Republic of China and the Government of Japan on cooperation of fisheries on November 11, 1997 (effective June 1, 2000), the Agreement on Fisheries between the PRC and the State of Japan (effective June 1, 2000), and Principled Consensus on the East China Sea Issue between China and Japan issued by the foreign affairs departments of the two countries (June 18, 2008). Furthermore, the Agreement on Fisheries between the Government of the PRC and the Government of the Republic of Korea was signed by both governments on August 3, 2000 (effective June 30, 2001). China has further conducted negotiations with the Republic of Korea on the delimitation of the maritime boundary in the Yellow Sea. These achievements, documents, and acts have played a role in effectively resolving and deferring disputes over China's surrounding marine environment and oceans, reflecting the practical

---

[4] See Chinese Society of International Law. 2018. *The South China Sea Arbitration Awards: A Critical Study*. Beijing: Foreign Languages Press. p. 34.

[5] See Department of Boundary and Ocean Affairs of the Ministry of Foreign Affairs of the People's Republic of China. 2016. *Compilation of documents on China's response to the South China Sea arbitration case*. Beijing: World Affairs Press. pp. 86–90.

[6] For relevant documents, see Department of Boundary and Ocean Affairs of the Ministry of Foreign Affairs of the People's Republic of China. 2017. *Compilation of relevant documents on China's neighboring maritime issues*. Beijing: World Affairs Press. pp. 69–94.

effectiveness of China's insistence on resolving disputes through peaceful, political means and deferring disputes through crisis management mechanisms.

The aforementioned statutes and declarations, as well as agreements and consensus, have safeguarded China's maritime rights and interests and fulfilled its international responsibilities and obligations, safeguarding the smooth progress of the reform and opening-up and forming the foundation of China's law of the sea regime.

2.1.4 Enrichment Phase of the Rule of Law for the Oceans (2010–2019)

During this period, in addition to the second revision of the Marine Environmental Protection Law (December 28, 2013, November 7, 2016), the important internal and external legal measures include the following:

First, the Seabed Disputes Chamber of the ITLOS issued the advisory opinion on February 1, 2011, concerning the responsibilities and obligations of states sponsoring persons and entities with respect to activities in the Area. On August 18, 2010, the Department of Treaty and Law of the Ministry of Foreign Affairs of the People's Republic of China (MFA) submitted the Written Statement of the People's Republic of China on the Responsibilities and Obligations of States Sponsoring Persons and Entities with respect to Activities in the International Seabed Area. The written submission was generally adopted by the International Seabed Disputes Chamber in its advisory opinion and contributed to advancing the implementation of the regime for the international seabed area.[7]

Second, in response to Japan's "nationalization" of the three islands of Diaoyu Dao, the Chinese Government issued the Statement of the Government of the People's Republic of China on the Baselines of the Territorial Sea of Diaoyu Dao and Its Affiliated Islands (September 10, 2012).[8] The first group of the straight baselines of the territorial sea is adjacent to Diaoyu Dao, Huangwei Yu, Nanxiao Dao, Beixiao Dao, Nan Yu, Bei Yu and Fei Yu; and the second group of straight baselines is adjacent to Chiwei Yu. Meanwhile, on December 14, 2012, the Chinese Government presented a Submission to the Commission on the Limits of the Continental Shelf in part of the ECS to the Secretary-General of the UN, in order to supplement the Preliminary Information on May 11, 2009 and fulfill its responsibility.[9]

---

[7] See Department of Treaty and Law of the Ministry of Foreign Affairs of the People's Republic of China. 2018. China's participation in the relevant procedures concerning the advisory opinion on the responsibilities of the sponsoring states of the International Tribunal for the Law of the Sea, in *Selected cases of China's international law practice*. Beijing: World Affairs Press. pp. 53–80.

[8] See China's Statement of the Government of the People's Republic of China on the Baselines of the Territorial Sea of Diaoyu Dao and its Affiliated Islands, http://www.gov.cn/jrzg/2012-09/10/content_2221140.htm, accessed October 18, 2018.

[9] Submission on the outer limits of the continental shelf in parts of the East China Sea, https://www.un.org/Depts/los/clcs_new/submissions_files/chn63_12/executive%20summary_EN.pdf, accessed

Furthermore, to address flight safety in the airspace of the ECS, including the waters around the Diaoyu Dao, the Ministry of National Defense of the People's Republic of China (MND) of the PRC issued the Statement on the Establishment of the East China Sea Air Defense Identification Zone and the Announcement of the Aircraft Identification Rules for the East China Sea Air Defense Identification Zone of the People's Republic of China on November 23, 2013, in light of international practice and domestic law, ensuring its sovereignty and interests in the area.[10]

Third, after years of efforts, representatives of the Governments of China and Japan reached a four-point principled consensus for handling and improving relations between the two countries on November 7, 2014, known as the Four-Point Principled Agreement on Handling and Improving Bilateral Relations.[11] Despite the fact that China and Japan reached the above four-point principled agreement after many diplomatic consultations, there are still different divergences and interpretations of the content. To maintain maritime and air security in the ECS, after years of consultations, including negotiations at the China-Japan High-level Consultation Mechanism on Maritime Affairs, the MND and the Ministry of Defense of Japan signed the Memorandum of Understanding on Maritime And Air Liaison on May 9, 2018 (entered into force on June 8, 2018), and the Agreement on Maritime Search and Rescue Cooperation between the Government of Japan and the Government of the People's Republic of China (October 26, 2018), which was signed and entered into force on February 14, 2019).

The fourth legal measure is the Law of the People's Republic of China on the Exploration and Development of Resources in the Deep Seabed Area (adopted on February 26, 2016, effective May 1, 2016). To implement the Convention, States are required to sponsor a natural or juridical person of their nationality or under their control to carry out activities in the Area in accordance with the Convention and to clarify the responsibility of the sponsoring State to take measures to effectively control the activities of the contractors it sponsors in the Area. As a concrete measure taken by States, China enacted the above-mentioned law on February 26, 2016, to implement and enforce the obligations and requirements of the Convention.[12] Meanwhile, the Notice on Issuing the Measures for the Administration of Licensing for the Exploration and Development of Resources in Deep Seabed Areas (April 27,

---

October 18, 2018. China's Preliminary Information on the establishment of the outer limits of the continental shelf beyond 200 Nautical Miles, https://www.un.org/Depts/los/clcs_new/submissions_files/chn63_12/clcs_63_2012.pdf, accessed October 18, 2018.

[10] China's Statement on the Establishment of the East China Sea Air Defense Identification Zone and the Announcement of the Aircraft Identification Rules for the East China Sea Air Defense Identification Zone, http://www.gov.cn/jrzg/2013-11/23/content_2533099(or252533101).htm, accessed October 18, 2018.

[11] For the Four-Point Principled Agreement on Handling and Improving Bilateral Relations, see http://www.fmprc.gov.cn/mfa_chn/zyxw_602251/t1208349.shtml; or https://www.MFA.go.jp/a_o/c_m1/cn/page4e_000150.html, accessed November 11, 2014.

[12] The Law of the PRC on Exploration and Exploitation of Resources in the Deep Seabed Area comprises 7 chapters and 29 articles. For details, see the *Law of the People's Republic of China on Exploration and Exploitation of Resources in the Deep Seabed Area (including draft explanations)*. 2016. Beijing: China Legal Publishing House. pp. 2–12.

2017), the Interim Measures for the Management of Samples in the Exploration and Development of Deep-sea Submarine Area Resources (December 29, 2017), and the Interim Measures for the Management of Data in the Exploration and Development of Deep-sea Submarine Area Resources.(December 29, 2017) were formulated in accordance with the aforementioned Law, further enriching the practice of the Area regime in China.

Fifth, in the area of polar affairs, the more important regulations are the Provisions on Administrative Licensing Management of Antarctic Expedition issued by the State Oceanic Administration (SOA) on May 30, 2014, the Provisions on Administration of Environmental Impact Assessment of Antarctic Expedition Activities issued by the SOA on May 18, 2017, the Provisions on Administration of Environmental Protection of Antarctic Activities issued by SOA on February 8, 2018, the Provisions on Administrative Licensing Management of Arctic Expedition issued by SOA on August 30, 2017. These are regulations on the licensing of expedition activities and environmental protection in the Antarctic and Arctic, which are insufficient for in-depth scientific research activities or for strengthening the protection and utilization of polar resources, including the possibility of utilizing Arctic shipping lanes. Thus, it is necessary to take further measures to accelerate the upgrading of the legal status of polar initiatives.

With regard to the Antarctic cause, the legislative plan of the Standing Committee of the Thirteenth NPC (116 items), published on the NPC's website on September 10, 2018, divides legislative projects into three categories. In the first category (draft laws to be submitted for consideration during the term of office under relatively mature conditions) is "legislation on Antarctic activities and environmental protection," which is to be submitted for consideration by the Commission on Environment and Resources Management of the NPC or to take the lead in drafting. This clarification of the responsibilities of the main body and scope will help guarantee and promote the timely formulation of a system to protect Antarctic scientific research activities, resources, and the environment.

2.2 New China's Ocean Policy Achievements

In the process of building the legal system for the sea in New China, especially at the shaping and enriching stage, the role of marine policy is indispensable. To a certain extent, China's marine policy and the construction of the legal system are inextricably linked; indeed, marine policy contributed to the formulation and modification of the law of the sea.

New China's ocean policy is expressed in various forms, mainly in the documents of the Party Central Committee, the SC, and relevant departments, as well as in government work reports and speeches by state leaders. During the 70 years of New China's development, and especially after the reform and opening-up period, as China's ocean affairs have developed and expanded, the definition of ocean policy has been continuously upgraded, with a gradual transition from the policies of the various sea-related departments and single-field policies of to a comprehensive and all-encompassing ocean policy that has the goal of the overall development of the sea.

In the early years of the founding of New China, however, marine policy focused on defending national security, safeguarding sea transportation routes, preventing imperialist aggression at sea, and building up strength to unify the motherland. Thus, for many years after the founding of New China, constructing a strong navy and the defense of the territorial integrity of the motherland dominated maritime policy.

Guided by the basic policy of constructing national defense and the economy, the SOA was approved by the 124th meeting of the Standing Committee of the Second NPC at its 22nd meeting in July 1964 and was placed under the authority of the Navy to manage national ocean affairs, with the main duties of oceanographic investigation and scientific research. The SOA established the institutional foundation to develop China's ocean affairs.

Since China's reform and opening-up, there has been an increasing demand for marine resources for national economic and social development, and surveys of China's marine environmental resources have become particularly important. China's marine policy has also gradually transitioned from its early focus on naval construction to the national economy and social development. The continuous enrichment of marine policy has covered such areas as marine science and technology, marine resources, marine industry, and polar and oceanic expeditions, realizing the goal of leapfrogging development.

New China's performance in ocean policy is highlighted in the following:

2.2.1 Formulation of China's Comprehensive Ocean Policy

First, in accordance with the spirit of the 1992 UN Conference on Environment and Development, the Chinese Government formulated China's Agenda 21 as a sustainable development strategy for China's future development. To better implement the spirit of China's Agenda 21 in the marine sector and to promote the sustainable development and utilization of the oceans, in May 1996, the SOA prepared China Ocean Agenda 21, which deepened the China's Agenda 21 in the marine sector,[13] serving as a policy guideline and course of action for the sustainable development and utilization of the seas.

Second, on February 7, 2008, the SC published the Outline of the National Ocean Economy Development Plan. It systematically planned China's marine industry development goals from 2006 to 2010 in 10 areas: opportunities and challenges; guiding ideology, basic principles, development goals; sustainable utilization of marine resources; protection of the marine environment and ecology; integration and coordination of the marine economy; services for the public welfare of the

[13] State Oceanic Administration. 1996. *China's ocean agenda for the twenty-first century*. Beijing: Ocean Press. pp. 1–75.

oceans; maritime law enforcement and rights and interests safeguarding; international marine affairs; marine science, technology and education, and measures for the Plan's implementation. The Outline systematically planned the goal of developing marine undertakings in China from 2006 to 2010, which has important guiding significance.

Third, the report of the Eighteenth National Congress of the Communist Party of China (CPC), for the first time, completely advances China's strategic goal of becoming a maritime country. It states that China "should enhance our capacity for exploiting marine resources, develop the marine economy, protect the marine ecological environment, resolutely safeguard China's maritime rights and interests, and build China into a maritime country."[14] These elements are fundamental to becoming a strong maritime country.

General Secretary Xi Jinping, while presiding over the eighth collective study of the Political Bureau of the Central Committee of the CPC on building a strong maritime country (July 30, 2013), emphasized the basic requirements for building strong marine capacity. China's strategy for developing a strong maritime country comprises "four transformations": improving the capacity for resource development, and promoting a quality and efficiency-oriented marine economy; protecting the ecological environment, and promoting recycling-oriented marine development; developing marine science and technology, and focusing on promoting innovation-led marine science and technology; and safeguarding the country's maritime rights and interests, and striving to promote the transformation of maritime rights and interests to an overall consideration.

China's progress toward achieving the strategy of becoming a maritime country is reflected in the 19th Party Congress' report. This report points out that China "will pursue coordinated land and marine development, and step up efforts to build China into a strong maritime country; should pursue the Belt and Road Initiative (BRI) as a priority, and make new ground in opening China further through links running eastward and westward, across land and over sea."[15] Therefore, the strategic goal of China's maritime country has been deepened in the report of the 19th National Congress of the CPC and has become an important guideline and policy choice for accelerating China's maritime country strategy.

Fourth, the BRI was proposed by Chinese President Xi Jinping in his speeches during his visits to Kazakhstan and Indonesia in September 2013 and October 2013, respectively, in which he mentioned launching the Silk Road Economic Belt and the twenty-first Century Maritime Silk Road.[16]

---

[14] Jintao, Hu. 2012. Firmly march on the path of socialism with Chinese characteristics and strive to complete the building of a moderately prosperous society in all respects. Beijing: People's Publishing House. pp. 39–40.

[15] Jinping, Xi. 2017. Secure a decisive victory in building a moderately prosperous society in all respects and strive for the great success of socialism with Chinese characteristics for a new era. Beijing: People's Publishing House. pp. 33–34.

[16] Chinese President Xi Jinping proposed to "jointly build the Silk Road Economic Belt" in his speech "Promote People-to-People Friendship and Create a Better Future" at the Nazarbayev University, Kazakhstan on September 7, 2013, see Jinping, Xi. 2018. *President Xi Jinping's discourses*

For China's reform and opening up under the background of major changes and adjustments in the current international situation, the BRI is a new development model relying on the achievements and experience made since China's reform and opening up, in order to give full play to China's multiple identities and roles, with the goal of further integration and promotion of international and regional development, that is, the BRI is an upgraded version of China's reform and opening up. The BRI has been actively corresponded by the international community and achieved good practical results, thanks to the continuous enrichment and improvement of the BRI by the CPC and government, including speeches by national leaders on important occasions, and the establishment of important documents and platforms.

The documents on the basic objectives, areas of cooperation, specific paths, and implementation effects of the BRI include the following: Vision and Actions on Jointly Building Silk Road Economic Belt and twenty-first Century Maritime Silk Road, was authorized by the SC and jointly issued by the National Development and Reform Commission (NDRC), the MFA, and the Ministry of Commerce of the People's Republic of China (MOFCOM) on March 28, 2015[17]; Building the Belt and Road: Concept, Practice and China's Contribution, was jointly issued by the Office of the Leading Group for Promoting the Belt and Road Initiative, May 10, 2017[18]; Vision for Maritime Cooperation under the Belt and Road Initiative, was jointly released by the NDRC and the SOA on June 20, 2017[19]; The Belt and Road Initiative: Progress, Contributions and Prospects, was released by the Office of the Leading Group for Promoting the Belt and Road Initiative on April 22, 2019.[20]

The main platforms that strengthen the BRI are the Asian Infrastructure Investment Bank (AIIB), the Silk Road Fund, the Office of the Leading Group for Promoting the Belt and Road Initiative, the Belt and Road Forum for International Cooperation, the Belt and Road Media Cooperation Alliance, and the Belt and Road Think Tank Cooperation Alliance, as well as the China International Import Expo (CIIE).

The deepening and development of the BRI has also played an important role in solidifying and safeguarding its standardization and guidance in important domestic documents (such as the Report on the Work of the Government). For example, the Report on the Work of the Government in 2015) recommended that China should

on the Belt and Road Initiative. Beijing: Central Party Literature Press. pp. 1–5. For the content of "jointly building the twenty-first Century Maritime Silk Road" proposed by Chinese President Xi Jinping in his speech "Jointly Building a China-Asean Community of Common Destiny" in the Indonesian parliament on October 3, 2013, see Jinping, Xi. 2018. *President Xi Jinping's discourses on the Belt and Road Initiative.* Beijing: Central Party Literature Press. pp. 1–5.

[17] See Vision and Actions on Jointly Building Silk Road Economic Belt and twenty-first Century Maritime Silk Road, http://www.gov.cn/xinwen/2015-03/28/content_2839723.htm, accessed March 28, 2015.

[18] See Building the Belt and Road: Concept, Practice and China's Contribution, http://www.china.com.cn/news/2017-05/11/content_40789833.htm, accessed May 11, 2017.

[19] See Vision for Maritime Cooperation under the Belt and Road Initiative, https://www.gov.cn/xinwen/2017-11/17/content_5240325.htm, accessed June 21, 2017.

[20] See The Belt and Road Initiative: Progress, Contributions and Prospects, http://www.xinhuanet.com/world/2019-04/22/c_1124400071.htm, accessed April 22, 2019.

develop the Silk Road Economic Belt and the twenty-first Century Maritime Silk Road; Preparations have been made for establishing the AIIB, and the Silk Road Fund has been set up; China will move faster to strengthen infrastructure connectivity with China's neighbors, simplify customs clearance procedures, and build international logistics gateways.[21] The Report on the Work of the Government in 2016 confirmed that the Asian Infrastructure Investment Bank was officially inaugurated, and the Silk Road Fund opened for business; Progress was made in the BRI, the pace of our industrial-capacity cooperation with other countries was stepped up, and breakthroughs were made in China's export of high-speed railway and nuclear power equipment; China will work to secure solid progress in pursuing the BRI, promote domestic regional development and opening up and international economic cooperation in a coordinated way, work with other countries and regions to build overland economic corridors and maritime cooperation hubs, and promote connectivity, economic and trade cooperation, and cultural exchange; China will work to develop cooperative mechanisms for achieving compatibility in customs clearance procedures along the routes and build international logistics networks; China will promote the development of border economic cooperation zones, cross-border economic cooperation zones, and overseas economic and trade cooperation zones; With a commitment to achieving common development and shared growth through joint consultation, China will ensure that the BRI creates bonds of peace, friendship, and common prosperity.[22]

In addition to regulating the process and direction of the BRI in important Chinese Government documents, government leaders have further deepened and expanded the cooperation and action plan of the BRI on a number of occasions, guaranteeing its progress and effectiveness. In other words, the Chinese Government and its leaders have made many efforts to construct and advance the BRI and secured understanding and support from the international community. The results of the Belt and Road Forum for International Cooperation and the First CIIE, including the large number of representatives from participating countries and international organizations, and the development, leadership, and comprehensive interpretations of the initiative, are concrete manifestations of this.[23] For example, the first Belt and Road Forum for International Cooperation (conducted in May 2017) was was attended by heads of state and government of 29 countries as well as more than 1,600 representatives from over 140 countries and 80-plus international organizations. The forum produced 279 deliverables, involving 76 major items in five key areas.[24]

---

[21] Keqiang, Li. 2015. Report on the work of the government—March 5, 2015 at the 3rd Session of the 12th National People's Congress. Beijing: People's Publishing House. p. 9, 20.

[22] Keqiang, Li. 2016. Report on the work of the government—March 5, 2016 at the 4th Session of the 12th National People's Congress. Beijing: People's Publishing House. pp. 5, 30–31.

[23] Yongming, Jin. 2018. *Research on China's ocean power strategy in the new era.* Beijing: Ocean Press. pp. 10–12.

[24] Office of the Leading Group for Promoting the Belt and Road Initiative. 2019. The Belt and Road Initiative: Progress, Contributions and Prospects, http://www.xinhuanet.com/world/2019-04/22/c_1124400071.htm. Accessed April 22, 2019.

2.2.2 *Formulation of National Ocean Development Plans*

First, the SC approved the National Ocean Development Plan in May 1995, aiming for the best form of coordination between the population, resources, and the environment, as well as between the economy, society, and ecology, based on the country's economic development needs and the current situation of marine resources. Currently, it seeks to achieve its strategic objective of making integrated arrangements for the development, utilization, and protection of marine resources and coordinating and resolving the contradictions and problems of marine development. Further, it seeks to macro-guide and regulate national marine development activities, accelerate the process of marine development, and play a role in achieving the national economic construction objectives.

Second, China's government formulated the National Marine Functional Zoning in 2002, in accordance with the Law on the Administration of Sea Areas, the Marine Environmental Protection Law, and relevant regulations and policies.

Third, on May 9, 2003, the SC approved the Outline of the National Ocean Economy Development Plan and requested all regions to consider the actual situation and conscientiously implement it. The Outline is the first guiding document with a macroscopic role formulated by the Government of China to promote the marine economy's comprehensive development. It is important for China to accelerate the development and utilization of marine resources, promote the rational distribution of the economy of the coastal areas and the adjustment of the industrial structure, and drive the various industries of the marine economy to form a new point of growth in the national economy. It is of great significance to maintain the sustained, healthy and rapid development of the national economy and achieve the goal of building a well-off society in an all-round way.

To implement China's strong maritime country strategy and the Outline of the 13th Five-Year Plan (2016–2020) for National Economic and Social Development, the NDRC and the SOA jointly issued the National 13th Five-Year Plan for the Development of the Marine Economy on May 4, 2017, which is oriented to the current problems and needs of China's marine economic development. The plan takes the initiative in applying and leading the new normal phase of marine economic development, accelerates supply-side structural reform, focuses on optimizing the regional layout of the marine economy, upgrades the structure and level of the marine industry, expands the opening-up of the marine economic sector, and promotes the transformation of the marine economy from a speed-based model to one that is oriented toward quality and efficiency.[25]

In terms of safeguards and foundations for marine development activities, the Ministry of Science and Technology of the People's Republic of China (MOST), the Ministry of Land and Resources of the People's Republic of China (MLR), and SOA jointly issued the 13th Five-Year Plan for Special Projects on Scientific and Technological Innovation In The Marine Field on May 8, 2017, aiming to further

---

[25] Research Group of the China Institute For Marine Affairs of the State Oceanic Administration. 2018. *China's Ocean Development Report (2018)*. Beijing: Ocean Press. p. 54.

build and improve the national system of marine science and technology innovation and upgrade China's marine science and technology innovation capacity. It proposes specific safeguards in four areas: organizational and implementation mechanisms and modes; funding modes; monitoring, assessment and evaluation mechanisms; and risk assessment.[26]

2.2.3 *External Publicity for the Oceans*

To introduce the development of China's oceanic endeavors and elaborate upon China's position on oceanic issues, the Chinese Government has issued white papers on ocean policy.

(1) The development of China's ocean affairs. In the International Year of the Ocean (1998), the Chinese Government published a white paper on the development of China's ocean affairs. It comprises the "Foreword," "Strategy for the sustainable development of the ocean," "Rational development and utilization of marine resources," "Protection and preservation of the marine environment," "Marine science development, technology and education," "Comprehensive marine management implementation," and "International cooperation in ocean affairs." As the first report on China's achievements and policies in the field of the ocean, it enables other countries to understand China's marine policy; meanwhile, it comprehensively and systematically elaborates on the basic policies and principles that should be followed in the process of China's development of its marine endeavors.

(2) Safeguarding sovereignty over the Diaoyu Dao. To safeguard China's rights and interests over its sovereignty over the Diaoyu Dao, The SC Information Office of the People's Republic of China (SCIO) issued a white paper in September 2012 titled "Diaoyu Dao, an Inherent Territory of China."

It consists of the following parts: "Foreword;" "Diaoyu Dao is China's Inherent Territory; Japan Grabbed Diaoyu Dao from China;" "Backroom Deals Between the United States and Japan Concerning Diaoyu Dao are Illegal and Invalid;" "Japan's Claim of Sovereignty over Diaoyu Dao is Totally Unfounded;" "China has Taken Resolute Measures to Safeguard its Sovereignty over Diaoyu Dao;" "Conclusion." It argues that Diaoyu Dao and its affiliated islands are an inseparable part of the Chinese territory; Diaoyu Dao is China's inherent territory in all historical, geographical and legal terms, and China enjoys indisputable sovereignty over Diaoyu Dao; China is firmly opposed to Japan's violation of China's sovereignty over Diaoyu Dao in whatever form and has taken resolute measures to curb any such act; China strongly urges Japan to respect history and international law and immediately stop all actions that undermine China's territorial sovereignty. The Chinese government has the unshakable resolve and will to uphold the nation's territorial sovereignty. It

[26] Research Group of the China Institute For Marine Affairs of the State Oceanic Administration. 2018. *China's Ocean Development Report (2018)*. Beijing: Ocean Press. pp. 116–117.

has the confidence and ability to safeguard China's state sovereignty and territorial integrity.[27]

(3) Safeguarding the rights and interests of the islands in the SCS. To safeguard China's sovereignty and maritime rights and interests in the Nanhai Zhudao, especially in response to the *SCS* Arbitration initiated by the Philippines, the SCIO issued a white paper in July 2016 titled China Adheres to the Position of Settling Through Negotiation the Relevant Disputes Between China and the Philippines in the South China Sea. It consists of the following aspects: "Introduction;" Nanhai Zhudao are China's Inherent Territory;" "Origin of the Relevant Disputes Between China and the Philippines in the South China Sea;" "China and the Philippines Have Reached Consensus on Settling Their Relevant Disputes in the South China Sea;" "The Philippines Has Repeatedly Taken Moves that Complicate the Relevant Disputes;" "China's Policy on the South China Sea Issue." The document aims to restore the truth of the China–Philippines dispute over the SCS, reiterate China's consistent position and policy on the issue, trace back to the origin of the conflict, and set the record straight. The document is summarized as follows:

In the course of history, the Chinese people have since ancient times lived and engaged in production activities on Nanhai Zhudao and in relevant waters. China is the first to have discovered, named, explored and exploited Nanhai Zhudao and relevant waters, and the first to have continuously, peacefully and effectively exercised sovereignty and jurisdiction over them, thus establishing sovereignty over Nanhai Zhudao and the relevant rights and interests in the South China Sea; China's sovereignty over Nanhai Zhudao had never been challenged before the twentieth century. When France and Japan invaded and illegally occupied by force some islands and reefs of China's Nansha Qundao in the 1930s and 1940s, the Chinese people rose to fight back strenuously and the Chinese government took a series of measures to defend China's sovereignty over Nansha Qundao.

After the end of the Second World War, China recovered and resumed the exercise of sovereignty over Nanhai Zhudao. Many countries recognize that Nanhai Zhudao are part of China's territory. The core of the relevant disputes between China and the Philippines in the SCS lies in the territorial issues caused by the Philippines' invasion and illegal occupation of some islands and reefs of China's Nansha Qundao. In addition, with the development of the international law of the sea, a maritime delimitation dispute also arose between the two states regarding certain sea areas of the SCS.

From the perspective of history and international law, the Philippines' territorial claims to some maritime features in the Nansha Qundao are groundless. There are following reasons: The Philippines' territorial claim over part of Nansha Qundao is groundless from the perspectives of either history or international law. The claim that "Kalayaan Island Group" is "*terra nullius*" discovered by the Philippines is groundless. Nansha Qundao is not "trust territory" either. Neither "contiguity or proximity" nor national security is a basis under international law for acquiring

[27] The State Council Information Office of the People's Republic of China. 2012. *Diaoyu Dao, an inherent territory of China.* Beijing: People's Publishing House. pp. 1–16.

territory. The Philippines claims that some islands and reefs of China's Nansha Qundao are located within its exclusive economic zone and continental shelf and therefore should fall under its sovereignty or form part of its continental shelf. The Philippines' so-called "effective control" on the basis of its illegal seizure is null and void. China has conducted consultations with the Philippines on managing maritime differences and promoting practical maritime cooperation, and the two sides have reached important consensus on settling through negotiation relevant disputes in the SCS and properly managing relevant disputes.

Since the 1980s, the Philippines has repeatedly taken moves that complicate the relevant disputes, including the following aspects: "The Philippines attempts to entrench its illegal occupation of some islands and reefs of China's Nansha Qundao, has increasingly intensified its infringement of China's maritime rights and interests, has territorial pretensions on China's Huangyan Dao, and the Philippines' unilateral initiation of arbitration is an act of bad faith. China consistently abides by the purposes and principles of the UN Charter and is committed to upholding and promoting international rule of law. It respects and acts in accordance with international law. While firmly safeguarding its territorial sovereignty and maritime rights and interests, China adheres to the position of settling disputes through negotiation and consultation and managing differences through rules and mechanisms. China endeavors to achieve win-win outcomes through mutually beneficial cooperation, and is committed to making the SCS a sea of peace, cooperation and friendship."[28] This is the consistent position and attitude of the Chinese Government toward the South China Sea issue.

(4) With regard to polar affairs, in May 2011, China issued the 12th Five-Year Plan for the Development of China's Polar Expeditions. It puts forward four development goals, five major tasks, and four safeguard measures for China's polar expedition during the period of the 12th Five-Year Plan.

The four development objectives are as follows: first, to carry out in-depth research on polar strategies, further strengthen the construction of policies, regulations and planning systems, and guide China's polar expeditions in a scientific and orderly way; second, to carry out comprehensive environmental expeditions to key polar regions, strengthen the monitoring of changes in polar climate and environment, open up research in the frontier fields of polar science and technology, and deepen the scientific knowledge of the North and South Polar regions; and third, continue to strengthen the capacity-building of polar expeditions, promote the application of high and new technologies, enhance the protection capacity of polar research stations, establish China's polar scientific research fleet, upgrade the capacity of polar oceanographic expeditions, and construct China's polar aviation protection capacity and safety and emergency response system, to enhance China's strength in polar expeditions; and fourth, to participate extensively in international polar affairs, safeguarding the international legal system of the polar field, and fulfilling

---

[28] The State Council Information Office of the People's Republic of China. 2016. China adheres to the position of settling through negotiation the relevant disputes between China and the Philippines in the South China Sea (July, 2016). Beijing: People's Publishing House. pp. 1–49.

corresponding international obligations to enhance China's international role in polar affairs.

There are five major tasks: first, focus on national needs and implement key special projects, including comprehensive expeditions to the North and South Poles and constructing new icebreakers for polar scientific research; second, enhance the level of polar scientific research and update the technical means of polar observation, including North and South Polar scientific research and polar observation technology and research; third, strengthen the basic platform and enhance the capacity of polar expeditions, including constructing polar research stations and domestic bases, the East and South Polar continental aviation system, the polar expedition transportation system, the real-time monitoring and emergency command system for polar expeditions, the polar logistic support system and research on basic technologies, the communication network system for polar expeditions, and the information-sharing platform for polar scientific expeditions, among others; fourth, carry out research on polar policies and soft sciences, and develop the administration in accordance with the law; and fifth, strengthen international cooperation to enhance China's influence in the polar field.

To complete the tasks of polar expeditions during the 12th Five-Year Plan period, four safeguard measures have also been proposed, including strengthening organizational leadership, reforming and improving the management system and operational mechanism, establishing a mechanism for evaluating and supervising the planning process, raising funds through multiple channels to increase investment in polar work, and building a team of researchers and promoting the spirit of polar culture.[29]

On May 22, 2017, the SCIO released the White Paper "China's Antarctic Activities." This is the first white paper by the Chinese Government on Antarctic activities development. It comprehensively reviews China's Antarctic activities development achievements over the past 30 years, including the national Antarctic observation network covering air-, shore-, sea-, ice-, and seabed-based activities, and a "one-ship, four-station, and one-base" Antarctic expedition guarantee platform, which basically guarantees the needs of Antarctic expedition activities. China has made a number of breakthrough achievements in the fields of Antarctic glaciology, space science, biology and ecology, and climate change science and has promoted the development of Antarctic scientific research from single-discipline research to interdisciplinary and comprehensive research. China is committed to peacefully utilizing Antarctica, resolutely safeguarding the Antarctic Treaty system, increasing its investment in the Antarctic, and enhancing its participation in the global governance of Antarctica.

In January 2018, the SCIO issued a white paper on China's Arctic Policy. The white paper aimed to expound its basic positions on Arctic affairs, to elaborate on its policy goals, basic principles, and major policies and positions regarding its engagement in Arctic affairs, to guide relevant Chinese government departments and institutions in Arctic-related activities and cooperation, to encourage relevant parties to get better involved in Arctic governance, and to work with the international

---

[29] Research Group of the Institute for Marine Development Strategy of the State Oceanic Administration. 2012. *China ocean development report (2012)*. Beijing: Ocean Press. pp. 298–299.

community to safeguard and promote peace and stability in, and the sustainable development of, the Arctic. It consists of the "Foreword;" "The Arctic Situation and Recent Changes;" "China and the Arctic;" "China's Policy Goals and Basic Principles on the Arctic;" "China's Policies and Positions on Participating in Arctic Affairs;" "Conclusion."[30] Regarding Arctic issues, on the basis of the principles of "respect, cooperation, win-win result and sustainability," China, as a responsible major country, is ready to cooperate with all relevant parties to seize the historic opportunity in the development of the Arctic, to address the challenges brought by the changes in the region, jointly understand, protect, develop and participate in the governance of the Arctic, and advance Arctic-related cooperation under the Belt and Road Initiative, so as to build a community of shared future for mankind and contribute to peace, stability and sustainable development in the Arctic.

2.3 New China's Achievements and Tasks Involving Ocean Management Institutions and Reforms

2.3.1 Creation and Development of China's Ocean Management Institutions

Since the SOA was established, which was approved by the 124th Standing Committee of the Second NPC in July 1964, it has undergone a number of institutional reforms. At the time of its establishment, the main responsibilities of the SOA were to unify the management of marine resources and marine environment surveys, data collection and compilation, and marine public welfare services, with the aim of transforming a decentralized and temporary collaborative force into a stable force for marine work.

The 1983 institutional reform made it clear that the SOA was a functional department of the State Council in the management of national marine work and that its main responsibilities included organizing and implementing marine surveys, scientific research, management, and public welfare services, along with coordinating national marine work.

In 1998, the basic functions of the SOA were reorganized into three main areas—marine legislation, planning, and management. Its main responsibilities were developed into six areas: management of the use of sea areas, marine environmental protection, marine science and technology, international cooperation in the oceans, marine disaster prevention and mitigation, and safeguarding of the country's maritime rights and interests.

On July 10, 2008, the General Office of the State Council issued document No. 63, "Provisions on the Main Functions, Internal Bodies and Staffing of the State Oceanic

[30] The State Council Information Office of the People's Republic of China. 2018. *China's Arctic policy*. Beijing: People's Publishing House. pp. 1–22.

Administration" (the "Three-Rules" Plan). It expanded the main responsibilities of the SOA from 7 to 11 provisions, and in the "Adjustment of Duties," it assigned the SOA the task of "strengthening the study of ocean strategy and the comprehensive coordination of ocean affairs." The newly added responsibilities represent a historic starting point toward the goal of comprehensive ocean management and a new milestone in China's ocean affairs and are important to the healthy and rapid development of China's ocean affairs in the coming period.

In the 2008 government institutional reform, the basic functions and duties of the SOA were adjusted and strengthened, with additional duties including the monitoring, assessment, and information dissemination of marine economy operations; energy conservation and emission reduction in the marine field and the response to climate change; ecological protection of islands and the lawful use of uninhabited islands; research, application, and management of the use of seawater and marine renewable resources; the organization of special projects; construction and daily operation management of the marine environmental safety and security system; and the implementation of regular rights protection patrol law enforcement system in China's jurisdictional waters, etc. In the adjustment of its basic duties, the SOA was assigned the basic duty of "strengthening marine strategic research and comprehensive coordination of marine affairs." This change has far-reaching significance in strengthening the comprehensive coordination of ocean development and utilization activities and promoting comprehensive ocean management.[31]

In addition, in October 1998, with the approval of the State Commission Office for Public Sector Reform, the SOA established the China Marine Surveillance (CMS, the Ministries and Commissions Bureau-Director level China), which was administered with reference to the national civil service system. According to the Notice on Printing and Distributing the Regulations on the Main Responsibilities, Internal Institutions, and Staff of the CMS (Guo Hai Ren Zi [2010] No. 359) issued by the SOA, the CMS' main functions are building and managing marine surveillance teams on behalf of the SOA, organizing, guiding, and supervising administrative enforcement of the sea, and organizing and implementing the enforcement of the rights of the sea. Its main duties include formulating strategies, plans, and policies for the development of CMS; supervising the implementation of the work plan and regulations of CMS; organizing and implementing rights safeguarding patrol law enforcement in the waters under China's jurisdiction, coordinating and directing major maritime law enforcement operations; organizing and conducting maritime administrative law enforcement, investigating and punishing unlawful activities in accordance with the law, compiling maritime law enforcement communiqués, bulletins, and circulars; being responsible for the construction of China's CMS system; being responsible for the capacity building, supervision and management of China's CMS ships, aircrafts, special equipment and land-shore facilities; organizing and carrying out the supervision and training of China's CMS teams; undertaking the emergency management

[31] Research Group of the China Institute For Marine Affairs of the State Oceanic Administration. 2012. *China ocean development report*, Beijing: Ocean Press. pp. 311–312.

related work of the SOA, organizing and coordinating the emergency response actions for major maritime emergencies, etc.

Since July 2006, the CMS has launched regular rights safeguarding patrol law enforcement missions in the ECS; by December 2007, the CMS realized regular rights protection patrol in all areas under China's jurisdiction, including the Yellow Sea, the ECS, and the SCS, and made a historically significant step in safeguarding the rights and interests of the sea.[32]

2.3.2 *Reforms and Tasks of China's Ocean Management Organizations*

On March 10, 2013, the 12th NPC considered and adopted the Decision on the Plan for Restructuring the State Council and Transforming Functions, reconstructing the SOA. The plan states that in order to promote unified maritime law enforcement and improve law enforcement efficiency, the current SOA and its CMS, the Coast Guard of the Ministry of Public Security, the China Fishery Administration (CFA), and the General Administration of Customs of the People's Republic of China (GACC)' Maritime Anti-Smuggling Police teams and responsibilities will be integrated. The SOA will be reorganized to carry out maritime rights safeguarding law enforcement in the name of the China Coast Guard (CCG) Bureau, and receive professional guidance from the Ministry of Public Security of the People's Republic of China (MPS).

To strengthen the overall planning and comprehensive coordination of ocean affairs, the State Oceanic Commission, a high-level deliberative and coordinating body, has been established to formulate a national strategy for the ocean development and coordinate and cooperate for major ocean-related matters. The work of the State Oceanic Commission is undertaken by the SOA.

The main responsibilities of the reorganized SOA contain the following aspects: Being responsible for drafting laws and regulations concerning sea area uses, environmental protection, scientific research and island protection in China's internal sea, territorial waters, contiguous zone, exclusive economic zone, continental shelf and other sea areas; formulating and supervising the implementation of the plans of marine function zoning and the management system of sea area uses; formulating and supervising the implementation of regulations concerning island protection and the development and utilization of uninhabited islands; carrying out plans concerning marine ecological environment protection; formulating and supervising the implementation of regulations for marine monitoring and observance and forecasting, as well as hazard forecasting and early warning, participating in emergency response to major marine disasters; conducting international marine cooperation and exchanges.

In accordance with the overall deployment of the SC to strengthen the reform of the administrative system and accelerate the transformation of government functions,

[32] Research Group of the China Institute For Marine Affairs of the State Oceanic Administration. 2013. *China ocean development report*. Beijing: Ocean Press. p. 59.

in June 2013, the SC issued the Provisions on the Main Functions, Internal Bodies and Staffing of the SOA. These provisions streamlined the division of responsibilities between the SOA and other major sea-related departments, such as the NDRC, the MFA, the MLR, the Ministry of Environmental Protection of the People's Republic of China (MEP), the MOST, the Ministry of Transport of the People's Republic of China (MOT), the Ministry of Agriculture of the People's Republic of China (MOA), the Ministry of Water Resources of the People's Republic of China (MWR), the MPS, the Ministry of Industry and Information Technology (MIIT), the National Tourism Administration (NTA), the National Forestry and Grassland Administration (NFGA), the National Cultural Heritage Administration (NCHA), and the GAOC.

According to the Decision of the CPC Central Committee on Deepening the Reform of the Party and State Institutions adopted by the Third Plenary Session of the 19th Central Committee of the CPC on February 28, 2018, and the Plan for Deepening the Reform of Party and State Agencies issued by the Central Committee of the CPC on March 21, 2018, the main elements of the reform of the sea-related institutions include the following aspects:

First, with regard to deepening the reform of party central agencies, the Central Leading Group for Safeguarding Maritime Rights and Interests will no longer exist. In order to resolutely safeguard national sovereignty and maritime rights and interests, better coordinate the resources and forces of foreign affairs and maritime-related departments, the protection of maritime rights and interests will be incorporated into the overall situation of the central foreign affairs work for unified planning and unified deployment. The Central Leading Group for Safeguarding the Maritime Rights will no longer be established. The relevant responsibilities will be entrusted to the Central Commission for Foreign Affairs and its office, and the Office for Safeguarding Maritime Rights and Interests will be set up in the Office of the Central Commission for Foreign Affairs (CCFA). After the adjustment, the main responsibilities of the CCFA and its office in safeguarding maritime rights and interests are to organize, coordinate, guide and urge all relevant parties to implement the Party Central Committee's decision-making and deployment on safeguarding maritime rights and interests, collect, summarize, analyze and judge intelligence information related to the country's maritime rights and interests, coordinate and deal with emergencies, organize research on major issues in safeguarding maritime rights and interests and put forward countermeasures and suggestions, etc.

Second, regarding deepening the reform of SC institutions, the MNR will be established. In order to uniformly exercise the responsibilities of owners of natural resources assets owned by the whole people, uniformly exercise all the responsibilities of land and space use control and ecological protection and restoration, and strive to solve the problems of inadequate owners of natural resources and overlapping spatial planning, the responsibilities of the MLR, the organization and planning responsibilities for main functional areas of the NDRC, the urban and rural planning management responsibilities of the Ministry of Housing and Urban–Rural Development of the People's Republic of China (MOHURD), the water resources investigation and ownership confirmation registration management responsibilities of the MWR, the grassland resources investigation and ownership confirmation registration management responsibilities of the MOA, the forest, wetland and other resources investigation and ownership registration management responsibilities of the NFGA, the responsibilities of the SOA, and the responsibilities of the National Administration of Surveying, Mapping and Geoinformation (NASG) are integrated, and the MNR is established as a constituent department of the State Council. The MNR retains the name of the SOA for external purposes.

The main responsibilities are to supervise the development, utilization and protection of natural resources, establish a spatial planning system and supervise its implementation, perform the duties of owners of all kinds of natural resource assets owned by the whole people, unify investigation and registration of rights confirmation, establish a paid use system of natural resources, and be responsible for the management of surveying and mapping and geological exploration industries. The MLR, the SOA and the NASG will no longer be retained.

Third, regarding deepening the reform of SC institutions, the MEE was formed. In order to integrate the scattered responsibilities of ecological and environmental protection, unify the supervision and administrative law enforcement of various types of pollution emissions in ecology and urban and rural areas, strengthen environmental pollution control, ensure national ecological security, and build a beautiful China, the responsibilities of the MEP, the NRDC's response to climate change and emission reduction responsibilities, the MLR's supervision and prevention of groundwater pollution responsibilities, the MWR's preparation of water function zoning, sewage outlet setting management, and basin water environment protection responsibilities, the MOA's supervision and guidance of agricultural non-point source pollution control responsibilities, the SOA's marine environmental protection responsibilities, and the South-to-North Water Diversion Project Area Environmental Protection responsibilities of the General Office of the SC South-to-North Water Diversion Project Construction Committee are integrated to form the MEE as a constituent department of the SC. The MEE retains the name of National Nuclear Safety Administration for external purposes.

The MEE's main responsibilities are to formulate and organize the implementation of ecological environment policies, plans, and standards, be responsible for ecological environment monitoring and law enforcement, supervise and manage pollution prevention and control, nuclear and radiation safety, and organize central environmental protection inspections. The MEP will no longer be retained.

Fourth, with regard to deepening the reform of administrative law enforcement, a comprehensive law enforcement team for ecological environmental protection will be integrated and formed by the MEE. The law enforcement responsibilities and teams of environmental protection, land, agriculture, water conservancy, ocean and other departments related to pollution prevention and ecological protection are integrated, and the implementation of ecological environment protection law enforcement is unified under the guidance of the MEE.

Fifth, in the context of deepening cross-service and cross-regional reform, the Maritime Corps, under the leadership and management of the SOA, will be transferred to the Chinese People's Armed Police Force (PAP). Implementing the Party Central Committee's decision on adjusting the leadership and command system of the PAP, in accordance with the principle that the army is the army, the police is the police, and the people are the people, all active forces listed in the sequence of the PAP and managed by the SC department leaders will be withdrawn from the PAP, the coast guard under the leadership and management of the SOA will be transferred to the PAP, and the Gold Corps, Forestry Corps, and Hydropower Corps of the PAP that are responsible for civil tasks will be transferred to the relevant functional areas of business of the country and reorganized into non-active professional corps. Meanwhile, the customs duty force of the PAP will be withdrawn, and the relationship between the leadership, management, command and use of the PAP will be thoroughly straightened out. In addition, the Maritime Corps was transferred to the Armed Police Force, and all the Maritime Corps and related functions under the leadership of the SOA (the CCG Bureau) were transferred to the Armed Police Force in the manner of first transfer and then reorganization.[33]

Based on the Decision of the CPC Central Committee on Deepening the Reform of the Party and State Institutions, the Plan for Deepening the Reform of Party and State Agencies and the Program for the Institutional Reform of the State Council approved at the First Meeting of the Thirteenth NPC, the MNR published the Provisions on the Configuration of the Functions, Internal Organizations and Staffing. The MEE published the Provisions on the Configuration of the Functions, Internal Organizations and Staffing (September 11, 2018).[34]

Meanwhile, in order to enable the CCG Bureau to perform its maritime rights protection law enforcement duties in accordance with the decision-making arrangements of the Deepening the Reform Plan of Party and State Institutions and the Implementation Plan for the Reform of the Armed Police Force (December 27, 2017) (the entire Coast Guard Force is under the leadership and command of PAP, and the establishment of the CCG Bureau, unified performance of maritime rights protection law enforcement duties), the Third Meeting of the Standing Committee of the 13th NPC passed the Decision on the Exercise of Maritime Rights Protection Law Enforcement Duties by the Chinese Coast Guard Bureau on June 22, 2018 (effective from July 1, 2018).[35]

The aforementioned decision stipulated the scope or tasks of the CCG Bureau's rights protection and law enforcement, as well as the relationship with other relevant administrative agencies during the execution of tasks, were stipulated, thus coordinating the powers of the CCG Bureau between the leadership of the Central Military Commission and other administrative agencies in law enforcement. In particular, a coordination mechanism between the CCG Bureau and other administrative organs

---

[33] See http://www.xinhuanet.com/politics/2018-03/21/c_1122570517.htm, accessed March 21, 2018.

[34] For the Ministry of Natural Resources' "Three-Rules" contents, see http://www.mnr.gov.cn/bbgk/sdfa/, accessed September 11, 2018; for the Ministry of Ecology and Environment's "Three-Rules" contents, see http://www.cenews.com.cn/news/201809/t20180911_884728.html, accessed September 12, 2018.

[35] For the content of the Decision of the Standing Committee of the NPC on the Exercise of Maritime Rights Protection Law Enforcement Powers by the China Coast Guard Bureau, see http://www.npc.gov.cn/npc/xinwen/2018-06/22/content_2056585.htm, accessed on June 22, 2018.

(e.g., the MNR, the MEE, the Ministry of Agriculture and Rural Development of the People's Republic of China (MARA), and the GAOC) must be refined in future laws and regulations, including amending existing laws and regulations related to the maritime field. More importantly, in order to exercise the powers of the CCG Bureau in maritime rights protection and law enforcement, the Organizational Law of the Chinese Coast Guard should be formulated as soon as possible to further clarify its powers and scope or tasks at a higher level of law.[36]

Undeniably, one of the important tasks of our country's ocean management agencies is to further clarify the specific powers and obligations of sea-related agencies, which need to be solidified by law, including amending previous relevant regulations, as well as supplementing and formulating new regulations, such as the Basic Law of the Sea, to define the coordinating function of maritime agencies, especially the State Oceanic Commission, and play its leading role.

2.4 China's Policy and Position on Maritime Issues

For a number of subjective and objective reasons, including low awareness of the oceans for a long duration; backwardness in marine science, technology, and equipment; and a relatively unfavorable marine geographic environment, China has accumulated many marine problems. With the increased demand for and efforts to exploit and utilize the oceans and their resources by the international community, particularly with the entry and implementation of the UNCLOS, several controversies over marine issues, especially in the SCS and ECS, are becoming increasingly prominent, jeopardizing the order of the oceans and regional security.

China has proposed specific principles and methods to solve these issues, however, despite having made certain achievements, it has faced difficulties and challenges. China's ocean policy includes a commitment to consultation and negotiation, the principle of "sovereignty belongs to China, disputes can be shelved, and we can pursue joint development," the "dual-track approach" (disputes related to the SCS should be addressed properly through negotiations and consultations among countries directly concerned, and China and the ASEAN countries should work together to safeguard peace and stability in the SCS), the formulation of rules and regulations, crisis management, resource sharing and win–win cooperation, a desire for a sea of peace, amity, and cooperation, and achieving a "harmonious sea." These are policy choices based on China's own national conditions and realities, which reflect its cultural influences and a will for peace, inclusiveness, and cooperation. They are further based on applying and developing China's culture of peace and harmony, including the idea of seeking common ground while resolving differences

[36] The Coast Guard Law of the People's Republic of China was adopted by the 25th Meeting of the Standing Committee of the 13th NPC on January 22, 2021, and came into force on February 1, 2021. See *Law of the People's Republic of China on Maritime Police*. 2021. Beijing: Law Press. pp. 3–22.

and valuing peace in ocean policy above all. This is fully in line with the development process of the international community, including the order of the sea, and should be understood and respected. The principles of peace, inclusiveness, and cooperation embedded in China's ocean policy reflect not only the application and development of its traditional culture in the oceans but also Chinese culture's status and role in the governance of the oceans and have research value.

This section provides a preliminary look at the principles or approaches of China's ocean policy based on national initiatives, highlighting their rationality and feasibility and differentiating them from analyses based on the perspectives of ocean culture and soft power. The aim is to enable people to understand the reasons for, and the position and role of cultural elements in, China's ocean policy.[37]

2.4.1 Peace: Consistent with the Principles and Aspirations of the International Community

With regard to maritime issues involving vital national interests, China insists on prioritizing maritime dispute resolution with other countries through peaceful political or diplomatic methods, including direct consultation and negotiation. The peaceful nature of such a policy is fully in line with the institutional requirements of international law and China's national practice and is worth complying with.

The use of peaceful means to settle disputes between states is not only a normative requirement of the UN Charter, e.g., Articles 2(3) and 33, but is also in line with the principle of peaceful settlement of disputes of the UNCLOS, e.g., Article 279.[38] It is also in accordance with the requirements of the regional regime, e.g., Article 4 of the DOC, as well as the requirements of other bilateral documents, including the China-Philippines Joint Statements (Joint Declarations), China–Vietnam Joint Declarations, Article 6 of the Sino-Japanese Joint Communique, and Article 1(2) of the Sino-Japanese Treaty of Peace and Friendship.[39]

---

[37] For research on marine culture, see Jilu, Wu. 2008. On the content, positioning and perspective of marine culture research, *Ningxia Social Science* 4; for marine soft power, see Qi, Wang and Jianshan, Liu. 2013. Marine Soft Power: Definition and Interpretation, *Journal of University of Jinan (Social Science Edition)* 2; for the relationship between the ocean and history, culture, and consciousness, see Wenhe, Yang, and Boyong, Chen. 2014. *Ocean and Modern China.* Beijing: Ocean Press.

[38] For example, Article 279 of the UNCLOS provides that "States Parties shall settle any dispute between them concerning the interpretation or application of this Convention by peaceful means in accordance with Article 2, paragraph 3, of the Charter of the United Nations and, to this end, shall seek a solution by the means indicated in Article 33, paragraph 1, of the Charter."

[39] Article 4 of the Declaration on the Conduct of Parties in the South China Sea provides that "The Parties concerned undertake to resolve their territorial and jurisdictional disputes by peaceful means, without resorting to the threat or use of force, through friendly consultations and negotiations by sovereign states directly concerned, in accordance with universally recognized principles of international law, including the 1982 UN Convention on the Law of the Sea." Article 6 of the Sino-Japanese Joint Communique, and Article 1(2) of the Sino-Japanese Treaty of Peace and Friendship

The use of peaceful methods, especially political methods, to settle interstate maritime disputes is also in line with China's theory and practice. For example, Article 2 of the Decision of the Standing Committee of the NPC on the Ratification of the UNCLOS (May 15, 1996)[40]; Article 2(3), of the Law of the People's Republic of China on the Exclusive Economic Zone and the Continental Shelf[41]; and the written declaration submitted by China to the UN Secretary-General on August 25, 2006 in accordance with Article 298 of the UNCLOS to exclude from compulsory jurisdiction such matters as territorial sovereignty, the sea boundary delimitation, historical title, and other law enforcement activities. Meanwhile, over the past 50 years, China has solved boundary issues with 12 land neighbors and signed 29 land boundary treaties through negotiation and consultation.[42] China and Vietnam concluded the China and Vietnam Initial Agreements on Delimitation of Beibu Bay/Fishery Cooperation (which entered into force on June 30, 2014). China has insisted on prioritizing the use of political methods to resolve territorial disputes with neighboring countries and has achieved positive results.

2.4.2 *Inclusiveness: The Rationality and Difficulty of "Shelving Disputes and Carrying Out Joint Development" Solutions*

With regard to the ECS and the SCS, China has proposed the principle or guideline of "sovereignty belongs to China, disputes can be shelved, and we can pursue joint development," which embodies the position of respecting and understanding the claims of other countries. It also reflects the cultural characteristic of inclusiveness, especially the concept of "sovereignty is indivisible and resources can be shared."

With regard to the ECS, especially the Diaoyu Dao, although "shelving disputes" is not found in the Sino-Japanese Joint Communique (September 29, 1972) or the Sino-Japanese Treaty of Peace and Friendship (August 12, 1978), However, on October 25, 1978, after the exchange of the Sino-Japanese Treaty of Peace and Friendship

provides that "The two Governments confirm that, in their mutual relations settle all disputes by peaceful means and shall refrain from the use or threat of force."

40 Article 2 of the Decision of the Standing Committee of the NPC on the Ratification of the UNCLOS stipulates that the PRC will, via consultations with States with opposite or adjacent coasts, delimit their respective maritime jurisdictions as per the principle of equity on the basis of international law.

41 Article 2(3) of the Law on the Exclusive Economic Zone and the Continental Shelf stipulates that "Conflicting claims regarding the exclusive economic zone and the continental shelf by the People's Republic of China and States with opposite or adjacent coasts shall be settled, on the basis of international law and in accordance with the principle of equity, by an agreement delimiting the areas so claimed."

42 See Director-General of the Department of Boundary and Ocean Affairs of the Ministry of Foreign Affairs Ouyang Yujing Gives Interview to Chinese and Foreign Media on South China Sea Issue, 2016, http://www.fmprc.gov.cn/web/wjbxw_673019/t1361270.shtml, accessed May 8, 2016.

(October 23, 1978), Chinese Vice Premier Deng Xiaoping's response at the Japan Press Club indicated that there was an agreement between the two countries not to involve the Diaoyu Dao issue in the negotiations to normalize Sino-Japanese diplomatic relations and the Sino-Japanese Treaty of Peace and Friendship,[43] otherwise, in response to Deng Xiaoping's response at the Japan Press Club, the Japanese government could have given a different answer, but they did not express a different opinion or raise objections, indicating that the Japanese government tacitly agreed to "shelving disputes". It should be noted that since Vice Premier Deng Xiaoping's response at the Japan Press Club was held after the exchange of the approval documents of the China-Japan Treaty of Peace and Friendship on October 23, 1978, the response to the Diaoyu Dao issue has the defect of supplementing the content of the China-Japan Treaty of Peace and Friendship in principle and abstraction, and has the function and effect of interpretation, that is, the response to the Diaoyu Dao issue also has certain effectiveness. Article 32(2), of the VCLT provides that the *travaux prếparatoires* of the treaty and the circumstances of its conclusion may also serve as supplementary information for the interpretation of the treaty.[44]

Meanwhile, Articles 1–3 of the Sino-Japanese Fisheries Agreement (signed on November 11, 1997, and entered into force on June 1, 2000) regard the waters surrounding the Diaoyu Dao as disputed waters, recognizing the existence of a dispute between the two countries over the waters surrounding the Diaoyu Dao, and reflecting that it is based on the consensus of "shelving disputes." Since then, the Government of Japan has also dealt with the Diaoyu Dao issue on the basis of this "shelving" approach, which has been manifested in the form of "no visit to the islands, no investigation, no exploitation and no punishment."

Even in the China and Japan Reach Principled Consensus on the East China Sea Issue, issued by the foreign affairs departments of China and Japan on June 18, 2008, the issue of the delimitation of the maritime areas of China and Japan in the ECS was shelved, implying joint development of the matter. It states that, after serious consultations, China and Japan have agreed to cooperate, without prejudice to the legal positions of the two sides, during the transitional period before demarcation is realized, including cooperative development in the Chunxiao Oil and Gas Field and joint development in other areas of the ECS.

Regarding the disputes over the SCS, especially the Nansha Qundao, Chinese Vice Premier Deng Xiaoping proposed the approach of "sovereignty belongs to China,

---

[43] See The Editorial Team of Deng Xiaoping's Conversations with Foreign Heads of State and Press Conferences. 2011. Deng Xiaoping's Conversations with Foreign Heads of State and Press Conferences. Beijing: Taihai Publishing House. pp. 315–320. Vice Premier Deng Xiaoping pointed out at the Japan Press Club: "This issue is temporarily shelved, it doesn't matter if it is left for ten years; our generation lacks wisdom, and once this issue is discussed, there will be no results; the next generation will definitely be smarter than us, and I believe that we can find a good solution that both sides can accept at that time." See Japan Press Club. 1978. Friendly Relations towards the Future, http://www.jnpc.or.jp/files/opdf/117, accessed August 12, 2014.

[44] On "shelving disputes" in the Diaoyu Dao, see Yongming, Jin. 2016. Analysis of China's maintenance of rights and interests in East China Sea according to international law, *Journal of Shanghai University (Social Sciences Edition)* 4: 5–7.

disputes can be shelved, and we can pursue joint development" in 1984. In a June 1986 meeting with Philippine Vice President Salvador Laurel, Chinese leader Deng Xiaoping pointed out that Nansha Qundao belongs to China, and when referring to the matter of differences, stated that, "This issue can be shelved for now. Several years later, we can sit down and work out a solution that is acceptable to all in a calm manner. We shall not let this issue stand in the way of our friendly relations with the Philippines and with other countries." In April 1988, when meeting with Philippine President Corazón Aquino, Deng Xiaoping reiterated that "with regard to the issue concerning Nansha Qundao, China has the biggest say. Nansha Qundao has been part of China's territory throughout history, and no one has ever expressed objection to this for quite some time;" and "For the sake of the friendship between our two countries, we can shelve the issue for now and pursue joint development." Since then, when handling the relevant SCS issue and developing bilateral ties with other littoral countries around the SCS, China has all along acted in keeping with Deng Xiaoping's idea: "Sovereignty belongs to China, disputes can be shelved, and we can pursue joint development."[45]

In addition, through the efforts of all parties, China and some ASEAN countries have achieved results based on the policy of "pursuing joint development while shelving disputes," including concluding the China and Vietnam Initial Agreements on Delimitation of Beibu Bay/Fishery Cooperation. On March 14, 2005, China signed the Tripartite Agreement for Joint Marine Seismic Undertaking in the Agreement Area in the South China Sea with the Philippines and Vietnam. Based on the DOC (November 4, 2002), China and ASEAN countries reached a unanimous consensus on the Guidelines for Implementing the Declaration on the Conduct of Parties in the South China Sea on July 20, 2011.[46] On October 11, 2011, China and Vietnam concluded an Agreement on the basic principles guiding the settlement of maritime issues and issued the Sino-Vietnamese Joint Declaration on October 15, 2011, which provided political guarantees of utilizing peaceful methods to resolve disputes in the SCS between China and ASEAN countries and reflect the function and significance of reference and inspiration, reflecting the cultural thought of valuing harmony.

While the policy of "pursuing joint development while shelving disputes" has a theoretical basis in international law, such as Articles 74(3) and 83(3) of the UNCLOS, it is also in line with the practices of the international community.[47] However, due to the complexity and sensitivity of the disputes in the SCS, the policy

---

[45] The State Council Information Office of the People's Republic of China. 2016. White paper on China Adheres to the Position of Settling Through Negotiation the Relevant Disputes Between China and the Philippines in the South China Sea. Beijing: People's Publishing House. p. 25.

[46] For example, the Guidelines for the Implementation of the Declaration on the Conduct of Parties in the South China Sea between China and ASEAN Countries state: "The implementation of the DOC should be carried out in a step-by-step approach in line with the provisions of the DOC. The Parties to the DOC will continue to promote dialogue and consultations in accordance with the spirit of the DOC. The decision to implement concrete measures or activities of the DOC should be based on consensus among parties concerned, and lead to the eventual realization of a Code of Conduct."

[47] For example, Article 74(3) of the UNCLOS provides that, "Pending agreement as provided for in paragraph 1, the States concerned, in a spirit of understanding and cooperation, shall make every

of "pursuing joint development while shelving disputes" has not been effectively respected. There are a few reasons for this: some ASEAN countries lack the political will to implement the policy of "pursuing joint development while shelving disputes," making it difficult to start. There is no need for practical interests because some ASEAN countries have already made great efforts to develop resources in the SCS. The disputes in the SCS, especially the dispute over Nansha Qundao, involve a number of parties, making it difficult to reach a consensus, and there are difficulties in the actual operation of the policy.[48] Therefore, there are still difficulties in the implementation of the principle or policy of "pursuing joint development while shelving disputes" in Nansha Qundao.

In this context, the approach of "resolving simple issues before the difficult ones" should be followed, with a focus on making a breakthrough for less sensitive areas, including strengthening cooperation in the areas of marine environmental protection, marine scientific research, the safety of maritime navigation and transportation, search and rescue operations, and combating transnational crime includes but is not limited to combating drug trafficking, piracy and armed robbery at sea, and arms smuggling. This is in line with Article 6 of the DOC and the normative requirements of Article 123 of the UNCLOS. In other words, despite the rationality of the principle of "pursuing joint development while shelving disputes", its practical implementation in the SCS still faces challenges and difficulties, especially in the Nansha Qundao. Thus, it is still an important and arduous task for China and ASEAN countries to find feasible ways that can be accepted by multiple parties. In this regard, extraterritorial countries in the SCS region should respect the "dual-track approach" policy adopted by China and the ASEAN countries and encourage and promote the consensus reached between them to enhance mutual trust and contribute to a resolution of the SCS issue. This is also the proper meaning of China's cultural inclusiveness.

2.4.3 Cooperativeness: Building a Platform for Ocean Cooperation to Achieve a Multi-Win Goal

Due to the complexity and comprehensiveness of the ocean itself, the governance of the ocean and the resolution of ocean issues require a cooperative attitude from multiple parties in order to reasonably handle ocean issues and achieve the goal of sustainable use of the ocean and its resources. The preamble to the UNCLOS states that "The States Parties to this Convention are conscious that the problems of ocean

---

effort to enter into provisional arrangements of a practical nature and, during this transitional period, not to jeopardize or hamper the reaching of the final agreement. Such arrangements shall be without prejudice to the final delimitation."

[48] See Yongming, Jin. 2012. Nature of the dashed line and legal status of internal water areas in South China

Sea, China Legal Science 6: 46.

space are closely interrelated and need to be considered as a whole." Meanwhile, cooperation in dealing with the problems of the sea is a normative requirement of the UNCLOS and is reflected in a number of articles, such as Articles 100, 108, 117, 118, 123, 197, 242, 266, 270, 273, and 287. This principle is also consistent with the requirements of the UN Charter, for example, Articles 1, 2, 11, and 49. Moreover, "the duty of states to cooperate with one another" was recognized in the Declaration on Principles of International Law concerning Friendly Relations and Co-operation among States in accordance with the Charter of the United Nations adopted by the UNGA on 24 October 1970. In other words, cooperation in dealing with maritime issues is a basic principle of international law, including the UN Charter and the UNCLOS, and must be respected and implemented. This principle is in line with the requirements of China's harmonious culture.

To effectively implement the principle of cooperation, specific paths or platforms must be provided, in this regard, China has provided excellent public services to enhance the potential and effectiveness of cooperation. For example, platforms such as the AIIB, and the China–ASEAN Investment Cooperation Fund have promoted the BRI and strengthened interfacing with regional countries' development strategies to achieve cooperation that is beneficial to all parties.

The main purpose of China's establishment of these platforms is to build the ocean, including the ECS and the SCS, into a sea of "peace, friendship, and cooperation," and to achieve the goal of "harmonious oceans." In 2009, China proposed an initiative to build "harmonious oceans," reflecting a new understanding of and requirements for ocean issues and marking China's contribution to the development of marine order and the law of the sea. Because this concept is a product that combines the development of domestic and foreign maritime situations and meets the needs of the times, it is necessary to work together to maintain lasting peace and security in the oceans. The content of harmonious oceans includes: adhering to the leadership of the UN, establishing a fair and reasonable ocean; adhering to equal consultation, building a free and orderly ocean; adhering to treating both symptoms and root causes, building a peaceful and peaceful ocean; adhering to communication and cooperation, building a harmonious and coexisting ocean; adhering to respecting and loving the sea, and building a unified ocean. That is, by standardizing and defining the goals, principles, directions, paths, attitudes, etc. of "harmonious oceans," it reflects the beautiful desire of human beings to develop and utilize ocean space and its resources, and cooperates to deal with the fundamental trend and inevitable requirements of the ocean, in order to achieve the win–win goal of human use of the ocean and the goal of harmonious coexistence between human beings and the ocean.

2.4.4 Consistency: Adherence to the Principle of Sovereign Equality of States in Dealing with Maritime Issues

China's position and attitude towards ocean policy are not only consistent, but also long-term and have the characteristics of continuity. That is to say, China's policy of dealing with ocean issues always contains several elements of culture: peace, inclusiveness, and cooperation, reflecting the idea and essence of peace and harmony.

Even after the Philippines unilaterally initiated the *SCS* Arbitration on January 22, 2013, the Tribunal of the *SCS* Arbitration, ignoring the Chinese Government's rejection of the arbitration, insisted on advancing arbitration to make the so-called final award on July 12, 2016. The Chinese government still adheres to the position of resolving disputes in the SCS through consultation and negotiation with relevant countries in a series of documents or statements, reflecting the consistency and consistency of policies in dealing with major maritime disputes.

For example, the Position Paper of the Government of the PRC on the Matter of Jurisdiction in the South China Sea Arbitration Initiated by the Republic of the Philippines (December 7, 2014) states that "The unilateral initiation of the present arbitration by the Philippines will not change the history and fact of China's sovereignty over the South China Sea Islands and the adjacent waters; nor will it shake China's resolve and determination to safeguard its sovereignty and maritime rights and interests; nor will it affect the policy and position of China to resolve the relevant disputes by direct negotiations and work together with other States in the region to maintain peace and stability in the South China Sea."[49]

The Statement of the Ministry of Foreign Affairs of the People's Republic of China on the Award on Jurisdiction and Admissibility of the South China Sea Arbitration by the Arbitral Tribunal Established at the Request of the Republic of the Philippines (October 29, 2015) states that "The Philippines' attempt to negate China's territorial sovereignty and maritime rights and interests in the South China Sea through arbitral proceeding will lead to nothing. China urges the Philippines to honor its own commitments, respect China's rights under international law, change its course and return to the right track of resolving relevant disputes in the South China Sea through negotiations and consultations."[50]

The Statement of the Ministry of Foreign Affairs of the People's Republic of China on Settling Disputes Between China and the Philippines in the South China Sea Through Bilateral Negotiation (June 8, 2016) states that "China is firmly opposed to the Philippines' unilateral actions. China adheres to the solemn position of non-acceptance of and non-participation in the arbitration, and will stay committed to

---

[49] Position Paper of the Government of the People's Republic of China on the Matter of Jurisdiction in the South China Sea Arbitration Initiated by the Republic of the Philippines, http://www.gov.cn/xinwen/2014-12/07/content_2787671.htm, accessed December 8, 2014.

[50] Statement of the Ministry of Foreign Affairs of the People's Republic of China on the Award on Jurisdiction and Admissibility of the South China Sea Arbitration by the Arbitral Tribunal Established at the Request of the Republic of the Philippines, http://www.fmprc.gov.cn/web/zyxw/t1310470.shtml, accessed October 30, 2015.

settling the relevant disputes with the Philippines in the South China Sea through bilateral negotiation.."[51]

The Statement of the Government of the People's Republic of China on China's Territorial Sovereignty and Maritime Rights and Interests in the South China Sea (July 12, 2016) states that "China stands ready to continue to resolve the relevant disputes peacefully through negotiation and consultation with the states directly concerned on the basis of respecting historical facts and in accordance with international law. Pending final settlement, China is also ready to make every effort with the states directly concerned to enter into provisional arrangements of a practical nature, including joint development in relevant maritime areas, in order to achieve win-win results and jointly maintain peace and stability in the South China Sea.."[52]

The Statement of the Ministry of Foreign Affairs of the People's Republic of China on the Award of 12 July 2016 of the Arbitral Tribunal in the South China Sea Arbitration Established at the Request of the Republic of the Philippines (July 12, 2016) states that "The Chinese government will continue to abide by international law and basic norms governing international relations as enshrined in the Charter of the United Nations, including the principles of respecting state sovereignty and territorial integrity and peaceful settlement of disputes, and continue to work with states directly concerned to resolve the relevant disputes in the South China Sea through negotiations and consultations on the basis of respecting historical facts and in accordance with international law, so as to maintain peace and stability in the South China Sea."[53]

In this context, China's right to independently choose its own method of dispute settlement based on the principle of sovereign equality of states should be respected. This position is consistent with the principles of international law and is recognized by most countries. For example, the Doha Declaration (May 12, 2016) adopted at the 7th Session of Ministerial Meeting of Arab-Chinese Cooperation Forum emphasized that Arab states support China to peacefully settle territorial and maritime disputes with concerned countries though friendly consultation and negotiation in accordance with bilateral agreements and relevant regional consensus, and stresses that the rights entitled to sovereignty states and State Parties of the United Nations Convention

[51] Statement of the Ministry of Foreign Affairs of the People's Republic of China on Settling Disputes Between China and the Philippines in the South China Sea Through Bilateral Negotiation, http://www.fmprc.gov.cn/web/zyxw/t1370477.shtml, accessed June 8, 2016.

[52] Statement of the Government of the People's Republic of China on China's Territorial Sovereignty and Maritime Rights and Interests in the South China Sea, http://world.people.com.cn/n1/2016/0712/c1002-28548370.html, accessed July 12, 2016.

[53] Statement of the Ministry of Foreign Affairs of the People's Republic of China on the Award of 12 July 2016 of the Arbitral Tribunal in the South China Sea Arbitration Established at the Request of the Republic of the Philippines, http://www.fmprc.gov.cn/web/zyxw/t1379490.shtml, accessed July 12, 2016.

of the Law of the Sea to choose dispute settlement ways independently should be respected.[54]

The Declaration of the People's Republic of China and the Russian Federation on the Promotion of International Law (June 26, 2016) states that China and Russia "reaffirm the principle of peaceful settlement of disputes and express their firm conviction that States shall resolve their disputes through dispute settlement means and mechanisms that they have agreed upon, and all means of settlement of disputes should serve the goal of resolving disputes in a peaceful manner in accordance with applicable international law, thus leading to de-escalation of tensions and promotion of peaceful cooperation among disputing parties. This applies equally to all types and stages of dispute settlement, including political and diplomatic means when they serve as a pre-requisite to the use of other mechanisms of dispute settlement. It is crucial for the maintenance of international legal order that all dispute settlement means and mechanisms are based on consent and used in good faith and in the spirit of cooperation, and their purposes shall not be undermined by abusive practices."[55]

The Joint Statement of The Foreign Ministers of ASEAN Member States and China on The Full and Effective Implementation of The Declaration on The Conduct of Parties in The South China Sea (July 25, 2016) states that "The Parties concerned undertake to resolve their territorial and jurisdictional disputes by peaceful means, without resorting to the threat or use of force, through friendly consultations and negotiations by sovereign states directly concerned, in accordance with universally recognised principles of international law, including the 1982 UNCLOS."[56]

The above-mentioned regional and bilateral documents demonstrate that China's consistent commitment to resolving disputes by political or diplomatic means with the sovereign states directly concerned is recognized by most countries. Therefore, China's ocean policy is consistent and fully in line with the principles of international law and must be respected. Furthermore, it reflects the inheritance of Chinese culture.

2.4.5 *China's Basic Path and Key Points in Resolving Maritime Disputes*

As mentioned above, China's position and attitude toward maritime issues enjoys the support of most countries and is in line with international maritime development trends. To maintain order, peace, and security in the oceans, China has exercised the utmost restraint, including refraining from developing resources in the SCS,

---

[54] 70 countries around the world clearly state their support for China's position on the South China Sea, 2016, http://world.people.com.cn/n1/2016/0711/c1002-28544870.html, accessed July 12, 2016.

[55] Declaration of the People's Republic of China and the Russian Federation on the Promotion of International Law, http://www.fmprc.gov.cn/web/zyxw/t1375313.shtml, accessed June 26, 2016.

[56] Joint Statement of The Foreign Ministers of ASEAN Member States and China on The Full and Effective Implementation of The Declaration on The Conduct of Parties in The South China Sea, http://www.fmprc.gov.cn/web/zyxw/t1384157.shtml, accessed July 25, 2016.

especially in the Nansha Qundao. Additionally, it has not taken threatening measures preventing other countries from developing resources in the Nansha Qundao and has striven to build mechanisms for peaceful settlement, including actively promoting the process of the "COC," in accordance with the principles and requirements of the DOC and principles and requirements of the guidelines for its follow-up. In doing so, it aims to functionally and normatively unify the SCS and its resources and to contribute to regional development. Specifically, China's path to maritime issues is formulating rules, managing crises, and implementing joint development regimes to ultimately rationally resolve major maritime disputes, such as those in the SCS and ECS and become a regional maritime country and contribute to advancing the maritime silk road.

In short, China is a firm defender of the law of the sea system and maritime order, as well as a defender and builder of enriching and developing the international legal system, including the law of the sea. China's actions and practices should be understood and supported. Given China's development process and major country status, it is also in line with the needs of practical development to require it to make greater international contributions and assume more responsibilities. Peaceful joint efforts to deal with maritime issues are the common expectation of the international community, with the aim of maintaining maritime security and order, making the oceans better serve humanity, and giving full play to the unique contributions of the oceans. This is the common expectation of the international community and must be achieved through cooperation. The above-mentioned maritime policies and guidelines also reflect the basic requirements of Chinese culture, showing a trend of cooperation at multiple levels to reflect the essence of harmony and harmony culture.

Finally, it should be emphasized that China's recovery of territorial sovereignty, including the Nanhai Zhudao and the Diaoyu Dao, and the achievement of sovereignty and territorial integrity goals is not only a just and reasonable demand of the Chinese government, but also a legitimate requirement of Chinese culture, and a reasonable destination for maintaining the international legal system and international order established after World War II. It should receive strong support from the international community; otherwise, the international rules and security order established after World War II will face major challenges and crises, and China's cultural essence will face major impacts, which is a reality that the international community does not want to see.

Chapter 3
Measures and Effects of New China in the Ocean Project

New China's policy achievements in the area of oceans and seas have mainly been accomplished with regard to the concept of harmonious oceans, the strategic goal of a strong maritime country, and the BRI.

3.1 The Harmonious Oceans Concept of New China

In celebration of the 60th anniversary of the founding of the People's Liberation Army Navy (PLAN), and consistent with international and domestic development needs, China proposed the harmonious oceans and seas initiative with a view to jointly safeguarding lasting peace and security in the oceans. The harmonious oceans concept crystalizes the concept of building a harmonious world proposed by Chinese President Hu Jintao at the UN Summit on September 15, 2005, reflecting the international community's new understanding of and demands related to the oceans and marking China's new contribution to international law, in particular the law of the sea.

3.1.1 The Need for the Concept of Building Harmonious Oceans

The twenty-first century has been called the century of the oceans. The rational development and utilization of ocean space and resources will ensure the supply of resources and space needed for the development of human society. The rational planning and strategic use of the oceans and seas is expected to achieve both maritime and national security. For the foreseeable future, China's national security will come mainly from the sea, especially the nontraditional security of the sea. The main reasons for this are, first, that the survey of the land borders between China and the

Y. Jin, *Ocean Law and Policy of the People's Republic of China*,
https://doi.org/10.1007/978-981-95-3166-0_3

major neighboring countries has been completed, and the security problems stemming from the land borders will be reduced accordingly. Second, with the deepening of globalization, the breadth and depth of China's use of the oceans and seas will expand, which will inevitably lead to an increase in the number of maritime problems. For example, the safety of sea passage affected by piracy, marine pollution caused by ship navigation and collision, information security challenged by the investigation activities of ships and warships, and the safety of the lives and properties of residents caused by tsunamis. Third, China is a country with relatively unfavorable marine geography and has maritime boundary delimitation problems with most of its neighboring countries. This is especially acute in disputes over the sovereignty of islands, which are vital to address in a reasonable and fair manner to ensure a safe marine environment for China. Therefore, it is urgent for China to further increase the strength of marine protection and rights defense. To ensure a period of strategic opportunity for China's development and to maintain international, regional, and neighborhood stability, the concept of building harmonious oceans is essential.

3.1.2 International Law Analysis of the Meaning of Harmonious Oceans

China's concept of harmonious oceans comprises the following aspects: adhere to the auspices of the UN and establish a just and equitable ocean; adhere to equal-footed consultation and build a free and orderly ocean; adhere to treating both the symptoms and the root causes of problems and build the ocean environment with peace and tranquility; adhere to exchanges and cooperation and build a harmonious coexistence of oceans; and adhere to respect for and love of the sea and build an ocean environment in which humans are part of nature.

Thus, the harmonious oceans concept is not only a current necessity but is also deeply rooted in international law. Because ocean issues are complex, sensitive and interrelated, they require comprehensive consideration and response. Evidence shows that it is impossible for a single country to cope with and deal with these issues; thus, it is necessary to play the leading role in international organizations, especially the UN, to build a just and equitable ocean management system. When developing and utilizing the oceans, countries are bound to have disputes due to their different interests and positions. When encountering such disputes over ocean issues, they must be solved through consultation, where equal status should be ensured during negotiations, and the basic principle of international law—the sovereign equality of states—should be respected to maintain the order of the ocean system. At the same time, due to the interrelatedness and complexity of ocean issues, there is a need to implement integrated management, especially the categorization and synthesis of the functional matters of the oceans and seas, which requires treating both the symptoms and the root causes of the problem. In addition, solving international problems requires a combination of forces at all levels, especially through cooperation, which has a basis in international law. For example, Article 1 of the UN Charter provides that "the purposes of the United Nations is to achieve international co-operation in solving international problems;" Article 2 provides that "all Members shall give the United Nations every assistance in any action it takes in accordance with the present Charter;" Article 11 provides that "the General Assembly may consider the general principles of co-operation in the maintenance of international peace and security;" and Article 49 provides that "the Members of the United Nations shall join in affording mutual assistance in carrying out the measures decided upon by the Security Council."

A variety of cooperation methods also exist in the UNCLOS, including in subject matter, cooperation among all states, among the states concerned, and among states and international organizations. Cooperation involves the repression of piracy on the high seas by all states, the repression of illicit traffic of narcotic drugs or psychotropic substances at sea by ships in violation of international conventions, the adoption of measures for the conservation of the living resources of the high seas, and the protection of objects of an archaeological and historical nature found at sea; the protection of cooperation between states concerned with anadromous stocks in the EEZ, flag state jurisdiction, control over ships on the high seas and the investigation of marine casualties or incidents of navigation, conservation and management of living resources on the high seas, the right of access of landlocked states to and from the sea and freedom of transit, and the avoidance of delays or other difficulties of a technical nature in traffic in transit. Cooperation between states and international organizations also entails the designation of sea lanes and traffic separation schemes in straits used for international navigation, the conservation and management of living resources in the EEZ, the protection and preservation of the marine environment and marine scientific research.[1]

To rationally develop and utilize ocean space and resources in a sustainable manner to reduce disasters and risks, various measures should be taken to achieve harmony between humans and nature, sustainable development, and the goal of forming a maritime community with a shared future.

3.1.3 Harmonious Oceans as a Refinement of the Harmonious World

While proposing the concept of building a harmonious world, China has proposed specific principles for this purpose, such as adherence to multilateralism, mutually beneficial cooperation, and the spirit of inclusiveness and prudence. These principles are consistent with those implied by a harmonious ocean, reflecting that harmonious oceans are a derivative of the concept of a harmonious world—therefore, these

[1] See Yongming, Jin. 2018. Modern system of the law of the sea and China's practice, *Chinese Review of International Law* 6: 43–44.

principles reflect the deepening and development of the concept. To build a harmonious ocean, one of China's key tasks is formulating and implementing a national ocean strategy and enforcing it as a national state policy, with a focus on clarifying the related initiatives, including coordinating, improving, and implementing international, regional, and bilateral regimes on ocean issues. As the major countries of the world have already formulated relevant marine strategies and policies and constantly enrich and improve their marine legal systems, a national marine strategy needs to be formulated and implemented as soon as possible to rationally develop and utilize oceans and ocean-related resources and safeguard the rights and interests of the oceans and ensure maritime security, with a view of achieving the goal of a harmonious ocean.

3.2 Expansion and System of China's Strong Maritime Country Strategy in the New Era

As mentioned above, China's strong maritime country strategy was deepened in the Report to the 19th CPC National Congress; however, we should analyze the background, basic connotations, and specific objectives of the Report to the 18th CPC National Congress, which proposed the strategic goals of China's strong maritime country in the new era for the first time, to comprehensively and accurately understand China's strong maritime country strategy.

3.2.1 Contents and Development Process of China's Strong Maritime Country Strategy

Based on the strategic objectives of the Report to the 18th CPC National Congress on becoming a strong maritime country, analyzing its contents, which address the necessity and potential of becoming a strong maritime country and the related development of the national marine policy and strategy, is necessary.

3.2.1.1 The Specific Content Regarding China's Strong Maritime Country and its Interrelations

The Report to the 18th CPC National Congress on becoming a strong maritime country indicates that the development of the marine economy through continuous enhancement of the capacity for exploiting marine resources is the specific path to achieving China's goals of building a strong maritime country. These include resolving its major marine problems (i.e., the ECS issue and the SCS issue); firmly safeguarding national sovereignty, territorial integrity, and maritime rights and interests; and guaranteeing a safe environment to develop the oceans and their resources. The overarching goal is to protect the marine ecosystem and build a strong maritime country.

3.2.1.2 China's Need and Potential for Becoming a Strong Maritime Country

China has historically focused on the development of land resources, neglecting the development and utilization of marine resources. In particular, it has poor awareness of the oceans; relatively less advanced marine science, technology, and equipment; and weak policies and measures to develop and utilize the oceans and their resources, which delay the development of China's maritime cause. Coupled with China's geographic location, history, and subjective and objective factors, China's initiatives on ocean issues have not been adequate or vigorous, resulting in the accumulation of many conflicts that worsen and jeopardize China's sovereignty and territorial integrity.

Since the deepening of the reform and opening-up, China's economic strength, marine technology, and scientific research have continued to improve (for example, the completion and use of the Haiyang Shiyou 201, Haiyang Shiyou 981, and "Jiaolong" manned submersible 7000-meter sea test in the Mariana Trench test area), facilitating the development of its ocean strategy. Given that land resources cannot support China's further development, developing and utilizing the oceans and their resources is necessary, including relying on them for the international exchange of raw materials and products. Amid the backdrop of deepening international trade and economic integration, China's oceans and ocean resources continue to strengthen, as do the conditions to develop and utilize them. With the implementation of the UNCLOS, including the EEZ, continental shelf, and regime of islands, the ambiguities and shortcomings of the regional maritime regimes (e.g., the DOC), various countries have intensified the development and protection of the ocean space and its resources, triggering sensitive conflicts in the ECS and SCS and worsening China's maritime security. As many countries strengthen their marine activities and develop marine strategies, legal systems, and management, China should take concrete measures to accelerate the formulation and implementation of its national marine strategy based on current situations and trends. The strategic goal of becoming a strong maritime country, as proposed by the Report to the 18th CPC National Congress, is consistent with current trends.

3.2.1.3 The Development of China's Strategy for a Strong Maritime Country

Undeniably, the strategic goal of building a strong maritime country is the deepening and upgrading of China's party and government's response to marine issues, especially the deepening and upgrading of marine policies, especially marine economic development policies, since the new century, and has the characteristics of continuity and consistency. For example, as early as in the Report to the 16th CPC National Congress (2002), the CPC Central Committee proposed "promoting marine development." The SC, in its 2004 Report on the Work of the Government, issued the policy of "emphasizing the development and protection of marine resources." The Outline of the 11th Five-Year Plan for National Economic and Social Development of the PRC (2006) stated that China should "promote the development of the marine economy." The 2009 Report on the Work of the Government emphasized the importance of "developing and using marine resources wisely." The Recommendations of the 12th Five-Year Plan for China's National Economic and Social Development (2011) states that China should "develop the marine economy." Based on this statement, chap. XIV of the Outline of the 12th Five-Year Plan for National Economic and Social Development of the PRC (2012) states that China will persist in land and sea coordination, formulate and implement the strategy on ocean development, and raise the capability of maritime development, control, and comprehensive management. These reports and plans provide an important political guarantee of China becoming a strong maritime country. This goal is proposed in the context of China's combination of international and domestic development, particularly the development of the oceans, and the need to enhance the related long-standing policies and measures. It is a vital political task that has become a major strategy at the national level.

3.2.1.4 China's Efforts to Become a Strong Maritime Country Are Closely Linked to the Concept of a "Harmonious Oceans"

The goal of becoming a "strong maritime country" proposed by China at the domestic level echoes the concept of building "harmonious oceans" at the international level and is an important domestic measure to improve its responses to international maritime issues and conflicts. As mentioned above, in 2009, on the 60th anniversary of the founding of the Chinese PLAN and in line with the international and domestic situation, China proposed the "harmonious oceans" concept to safeguard lasting peace and security in the oceans via cooperation and mutual trust. The concept of "harmonious oceans" is a materialization of the "harmonious world" in the field of oceans and seas proposed by the President of China at the 60th anniversary Summit of the UN on September 15, 2005, reflecting the international community's new understanding and requirements of the management of oceans and seas and marking China's contribution to the development of the law of the sea.[2]

3.2.2 *Basic Path and Characteristics of China's Strong Maritime Country Construction*

China has taken the path of developing its ocean economy to promote its national maritime cause and enhance its ability to develop and utilize the oceans and their resources, providing services and guarantees for a strong maritime country. This is determined by the status of the ocean economy in China's economic and social development and is easily accepted by the international community, making it an appropriate and readily acceptable path.

3.2.2.1 The Choice of the Path to Become a Strong Maritime Country

China's marine economic output in its gross domestic product (GDP) is increasing, which is an important pathway toward becoming an "strong maritime country." Especially in the twenty-first century, the total size of China's marine economy has continued to grow, for example, during 2001–2006, the marine GDP's contribution to the national economy rose from 8.71% to 10.06%. In 2007, China's marine GDP was 2493.9-billion-yuan, accounting for 10.11% of the national GDP.[3] In 2008, China's marine GDP was 2966.2-billion-yuan, accounting for 10.11% of the GDP. Gross Marine Product (GMP) was 2966.2-billion-yuan, accounting for 9.87% of GDP. In 2009, China's GMP was 319.64-billion-yuan, accounting for 9.53% of GDP. In 2010, China's GMP was 3843.9-billion-yuan, accounting for 9.70% of GDP.[4] In 2011, China's GMP was 4557-billion-yuan, accounting for 9.70% of GDP.[5] In 2012, China's GMP was 5008.7-billion-yuan, accounting for 9.60% of GDP.[6] In 2013, China's GMP was 543.13-billion-yuan, accounting for 9.5% of GDP.[7] In

[2] The concept of "harmonious oceans" proposed by China consists of the following elements: "Adhere to the auspices of the UN and establish a just and equitable ocean; adhere to euqal-footed consultation and build a free and orderly ocean; adhere to treating both the symptoms and the root causes of problems and build the ocean environment with peace and tranquility; adhere to exchanges and cooperation and build a harmonious coexistence of oceans; and adhere to respect for and love of the sea and build an ocean environment in which humans are part of nature.. The concept of "harmonious oceans" is not only a requirement and product of current trends but it also has a deep foundation in international law. See Yongming, Jin, 2011. *Monographs on ocean issues (Volume I)*. Beijing: Ocean Press. pp. 376–377.

[3] See China Ocean News, May 23, 2008, p. 1.

[4] See China Ocean News, March 4, 2011, p. 1.

[5] See China Ocean News, December 7, 2012, p. 3.

[6] See China Ocean News, March 27, 2013, p. 1.

[7] See China Ocean News, March 12, 2014, p. 1.

2014, China's GMP was 5993.6-billion-yuan, accounting for 9.4% of GDP.[8] In 2015, China's GMP was 6466.9-billion-yuan, accounting for 9.6% of GDP.[9] In 2016, our GMP was 7050.7-billion-yuan, accounting for 9.5% of GDP.[10] In 2017, China's GMP was 7761.1-billion-yuan, accounting for 9.4% of GDP.[11] In 2018, China's GMP was 8341.5-billion-yuan, accounting for 9.3% of GDP.[12] According to the China Marine Economy Statistical Bulletin (May 2020) by the Department of Marine Strategic Planning and Economy of the MNR, China's 2019 ocean GDP was 8941.5-billion-yuan, accounting for 9.0% of GDP. China's marine GDP is thus clearly increasing, accounting for about 10% of the national GDP, making it a significant industry and an important area for promoting green development, which is conducive to building an ecological civilization. Thus, it is important for China to understand the marine economic sector and strengthen the development of the marine economy.[13]

3.2.2.2 Basic Indicators of China's Strong Maritime Country Strategy

The international community has no specific indicators or characteristics of a "strong maritime country," and there is no uniform and standardized definition. Traditionally, a maritime country referred to a country with strong sea power, referring to a comprehensive influence in commerce, maritime country, naval power, and the ability to utilize marine resources. That is, a traditional maritime country established its hegemony based on maritime commerce and naval power. In contrast, the maritime countries of today are countries that contribute to the international comanagement of ocean corridors and whose survival and development depend on the ocean, especially on marine science and technology. A country that relies on the sea, in particular, relies on marine science and technology (hard power) and marine management (soft power) to realize the goal of "ruling the sea according to law." The requirements for becoming a maritime country include the following aspects: (1) geographic requirements, which entail belonging to a geographical island or coastal country, which is constant; (2) the idea of the elements, which entails relying on technology and consciousness to change humans' geographic senses, affecting their mode of action and decision-making; and (3) technological essentials, which enable us to connect geographically and ideologically, which is variable.[14] Therefore, for coastal States to become maritime countries, they must organically combine constants and variables,

[8] See China Ocean News, March 19, 2015, p. 1.

[9] See China Ocean News, March 3, 2016, p. 1.

[10] See China Ocean News, March 17, 2017, p. 1.

[11] See China Ocean News, March 2, 2018, p. 1.

[12] See China Ocean News, April 12, 2019, p. 1.

[13] Keqiang, Li. 2018. Report on the work of the government - March 5, 2018, at the first Session of the 13th National People's Congress. Beijing: People's Publishing House. p. 31.

[14] See [Japanese] Okuyama, Shinji. 2013. The theory of classical geopolitics and the construction of safety and security in the East Asian Seas, in *East Asian seas in a mixed-up world: Toward the construction of a new maritime order*, ed. Japan Ocean Policy Research Foundation. Tokyo: Japan Ocean Policy Research Foundation. pp. 191–193.

attach significance to ocean awareness and culture, and establish a correct view of the ocean, including respect for the ocean's freedom and democracy and the openness and equality of ocean management.

Given the importance of the ocean space and resources in the development of the international community, especially the entry into force of the UNCLOS (November 16, 1994), which has become a comprehensive code for regulating ocean issues, the basic indicators of "strong maritime country" can be based on the principles and institutions of the UNCLOS. In this regard, considering China's national conditions and economic and social development, the basic indicators of China's strategy for becoming a strong maritime country are as follows:

First, the marine economy is well-developed. The marine economy is a broad concept referring to industries related to marine economic activities, including in the fields of exploration, development, and transportation of marine oil and gas resources; shipbuilding and restoration technology; fishery processing, manufacturing, and aquaculture; and environmental protection industries. There is a particular need to develop strategic marine emerging industries, such as the marine biomedicine industry, seawater desalination and comprehensive utilization of seawater, the marine renewable energy industry, the marine major equipment industry, and the deep-sea industry, to sustainably support the development of the marine economy and make it efficient and of a high quality.

Second, China's marine science and technology are at an advanced level. It has advanced scientific and technological equipment to support the development and utilization of the oceans and their resources, aid the protection of the marine environment, and deal with marine environmental monitoring, pollution, and disasters. Having marine science, technology, and equipment that are commensurate with the level of development of the marine economy is necessary to safeguard the strength of the marine economy and transform the country's marine science and technology into an innovative model.

Third, the marine ecological environment is beautiful. China has the capacity to manage the oceans and their resources in an integrated manner and prevent, protect, and repair the pollution of the marine environment to enhance sustainability. To that end, improving data monitoring, gathering, and processing from ocean waters and increasing the penalties imposed on those who pollute or cause damage is crucial. At the same time, marine recreation projects should be developed to better serve national needs, enjoy the benefits of the beautiful marine ecosystem, and transform marine development into a recycling-oriented model.

Fourth, there is a team of high-level human resources for the construction of ocean regimes and systems. The availability of talent is the key element for the smooth progress of all work. As a "strong maritime country," China should have the right to speak and have input in the construction of international, regional, and bilateral marine systems to reflect the country's position, claims, needs, and interests. Thus, it should actively create conditions to develop teams of high-level talent in the field of ocean affairs, reflecting the advantages of a large maritime country and providing a guarantee for the improvement of maritime regimes and systems.

Fifth, there is a strong capacity for maritime national defense. According to the Report to the 18th CPC National Congress, China should "build strong national defense and powerful armed forces that are commensurate with China's international standing and meet the needs of its security and development interests is a strategic task of China's modernization drive."[15] On maritime issues, in line with China's survival, development, and expanding maritime interests, the country should strengthen the construction of its maritime national defense to protect its national sovereignty, territorial integrity, and maritime rights and interests. It should follow the principles of adopting a holistic approach and overall coordination. Building a strong maritime national defense will guarantee China's ability to address maritime disputes, disasters, and accidents and respond to emergencies to ensure a safe and secure maritime environment. This is an important consideration of a strong maritime country, with a view to achieving a holistic approach toward maritime rights and interests.

The Report to the 19th CPC National Congress points out that China must "fully implement the Party's thinking on strengthening the military for the new era and the military strategy for new conditions" and "modernize the military across the board in terms of theory, organizational structure, service personnel, and weaponry." China will "make it our mission to see that by 2035, the modernization of the national defense and the forces is basically completed; and that by the mid-21st century the people's armed forces have been fully transformed into world-class forces."[16]

These are the main indicators of the strategy to develop a strong maritime country. Developing the marine economy is an important means of becoming a strong maritime country. Marine science and technology are technological guarantees of a strong maritime country and pillars for enhancing marine development capacity. A beautiful marine ecological environment is an important goal for becoming a strong maritime country. The development of high-level marine talent is a sustained impetus and an important aspect of becoming a strong maritime country. Finally, a strong maritime defense force is necessary for a strong maritime country. In short, these factors are closely interrelated and should be comprehensively planned, implemented, promoted, and upgraded, with no aspect being neglected.

3.2.2.3 Basic Features of China's Strategy for Becoming a Strong Maritime Country

China's strategy for becoming a strong maritime country is an important component of China's strategy for peaceful development and should be in line with China's conditions and realities. Its basic features entail the following:

---

[15] Jintao, Hu. 2012. Firmly march on the path of socialism with Chinese characteristics and strive to complete the building of a moderately prosperous society in all: Report to the 18th National Congress of the Communist Party of China. Beijing: People's Publishing House. p. 41.

[16] Jinping, Xi. 2017. Secure a decisive victory in building a moderately prosperous society in all respects and strive for the great success of socialism with Chinese characteristics for a new era: Report to the 19th National Congress of the Communist Party of China. Beijing: People's Publishing House. p. 53.

First, peacefulness. China's strategy for becoming a strong maritime country has adhered to the principle of continuous enrichment and improvement through peaceful means. This is fully in line with current trends and a new security vision of China featuring mutual trust, mutual benefit, equality and coordination, as well as with the goals of China's peaceful development process.

Second, mutual benefit. The implementation of China's maritime country strategy does not aim to maximize China's access to marine resources and interests but rather considers the reasonable demands and concerns of other countries and seeks an appropriate balance of interests to ensure mutual benefits and win–win cooperation.

Third, cooperation. Marine issues are complex and closely interrelated, and it is difficult for a single country to properly respond to and deal with them; thus, various cooperative approaches should be adopted to advance China's strategic goal of becoming a strong maritime country.

Fourth, the phased approach. Maritime issues are complex and sensitive, and it is generally difficult for countries to make compromises, especially on the issue of sovereignty. Thus, China, in implementing its strategy of becoming a strong maritime country, should adopt stage-by-stage steps to resolve them in a fairer manner, adhering to the principle of resolving maritime issues fairly and reasonably when the conditions are ripe and, in contrast, avoiding forcible measures to resolve maritime issues when the conditions are not ripe.

Fifth, security. In its efforts to become a strong maritime country, China will take vigorous measures to ensure safe access to international waters, including the continued dispatch of naval forces to participate in the fight against piracy to ensure the security of the maritime areas used by the international community and the interests of the oceans, in particular, freedom of navigation and overflight.

The above features of China's strategy for becoming a strong maritime country are consistent with China's advocacy and goals and are also in line with the principles and requirements of international law, including the UN Charter, UNCLOS, the DOC, and other norms, which should be easily accepted by the international community. Therefore, it is particularly important and urgent to further publicize China's strategy of strengthening the country by sea and to establish a view of the sea in line with the development of the situation.

The new ocean concept (peace, cooperation and harmony) advocated by Li Keqiang, Premier of the SC of the PRC in his remarks at the China-Greece Marine Cooperation Forum: For Peace, Cooperation and Harmony in the Ocean is easily accepted by the international community as it reflects the requirements of the international community in terms of ocean governance. It is also in line with the concept of the oceans that China has always advocated and practiced, and reflects China's interest in an ocean order and management system that must be followed in practice.[17]

As can be seen from the characteristics of China's strong maritime country strategy, the steps in China's strategic process of becoming a strong maritime country

[17] Keqiang, Li. 2014. For Peace, Cooperation and Harmony in the Ocean - Remarks at the China-Greece Marine Cooperation Forum, http://www.gov.cn/xinwen/2014-08/01/content_2728512.htm, accessed August 18, 2014.

will be orderly, the objectives will be limited, the focus will be on safeguarding and securing China's rights and interests at sea, and the way in which power is utilized will be peaceful and comprehensive. This is in contrast to the traditional maritime hegemonic model, which relies more on military power, including establishing military bases and overseas strongholds and overseas colonies as a model of expanding maritime hegemony. In other words, China will adopt a comprehensive approach to power, including political, diplomatic, economic, legal and cultural, and military means, as well as a cooperative approach and the development of military power commensurate with China's strength, to resolve in an orderly manner the challenges encountered in the process of advancing its goal of becoming a strong maritime country and to safeguard its maritime rights and interests.

Summarizing the above views, the concept of China's strong maritime country strategy can be defined as follows: based on the principles and requirements of the international community's norms and standards, China will peacefully develop its marine economy and marine scientific and technological equipment, enhance its ability to develop and utilize marine resources, strengthen the comprehensive management of marine resources and interests, including improving the construction of marine institutions and mechanisms, and moderately develop its maritime military force. On the basis of not harming its core interests, China strives to use peaceful methods to resolve maritime disputes and to maximize the relative benefits of the oceans so as to protect the marine environment, safeguard the country's rights and interests in the oceans, and ensure national maritime security, and to build China into a maritime country that is compatible with its national conditions and development needs. Thus, China will achieve its dream of becoming a strong maritime country with Chinese characteristics.

In short, the political and security goals of China's strategy for a strong maritime country can be defined as no hegemony and peaceful development, i.e., adhering to the overall concept of national security and resolutely safeguarding the country's sovereignty, security and development interests; economically, applying the new concept of innovative, coordinated, green, open, and shared development to develop and strengthen the maritime economy; culturally promoting the core values of socialist culture with Chinese characteristics, a marine culture of inclusiveness and mutual learning; and ecologically, through the protection of the marine environment, a sustainable marine environment will be constructed, thus realizing the goal of unity between people and the sea advocated by the harmonious oceans initiative.

3.2.2.4 Positioning of China's Strong Maritime Country Strategy

The Report to the 18th CPC National Congress points out that "China is still in the primary stage of socialism and will long remain so. This basic condition of China has not changed; nor has the principal problem in the society, that is, how to meet the ever-growing material and cultural needs of the people with backward social production; nor has China's international position as the largest developing country in the world."[18]However, as pointed out in the Report to the 19th CPC National Congress, "the evolution of the principal contradiction facing Chinese society does not change our assessment of the present stage of socialism in China. The basic dimension of the Chinese context—that our country is still and will long remain in the primary stage of socialism—has not changed. China's international status as the world's largest developing country has not changed."[19] In view of this national situation and status, China should advance the goal of becoming a strong maritime country in a phased and step-by-step manner.

(1) A regional strong maritime country. The Report to the 18th CPC National Congress points out that "An examination of both the current international and domestic environments shows that China remains in an important period of strategic opportunities for its development, a period in which much can be achieved." In this regard, to position itself as a strong maritime country, China should minimize the impact of maritime threats on the marine development process.[20] In the author's view, during this period of strategic opportunity, the focus should be on resolving the disputes in the SCS with the ASEAN countries to establish China's status as a regional strong maritime country.

The DOC and the subsequent principles and systems regulated among countries should be observed in dealing with the disputes in the SCS and resolving the issues through peaceful, political, or diplomatic methods in accordance with the principles and systems of international law including the UNCLOS should be prioritized. While pursuing its national interests, China should reasonably accommodate the concerns and claims of other countries to strike a better balance and ensure the interests of all countries in the SCS regarding the sea and the resources are achieved to realize the goal of sustainable development.[21] To this end, China should accelerate the pace of constructing the China–ASEAN Maritime Silk Road, including active consultation with ASEAN countries, and formulate a Code of Conduct in the SCS to prudently deal with issues in the region. In particular, China should strengthen the pace of

[18] Jintao, Hu. 2012. Firmly March on the Path of Socialism with Chinese Characteristics and Strive to Complete the Building of a Moderately Prosperous Society in All: Report to the Eighteenth National Congress of the Communist Party of China. Beijing: People's Publishing House. p. 16.

[19] Jinping, Xi. 2017. Secure a Decisive Victory in Building a Moderately Prosperous Society in All Respects and Strive for the Great Success of Socialism with Chinese Characteristics for a New Era: Report to the 19th National Congress of the Communist Party of China. Beijing: People's Publishing House. p. 12.

[20] "China's overall goal of pursuing peaceful development is to pro-mote development and harmony domestically and pursue cooperation and peace internationally. Specifically, this means that China will endeavor to make life better for its people and contribute to human progress through hard work, innovation and reform carried out by the Chinese people and growing long-term friendly relations and promoting equality and mutually-beneficial cooperation with other countries. This has become a national commitment which is manifest in strategies for national development, and progress made in the course of China's development." See China's State Council Information Office. 2011. *China's peaceful development*. Beijing: People's Publishing House. p. 9.

[21] For more information on the disputes and solutions to the South China Sea issue, see Yongming, Jin. 2012. Empirical researches on non-application of legal means to territorial disputes over Nansha Islands and Reefs, *Pacific Journal* 20 (4): 20–30.

cooperation; avoid complexity, enlargement, and internationalization; and seek to actively utilize the SCS marine resources and space to stabilize the security of the region, aiming to unify the region's functions and norms and realize the functionality and normative unity of the space and resources.[22]

(2) A global strong maritime country. To achieve the strategic goal of building a strong maritime country, China should, based on being a regional strong maritime country, address and resolve the ECS and the Taiwan Strait issues to achieve peaceful reunification and establish China's status as a global strong maritime country.

Regarding the ECS, including the Diaoyu Dao, China initially established a territorial seas and airspace regime for the Diaoyu Dao, their affiliated islands, and the surrounding waters.[23] For this reason, China should take further measures to improve the domestic legal system, in particular law enforcement and management, for China's cruises in the waters surrounding the Diaoyu Dao and their affiliated islands, including rules and regulations pertaining to the passage of foreign ships in its territorial waters and to identify aircraft in China's East China Sea Air Defense Identification Zone. At the same time, China should supplement and improve institutional norms, such as the Organic Law on the Establishment of CCG, to firmly defend its national sovereignty and territorial integrity. Regarding other issues in the ECS, such as the development of the ECS waters, China should continue to consult and negotiate with Japan to effectively fulfill the requirements and obligations stipulated in the "China and Japan Reach Principled Consensus on the East China Sea Issue" announced by China and Japan's diplomatic departments on June 18, 2008, to achieve the goal of sharing the seabed resources in the ECS and providing stability. To this end, China should rapidly formulate institutional norms that can be applied in the future within the joint development regime in the ECS.

To realize the goal of turning the ECS into a sea of peace, cooperation, and friendship, China and Japan should continue to use the existing bilateral dialogue and consultation mechanisms, such as the China-Japan High-level Consultation Mechanism on Maritime Affairs, the China-Japan Strategic Dialogue Mechanism, the China-Japan Dialogue Mechanism at Vice Foreign Minister-level, and the China-Japan Intergovernmental Exchange of Notes on the Consensus of Principles on East China Sea Issues. In particular, the issue of the Diaoyu Dao should be incorporated into the China-Japan Dialogue and Consultation, such that these disputes on the ECS issues can be comprehensively resolved.

---

[22] On the goal of the South China Sea resource development, see Yongming, Jin. 2013. On the goal orientation of resource development in the South China Sea: Functionality and Normativity, *Journal of Hainan University (Humanities & Social Sciences)* 4: 1–6.

[23] For China's statement on the baselines of the territorial waters of the Diaoyu Dao and their affiliated islands, see http://www.go.cn/jrzg/2012-09/10/content_2221140.htm, accessed September 11, 2012. Statement of the PRC on the establishment of the East China Sea Air Defense Identification Zone (November 23, 2013), Announcement of the PRC on the Rules for the Identification of Aircrafts in the East China Sea Air Defense Identification Zone (November 23, 2013), see http://www.gov.cn/jrzg/2013-11/23/content_2533099.htm, http://www.gov.cn/jrzg/2013-11/23/content_2533101.htm, accessed November 25, 2013.

To realize the strategic goal of becoming a strong maritime country, which is regional as well as global, China's strategic goals (comprehensive goals and milestones) in various periods can be divided into the following stages:

First, immediate strategic objectives (2019–2020). The main objective is stabilizing the escalation or eruption of maritime issues, adopting a position of keeping the status quo, and gradually taking feasible measures to minimize further maritime threats or damage such that China can take advantage of the strategic opportunity in this period. The specific objectives are improving the construction of marine institutions and mechanisms, including the improvement of organizational structures such as the State Oceanic Commission, the coordination of the powers of the MNR, and the development of policies and legal systems in the field of the oceans, to create the conditions for the recovery of islands and reefs.

Second, medium-term strategic objectives (2021–2035). To create conditions and utilize China's comprehensive strength to find solutions to specific issues (e.g., the SCS issue) and achieve the goal of becoming a regional strong maritime country. The specific objectives are to gradually recover, resume, and develop the islands and reefs seized by other countries and adopt a strategy of self-development, supplemented by cooperative and joint development.

Third, long-term strategic goals (2036–2050). Once China possesses sufficiently comprehensive economic, scientific, and technological strength, it will comprehensively address and resolve the issue of oceans and seas, complete peaceful reunification, and achieve the goal of becoming a global maritime country. The specific objectives are unimpeded management of the sea areas under China's jurisdiction within three million square kilometers and moderately free use of global oceans and their resources.[24]

Fourth, the end-term strategic goal (2051–2080). On the occasion of the 100th anniversary of the country's reform and opening-up, China will utilize its comprehensive strength to achieve the goal of becoming a global strong maritime country. The specific objectives are to develop the ability to rapidly respond to various marine disasters, accidents, and other delivery and disposal capabilities in a timely and effective manner and provide the international community with a variety of products, including the institutional design of the governance of the oceans, to achieve the goals of a harmonious ocean and comprehensive ocean governance.

3.3 Contemporary Practice of the BRI

Since its introduction in 2013, the BRI has been a guide to action for the Chinese Government, especially after it hosted the Belt and Road Forum for International Cooperation on May 14, 2017, which identified the nature, content, goals, and vision of the BRI.

---

[24] See Yongming, Jin. 2012. Study on the strategy of the ocean security of China, *Global Review* 4: 2–3.

3.3.1 Nature and Task of the BRI

Chinese President Xi Jinping pointed out in the Toast at thc Welcoming Banquet in honor of the distinguished guests attending the Belt and Road Forum for International Cooperation that the initiative "renews the Silk Road spirit and discusses the Belt and Road development for international cooperation. This is both a continuation of our shared legacy and a correct choice for the future." At the same time, "the BRI embodies our aspiration for inter-civilization exchanges. As a vehicle that facilitates communication between different civilizations, the Initiative will promote mutual learning and add splendor to human civilization." Additionally, "the BRI embodies our yearning for peace and stability. As a bond bringing countries closer to each other, the Initiative will encourage solidarity, mutual respect and mutual trust between countries, and inspire our people to work together to build a harmonious and peaceful world. Then, it embodies our pursuit of common development. The Initiative aims to break development bottlenecks, narrow development gaps and promote the sharing of development achievements among countries. It envisions a community of common development where we work together through thick and thin for a shared future." Finally, it "embodies our shared dream for a better life. The Initiative weaves into a common vision the dreams of different countries and peoples. We will work to translate this vision into reality and deliver greater happiness and well-being to our peoples."[25] This explanation indicates the nature of the BRI. As a major step of China's reform and opening-up in the current era, the BRI is an important practical platform for building of a community of shared future for mankind.

3.3.2 Spatial Scope of the BRI

The Chinese Government has established the General Office of the Leading Group for Advancing the Development of the Belt and Road for the purpose of jointly constructing the Belt and Road under the NDRC. According to Building the Belt and Road: Concept, Practice and China's Contribution released on May 10, 2017, "China has determined five routes for the Belt and Road. The Silk Road Economic Belt has three routes: one from Northwest China and Northeast China to Europe and the Baltic Sea via Central Asia and Russia; one from Northwest China to the Persian Gulf and the Mediterranean Sea, passing through Central Asia and West Asia; and one from Southwest China through the Indochina Peninsula to the Indian Ocean. The 21st-Century Maritime Silk Road has two major routes: one starts from coastal ports of China, crosses the South China Sea, passes through the Malacca Strait, and reaches the Indian Ocean, extending to Europe; the other starts from coastal ports of China,

[25] Toast at the Welcoming Banquet in honor of the distinguished guests attending the Belt and Road Forum for International Cooperation. See http://www.gov.cn/xinwen/2017-05/15/content_5193787.htm#1, accessed May 15, 2017.

crosses the South China Sea, and extends to the South Pacific."[26] This is of important guiding and practical significance to understand the spatial and geographical scope of the BRI.

3.3.3 *Basic Contents of the BRI*

The Belt and Road is a systematic project that adheres to the principles of extensive consultation, joint contribution, and shared benefits and actively promotes the coordination of development strategies of the countries along the route. According to the "Vision and Actions on Jointly Building Silk Road Economic Belt and 21st-Century Maritime Silk Road," formulated and released by the Chinese Government in March 2015, the key areas of cooperation are the "five cooperation priorities," i.e., policy coordination, an important guarantee for implementing the Initiative; Facility connectivity, a priority area for implementing the Initiative; Unimpeded trade, a major task in building the Belt and Road; Financial integration, an important underpinning for implementing the BRI; and People-to-people bond, the public support for implementing the Initiative.[27] In other words, China will work with countries along the Belt and Road route to promote the initiative and all benefit from this Initiative at five different levels of cooperation.

3.3.4 *Objectives and Vision of the BRI*

According to the Chinese Government's policy documents, the goals and visions of the Belt and Road can be summarized in the following five areas:

First, China should promote win–win cooperation by building partnerships based on dialogue rather than confrontation, and friendship rather than alliance. The political objective of the BRI is building a road of peace.

Second, China should focus on the fundamental issue of development by encouraging economic integration, interconnected development, and the sharing of achievements and building a road toward prosperity—the economic goal of the initiative.

Third, efforts should be made to build an open platform for cooperation by facilitating the orderly flow of production factors, the efficient allocation of resources, deep integration of markets so as to create a road of openness, the goal of the openness model.

---

[26] See https://eng.yidaiyilu.gov.cn/wcm.files/upload/CMSydylyw/201705/201705110537027.pdf, accessed May 11, 2017.

[27] Party Documents Research Office of the CPC Central Committee. 2016. *Vision and Actions on Jointly Building Silk Road Economic Belt and twenty-first-Century Maritime Silk Road*. Beijing: Central Party Literature Press. pp. 442–455.

Fourth, efforts should be made to promote innovation-led development, optimizing the innovation-enabling environment, and pooling innovation resources, creating innovation hubs, and creating a road of innovation, which is the goal in terms of development.

Fifth, efforts should be made to deepen multilevel human exchanges by promoting mutual understanding, respect, and trust among countries and creating the road of civilization, which is the goal in terms of culture.[28]

In other words, the vision of the BRI embodies peace in terms of political security, prosperity in terms of economic development, openness in terms of development, innovation in terms of development means, and cultural preservation of civilization. The BRI undertaking is a systematic, comprehensive project that requires all parties to work together and take concrete and effective measures to achieve the goals of common development and benefits.

The international community has reached a consensus on the specific objectives and vision for the construction of the BRI: "Promoting peace, mutually-beneficial cooperation, and honoring the purposes and principles of the UN Charter and international law are our shared responsibilities; achieving inclusive and sustainable growth and development, and improving people's quality of life are our common goals; creating a prosperous and peaceful community with shared future for mankind is our common aspiration."[29] These goals and aspirations are fully in line with the international community's development trends and the common interests and well-being of humanity and should be followed and recognized by all countries. This is because they are in line with the laws of human development and common expectations. Specifically, "the Belt and Road will become a road of peace, prosperity, opening-up, green development, innovation, connected civilizations, and clean government. It will make economic globalization become more open, inclusive, balanced and beneficial to all."[30]

3.3.5 Cooperation and Safeguards for the BRI

To build the "Belt and Road," focusing on promoting the process of policy coordination, connectivity of infrastructure, unimpeded trade, financial integration, and closer people-to-people ties, actively promoting the process based on the laws and regulations of each country and relevant international obligations of cooperation with

---

[28] Vice-Premier Zhang Gaoli's Speech at High-level Plenary Meeting of the Belt and Road Forum for International Cooperation http://www.gov.cn/guowuyuan/2017-05/14/content_5193708.htm, accessed May 15, 2017.

[29] Joint Communique of the Leaders Roundtable of the Belt and Road Forum for International Cooperation, 2017, http://ydyl.people.com.cn/n1/2017/0516/c411837-29277121.html, accessed May 16, 2017.

[30] The Belt and Road Initiative: Progress, Contributions and Prospects, http://www.xinhuanet.com/world/2019-04/22/c_1124400071.htm. Accessed April 22, 2019.

countries along the routes, at the multilateral, regional, and bilateral levels. Additionally, following the five major principles of equality and consultation, mutual benefit, cooperation, harmony and inclusiveness, market operations, and balance and sustainability will accelerate cooperation and achieve results is necessary. The Belt and Road project follows the basic principles of openness, inclusiveness, voluntariness, and mutual benefit, which are in line with the norms of international relations and the principles of international law. Furthermore, it is crucial and operational, as evidenced by the international community's participation.

In building the Belt and Road and achieving sustained positive effects, the creation and enrichment of operational platforms and safeguards is an important foundation toward which China has made great contributions. For example, based on the original organizational structure, China's NDRC established the Facilitating Center for Building the Belt and Road, launched the official Belt and Road portal on the Internet and the Marine Silk Road Trade Index. China has hosted the CIIE from 2018 onwards, added 100-billion-yuan to the Silk Road Fund, and established the China–Russia Regional Development Investment Fund. Furthermore, the Ministry of Finance of China and multilateral development banks established the Multilateral Development and Financing Cooperation Center. The China Development Bank has organized the Belt and Road Multi-currency Special Lending Scheme for Infrastructure Development, the Belt and Road Multi-currency Special Lending Scheme for Industrial Cooperation, and the Belt and Road Multi-currency Special Credit Lines for Overseas Financial Institutions. Meanwhile, the Export-Import Bank of China will set up the Belt and Road Multi-currency Special Lending Scheme and the Belt and Road Multi-currency Special Lending Scheme for Infrastructure Development. The Asian Financial Cooperation Association has been officially established. The Chinese government will increase its assistance to developing countries along the Belt and Road, with an overall assistance scale of no less than RMB 60 billion over the next three years (2018–2021). Additionally, China Central Television will set up the "Belt and Road News Alliance" with mainstream media of relevant countries. Silk Road Think Tank Association (SRTA) launched the International Think Tank Cooperation Program on Enhancing People-to-People Connectivity along the Belt and Road and establish the Belt and Road international commercial dispute settlement mechanism and institutions.[31] The creation and expansion of these comprehensive measures and platforms guarantee the effectiveness of the BRI.

[31] Opinions on the Establishment of International Commercial Dispute Settlement Mechanisms and Institutions for the "Belt and Road," issued by the General Office of the CPC Central Committee and the General Office of the State Council (June 2018), see People's Daily, June 28, 2018, pp. 1 and 3.

3.3.6 *Effects of the BRI*

The BRI has become an important part of China's strategy for peaceful development, a core concept and a new initiative of major-country diplomacy with Chinese characteristics, and an important practical platform for building a community of shared future for mankind. At the same time, worldwide consensus has emerged about its importance as a means for economic cooperation and development.

Since its inception and subsequent enrichment, the BRI has received a positive response and participation from most countries, reflecting its vitality and innovativeness. In terms of effectiveness, "the Belt and Road cooperation has opened up new space for global economic growth, produced new platforms for international trade and investment and offered new ways for improving global economic governance. Indeed, this initiative has helped improve people's lives in countries involved and created more opportunities for common prosperity."[32] Characterized by the spirit of traditional Chinese culture, Belt and Road embodies Chinese wisdom and is worth adhering to and deepening.

However, as the countries along the BRI and other participating countries are different, with varying levels of development and needs and diverse cultures, difficulties, challenges, and controversies are bound to arise in the course of constructing the BRI. However, if China adheres to the principles and spirit of the BRI and the norms of international law and international relations, including the international commercial dispute resolution mechanisms, we will be able to resolve the challenges and enhance the confidence and responsibility of all countries participating in the BRI. This is the proper approach to the BRI and its construction.

The Opinions on the Establishment of International Commercial Dispute Settlement Mechanisms and Institutions for the "Belt and Road" issued by the General Office of the CPC Central Committee and the General Office of the SC in June 2018, and the Statement of the Co-Chairs of the Forum on the Belt and Road Legal Cooperation in the Forum on the Belt and Road Legal Cooperation organized by the MFA of China and the Chinese Law Society in July 2018, is important for the application of rule of law thinking and legal methods to resolve disputes, especially commercial disputes, in the course of the construction of the "Belt and Road."[33]

---

[32] Jinping, Xi. 2019. Working Together to Deliver a Brighter Future For Belt and Road Cooperation—Keynote speech at the opening ceremony of the second Belt and Road Forum for International Cooperation, http://www.xinhuanet.com/politics/leaders/2019-04/26/c_1124420187.htm, accessed April 26, 2019.

[33] For the reply of the Supreme People's Court to a reporter's question on the Opinions on the Establishment of International Commercial Dispute Settlement Mechanisms and Institutions for the "Belt and Road". See People's Daily, June 28, 2018, page 3; and for Statement of the Co-Chairs of the Forum on the Belt and Road Legal Cooperation, http://www.fmprc.gov.cn/web/wjbxw_673019/t1573634.shtml, accessed July 5, 2018.

Chapter 4
Problems and Tasks of New China in the Ocean Legal System

To realize its strategic goal of becoming a strong maritime country in the new era, China must consider international maritime development trends and, in particular, comply with the systems and rules of the international law of the sea and incorporate them into its domestic law to advance China's strategy of becoming a strong maritime country. This is an obligation of member States of the international community, in particular of the Treaty, as well as an outcome and requirement for enhancing the national ocean governance system and upgrading the ocean governance capacity.

4.1 Development Stages and Trends of the System of the UNCLOS

The UNCLOS system has an important place in the international rules and laws of the sea system. The development UNCLOS went through the following stages of development and exhibited these trends.

4.1.1 Development Stages of the System of the UNCLOS

The first stage of UNCLOS was that of its adoption. The Convention comprises a preamble, a body of 320 articles, and nine annexes. In accordance with Article 318, the annexes are an integral part of the Convention, and unless otherwise provided, a reference to the Convention or to one of its parts includes a reference to the annexes to which it relates.

The second stage was the development of the Convention, namely the 1994 Agreement relating to the Implementation of Part XI of the UNCLOS of December 10, 1982 (the "Part XI Implementing Agreement," which entered into force on July 28, 1996)

Y. Jin, *Ocean Law and Policy of the People's Republic of China*,
https://doi.org/10.1007/978-981-95-3166-0_4

and the 1995 Agreement for the Implementation of the Provisions of the UNCLOS Agreement for the Implementation of the Provisions of the UNCLOS of December 10, 1982 relating to the Conservation and Management of Straddling Fish Stocks and Highly Migratory Fish Stocks ("Straddling Fish Implementing Agreement," entered into force on December 11, 2001). Together, they constitute the Convention's development and form a new integral part of the Convention.[1]

The third stage is the deepening of the Convention, manifested by the resolution adopted by the UNGA on June 19, 2015 (A/RES/69/292), titled "Development of an international legally binding instrument under the United Nations Convention on the Law of the Sea on the conservation and sustainable use of marine biological diversity of areas beyond national jurisdiction." In this regard, the UN intended to negotiate and consider the above-mentioned issues at an intergovernmental meeting to be convened between 2018 and 2020. The development of such an international legally binding instrument by the intergovernmental meeting within a specified time frame represents a deepening of the Convention regime, addressing the gaps in the Convention's biodiversity norms by enhancing the functioning and effectiveness of the conservation and sustainable use of marine biodiversity beyond national jurisdictions.[2]

4.1.2 Development Trends of the System of the UNCLOS

Development trends of the Convention system are reflected in the following areas:

First, the developmental nature of the legislative model. As can be seen from the development of the Convention system, supplementing and refining the Convention by formulating "implementing agreements" can be regarded as an innovation in the legislative model.[3] This approach avoids the difficulty of utilizing the "Amendment" procedure under Article 312 and the "Amendment by simplified procedure" under Article 313 of the Convention and is also efficient. At the same time, it is reasonable and in line with the normative content of Articles 30 and 59 of the VCLT.

Second, the developmental nature of legislative thinking. The developmental nature of legislative thinking is characterized by the principle of limiting freedom on the high seas, applying the principles of the common heritage of mankind, and

---

[1] The relationship between Part XI Agreement and the UNCLOS is established in Article 2(1), of the Part XI Agreement, while the relationship between the Straddling Fish Stocks Agreement and the UNCLOS is established in Article 4 of the Straddling Fish Stocks Agreement. The relationship between the Part XI Agreement and the UNCLOS is established in Article 4 of the Straddling Fish Stocks Implementation Agreement.

[2] See Yongming, Jin. 2018. Issues relating to the conservation and sustainable use of marine biological diversity beyond areas of national jurisdiction, *Journal of Social Sciences* 9: 12–21.

[3] The legislative model in this context refers to the method by which customary international law is codified and developed into treaties. For example, Article 13(1)(a), of the UN Charter provides that "the General Assembly shall initiate studies and make recommendations for the purpose of promoting international cooperation in the political field and encouraging the progressive development of international law and its codification."

strengthening management of the oceans and seas by international institutions. The purpose is to achieve integrated management of the oceans and seas and eliminate the drawbacks of having jurisdiction over the oceans and seas in a single matter.[4] This change in legislative thinking is reflected, in particular, in discussions on the conservation and sustainable use of marine biodiversity in areas beyond national jurisdictions.

Third, the need for multidimensional cooperation. The Convention provides for multiple modes and paths of cooperation. These include cooperation between the states (e.g., Articles 66, 94, 118, and 130), cooperation among all states (e.g., Articles 100, 108, 117, and 303), and cooperation between states and international organizations (e.g., Articles 41, paragraph 4–5, 61, and 64–65, Article 197, Articles 200–201, and 242–244). As noted above, the content, involves the repression of piracy on the high seas by all states, the repression of illicit traffic of narcotic drugs or psychotropic substances at sea by ships in violation of international conventions, the adoption of measures for the conservation of the living resources of the high seas, and the protection of objects of an archaeological and historical nature found at sea; the protection of cooperation between states concerned with anadromous stocks in the EEZ, flag state jurisdiction, control over ships on the high seas and the investigation of marine casualties or incidents of navigation, conservation, and management of living resources on the high seas, the right of access of landlocked states to and from the sea and freedom of transit, and the avoidance of delays or other difficulties of a technical nature in traffic in transit. Cooperation between states and international organizations also entails the designation of sea lanes and traffic separation schemes in straits used for international navigation, the conservation and management of living resources in the EEZ, the protection and preservation of the marine environment, and marine scientific research.[5] Therefore, there are multiple levels and aspects of cooperation and requirements in the Convention, which are determined by the comprehensive nature of the oceans and seas and represent the summation of the international community's understanding of the principle of cooperation and its applicability in managing the oceans and seas.

[4] See Atsuko Kanehara. 2016. What does a new international legally binding instrument on marine biological diversity of areas beyond national jurisdiction "under the UNCLOS" mean? *Sophia Law Review*, 59(4): 53–73.

[5] See [Japanese] Okuwaki, Naoya. 2015. The duty to cooperate in the United Nations Convention on the Law of the Sea" - Centering on the duty to collect, provide, and share information, in *The practice of international law*, eds. Shunji Yanai, Shinya Murase. Tokyo: Shinzansha Publishing. pp. 412–442.

4.2 China's Specific Legislative Practice in Accordance with International Ocean Rules

As mentioned above, states have an important responsibility to incorporate and apply the principles and spirit of the modern law of the sea system, in particular the UNCLOS, into domestic laws.[6] Moreover, it is the common call of the international community to promote the rule of law at the international level.[7] After a brief description of the relationship between international and domestic law, we will discuss China's specific practices regarding the law of the sea based on the international laws of the sea (customary and statutory laws).

4.2.1 Relationship Between International Law and Domestic Law

4.2.1.1 The Doctrine of the Relationship Between International Law and Domestic Law

There are two major theoretical schools of thought regarding law: monism and dualism. Monism advocates that international law and domestic law belong to the same legal system; dualism believes that international law and domestic law are two different legal systems. There are three theories on the effectiveness of international law and domestic law in relation to each other: domestic law is superior to international law, international law is superior to domestic law, and international law and domestic law are independent and not subordinate to each other.[8]

In fact, the doctrinal debate over the relationship between international and domestic law is not practically productive; it is necessary to examine their specific paths and practices.[9] The important question is how each country applies the rules of international law within their internal legal framework and how conflicts between

---

[6] For example, Article 300 of the UNCLOS provides that "States Parties shall fulfil in good faith the obligations assumed under this Convention and shall exercise the rights, jurisdiction and freedoms recognized in this Convention in a manner which would not constitute an abuse of right."

[7] For example, the United Nations General Assembly adopted a resolution (A/RES/70/118) on the "The rule of law at the national and international levels" on December 14, 2015, based on the Sixth Committee of the United Nations' report (A/70/511) stating that "Reaffirming also the need for universal adherence to and implementation of the rule of law at both the national and international levels and its solemn commitment to an international order based on the rule of law and international law, which, together with the principles of justice, is essential for peaceful coexistence and cooperation among States."

[8] See Tieya, Wang. 2004. *International law*. Beijing: Law Press. pp. 19–20.

[9] Jennings, Watts. 1995. *Oppenheim's international law (Volume I, Subtitle I)*, translated by Tieya, Wang., Gongchuo, Chen., et al. Beijing: Encyclopedia of China Publishing House. pp. 31–32; [Japanese] Sugihara, Takane. 2017. *Fundamental international law (2nd ed.)*. Tokyo: Yuhikaku Publishing. pp. 77–78.

international and domestic laws are resolved, that is, the status of international law in domestic law and the question of what takes precedence in the event of a conflict. In this regard, the status of international law in domestic law and the priority of its application in case of conflict are not the same among countries due to differences in their constitutions and basic legal systems. However, according to Article 27 of the VCLT, a party may not invoke the provisions of its internal law as justification for its failure to perform a treaty. This means that the provisions of domestic law cannot take precedence over international treaties, or, in other words, the "principle of prohibition of invocation of domestic law."[10]

4.2.1.2 The Status of International Law, Especially Treaties, in Chinese Law

Although the Constitution of the PRC[11] does not directly stipulate the status of international treaties, there are provisions on the right to conclude treaties and procedures for doing so. For example, Article 89(9) provides that the SC has the power to "manage foreign affairs and conclude treaties and agreements with foreign countries," and the Standing Committee of the NPC "could decide on the ratification or abrogation of treaties and important agreements concluded with foreign countries;" (Article 67, para. 15). "The president of the People's Republic of China engages in affairs of state and receives foreign diplomatic envoys on behalf of the People's Republic of China and, pursuant to decisions of the Standing Committee of the National People's Congress, appoints or recalls plenipotentiary representatives abroad and ratifies or abrogates treaties and important agreements concluded with foreign countries" (Article 81). Meanwhile, laws are enacted and amended by the Standing Committee of the NPC (Article 67(2)) and promulgated by the President pursuant to decisions of the National People's Congress and the National People's Congress Standing Committee (Article 80). The treaty-making and law-making procedures are largely the same according to the above-mentioned constitutional provisions.

As the Constitution does not explicitly provide for international law in the legal system, it is necessary to analyze the provisions for international law in terms of China's general laws. In Chinese law, the provisions for international treaties are roughly categorized into three types: first, domestic law stipulating that international treaties shall be directly applied, for example, Article 19 of the 1982 Trademark Law of the PRC, Article 19 of the 1985 Law of Succession of the PRC, Articles 239 and 247 of the 1986 Civil Procedure Law of the PRC, and Article 18 of the Patent Law of the PRC (1992 Amendment). Second, domestic law stipulates that international treaties shall take precedence in case of conflict, for example, Article

[10] [Japanese] Sugihara, Takane, 2017. *Fundamental international law (2nd ed.)*. Tokyo: Yuhikaku Publishing. pp. 78–79.

[11] China's Constitution was adopted on December 4, 1982, and has been amended five times, on April 12, 1988, March 29, 1993, March 15, 1999, March 14, 2004, and March 11, 2018, respectively.

142 of the 1986 General Principles of the Civil Law of the PRC.[12] Third, domestic law does not provide for the direct application of international treaties; instead, it adopts the method of amending or supplementing legislation to make the provisions of international treaties domestically applicable.[13]

For a treaty to be implemented domestically, it must be given domestic effect. There are two ways of incorporating treaties into domestic law: absorption/incorporation or direct application (i.e., recognizing the domestic effect of a treaty through its publication) and transformation (i.e., transforming the treaty into domestic law through the legislative process of the Parliament or the Standing Committee of the NPC). That is, the effects of international law, especially treaties, in domestic law are integrated by means of recognition or transformation, and the transformation mode, in particular, is aligned with the practice of the law of the sea in China.[14]

4.2.2 China's Specific Practice Based on the Modern System of the Law of the Sea

Based on customary law and the basic principles of the modern law of the sea, in particular the Convention system, China has established several practices in formulating and implementing its domestic law of the sea.

4.2.2.1 Legislation (Policy) on General and Principled Regime and Core Content

(1) Declaration of the Government of the People's Republic of China on China's Territorial Sea (September 4, 1958).[15] This declaration stipulates that the territorial sea of the Chinese mainland and its coastal islands is based on straight baselines and that its width is 12 nautical miles. Foreign airplanes and military vessels are not allowed to enter the territorial sea and its corresponding airspace without the permission of the Government. Any foreign vessel navigating China's territorial seas must comply with the relevant decrees of the Government.

---

[12] However, the General Provisions of the Civil Law of the PRC adopted at the Fifth Session of the 12th National People's Congress on March 15, 2017 (effective October 1, 2017) do not contain provisions such as Article 142 of the General Principles of the Civil Law. Whether these elements will be incorporated into the Civil Code in the future is subject to change. Until then, the General Principles of the Civil Law shall apply.

[13] See Lingliang, Zeng, and Geping, Rao. 2005. *International law*. Beijing: Law Press. pp. 110–113.

[14] Although there are disputes in China about the rank and effect of international and domestic law, Chinese legislation and practice show that treaties have precedence over domestic laws. See Zhonghai, Zhou. 2004. *International law*. Beijing: China University of Political Science and Law Press. pp. 64–66.

[15] This declaration was issued prior to the UNCLOS and is based on the customary rules of the law of the sea at the time.

(2) Declaration of the Government of the People's Republic of China on the Baselines of the Territorial Sea of the PRC (May 15, 1996). This declaration issued a statement on partial baselines of the mainland territorial sea and baselines of the territorial sea of the Xisha Qundao of the PRC. These territorial sea baselines are shown in the form of straight lines; the Government of the PRC will further announce the remaining baselines of the territorial sea.

(3) The 1996 Decision of the Standing Committee of the National People's Congress of the People's Republic of China on the Ratification of the UNCLOS (May 15, 1996). According to this declaration, the PRC will delimit its respective maritime jurisdictions based on international law and the principle of equity via consultations with states with opposite or adjacent coasts. This reflects the requirement of the Convention that delimitation be based on the principle of equity. Further, the PRC reaffirms that the provisions of the Convention on innocent passage through the territorial sea are without prejudice to the right of a coastal State to require a foreign warship to obtain prior authorization or give notification in accordance with its laws and regulations before passing through its territorial sea. This is not entirely consistent with the Declaration of the Government of the PRC on China's Territorial Sea.

(4) Statement of the Government of the People's Republic of China on the Baselines of the Territorial Sea of Diaoyu Dao and Its Affiliated Islands (September 10, 2012).[16] The baselines are divided into two groups: the first group of straight baselines connects the Diaoyu Dao, Huangwei Yu, Nanxiao Dao, Beixiao Dao, Nan Yu, Bei Yu and Fei Yu; the second group is the straight baselines delineated around Chiwei Yu.

4.2.2.2 Legislation on the Basic Maritime Zone Regime

(1) Law of the People's Republic of China on the Territorial Sea and the Contiguous Zone (February 25, 1992). It stipulates that "The breadth of the territorial sea of the People's Republic of China is twelve nautical miles, measured from the baselines of the territorial sea. The method of straight baselines composed of all the straight lines joining the adjacent base points shall be employed in drawing the baselines of the territorial sea of the People's Republic of China." At the same time, "foreign ships for military purposes shall be subject to approval by the Government of the People's Republic of China for entering the territorial sea of the People's Republic of China."

[16] For China's statement on the baselines of the territorial waters of the Diaoyu Dao and their affiliated islands, see http://www.gov.cn/jrzg/2012-09/10/content_2221140.htm, accessed October 18, 2018. Meanwhile, to address flight safety in the ECS airspace, including the waters around the Diaoyu Dao, China's Ministry of National Defense declared the "Statement of the Chinese Government on the Delineation of the East China Sea Air Defense Identification Zone" on November 23, 2013, in accordance with international practice and domestic law, and issued the "Announcement of Aircraft Identification Rules for China's East China Sea Air Defense Identification Zone." See http://www.gov.cn/jrzg/2013-11/23/content_2533099(or252533101).htm, accessed October 18, 2018.

(2) Law on the Exclusive Economic Zone and the Continental Shelf of the People's Republic of China (June 26, 1998). This stipulates that "The exclusive economic zone of the People's Republic of China covers the area beyond and adjacent to the territorial sea of the People's Republic of China, extending to 200 nautical miles from the baselines from which the breadth of the territorial sea is measured," and the continental shelf, "comprises the sea-bed and subsoil of the submarine areas that extend beyond its territorial sea throughout the natural prolongation of its land territory to the outer edge of the continental margin, or to a distance of 200 nautical miles from the baselines from which the breadth of the territorial sea is measured where the outer edge of the continental margin does not extend up to that distance." These provisions are based on the "principle of distance" in the Convention.

(3) Law of the People's Republic of China on the Administration of Sea Area (issued on October 27, 2001, effective January 1, 2002). According to Article 2, this law shall be applicable to any exclusive continuous use of the seas within specific sea areas of the interior waters or territorial seas for three months or longer. Articles 4–6 of the Law stipulate that the State shall implement the system of functional division of the sea, information for administering the use of sea areas, registration of the right to use the area, and statistics on the use of the area.

(4) Law of the People's Republic of China on the Exploration and Development of Resources in Deep Seabed Areas (issued on February 26, 2016, effective May 1, 2016). To implement the Convention, states are required to sponsor natural or juridical persons of their nationality or under their control to conduct activities in the deep seabed area as per the Convention and clarify the responsibility of the sponsoring state in taking measures to effectively control the activities of the contractors it sponsors. As a concrete measure taken by States, China enacted the above-mentioned law on February 26, 2016, as per the obligations and requirements of the Convention.[17]

4.2.2.3 Legislation on the Functional Regime for the Oceans and Its Core Content

(1) Marine Environmental Protection Law of the People's Republic of China (adopted on August 23, 1982, and amended three times on December 25, 1999, December 28, 2013, and November 7, 2016). According to Article 2, this Law shall apply to the internal waters, territorial seas, contiguous zones, exclusive economic zones and continental shelves of the People's Republic of China and all other sea areas under the jurisdiction of the People's Republic of China. This Law shall also apply to pollution to the sea areas under the jurisdiction of the PRC originating from areas beyond the sea areas under the jurisdiction of the People's Republic of China.

---

[17] The Law of the PRC on the Exploration and Development of Resources in Deep Seabed Areas consists of 7 chapters and 29 articles. For details, see Law of the People's Republic of China on Exploration and Exploitation of Resources in the Deep Seabed Area (Including Draft Explanations). 2016. Beijing: China Legal Publishing House. pp. 2–12.

Moreover, the Law makes corresponding provisions for the supervision and control over the marine environment, marine ecological protection, prevention and control of pollution damage to the marine environment caused by land-based pollutants, prevention and control of pollution damage to the marine environment caused by coastal construction projects, prevention and control of pollution damage to the marine environment caused by marine construction projects, prevention and control of pollution damage to the marine environment caused by dumping of wastes, and prevention and control of pollution damage to the marine environment caused by vessels and their related operations It further makes corresponding provisions for penalizing various illegal activities.

(2) Maritime Traffic Safety Law of the People's Republic of China (adopted on September 2, 1983, effective January 1, 1984). According to Articles 1–3, this Law is formulated in order to strengthen the control of maritime traffic; ensure the safety of vessels, installations, human life and property; and safeguard the rights and interests of the state. This Law shall apply to all vessels, installations and personnel and to the owners and managers of such vessels and installations that navigate, berth or operate in the coastal waters of the PRC. The harbour superintendency agencies of the PRC shall be the competent authorities responsible for the unified supervision and administration of traffic safety in the coastal waters.

(3) Provisions of the People's Republic of China on Administration of Foreign-related Marine Scientific Research (Adopted on June 18, 1996, effective October 1, 1996). Article 4 stipulates that the marine scientific research activities by the foreign side in the internal seas and territorial seas of the PRC shall be carried out in cooperation with the Chinese side. In other sea areas under the jurisdiction of the PRC, the foreign side may conduct such activities by itself or in cooperation with the Chinese side. Any marine scientific research activities conducted by the foreign side alone or in cooperation with the Chinese side shall be subject to approval from the State competent oceanic department or from the State Council through the State competent oceanic department and shall comply with the relevant laws and regulations of the PRC. Article 5 stipulates the date of acceptance of the written application, the organization examining it, and the duration for the decision on its approval.

4.2.2.4 Legislation on the Special Regime for the Oceans

The main legislation is the Island Protection Law of the People's Republic of China (adopted on December 26, 2009, effective March 1, 2010). This Law is formulated in order to protect the ecosystems of islands and their surrounding waters, rationally develop and exploit the natural resources of islands, protect the oceanic rights and interests of the state, and promote sustainable economic and social development (Article 1). The term "islands" as mentioned in this Law refers to the naturally formed land areas which are surrounded by seawater and above the surface of water at high tide, including inhabited islands and uninhabited islands (Article 2), and the state shall apply the principle of "scientific planning, giving priority to protection, rational development and sustainable utilization" to islands (Article 3). At the same time, in accordance with Article 22, the state shall protect the military facilities established on islands, and it shall be prohibited to damage or endanger such military facilities. The state shall protect the public facilities legally established on islands for navigation assistance or guidance, surveying, meteorological observation, marine monitoring, seismic monitoring, etc., and it shall be prohibited to damage, move without authorization or impede the normal use of such facilities. In accordance with the provisions of Article 28, the status quo of an uninhabited island shall be maintained if the use of it has not been approved; and such activities as quarrying, excavating sea sand, felling trees, production, construction and tourism shall be prohibited. Where the development and utilization of an uninhabited island involves the utilization of any special purpose island, or really needs any sea filling to connect islands or connect the island with continent or any serious change of the natural terrain or landform of the island, it shall be subject to the examination and approval of the State Council (Article 30). Of course, the state shall apply special protection to the islands where the territorial sea-base points are located, islands for the purpose of national defense, islands within the marine natural reserves and other islands for special purposes or with special conservation value (Article 36). These elements constitute the core of the protection of islands.

4.2.2.5 Policies (Legislation) of the Mechanism for Settling Maritime Disputes

It is well known that there are disputes over maritime territorial sovereignty and the delimitation of maritime boundaries between China and a number of countries, particularly in the ECS and the SCS. In addition to Article 2 of the Decision of the Standing Committee of the NPC on the Ratification of the UNCLOS and Article 2(3) of the Law on the Exclusive Economic Zone and the Continental Shelf, which provides for delimitation of maritime boundaries by agreement in accordance with the equitable principle and on the basis of international law. China has also stipulated a number of principled provisions for the settlement of disputes in other documents. The main ones are as follows:

On 25 August 2006, China made a declaration under article 298 of UNCLOS, stating that "China does not accept any of the procedures provided for in Section 2 of part XV of UNCLOS with respect to all the categories of disputes referred to in paragraph 1 (a), (b) and (c) of article 298" (i.e., disputes relating to delimitation of maritime boundaries, territorial sovereignty, military activities and the like). China has ruled out the possibility of applying international judicial or arbitral settlement to maritime disputes involving the vital interests of the State. This position is particularly reflected in the disposition of the SCS arbitration case.[18]

On 14 December 2012, the PRC submitted to the CLCS concerning the outer limits of the continental shelf beyond 200 nautical miles in part of the ECS to supplement and fulfill the responsibilities of "Preliminary Information Indicative of the Outer Limits of the Continental Shelf Beyond 200 Nautical Miles of the People's Republic of China," which had already been submitted to the UN Secretary-General by the Permanent Mission of China to the UN on May 11, 2009.[19]

In addition to these legal acts performed in accordance with the norms and requirements of the Convention, China also has specific practices dealing with the safeguarding of maritime rights and interests. These are mainly manifested in the following areas:

First, with regard to the status of the rock of Oki-no-Tori (Oki-no Tori-shima), the Permanent Mission of China to the United Nations submitted to the UN Secretary-General on February 6, 2009, a written statement of position with regard to the rock of Oki-no-Tori (Oki-no Tori-shima), pointing out that Oki-no-Tori (Oki-no Tori-shima) is a rock, not an island, and that it is not possible to use it as a base from which to claim the continental shelf or the outer continental shelf. Furthermore, the CLCS does not have the authority to consider the information relating to the outer continental shelf using the rock of Oki-no-Tori (Oki-no Tori-shima) as a base point.[20]

Second, in response to the joint submission made by Malaysia and Vietnam regarding the outer continental shelf (May 6, 2009) and the separate submission made by Vietnam on the outer continental shelf (May 7, 2009), the Permanent Mission of China to the UN submitted a note to the UN Secretary-General on May 7, 2009 (No. CML/17/2009), which stated that "China has indisputable sovereignty over the islands in the SCS and the adjacent waters, and enjoys sovereign rights and jurisdiction over the relevant waters as well as the seabed and subsoil thereof. The above position is consistently held by the Chinese Government, and is widely known by the international community." In response to the note of April 4, 2011, from the MFA of the Philippines to the Chinese Embassy in the Philippines, stating that the Republic of the Philippines has sovereignty and jurisdiction over the so-called "Kalayaan Islands Group" (in fact part of China's Nansha Qundao), the Permanent Mission of China to the United Nations once again addressed a note to the UN Secretary-General on April 14, 2011 (No. CML/8/2011), emphasizing that "China has indisputable sovereignty

---

[18] For China's position and attitude toward the *SCS* Arbitration, see Chinese Society of International Law. 2018. *Commentary on the South China Sea Arbitration awards: A critical study*. Beijing: Foreign Languages Press. pp. 1–446.

[19] For the Chinese Government's "Submission on the Outer Limits of the Continental Shelf in Parts of the East China Sea," see https://www.un.org/depts/los/clcs_new/submissions_files/submission_chn_63_2012.htm. accessed October 18, 2018. For Preliminary Information Indicative of the Outer Limits of the Continental Shelf Beyond 200 Nautical Miles of the People's Republic of China, see https://www.un.org/depts/los/clcs_new/submissions_files/preliminary/chn2009preliminaryinformation_english.pdf, accessed October 18, 2018.

[20] See http://www.un.org/deps/los/clcs_new/submission_files/jpn08/chn_6feb09_c.pdf, accessed October 18, 2018.

over the islands in the SCS and the adjacent waters, and enjoys sovereign rights and jurisdiction over the relevant waters as well as the seabed and subsoil thereof. China's sovereignty and related rights and jurisdiction in the South China Sea are supported by abundant historical and legal evidence."[21] This position and views were reaffirmed in the Statement of the Government of the People's Republic of China on China's Territorial Sovereignty and Maritime Rights and Interests in the SCS issued on July 12, 2016.[22]

Third, in response to the advisory opinion rendered by the International Seabed Disputes Chamber of the ITLOS on February 1, 2011, on the question of the responsibilities and obligations of States sponsoring persons and entities with respect to activities in the Area, the Department of Treaties and Laws of the MFA of the PRC submitted on August 18, 2010, a written opinion titled "Written Statement of the People's Republic of China - Responsibilities and obligations of States sponsoring persons and entities with respect to activities in the Area (Request for advisory opinion submitted to the seabed disputes chamber)." The written submission was generally adopted by the International Seabed Disputes Chamber in its advisory opinion, contributing to advancing the implementation of the regime for the international seabed area.[23]

Fourth, to manage the South China Sea issue, the DOC in the SCS was signed between China and ASEAN countries on November 4, 2002, the Guidelines for the Implementation of the DOC in the SCS were concluded on July 20, 2011, and the Joint Statement of the Foreign Ministers of ASEAN Member States and China on the Full and Effective Implementation of the Declaration on the Conduct of Parties in the South China Sea was issued on July 25, 2016."[24] At the same time, China and ASEAN countries launched the negotiation and formulation of the COC in August 2013 and have made substantial progress. The implementation of these measures and documents, as well as their concrete actions, have strongly stabilized the situation in the SCS and produced positive results.[25]

---

[21] See Chinese Society of International Law. 2018.*The South China Sea Arbitration Awards: A Critical Study*. Beijing: Foreign Languages Press. p. 34.

[22] See Department of Boundary and Ocean Affairs of the Ministry of Foreign Affairs of the People's Republic of China. 2016. A *compilation of documents related to China's handling of the South China Sea Arbitration*. Beijing: Beijing: World Affairs Press. pp. 86–90.

[23] See the Relevant Procedures of China's Participation in the "Advisory Opinion on the Responsibilities and Obligations of Sponsoring States" of International Tribunal for the Law of Sea. 2016. in *A Selection of Cases on International Law from China*, ed. Department of Treaties and Laws of the Ministry of Foreign Affairs of the People's Republic of China. Beijing: World Affairs Press. pp. 53–80.

[24] Border and Ocean Affairs Department, Ministry of Foreign Affairs of the People's Republic of China. 2017. *A Compilation of documents on the issues related to China seas*. Beijing: World Affairs Press. pp. 69–94.

[25] In addition, China and Vietnam signed the Agreement between the People's Republic of China and the Socialist Republic of Vietnam on the Delimitation of the Territorial Sea, Exclusive Economic Zone and Continental Shelf of the Two Countries in Beibu Bay and the Agreement between the People's Republic of China and the Socialist Republic of Vietnam on Fishery Cooperation in Beibu Bay.on December 25, 2000 (entered into force on June 30, 2004); the Fisheries Agreement between

4.3 Practical Problems and Response Measures of China's Ocean Legal System

4.3.1 Practical Challenges of China's Ocean Legal System

Although China has continuously enriched its domestic law of the sea system based on the principles of the modern law of the sea, especially the Convention system, some of its provisions and regimes have also been challenged by the international community, especially the U.S. This is mainly manifested in the following areas:

First, the challenge to the application of the straight baselines in the Xisha Qundao. China announced its straight baselines in the Xisha Qundao on May 15, 1996, which were challenged by the U.S. The U.S. considers this to be an "excessive maritime rights" claim, including the issuance of the report "Limits of the in the Seas Straight Baselines Claim: China" (No. 117) on June 9, 1996, as well as the implementation of a number of so-called Freedom of Navigation operations by warships the territorial waters of the Xisha Qundao in recent years, challenging the application of China's laws and legal norms.[26]

Second, procedural challenges to the innocent passage of warships in the territorial sea. The U.S. has mainly challenged China's application of prior authorization or notification to the coastal state for the innocent passage of foreign warships in the territorial sea in the above-mentioned Declaration on the Territorial Sea, the Law on the Territorial Sea and the Contiguous Zone, and the Decision on the Ratification of the UNCLOS, arguing that these provisions contravene the prevailing practices of the international community and insisting on the doctrine of the freedom of navigation, which stipulates that the innocent passage of warships in the territorial sea is not subject to prior authorization or notification to the coastal state.

the People's Republic of China and the State of Japan on November 11, 1997 (entered into force on June 1, 2000); the China–Japan Consensus of Principles on the East China Sea Issues issued by China and Japan (June 18, 2008); the China–Japan Four-Point Consensus of Principles on Handling and Improvement of Sino-Japanese Relations (November 7, 2014); the China–Japan Agreement on the Ministry of National Defense on May 9, 2018 by the Memorandum of Understanding on Maritime and Air Safety Liaison Mechanism between the Ministry of Defense of China and the Ministry of Defense of Japan (entered into force on June 8, 2018), the Agreement on Maritime Search and Rescue Cooperation between the Government of Japan and the Government of the People's Republic of China (signed on October 26, 2018, entered into force on February 14, 2019); the Agreement on Fisheries Between the Government of the People's Republic of China and the Government of the Republic of Korea signed on August 3, 2000 (entered into force on June 2001 entered into force on June 30, 2001); and negotiations with the Republic of Korea on the delimitation of the maritime area of the Yellow Sea, among others. All these achievements and documents have played a role in effectively resolving and delaying maritime disputes in China's maritime environment, reflecting the effectiveness of China's insistence on peacefully resolving disputes, especially with political means, and delaying disputes through crisis management mechanisms.

[26] For the so-called freedom of navigation operations carried out by U.S. warships in the waters of Xisha Qundao and Nansha Qundao, see Yongming, Jin. *How U.S. ships' freedom of navigation operations' challenge international law*, Pengpai News, 9 July, 2018.

Third, the challenge to jurisdiction over security matters in the contiguous zone. The U.S. believes that China's provision in Article 13 of the Law on the Territorial Sea and Contiguous Zone, which provides for jurisdiction over security matters in the contiguous zone to prevent and punish such matters, is contrary to the prevailing practice of most states and the normative content of the Convention.[27] The contiguous zone in Article 33 of the Convention inherits the provisions of the 1958 Convention on the Territorial Sea and the Contiguous Zone. The text submitted by Commission I of the First UN Conference on the Law of the Sea in 1958, which considered the regime of the contiguous zone, considered a reference to the "prevention and punishment of infringements of the security of the coastal state," but when this reference was considered in the plenary session, it was deleted from the final text because a majority of states opposed the inclusion of security matters. The reason given for the opposition was the abstract meaning of security, the expansive interpretations of all juridical interests to be protected, and the risk for abuse.[28] Consequently, Article 24 of the Convention on the Territorial Sea and the Contiguous Zone does not include jurisdiction and penalties for security-related matters.

Fourth, the challenge of China's construction and deployment in the SCS, especially in the Nansha Qundao and Reefs. The U.S.' position is that China's construction of the islands and reefs it occupies in the Nansha Qundao has harmed the surrounding maritime environment, especially after the completion of the land blowing and filling project, and has a tendency to militarize, posing a serious threat to the security of other countries, especially regarding freedom of navigation and security. Moreover, the U.S. argues that China cannot claim more jurisdictional waters based on the Nansha Qundao it occupies, as there are different and opposing claims on their status. In addition, the U.S. Department of State released the report "Limits of the Sea - China's Maritime Claims in the South China Sea" (No. 143) on December 5, 2014, and considers that China should clearly define the nature of the dotted line in the SCS and the legal status of the waters within the line.[29]

Fifth, the challenge to the binding effect of the *SCS* Arbitration Award. Some countries, led by the U.S., argue that China should comply with the *SCS* Arbitration Final Award (July 12, 2016) made by the arbitral tribunal.[30]

---

[27] Five states in the international community (Cambodia, China, Sudan, Syria, and Vietnam) claim jurisdiction over security matters within the contiguous zone. See Pedrozo, Raul. 2018. Military activities in the exclusive economic zone: East Asia focus, *The Journal of Island Studies* 7(2): 79.

[28] See [Japanese] Hayashi, Hisamura. 1995. *Studies on the law of the sea*. Tokyo: Nippon Hyoron Sha Publishers. pp. 89–92.

[29] For the refutation of the U.S. Department of State's "Limits of the Oceans" report, see Bingbing, Jia. 2016. Refuting State Department's Error on Historic Rights of South China Sea in No.143 of Limits in the Seas, *Law Review* 4: 76–82; and for the content of the dotted line in the South China Sea, see Zhiguo, Gao., Jia Bingbing. 2014. *The nine-dash line in the south China sea: history, status and implications*, Beijing: Ocean Press. pp. 1–49.

[30] For a comprehensive critique of the content of the South China Sea Arbitration Award, see Chinese Society of International Law. 2018. *The South China Sea Arbitration Awards: A Critical Study*. Beijing: Foreign Languages Press. pp. 1–395.

4.3.2 China's Response Measures to Improve Domestic Ocean Legal System

Based on customary international law and the modern law of the sea system, particularly the Convention, China has continuously developed and enriched its domestic law of the sea, which has played a positive role in the management and development of ocean affairs. Furthermore, this is a situation where the international community, especially the U.S., has challenged the principles and institutions of China's law of the sea. To further modernize China's ocean governance system and capacity and contribute to becoming a strong ocean state, it is particularly important to improve the construction of the domestic law of the sea system to achieve the goal of governing the oceans under the law.

First, the status of "oceans" in the national legal system should be established. In China's Constitution, there is no mention of the status of the oceans in the national legal system. To enhance the role of the oceans, their status must be elevated. The main way to do this could be to add that "oceans" are part of natural resources and should be protected in the Constitution or define and regulate the status of "oceans" through the enactment of the Basic Law on Oceans and Seas, to establish and elevate the status of "oceans."

Second, those elements of the domestic law of the sea that are challenged by other countries should be focused on. Doubts have been raised about China's systems of straight baselines in the Xisha Qundao, procedural authorization or notification of innocent passage by warships in the territorial sea, and authorization for military activities in the EEZ. China should strengthen its communication and coordination with other countries on these controversial issues by continuing to draw on the practices of other countries. In addition, China should prepare to further enrich the Convention, including formulating a new "implementing agreement" and the appropriate adaptation of the relevant domestic legal system.

Third, the development of legislation relating to functional matters of the oceans and seas should be supplemented. To develop and utilize the space and resources of the oceans sustainably, it is important to strengthen research and development in marine science and technology. This is the key to China becoming a strong maritime country. As marine science and technology play an important supporting role in the development and utilization of ocean space and resources, including the development of the ocean economy, China should pay more attention to these functional aspects, conduct research, and plan relevant legislative work to improve regulations such as the management of foreign-related marine scientific research and the formulation of laws such as the Marine Science and Technology Law and the Marine Safety Law.

Fourth, the institutional mechanism for the oceans should be improved. To enhance the modernization of the national governance system and capacity, China has reformed its marine mechanism institutions to utilize this national institutional reform to coordinate and clarify the functions of the sea-related management institutions (e.g., the SOA, the MNR, the MEE, the MARA, and the GACC and the CCG). Further, based on the Decision of Exercise of Maritime Rights Protection

Law Enforcement Powers by the China Coast Guard Bureau (adopted on June 22, 2018, and entered into force as of July 1, 2018), China further should develop and improve relevant laws and regulations such as the Basic Law of the Sea and the Organization Law of the CCG. These laws and regulations are important safeguards for the construction of a strong maritime country and comprehensive management of maritime affairs.[31]

4.4 Institutional Challenges of Innocent Passage in Territorial Waters and China's Response

The challenge of "freedom of navigation" in the Nanhai Zhudao, especially in the territorial waters of Xisha Qundao and the waters around the Nansha Qundao and Reefs, is undeniably an important issue that needs to be urgently addressed. This section discusses the regime of innocent passage in the territorial sea.

4.4.1 Questions Raised

On January 30, 2016, the guided-missile destroyer USS Curtis Wilbur (DDG-54) entered the territorial waters near China's Xisha Qundao without prior notification or permission, seriously undermining China's sovereignty and security in these territorial waters and its maritime rights and interests, and the Chinese MND and the MFA severely condemned this action. The spokesman for the China's MND pointed out that after the warship entered the territorial waters of Xisha Qundao in violation of Chinese laws, the Chinese troops guarding the islands and naval vessels and aircraft took immediate action to respond to the incident, warning and immediately driving it away. The U.S. committed a serious violation of the law, undermining the peace, security, and good order of the relevant sea areas. China promulgated the Law of the People's Republic of China on the Territorial Sea and the Contiguous Zone as early as 1992, stipulating that foreign ships for military purposes shall be subject to approval by the Government of the PRC for entering the territorial sea of the PRC. The unauthorized entry into China's territorial waters by a United States warship, knowing this law, is an intentional act of provocation.[32] In response to this serious

[31] Program for Deepening the Reform of the Party and State Institutions issued by the Central Committee of the Communist Party of China (Mar. 21, 2018), http://www.xinhuanet.com/politics/2018-03/21/c_1122570517.htm, accessed October 18, 2018. Decision of the Standing Committee of the 13th NPC on the Exercise of Maritime Rights Protection Law Enforcement Powers by the China Coast Guard Bureau, adopted on June 22, 2018, http://www.npc.gov.cn/npc/xinwen/2018-06/22/content_2056585.htm, accessed October 18, 2018.

[32] See Defense Ministry Spokesman Yang Yujun Speaks on U.S. Warship's Unauthorized Entry into Xisha Territorial Waters, http://news.mod.gov.cn/headlines/2016-01/30/content_4638189.htm, accessed January 31, 2016.

military and legal provocation by the U.S., China has exercised the utmost restraint and taken corresponding countermeasures, with a view to preserving China–United States relations and safety and order of navigation in the SCS.

The "freedom of navigation operations" carried out by the U.S. does not change the fact that they are in violation of international law, the agreement between the Ministries of Defense of China and the U.S.,[33] and Chinese law, and undermine the legislative purpose of the regime of innocent passage in territorial waters. Although domestic scholars have analyzed the system of innocent passage of foreign ships (including warships) in territorial seas, previous studies have seldom examined the purpose of the system of innocent passage in territorial seas and its relationship with other systems. Therefore, in light of the recent threatening behavior of the U.S. in China's Xisha Qundao territorial seas, it is necessary to discuss the innocent passage of foreign ships).[34]

4.4.2 Purpose of the Right of Innocent Passage and Its Relationship with Other Regimes

The right of "innocent passage" of warships in the territorial sea of other States is a matter of debate in theory and practice. Theoretically, it involves the system of territorial seas, the navigation system of international straits, and the freedom of navigation of ships. Practically, the controversy over the "innocent passage" of warships in territorial seas is reflected in disagreement as to whether it is necessary to notify or obtain prior permission from the coastal state or whether it is possible to navigate freely (without notification or permission). This is because the Convention on the Territorial Sea and the Contiguous Zone of the four Geneva Conventions on the Law of the Sea of 1958 and the UNCLOS adopted in 1982 do not have clear

[33] China's MND and the U.S. Department of Defense (DOD) signed the Memorandum of Understanding on the Notification of Major Military Activities and the Memorandum of Understanding Regarding the Rules of Behavior for Safety of Air and Maritime Encounters in November 2014. In 2015, the two countries agreed on the annexes on the Memorandum of Understanding on the Notification of Major Military Activities and the Memorandum of Understanding Regarding the Rules of Behavior for Safety of Air and Maritime Encounters.

[34] Upon the author's search in China National Knowledge Infrastructure (CNKI) on January 10, 2016, the academic papers in the domestic academic circles for the innocent passage system of foreign ships in the territorial sea include the following: Zhenguo, Chen. 1985. On the right of harmless passage in the territorial sea, *Political Science and Law* 2; Jianye, Zhu. 1993. Legal issues on the entry of foreign warships into China's territorial sea, *Law Science Magazine* 3; Hongyun, Li. 1997. Two Issues in the Regime of Innocent Passage in Territorial Sea, *Peking University Law Journal* 2; Hongyun, Li. 1998. The Right of Innocent passage of Foreign Warships in Territorial Sea, *Peking University Law Journal* 4; Junmin, Wang. 2002. On the legal position of warships in the law of the sea, *Journal of Ocean University of China (Social Science Edition)* 3; Jianwen, Zhao. 2005. On the Interpretative Declarations by the State Parties to United Nations Convention on the Law of the Sea concerning the Issue of Innocent Passage of Warships through the Territorial Sea, *China Oceans Law Review* 2; Shichen, Tian. 2007. The Legal Status of Foreign Warships in Territorial Seas *China Oceans Law Review* 2.

provisions on this issue; in particular, the two Conventions have ceded the standard for judging "innocent passage" to the coastal state, leading to different practices.[35] Therefore, before discussing the regime of innocent passage of warships in territorial seas, it is necessary to first define the right of innocent passage.

4.4.2.1 The Regime of Innocent Passage in Territorial Seas

According to Article 2 of the Convention, the territorial sea is the belt of the sea that "the sovereignty of a coastal State extends, beyond its land territory and internal waters;" "This sovereignty extends to the air space over the territorial sea as well as to its bed and subsoil." In other words, a State may exercise exclusive and comprehensive jurisdiction (legislative, executive, and judicial) over its own territory (territory, internal waters, and territorial sea) based on the principle of territorial sovereignty. The above provisions inherit from Articles 1 and 2 of the Convention on the Territorial Sea and the Contiguous Zone and reflect the view that the territorial sea is a natural and indivisible appendage of the coastal State; that is, the Convention adopts the view that the territorial sea is "the territory theory."[36]

Regarding the breadth of the territorial sea, Article 3 of the Convention provides that Every State has the right to establish the breadth of its territorial sea up to a limit not exceeding 12 nautical miles, measured from baselines determined in accordance with this Convention. This provision overcomes the shortcomings of the Convention on the Territorial Sea and the Contiguous Zone, which fails to provide for the breadth of the territorial sea, and creates a basis for determining the extent of other maritime areas of the Convention (such as the contiguous zone, the EEZ, and the continental shelf).[37]

To enable States to exercise exclusive and comprehensive jurisdiction in the territorial sea on the basis of the principle of territorial sovereignty, including jurisdiction

---

[35] See Nandan, S. N., Rosenne, S. 2014. *Commentary on the 1982 United Nations Convention on the Law of the Sea (Volume II)*, trans. Lv Wenzheng, Mao Bin. Beijing: Ocean Press. pp. 136–149.

[36] With regard to the jurisdiction of the coastal state over the territorial sea, there is an academic dichotomy between "the property theory" and "the territory theory "The property doctrine" means that the coastal state can only exercise jurisdiction over specific matters recognized in international law, while "the territory theory" means that the territorial sea is an extension of the territory of the coastal state, which has exclusive jurisdiction over it. The Convention on the Territorial Sea and the Contiguous Zone adopts "the territory theory". see O'Connel, D.P. 1971. The Juridical Nature of the Territorial Sea, *British Year Book of International law*, p. 381.

[37] Article 3 of the Convention on the Territorial Sea and the Contiguous Zone (adopted on April 29, 1958 and entered into force on September 10, 1964) provides that, "Except as otherwise provided in the articles of the Convention, the normal baseline from which the breadth of the territorial sea is measured is the low-water line, as shown on the large-scale charts officially recognized by the coastal state." In the Convention on the High Seas of the "Geneva Conventions on the Law of the Sea" (April 29, 1958), which includes the Convention on the Territorial Sea and the Contiguous Zone, the maritime areas are divided into internal waters, territorial sea, and the high seas only. Article 1 of the Convention on the High Seas provides that "The term 'high seas' means all parts of the sea that are not included in the territorial sea or in the internal waters of a State."

over living and non-living resources, particularly in the areas of cultures, finance, economic activities, immigration, health and safety, and security, the Convention grants coastal States the right to exercise necessary regulations in the territorial sea with respect to national and foreign vessels.[38] These rights reflect the fact that coastal States have legislative, enforcement, and judicial powers over the territorial sea.

In addition, to facilitate international maritime traffic, the Convention recognizes the right of innocent passage of foreign ships, including warships. Article 17 of the Convention provides that, "Subject to this Convention, ships of all States, whether coastal or land-locked, enjoy the right of innocent passage through the territorial sea."[39] The purpose of the Convention in providing for such a regime of innocent passage is to harmonize and balance the navigational interests of foreign ships and the sovereign interests of coastal States.[40] In other words, the Convention's regime on innocent passage is the product of a delicate balance and coordination between the navigational interests of ships' passage (the interests of the flag State) and the sovereignty of the coastal State on the premise of a dichotomy between them.[41] The theoretical basis for this design is to satisfy the requirement of balancing the requirements of "eliminating *de facto* actual harm to the coastal State" and "ensuring *de jure* the integrity of the sovereignty of the territorial sea of the coastal State."[42] The Convention's regime of innocent passage in the territorial sea is, therefore, a product of compromise and coordination.

Accordingly, the coastal State has the right to prescribe the conditions for the use of the territorial sea and the regime for the passage of ships, as provided in Article 21 of the Convention, which provides that "The coastal State may adopt laws and regulations, in conformity with the provisions of this Convention and other rules of international law, relating to innocent passage through the territorial sea" in respect of each or any of the following eight matters. Furthermore, Article 22(1) of the Convention provides that the "The coastal State may, where necessary having regard to the safety of navigation, require foreign ships exercising the right of innocent passage through its territorial sea to use such sea lanes and traffic separation schemes as it may designate or prescribe for the regulation of the passage of ships." The coastal State also has the obligation not to hinder innocent passage through the territorial sea to foreign ships.

The legal status of such "innocent passage" in the maritime domain was established in international law around the 1840s.[43] In fact, in the seventeenth and eighteenth centuries, when the dual structure of the sea (high seas and territorial sea) was

---

[38] See [Japanese] Yamamoto, Sōji. 1997. *Law of the sea.* Tokyo: Sanseido. p. 52.

[39] Article 24(1) of the UNCLOS provides that "The coastal State shall not hamper the innocent passage of foreign ships through the territorial sea except in accordance with this Convention."

[40] [Japanese] Yamamoto, Sōji. 2009. The maritime security law system—The intersection of the law of the sea and domestic law. Tokyo: Sanseido. pp. 131–132.

[41] [Japanese] Yamamoto, Sōji. 1997. *Law of the sea.* Tokyo: Sanseido. pp. 120–121.

[42] [Japanese] Sugihara,Takane. 1991. *The law of the sea and the right of navigation.* Tokyo: The Oceanographic Society of Japan. p. 65.

[43] See O'Connell., D. P.. 1982. *The international law of the sea, Vol. I.* Oxford: Clarendon Press, p. 19.

established, the concept of "innocent use" of the territorial sea was already advocated or affirmed in the doctrines of most scholars.[44] For example, Hugo Grotius, in the seventeenth century, argued that coastal states could not impede "unarmed navigation without intent to injure:" John Selden argued that even if the ocean is occupied, "inoffensive passage" should be allowed to foreigners. Emmerich de Vattel in the eighteenth century argued that ships without any suspicion should be allowed "innocent uses" in the territorial sea, and Henry Wheaton held that "innocent use" by other persons should be recognized as long as it did not bring harm and unreasonable conditions to the owner.[45]

Although in the case of non-innocent passage, the coastal State may regulate foreign ships to ensure the coastal State's right to protection, for example, Article 25(1), of the Convention provides that "The coastal State may take the necessary steps in its territorial sea to prevent passage which is not innocent." However, international law (especially the Convention) is not clear on how to deal with the harmful passage of foreign ships (especially warships) in the territorial sea, so it must be clearly stipulated in the domestic law of each State. At the same time, the regime of innocent passage in the territorial sea under the Convention is closely related to the regime of passage through international straits, both in terms of its content and in the process of its consideration and creation. Furthermore, the two are linked; that is to say, the regime of passage through international straits was agreed upon and established in conjunction with the regime of innocent passage in the territorial sea.

4.4.2.2 Regime of Passage Through International Straits in Relation to Innocent Passage Through Territorial Seas

International straits comprising the territorial sea are subject to a specific legal regime because they are major thoroughfares for maritime traffic. Article 16(4) of the Convention on the Territorial Sea and the Contiguous Zone provides that "There shall be no suspension of the innocent passage of foreign ships through straits which are used for international navigation between one part of the high seas and another part of the high seas or the territorial sea of a foreign State."

It has been argued that Article 16(4) of the Convention on the Territorial Sea and the Contiguous Zone, which deals with international straits, adopts the "mandatory right of innocent passage" or the "guaranteed right of innocent passage"[46] and has been recognized by the ICJ. For example, in its judgment in the *Corfu Channel* case (December 15, 1949), the ICJ stated: "It is generally recognized and in accordance

[44] It is generally recognized that the primary legal norm establishing the dualist structure of the oceans and seas is Article 1 of the Convention on the High Seas (adopted on April 29, 1958 and entered into force on September 30, 1962).

[45] [Japanese] Sugihara, Takane. 1991. *The law of the sea and the right of navigation.* Tokyo: The Oceanographic Society of Japan. pp. 56–58.

[46] [Japanese] Yamamoto, Sōji. 2009. The maritime security law system—The intersection of the law of the sea and domestic law. Tokyo: Sanseido. p. 132; Degong, Chen. 2009. Modern international law of the sea. Beijing: Ocean Press. p. 88.

with international custom that States in time of peace have a right to send their warships through straits used for international navigation between two parts of the high seas without the previous authorization of a coastal State, provided that the passage is innocent. Unless otherwise prescribed in an international convention, there is no right for a coastal State to prohibit such passage through straits in time of peace." As to the international character of a strait, the ICJ stated that "the decisive criterion is rather its geographical situation as connecting two parts of the high seas and the fact of its being used for international navigation."[47] In other words, in determining the nature of an international strait, the ICJ applied the geographical criterion of connecting two parts of the high seas and the functional criterion of being used, in fact, for international navigation.[48]

With the development of State practice concerning the regime of the territorial sea, during the Third UN Conference on the Law of the Sea, the breadth of the territorial sea has tended to be 12 nautical miles. Some straits with a width of 6 to 24 nautical miles have left open sea lanes when the territorial sea width was 3 nautical miles in the past[49]; whereas if a 12-nautical-mile territorial sea width is implemented, these straits will be completely within the territorial waters of coastal countries. Among the 116 straits in the world, more than 30 are considered "straits used for international navigation."[50]

In this regard, at the Third UN Conference on the Law of the Sea, to safeguard their national sovereignty and security, some coastal States argued that straits within the territorial sea, whether or not they were used for international navigation, should be an integral part of the territorial sea of the coastal State, and should therefore retain the legal status of the territorial sea and the regime of innocent passage should be implemented. In contrast, the U.S. and the then USSR, given their military-strategic interests, insisted that straits that were habitually used for international navigation should also be subject to "freedom of navigation on the high seas" even if they were within the territorial sea of the coastal State and that all foreign ships, including warships and airplanes, should be permitted to enjoy the freedom of navigation on the high seas. At the same time, the former Soviet Union claimed that its security depended on the free navigation of international straits as a condition for accepting

---

[47] *Corfu Channel Cases*, ICJ Reports 1949, p. 28. See Degong, Chen. 2009. *Modern international law of the sea*. Beijing: Ocean Press. p. 87.

[48] [Japanese] Sugihara, Takane. 1991. *The law of the sea and the right of navigation*. Tokyo: The Oceanographic Society of Japan. pp. 84–87.

[49] The Dutch jurist Bynkershoek proposed in 1703 that the rights of a land state are limited to the range of its artillery. This is known as the "Rule of Cannon Ranges"; In 1782, Galiani suggested that three nautical miles should be used as a uniform standard for cannon ranges. This principle was later widely practiced by Mediterranean countries, France, and England. From the 19th century to the early 20th century, most territorial sea widths established by various countries were 3 or 4 nautical miles, but did not exceed 12 nautical miles. See Degong, Chen. 2009. *Modern international law of the sea*. Beijing: Ocean Press. pp. 50–51; Min, Wei. 1987. *Law of the sea*. Beijing: Law Press. pp. 57–60.

[50] Degong, Chen. 2009. *Modern international law of the sea*. Beijing: Ocean Press. p. 79.

a 200-nautical-mile EEZ, while the U.S. stated that it would not recognize a 12-nautical-mile breadth of the territorial sea unless it was guaranteed the free navigation of straits used for international navigation and the freedom of overflight. In the event of irreconcilable disputes, the representative of Malta made proposals in 1973 to the Committee on the Peaceful Uses of the Seabed and Ocean Floor Beyond the Limits of National Jurisdiction to establish specific conditions for "passage," including compliance with the mandatory traffic diversion scheme, which required uninterrupted and expeditious passage; the requirement of three days' notice for the passage of a foreign submarine or warship; and the requirement that passage through the strait should not be made without notice. The proposal includes conditions for adherence to a mandatory traffic separation plan requiring nonstop and expeditious passage; a three-day advance notice requirement for the passage of foreign submarines or warships; and a condition that no aircraft be flown and that no research or intelligence-gathering activities be conducted during passage through the strait. This proposal provides the basis for the Convention to develop a new regime for straits used for international navigation that is distinct from "innocent passage" and "free passage,"[51] ensuring the integrity of the Convention.[52] Thus, as can be seen from the review process, the establishment of the regime of innocent passage in the territorial sea is closely linked to that of the 200-nautical-mile EEZ and that of passage through international straits.

Finally, the Convention established a new regime of passage through straits used for international navigation. Article 38(1) and (2), of the Convention provides that "In straits referred to in article 37, all ships and aircraft enjoy the right of transit passage, which shall not be impeded;" "Transit passage means the exercise in accordance with this Part of the freedom of navigation and overflight solely for the purpose of continuous and expeditious transit of the strait between one part of the high seas or an exclusive economic zone and another part of the high seas or an exclusive economic zone."

It should be noted that transit passage through straits used for international navigation does not require innocent passage and recognizes freedom of overflight and is therefore different from the "mandatory right of innocent passage" or the "guaranteed right of innocent passage" provided for in Article 16(4), of the Convention on the Territorial Sea and the Contiguous Zone.[53]" The Convention's regime of passage through straits for international navigation includes not only "transit passage" and "traffic separation" but also "innocent passage." For example, Article 45 provides that "The regime of innocent passage shall apply in straits used for international navigation excluded from the application of the regime of transit passage under article 38, paragraph 1 or between a part of the high seas or an exclusive economic zone and the territorial sea of a foreign State." Therefore, this regime is a hybrid one.

[51] Degong, Chen. 2009. *Modern international law of the sea*. Beijing: Ocean Press. pp. 85–92.

[52] The preamble to the UNCLOS states that "The States Parties to this Convention the problems of ocean space are closely interrelated and need to be considered as a whole."

[53] [Japanese] Yamamoto, Sōji. 2009. The maritime security law system—The intersection of the law of the sea and domestic law. Tokyo: Sanseido. p. 133.

4.4.3 *Legal Elements of Innocent Passage in Territorial Seas and Its Restrictions on Warships*

The author believes that when discussing the legal requirements for innocent passage within the territorial sea, it is helpful to further understand the innocent passage system of warships within the territorial sea by comparing it with the legal requirements for passage within the territorial sea.

The legal elements of passage in the Convention's territorial sea regime are established in Article 18. Paragraph 1 provides that "Passage means navigation through the territorial sea for the purpose of: (a) traversing that sea without entering internal waters or calling at a roadstead or port facility outside internal waters; or (b) proceeding to or from internal waters or a call at such roadstead or port facility." Paragraph 2 provides that "Passage shall be continuous and expeditious. However, passage includes stopping and anchoring, but only in so far as the same are incidental to ordinary navigation or are rendered necessary by force majeure or distress or for the purpose of rendering assistance to persons, ships or aircraft in danger or distress."

Meanwhile, the legal requirements for innocent passage through territorial seas are established in Article 19 of the Convention. Paragraph 1 provides that "Passage is innocent so long as it is not prejudicial to the peace, good order or security of the coastal State. Such passage shall take place in conformity with this Convention and with other rules of international law." Paragraph 2 provides that "Passage of a foreign ship shall be considered to be prejudicial to the peace, good order or security of the coastal State if in the territorial sea it engages in any of the following activities: (a) any threat or use of force against the sovereignty, territorial integrity or political independence of the coastal State, or in any other manner in violation of the principles of international law embodied in the Charter of the United Nations; (b) any exercise or practice with weapons of any kind; (c) any act aimed at collecting information to the prejudice of the defense or security of the coastal State; (d) any act of propaganda aimed at affecting the defense or security of the coastal State; (e) the launching, landing or taking on board of any aircraft; (f) the launching, landing or taking on board of any military device; (g) the loading or unloading of any commodity, currency or person contrary to the customs, fiscal, immigration or sanitary laws and regulations of the coastal State; (h) any act of willful and serious pollution contrary to this Convention; (i) any fishing activities; (j) the carrying out of research or survey activities; (k) any act aimed at interfering with any systems of communication or any other facilities or installations of the coastal State; (l) any other activity not having a direct bearing on passage."

From the content and structure of Articles 18 and 19 of the Convention, if the elements that do not meet the requirements of Article 18 are passed, they can be judged by the behavior of Article 19. That is to say, the Convention adopts the approach of separately legislating and stipulating the elements of passing and innocent passage, which is different from the approach of the Convention on the Territorial

Sea and the Contiguous Zone, which stipulates the elements of passing and innocent passage in the same article.[54] Article 14(2), of the Convention on the Territorial Sea and the Contiguous Zone provides that "Passage means navigation through the territorial sea for the purpose either of traversing that sea without entering internal waters, or of proceeding to internal waters, or of making for the high seas from internal waters;" paragraph 4 provides that "Passage is innocent so long as it is not prejudicial to the peace, good order or security of the coastal State. Such passage shall take place in conformity with these articles and with other rules of international law."

It can be seen that the difference between the UNCLOS and the Convention on the Territorial Sea and the Contiguous Zone in terms of the requirements for innocent passage is that the Convention has added enumerative provisions on harmful navigation, which has resulted in acts that do not meet the requirements of Article 18 of the Convention. These acts can be dealt with by either paragraph 1 of Article 19 of the Convention or one of the 12 harmful acts specified in paragraph 2 of Article 19 of the Convention. For example, prowling, cruising, anchoring, dropping anchor and other unspecified acts in the territorial sea, as they do not satisfy the requirement that the passage should continue uninterrupted and expeditiously, may be interpreted as not being acts of passage under Article 18 of the Convention, but as "any other activity not having a direct bearing on passage" (Article 19(2)(12) of the Convention).[55] Even if "other unspecified acts" do not fall under Article 19(2), of the Convention, they may be dealt with under Article 25(1) of the Convention. Thus, Articles 18, 19, and 25 of the Convention are complementary.

Likewise, there are two different views on the relationship between paragraphs 1 and 2 of Article 19 of the Convention. The first view (known as the "enumeration view") is that paragraph 2 regulates the behavior or state of a ship according to its classification, which is merely an enumeration of paragraph 1; therefore, the criteria of "peace, good order and security of the coastal State" should be judged in conjunction with the criteria of paragraph 2 and there is no room to judge and regulate according to the classification of ships. The second view (known as the "non-enumeration view") is that Article 19(2) does not require the coastal State to wait for evidence and that it is a "presumptive" provision based on the standard of conduct or state of affairs of a ship, not an exhaustive enumeration of the provisions of paragraph 1. For example, even if the passage of a ship carrying nuclear weapons is not enumerated in Article 19(2), the coastal State can claim that it is harmful to itself, and the action can thus be regulated by paragraph 1.[56]

In other words, if the "passage" of foreign ships is not a harmful act under Article 19(2) of the Convention or is likely to be considered as such under paragraph 1, the

---

[54] [Japanese] Yamamoto, Sōji. 1990. Violation of territorial sea not belonging to innocent passage, in *Japan's New Maritime Order (No. 3)*, ed, Japan Coast Guard Foundation. Tokyo: Japan Coast Guard Foundation. p. 72.

[55] [Japanese] Yamamoto, Sōji. 2009. The maritime security law system—The intersection of the law of the sea and domestic law. Tokyo: Sanseido. pp. 133–134.

[56] [Japanese] Yamamoto, Sōji. 1997. *The law of the sea*. Tokyo: Sanseido. pp. 125–127.

coastal State may exercise jurisdiction over the passage of such ships by prescribing conditions for the use of the territorial sea. This is because Article 21 of the Convention provides that "The coastal State may adopt laws and regulations, in conformity with the provisions of this Convention and other rules of international law, relating to innocent passage through the territorial sea, in respect of all or any of the following: (a) the safety of navigation and the regulation of maritime traffic; (b) the protection of navigational aids and facilities and other facilities or installations; (c) the protection of cables and pipelines; (d) the conservation of the living resources of the sea; (e) the prevention of infringement of the fisheries laws and regulations of the coastal State; (f) the preservation of the environment of the coastal State and the prevention, reduction and control of pollution thereof; (g) marine scientific research and hydrographic surveys; (h) the prevention of infringement of the customs, fiscal, immigration or sanitary laws and regulations of the coastal State. That is, as long as it is covered by one of the above eight acts or related to them, the coastal State can regulate the passage of foreign ships based on its domestic laws. Therefore, Articles 18 and 19 of the Convention should be considered as a whole, with Articles 21 and 25 to judge the nature of the passage of ships.

In addition, there are two different academic doctrines, the "combination doctrine" and the "separation doctrine," concerning the relationship between the criteria to determine whether the passage of a foreign ship is innocent or whether it violates the coastal state's domestic laws and regulations.[57] The "combination doctrine" means that when a foreign ship passes through a coastal state's territorial sea, as long as it acts in violation of the domestic law of the coastal State, such passage can be regarded as detrimental to the peace, good order or security of the coastal State, and, therefore, harmful. In contrast, the "separation doctrine" asserts that the passage of a foreign ship, irrespective of whether or not it violates the domestic law of the coastal State, is detrimental if it jeopardizes the vital interests of the coastal State. Therefore, based on the viewpoint of the "separation doctrine," the violation of the coastal State's domestic law by a foreign ship does not directly negate innocent passage of the ship. As long as it does not jeopardize the important interests of the coastal State, it does not negate the right of innocent passage, and only the responsibility of the foreign ship for violating the domestic law of the coastal State can be pursued. As for the "combined view," since the violation of the coastal State's domestic law by a foreign ship is linked to the determination of its harmfulness, it is necessary for the coastal State to protect the legal rights and interests of its territorial sea, to add regulating acts that do not fall into the category of innocent passage to its domestic law.[58]

Thus, regarding the criteria for determining the innocence of foreign ships passing through territorial seas, the provisions of the Convention have adopted the "combination theory" and the "separation theory" based on the acts and states of various

---

[57] [Japanese] Tanaka, Toshiyuki. 1998. Domestic rule of law not being an act of innocent passage, in *Developments in the United Nations Convention on the Law of the Sea Regime and Domestic Measures (No. 2)*, ed, Japan Coast Guard Foundation. Tokyo: Japan Coast Guard Foundation. p. 45.

[58] [Japanese] Yamamoto, Sōji. 1990, Violation of territorial sea not belonging to innocent passage, in *Japan's New Maritime Order (No. 3)*, ed, Japan Coast Guard Foundation. Tokyo: Japan Coast Guard Foundation. pp. 77–78.

ships, which can be called the "hybrid theory." This "hybrid theory" is adopted in the provisions of the Convention.

Despite the provisions on the innocent passage of foreign ships mentioned above, the fact that warships of other countries enter territorial seas under the regime of innocent passage does not mean that foreign warships can enter the territorial sea of the coastal State at will. According to the Convention, the innocent passage of warships in the territorial sea of other States is subject to the following restrictions:

First, compliance with regulations established by the coastal State. Article 25 of the Convention provides that "The coastal State may take the necessary steps in its territorial sea to prevent passage which is not innocent." Accordingly, warships of other States should comply with the laws and regulations on innocent passage established by the coastal State. The details are established in Article 21(1) of the Convention. The coastal State shall, of course, give due publicity to all such laws and regulations.

Second, navigation in sea lanes is designated or regulated by the coastal State. Article 22 provides that "The coastal State may, where necessary having regard to the safety of navigation, require foreign ships exercising the right of innocent passage through its territorial sea to use such sea lanes and traffic separation schemes as it may designate or prescribe for the regulation of the passage of ships." The coastal State shall clearly indicate such sea lanes and traffic separation schemes and shall give due publicity to them.

Third, measures to deal with violations of the regulations of the coastal State. Article 30 of the Convention provides that "If any warship does not comply with the laws and regulations of the coastal State concerning passage through the territorial sea and disregards any request for compliance therewith which is made to it, the coastal State may require it to leave the territorial sea immediately." Specifically, if the ship is found to be engaged in non-innocent navigational activities, it may be required to cease such activities and, if it still does not cease them, be required to leave the territorial sea.

The above are the general provisions of the Convention on the innocent passage of warships in the territorial sea of other States.[59] As mentioned above, the controversy over the innocent passage of warships in territorial seas centers on the confrontation and disagreement as to whether it is necessary to notify or obtain the prior consent of the coastal State or whether it is possible to navigate freely. This is due to the ambiguity of Article 17 of the Convention and the enumerative provisions of Article 19, which stipulate that all ships enjoy the right of innocent passage through territorial seas, and because Article 19 does not directly provide a clear definition of "innocent," but only establishes enumerative provisions on harmful activities. This has given rise to divergent State practices.

[59] In the UNCLOS regime of innocent passage in the territorial sea, there are not only rules applicable to all ships but also to merchant and government ships used for commercial purposes, as well as rules for warships and other government ships used for noncommercial purposes. In other words, UNCLOS adopts a categorized and differentiated approach to ships in their regime of innocent passage in the territorial sea. See Articles 17–32 of the United Nations Convention on the Law of the Sea.

Generally speaking, the "freedom of use doctrine" is emphasized by the large or strong maritime countries, while the "prior consent doctrine" is more often upheld by developing countries. This is a conclusion drawn from the declarations made by States when signing and ratifying the Convention, as well as from the information on national territorial sea laws provided by the UN Division for Ocean Affairs and the Law of the Sea.[60] The major maritime countries, led by the U.S., emphasize the "free use doctrine" to maintain the advantageous position of their naval forces, such that they can freely provide guarantees for the delivery of military weapons and equipment, support for military activities in emergency situations, and intelligence-gathering activities. Most developing countries adhere to the "prior consent doctrine" to protect their national defense and security and, accordingly, expand their military buffer zones and reduce threats. To eliminate this dichotomy and meet the requirements of Article 309 of the Convention, a State is not precluded from a State, when signing, ratifying or acceding to this Convention, from making declarations or statements.[61]

The interpretative declarations or statements already made by States range from those objecting to the right of innocent passage of warships in the territorial sea, as in the case of the Sudan, Cape Verde, Sao Tome and Principe, and Romania, to those requiring prior notification of the passage of warships through its territorial sea, as for Egypt, Malta, Croatia, Finland, Sweden, Serbia and Montenegro, and Bangladesh, and to those requiring prior authorization of the passage of warships, as in the case of Iran, Oman, Yemen, China, and Algeria. At the same time, there are also declarations by States in favor of the right of innocent passage of warships in their territorial seas, such as those of Argentina, the Netherlands, and Chile; declarations by Germany and Italy, which state that the Convention does not authorize the coastal State to require prior passage or authorization; and joint interpretations by the U. S. and the USSR, as well as declarations by the UK, which state that, according to the Convention and general international law, warships enjoy the right of innocent passage in territorial seas without prior notification or authorization.[62]

Some scholars consider that customary international law on the innocent passage of foreign warships through territorial seas is that the coastal State may allow innocent passage of foreign warships without any special requirements, or it may provide for prior notification or authorization, or fulfill other requirements, provided that the

---

[60] [Japanese] Tanaka, Norio. 2013. A Study of the UN Convention on the Law of the Sea: At the standpoint of 30th Anniversary of the Adoption of UNCLOS, *Journal of International Law and Diplomacy* 112(2): 18–20.

[61] Article 309 of the UNCLOS provides that no reservations or exceptions may be made to the Convention unless expressly permitted by other articles of this Convention. Article 310 of the UNCLOS provides that "Article 309 does not preclude a State, when signing, ratifying or acceding to this Convention, from making declarations or statements, however phrased or named, with a view, inter alia, to the harmonization of its laws and regulations with the provisions of this Convention, provided that such declarations or statements do not purport to exclude or to modify the legal effect of the provisions of this Convention in their application to that State."

[62] See Jianwen, Zhao. 2005. On the interpretative declarations by the state parties to United Nations Convention on the Law of the Sea concerning the issue of innocent passage of warships through the territorial sea, *China Oceans Law Review* 2(2): 5–13.

foreign warships carrying out such innocent passage comply with the domestic laws and regulations of the coastal State.[63] The legal basis for this view is Article 30 of the Convention. In other words, the international community holds two different views, the "free use doctrine" and the "prior consent doctrine," and there are different State practices. Even if the international community is unable to reach a consensus on this issue, there is no disagreement that the regime of innocent passage of foreign warships in the territorial sea should, at the very least, comply with the laws and regulations of the coastal State on innocent passage in the territorial sea. It has become a rule of international customary law so that even the U.S., which has not ratified or acceded to the Convention, should, at a minimum, comply with the domestic laws and regulations of the coastal State on innocent passage in the territorial sea.[64]

In response to the issue of innocent passage of warships in the territorial sea, Article 6(2) of the Law of the PRC on the Territorial Sea and the Contiguous Zone (February 25, 1992) stipulates that "To enter the territorial sea of the People's Republic of China, foreign military ships must obtain permission from the Government of the People's Republic of China;" and Article 10 stipulates that, "The relevant responsible organs of the People's Republic of China shall have the right to order an immediate eviction of foreign military ships or ships owned by foreign Governments and operated for non-commercial purposes that violate the laws or regulations of the People's Republic of China while passing through the territorial sea of the People's Republic of China. Losses or damage caused shall be borne by the nations whose flag is being flown by the ship in question." When China adopted its decision to ratify the Convention on May 15, 1996, it also made the following declaration, namely, that Further, the PRC reaffirms that the provisions of the Convention on innocent passage through the territorial sea are without prejudice to the right of a coastal State to require a foreign warship to obtain prior authorization or give notification in accordance with its laws and regulations before passing through its territorial sea.[65] These elements embody the principles and spirit of the Convention and constitute

---

[63] See Jin, Shao. 1990. General rules of international law concerning the innocent passage of foreign warships through the territorial sea, *Chinese Yearbook of International Law* (1989), p. 138.

[64] On the policy and practice of states regarding the innocent passage of warships in the territorial sea, see Jianwen, Zhao. 2005. "On the interpretative declarations by the state parties to United Nations Convention on the Law of the Sea concerning the issue of innocent passage of warships through the territorial sea, *China Oceans Law Review* 2(2): 1–17.

[65] The Constitution of the PRC does not contain clear provisions on the status of treaties in China's domestic law, nor do the Legislation Law of the PRC or the Law of the PRC on the Procedure of the Conclusion of Treaties. However, the application of treaties is provided for in a number of laws and regulations, which fall into three categories. First, the law explicitly provides that where an international treaty concluded or participated in by China has different provisions from those of the law, the provisions of the international treaty shall apply. For example, Article 142 of the General Principles of the Civil Law of the PRC (1982). Second, where the law provides that a treaty contains special or specific provisions, the provisions of the treaty shall apply. For example, Article 23 of the Measures on the Use of the Sign of Red Cross (1996). Third, the law directly stipulates the application of treaty provisions in certain fields. For example, Article 23 of the Rules for the Implementation of the Trademark Law of the PRC (1993 Revision) (1995 Revision). See Jielong, Duan, ed. *International Law in China: Cases and Practice*. Beijing: Law Press. pp. 215–216. Although there are disputes over the rank and effect of international and domestic law, Chinese

a manifestation of the State's will to protect its sovereignty over the territorial sea, which should be respected and observed by other States.

4.4.4 Illegality of the Unauthorized Entry of U.S. Warships into China's Territorial Waters of Xisha Qundao and China's Response Strategy

The unauthorized entry into territorial waters near China's Xisha Qundao by U.S. warships without China's permission or prior notification violates the principle of the peaceful settlement of disputes and of refraining from the use of force or the threat of force in accordance with Article 2 of the UN Charter. It also contravenes the principle of the obligation to settle disputes by peaceful means in accordance with Article 279 of the Convention, the rules of customary international law on the right of innocent passage through territorial seas, a number of Chinese laws (for example, the Declaration of the Government of the PRC on the Territorial Sea, September 4, 1958; the Law of the PRC on the Territorial Sea and the Contiguous Zone, February 25, 1992; and the Decision of the Standing Committee of the NPC on the Ratification of the UNCLOS, May 15, 1996), and the MND and the U.S. DOD signed the Memorandum of Understanding on the Notification of Major Military Activities and the Memorandum of Understanding Regarding the Rules of Behavior for Safety of Air and Maritime Encounters and its subsequent annexes. Such an act seriously undermines the stability and development of China–United States relations and is also detrimental to implementing the measures for settling the SCS issue.

The author is of the view that, as the harmless passage regime in the territorial waters of the Convention has become a rule of customary international law, even if the U.S. does not accede to the Convention, the unauthorized entry of its warships into the territorial waters of China's Xisha Qundao constitutes a violation of the rules of customary international law, which is mainly manifested in the following two aspects: first, the harmfulness of the navigational behavior of U.S. warships. The USS Wilbur has powerful electronic reconnaissance and jamming capabilities, strong regional defense and self-defense capabilities, and can be equipped with dozens of land-to-land cruise missiles and antisubmarine capabilities, in violation of Article 19(2)(a) and (c) of the Convention.[66] Second, the navigational acts of the U.S. warships are not "passage" acts, but harmful ones. Meaning of "passage" refers to navigation through the territorial sea: first, traversing that sea without entering internal waters or calling at a roadstead or port facility outside internal waters; or; and second, proceeding to or from internal waters or a call at such roadstead or port facility. In other words,

---

legislation and practice show that treaties are superior to domestic laws. See Zhonghai, Zhou. 2004. *International law*. Beijing: China University of Political Science and Law Press. pp. 64–66.

[66] See U.S. warships trespass in Xisha territorial waters, experts say China should boost military strength, http://military.people.com.cn/n1/2016/0201/c1011-28102014.html, accessed February 2, 2016.

the unauthorized entry of the U.S. warship into the territorial waters of Xisha is not an act of passage, nor is it an act of innocent passage, but rather a non-innocent passage since it is not directly related to the passage. It can be seen that such an act is essentially an act of political and legal provocation and should be severely condemned.

If this unilateral dispatch of warships by the U.S. to enter China's territorial waters of Xisha Qundao without authorization continues and expands in scope, China can take the following countermeasures at the international, bilateral, and domestic levels.

First, at the international level. As the unauthorized intrusion into the territorial waters of other states by warships carrying weapons and equipment is a harmful act that seriously undermines China's sovereignty and security and is highly susceptible to security mishaps, China may submit a written opinion to the UN Security Council recommending that it consider it an act that violates the domestic law of the coastal state and jeopardizes regional peace and security. Article 39 of the UN Charter stipulates that "The Security Council shall determine the existence of any threat to the peace, breach of the peace, or act of aggression and shall make recommendations, or decide what measures shall be taken in accordance with Articles 41 and 42, to maintain or restore international peace and security." Although the U.S. has a veto in the UNSC, which makes it difficult to pass such resolutions, the UNSC's resolutions will also be politically binding on the U.S. and, to a certain extent, limit its behavior.[67]

Second, at the bilateral level. There has been a long-standing dispute between China and the U.S. over military activities in the EEZ, centering on the dichotomy between whether military activities in the EEZ require prior consent or notification from the coastal state or can be used freely. As the Convention does not clearly regulate "military activities," even when analyzed from the point of view of peaceful uses of the sea and marine scientific research, there are different understandings and perceptions, leading to distinct and even opposing approaches in practice.[68] Considering that it is impossible to reach understanding and awareness within the framework of the Convention, disputes over military activities in the EEZ should be resolved through bilateral dialogue and consultation mechanisms to enhance mutual trust and consensus, and in particular, the Memorandum of Understanding on the Notification of Major Military Activities and the Memorandum of Understanding Regarding the Rules of Behavior for Safety of Air and Maritime Encounters and its subsequent annexes reached by the Ministries of Defense of the two countries should

[67] For example, Article 27(3) of the UN Charter provides that "Decisions of the Security Council on all other matters shall be made by an affirmative vote of nine members including the concurring votes of the permanent members; provided that, in decisions under Chapter VI, and under paragraph 3 of Article 52, a party to a dispute shall abstain from voting."

[68] For the issue of disputes over military activities in the exclusive economic zones of China and the United States, see Yongming, Jin. 2011. A dissection of disputes between china and the United States over military activities in exclusive economic zone by the law of the sea, *Pacific Journal* 11(1): 74–81.

be complied with.[69] Based on these assumptions, to avoid greater confrontation and disputes over the innocent passage of warships in the territorial sea, China and the U.S. should play a leading role through dialogues and consultations to reach a consensus so as to further enrich and improve the regime of innocent passage in the territorial sea ensure security and order in the SCS.

Third, at the domestic level. As it is difficult to reach a consensus quickly at the international and bilateral levels, China can continue to adhere to its diplomatic position and lodge a strong protest against the trespassing of United States warships in the territorial waters of the Xisha Qundao, make adequate preparations to respond militarily and strengthen its equipment, and more importantly, legally strengthen the regime of China's territorial waters as soon as possible. Because the Convention gives coastal states the right to enact laws and regulations on the innocent passage of foreign ships through its territorial seas, China should accordingly formulate a relevant domestic legal system that is in line with the Convention and improve its laws and regulations consistent with the goal of becoming a strong maritime country.[70] For example, the Fisheries Law (enforced in 1986 and last revised in 2013), which regulates the conservation of marine living resources; the Maritime Traffic Safety Law (enforced in 1983 and revised in 2021), which governs the safety of navigation and the management of maritime traffic; and the Marine Environmental Protection Law (adopted on August 23, 1982, revised on December 25, 1999, December 28, 2013, and November 7, 2016) regulates the preservation of the marine environment; the Provisions of the PRC on Administration of Foreign-related Marine Scientific Research (enforced in 1996); the Customs Law (enforced in 1987, last amended in 2013); the Regulations Governing Supervision and Control of Foreign Vessels by the PRC (enforced in 1979); and the Law on the Territorial Sea and the Contiguous Zone (enforced in 1992) regulates marine scientific research. It should further improve the system of laws and regulations on the passage of foreign ships through the territorial sea, including the formulation of regulations on the innocent passage of foreign warships in the territorial sea, the Organization Law of the CCG,[71] and the rules on overflight and navigation in the EEZ, and clarify its stance against the abuse of the right to freedom of navigation by foreign warships in China's coastal waters to increase its efficiency and functionality. At the same time, China's jurisdiction in the territorial sea and maritime interests should be strengthened, including through

---

[69] For the Notification of Major Military Activities between the U.S. and Chinese militaries, see https://dod.defense.gov/Portals/1/Documents/pubs/141112_MemorandumOfUnderstandingOnNotification.pdf, accessed February 10, 2015. For the Rules of Behavior for Safety of Air and Maritime Encounters between the U.S. and Chinese Militaries, see https://dod.defense.gov/Portals/1/Documents/pubs/141112_MemorandumOfUnderstandingRegardingRules.pdf, accessed February 10, 2015.

[70] The Law of the PRC on Safety of Maritime Traffic has been amended and adopted by the Standing Committee of the 13th NPC of the PRC at its Twenty-eighth Meeting on April 29, 2021, and shall come into force on September 1, 2021. See *Safety of maritime traffic law of the People's Republic of China*. 2021. Beijing: China Legal Publishing House. pp. 2–40.

[71] The Maritime Police Law of the PRC was adopted by the Twenty-fifth Meeting of the Standing Committee of the 13th NPC of the PRC on January 22, 2021, and shall come into force on February 1, 2021. See *Law of the People's Republic of China on Coast Guard*. Beijing: Law Press. pp. 3–22.

confirmation of nationality and innocent passage. Ensure compliance with domestic laws and regulations in the case of innocent passage, and remove non-innocent navigational practices in the territorial sea that violate domestic laws and regulations in administrative procedures for investigation and disciplinary action, and in criminal procedures for searches and arrests,[72] which provides legal safeguards for the effective protection of China's territorial sovereignty over the oceans.

Additionally, given that the threatening activities of the U.S. in the SCS involve the Nansha Qundao and Xisha Qundao and may involve the waters of Zhongsha Qundao, China may consider announcing the baselines of the territorial waters of some of China's islands and reefs in Nansha Qundao and the air defense identification zones based on the development of the security situation, including the scope, frequency, and extent of the implementation of the so-called freedom of navigation in the SCS by countries led by the U.S. This will reflect China's will and determination to safeguard its sovereignty, maritime rights, security and interests in the SCS. In other words, through the further formulation and improvement of domestic laws, such as the law on the territorial sea, the innocent passage of foreign ships, especially warships, China's territorial sea will be subject to China's domestic laws and regulations, reflecting that the Declaration of the Government of the People's Republic of China on the Baselines of the Territorial Sea of the PRC, the Law of the People's Republic of China on the Territorial Sea and the Contiguous Zone, the Declaration of the Government of the People's Republic of China on the Baselines of the Territorial Sea of the PRC, and the Statement of the Government of the People's Republic of China on the Baselines of the Territorial Sea of Diaoyu Dao and Its Affiliated Islands are effective and complete, and the position of "the prior consent doctrine" has been upheld. This forms a legal foundation for safeguarding China's sovereignty over its territorial sea, security, and maritime interests.

[72] For enforcement jurisdiction of the coastal state over the innocent passage of foreign ships, especially warships, in the territorial sea, see [Japanese] Tanaka, Toshiyuki. 1998. Domestic rule of law not being an act of innocent passage, in *Developments in the United Nations Convention on the Law of the Sea Regime and Domestic Measures (No. 2)*, ed, Japan Coast Guard Foundation. Tokyo: Japan Coast Guard Foundation. pp. 47–48.

Chapter 5
Challenges of New China on Ocean Strategic Issues

In the process of becoming a maritime country, China faces the major challenge of the SCS issue to achieve its goal. The challenges mainly involve the nature of the dotted line in the SCS, the attributes and status of the maritime features, the impact of the *SCS* Arbitration on the law of the sea, and the freedom of navigation in the waters surrounding the maritime features in the Nansha Qundao.

5.1 Nature of the Dotted Line in the SCS and the Legal Status of the Waters Within the Line

Recently, the question of the SCS has become an issue of concern to international and domestic communities, and the issue has tended to develop and deteriorate. There are many reasons for the emergence and escalation of the SCS issue, including the entry into force of the UNCLOS, the illegitimate intensification of the seizure of the Nanhai Zhudao by some ASEAN countries and their intensified efforts to exploit those resources and the involvement of and favoritism toward extraterritorial powers. In particular, the behavior of the Chinese Government in response to the map of the dotted line in the SCS in the note submitted to the UN Secretary-General on May 7, 2009—after the joint submission of the outer continental shelf by Malaysia and Vietnam (May 6, 2009) and Vietnam's submission of the outer continental shelf (May 7, 2009)—caused a number of countries to question the meaning or nature of the dotted line of the SCS in China and demand that China clarify its true intentions in the SCS.[1]

[1] The Permanent Mission of China to the UN presented its compliments to the Secretary-General of the UN and, with reference to the Joint Submission by Malaysia and Vietnam and the Submission by the Vietnam dated 6 May 2009, to the CLCS concerning the outer limits of the continental shelf beyond 200 nautical miles. China points out: "China has indisputable sovereignty over the islands in the South China Sea and the adjacent waters, and enjoys sovereign rights and jurisdiction over the

Y. Jin, *Ocean Law and Policy of the People's Republic of China*,
https://doi.org/10.1007/978-981-95-3166-0_5

At the same time, the filing of the *SCS* Arbitration and the so-called final award, as well as the U.S. Department of State's "Limits in the Seas: China's Maritime Claims in the South China Sea" released on December 5, 2014, have created a "necessity" for further clarification of the nature of the dotted line in the SCS. Since the Chinese Government has not yet publicly clarified the meaning of the dotted line in the SCS, this study will focus on this matter, including its nature, legal status, and the attributes of the waters within the line, considering history and jurisprudence, to make a modest academic contribution to the resolution of disputes over the SCS.

5.1.1 Theoretical Analysis Concerning the Concept of the Dotted Line in the SCS

Generally speaking, the SCS issue consists mainly of two disputes, namely, the maritime features of the Nansha Qundao and the delimitation of maritime areas. The former is the main dispute in the SCS, while the latter is a secondary dispute; nevertheless, they are closely linked and inseparable. In international law, the principle that the "land dominates the sea" takes precedence; therefore, only after determining to which State the land territory belongs can the specific sea area be determined and the corresponding maritime delimitation dispute be solved. In these disputes, the central issue is the nature of the dotted line in the SCS and the legal status of the waters within the line.

5.1.1.1 Theories of Domestic Scholars on the Meaning of the Dotted Line in the SCS

In view of the importance of the dotted line drawn by China in the SCS and marked on the map, Chinese scholars have long studied the meaning of the dotted line and published many insightful research results.[2] Scholars from Chinese Taiwan have also

---

relevant waters as well as the seabed and subsoil thereof (see attached map). The above position is consistently held by the Chinese Government, and is widely known by the international community." See China's note verbales to the Secretary-General of the United Nations on the continental shelf submissions and preliminary information of relevant countries. 2011. In *China Ocean Development Report (2011)*, ed. Research Group of the Institute for Marine Development Strategy of the State Ocean Administration. Beijing: Ocean Press. pp. 593–598.

[2] In recent years, the results (journal articles) of mainland Chinese scholars on the meaning of the dotted line in the South China Sea mainly include Jinming, Li. 2001. Problems and prospects for the Studies on Chinas Border in the South China Sea, *Southeast Asian Affairs* 3. Jinming, Li. 2011. Research on the 9 dotted line in the South China Sea and the related issues, *China's Borderland History and Geography Studies* 2. Yu, Jia. 2005. On the legal status of the dotted line in the South China Sea, *China Border History and Geography* 2. Yongzhi, Wang., Jun, Song., Xueshuang, Han., Guifang, Xue. 2008. Comprehensive discussion on the dotted line in the South China Sea, *Journal of Ocean University of China (Social Sciences)* 3. Jinming, Li. 2010. The legal status of the dotted line in the South China Sea: historic waters, maritime boundary or a line of Islands

published many relevant studies that can be used for reference.[3] These publications provide a good foundation for this paper. From the above observations and in combination with other studies, the doctrines or views on the meaning of the dotted line in the SCS include the following aspects:

(1) The theory of historic waters. According to this theory, China has historic rights to the islands, reefs, sands, beaches, and sea areas within the line, which comprise China's historic waters. The representative scholars are from China, such as Prof. Song Yann-Huei, Prof. Yu Jian-Hong, and Prof. Zhao Guozhai.[4] There are two favorable reasons for this argument: first, the 1948 map marking the dotted line in the SCS was published without any protests or objections; and second, the waters within the dotted line are historic waters and do not violate the provisions of Article 47(1) of the UNCLOS. At the same time, these arguments have also received support from the Policy Guidelines for the South China Sea published by Chinese Taiwan's executive branch on April 13, 1993. This policy declared that, in terms of history, geography, international law and facts, the Nansha Qundao, Xisha Qundao, Zhongsha Qundao and Dongsha Qundao, are part of inherent territory of China, the sovereignty over those islands belongs to China; The South China Sea area within the historic water limit is the maritime area under the jurisdiction of China, where China possesses all rights and interests."[5]

---

ownership?, *Southeast Asian Affairs* 4. Jinming, Li. 2011. The dotted line in the South China Sea: Its Background and Effectiveness, *Southeast Asian Studies* 1. Jinming, Li. 2011. Review of domestic and international studies on the legal status of the dotted line in the South China Sea, *Southeast Asian Affairs* 2. Yuan, Guo. 2011. The formation of the dotted line in the South China Sea and the analysis of its historical significance, *Journal of Zhejiang Ocean University (Humanities Sciences)* 3. Wei, Huang. 2011. On China's historic titles over the other waters within the U-shaped line of South China Sea, *Journal of Ocean University of China (Social Sciences)* 3. Jianqiang, Guan. 2012. Research on the legal status of nine dash line in the South China Sea, *International Review* 4. Keyuan, Zou. Some legal reflections on the U-shaped lines in the South China Sea. Nanlai, Liu. The legal status of the U-shaped lines from the perspective of the international law of the sea; and Haiwen, Zhang. The evolution of the traditional maritime boundary lines in the South China Sea, in *Proceedings of the South China Sea Issue Seminar*, Zhong Tianxiang, Han Jia, Ren Huaifeng, eds. 2002. Haikou: Hainan Institute for South China Sea Studies.

[3] The study of Chinese Taiwan scholars on the dotted line in the South China Sea mainly include Kuen Chen, Fu. 1995. *A study of the legal status of the South China Sea*. Taipei: Taipei 123 Information Publishing. Kuan-Hsiung, Wang. 2001. *Disputes over the islands in the South China Sea and fisheries co-operation*. Taipei: Showwe Information Publishing. Cikuan, Yu. The legal nature and status of the U-shaped Line in the South China Sea and the waters within the line, in *Proceedings of the South China Sea Issue Seminar*, Tianxiang, Zhong., Jia, Han., and Huaifeng, Ren., eds. 2002. Haikou: Hainan Institute for South China Sea Studies. Guocai, Zhao. 1999. Analyzing the sovereignty dispute over the Nansha Qundao from the contemporary law of the sea, *Asian Review* Spring/ Summer.

[4] See Jinming, Li. 2011. Review of domestic and international studies on the legal status of the dotted line in the South China Sea, *Southeast Asian Affairs* 2: 54–55. Nanlai, Liu. The legal status of the U-shaped lines from the perspective of the international law of the sea, in *Proceedings of the South China Sea Issue Seminar*, Zhong Tianxiang, Han Jia, Ren Huaifeng, eds. 2002. Haikou: Hainan Institute for South China Sea Studies. p. 51.

[5] See Litong, Chen. 2008. *A treatise on the international law of the sea*, Taipei: Angle Publishing. p. 18.

(2) The theory of Historic rights. According to this theory, China enjoys historic rights within the dotted line, including sovereignty over the islands, reefs, sands, and beaches, and sovereign rights over natural resources in the sea and seabed beyond the internal waters within the line, while recognizing the rights of other countries to freedom of navigation, overflight, and laying of submarine cables and pipelines, etc., in the sea area within the dotted line. Representative scholars are Prof. Pan Shiying and Prof. Xu Senan.[6]
(3) The theory of the Maritime Boundary Line. According to this view, the dotted line marks the scope of China's territorial sovereignty over the Nanhai Zhudao, confirming the maritime boundary of the Nanhai Zhudao that has been included in China's map since at least the fifteenth century. The islands and the adjacent waters within this line are subject to China's jurisdiction and control. In other words, the dotted line can be regarded as the maritime boundary line, and China enjoys historic rights over the natural resources, whether living or non-living, of the waters superjacent to the seabed and of the seabed and its subsoil within the dotted line. Representative scholars are Prof. Zhao Lihai, Prof. Chen Degong, and Prof. Fu Kuenchen.[7]
(4) The theory of the islands ownership line. According to this theory, the Nanhai Zhudao and their adjacent waters within the dotted line belong to China and are subject to China's jurisdiction and control, while the legal status of the waters within the dotted line depends on the legal status of the maritime features or archipelagos within the line. Representative figures are Prof. Gao Zhiguo, Prof. Li Jinming, Prof. Liu Nanlai, and Prof. Yu cikuan.[8]

The above-mentioned theories on the concept of the dotted line in the SCS basically reflect the academic views of Chinese scholars and are representative to a certain extent. These perspectives all agree that China has sovereignty over all the islands, reefs, sands and shoals within the dotted line in the SCS, as well as over the waters

[6] See Shiying, Pan. 1996. *Nansha Qundao—Petroleum Politics—International Law*. Hong Kong Economic Herald Publishing House. pp. 60–63; Senan, Xu. 2000. The connotation of the dotted national boundary line in the South China Sea, in *Selected Papers of the 21st Century South China Sea Issue and Prospects Seminar*, ed, Hainan Institute for South China Sea Studies. Haikou: Hainan Institute for South China Sea Studies. pp. 80–82.

[7] See Lihai, Zhao. 1995. *Research on the law of the sea*. Beijing: Peking University Press. p. 37. Jinming, Li. 2011. Review of domestic and international studies on the legal status of the dotted line in the South China Sea, *Southeast Asian Affairs* 2: 59. Kuen Chen, Fu. 1995. *A study of the legal status of the South (China) Sea*. Taipei: Taipei 123 Information Publishing. pp. 204–205.

[8] See Zhiguo, Gao. 1994. The South China Sea: From conflict to cooperation, *Ocean Development & International Law* 25: 136. Jinming, Li. 2011. Review of domestic and international studies on the legal status of the dotted line in the South China Sea, *Southeast Asian Affairs* 2(2): p. 61. Nanlai, Liu. The legal status of the U-shaped lines from the perspective of the international law of the sea, in *Proceedings of the South China Sea Issue Seminar*, Zhong Tianxiang, Han Jia, Ren Huaifeng, eds. 2002. Haikou: Hainan Institute for South China Sea Studies. p. 56. Cikuan, Yu. 2001. The legal status of the U-shaped lines from the perspective of the international law of the sea, in *Proceedings of the South China Sea Issue Seminar*, Zhong Tianxiang, Han Jia, Ren Huaifeng, Ren., eds. Haikou: Hainan Institute for South China Sea Studies. pp. 427–439.

adjacent to the Nanhai Zhudao. The distinction lies in the difference in the legal status of the waters within the dotted line in the SCS.

5.1.1.2 The Views of Foreign Scholars on the Meaning of the Dotted Line in the SCS

With regard to the SCS issue, foreign scholars are mostly concerned about the legal status of the dotted line. For example, Barry Wain argues that if China only claims sovereignty over the maritime features within the dotted line, the nine-dash line should be eliminated. Hasyim Djalal points out that the dotted line has neither definition nor coordinates, so their legitimacy and exact location are unclear; thus, China cannot claim sovereignty over all the waters within the dotted line. According to Singaporean scholar Tommy Koh, China's sovereignty claim is not clear, and if the dotted line in the SCS is the islands ownership line, they are consistent with UNCLOS; otherwise, they are inconsistent with the Convention. Regarding the question of whether the maritime features in the Nansha Qundao are entitled to maritime zones, Marius Gjetnes argues that, according to Article 121 of the UNCLOS, there are no islands but only rocks in the dotted line in the SCS, they are entitled to a maximum of 12 nautical miles of territorial waters. Robert Beckman (2011) attempts to delimit the SCS on the basis of the UNCLOS, completely ignoring the role of the dotted line in the SCS in the delimitation of the sea area and its implications for China's sovereignty. Other scholars believe that there are high seas and the Areas within the dotted line in the SCS, and so on.[9]

The aforementioned views reflect attempts to deny China's historic rights in the Nanhai Zhudao, to obliterate the validity and status of the dotted line in the SCS, and to resort to a one-sided interpretation of the regime and role of the UNCLOS, with the ultimate goal of curtailing China's territorial sovereignty over the Nanhai Zhudao, especially the Nansha Qundao, and China's maritime rights and interests in the SCS. It should be emphasized that these views seriously violate the important principle of intertemporal law in international law, which refers to the concept that for ancient international events, their effectiveness should be judged by the laws of the "time," rather than applying the international law of the "presence" (i.e. when international disputes arise or are judged).[10]

---

[9] See Wain, Barry. 2000. Beijing should erase the U-shaped Line, *The Asian Wallstreet Journal*: 10. Hasyim Djalal. 1995. Spratly dispute needs democratic settlement, *The Jakarta Post*: p. 5. Keyuan, Zou. 1999. The Chinese traditional maritime boundary line in the South China Sea and its legal consequences for the resolution of the dispute over the Spratly Islands, *International Journal of Marine and Coastal Law* 14. Gjetnes, Marius. 2000. *The legal regime of islands in the South China Sea.* Chemillier-Gendreau, Monique. 2000. *Sovereignty over the Paracel and Spratly Islands.* Hague/Boston: Kluwer Law International. Keyuan, Zou. 2007. South China Sea Studies in China: Achievements and Challenges, *Singapore Year Book of International Law* 11. Hong, Seoung-yong. 2009. *Maritime boundary disputes, settlement processes, and the law of the sea.* Leiden/Boston: Martinus Nijhoff Publishers.

[10] The concept of intertemporal law was originally used in domestic law to solve the problem of the scope of use of new and old laws in time. Nowadays, it is often mentioned in resolving

In addition, after the Chinese Government submitted a note verbale of objection to the UN Secretary-General in response to the joint submission made by Vietnam and Malaysia, Indonesia sent a note verbale to the UN Secretary-General on July 8, 2010, which raised objections to China's note verbale (attached by a map of the dotted line in the SCS), pointing out that the dotted line in the SCS was "clearly lacks international legal basis" and "encroaches the legitimate interest of the global community." Specifically, Indonesia is of the view that the dotted line in the SCS violates international law and that no maritime features in the Nansha Qundao can claim a 200-nautical-mile EEZ.[11] For this reason, it is necessary to examine the history of China's sovereignty over the Nanhai Zhudao and the process of the formation of the dotted line.

5.1.2 *Formation Process of the Dotted Line in the SCS*

Before discussing the formation of the dotted line in the SCS, it is necessary to examine China's sovereignty over the Nanhai Zhudao. China's sovereignty over the Nanhai Zhudao was gradually formed by the Chinese people in the course of long-term historical development, China is the first to have discovered, named, explored, and exploited Nanhai Zhudao and relevant waters, and the successive Chinese governments have exercised jurisdiction over Nanhai Zhudao in a continuous, peaceful and effective manner. This process of development has a sufficient and solid historical basis, has long been recognized by the international community,[12] and is fully consistent with international law.

---

territorial disputes between countries. In the *Palmas Island Arbitration* in 1928, Arbitrator Max Huber explicitly applied intertemporal law to the case for the first time. Intertemporal law has been repeatedly invoked by international judicial authorities in territorial dispute cases. In the process of applying intertemporal law, Huber distinguished the creation of rights and the existence of rights when resolving the relationship between rights and legal changes, thus deducing the two elements that intertemporal law principles should include. First, the creation of rights must be determined in accordance with the law at the same time; second, the existence of rights must be determined in accordance with the law at the critical moment when the right exists. The essence of the first element is "the law does not apply retroactively", which is generally accepted by international law scholars. According to the second element, rights obtained based on the first element may be lost if they are not correspondingly maintained according to the evolution of the law, even though new laws cannot retroactively render them invalid from the beginning. See Keju, Wang. 2012. Intertemporal law and the acquisition of territory-the theory and practice in dealing with territorial disputes, *Pacific Journal* 5: 20–26.

[11] See Guoxiang, Sun. 2011. New development of the South China Sea situation and the prospects and challenges of cross-strait cooperation, in *Proceedings of the South China Sea Issue Seminar*, Zhong Tianxiang, Han Jia, Ren Huaifeng, eds. 2002. Haikou: Hainan Institute for South China Sea Studies. p. 5.

[12] See Guoqiang, Li. 2011. The formation of China's sovereignty over the South China Sea Islands and the origin of the South China Sea issue, *Qiu Shi* 15.

5.1.2.1 China Has Indisputable Sovereignty Over the Nanhai Zhudao

Historically, the Nanhai Zhudao have been part of China since ancient times. *Yi Wu Zhi* (An Account of Strange Things) published in the Eastern Han Dynasty states that "twisted atolls are on the rising sea, the water is shallow and there are many shoals and reefs that have not yet surfaced. The people's big boats must be reinforced multiple times with iron anchors before they can be anchored." (*Zhanghaiqitou, Shuiqianer-duocishi, Jiaowaidazhou, Guyitieye, Zhiyiduoba*). *Nan Zhou Yi Wu Zhi* (An Account of Strange Things in Nan Zhou) during the period of the Three Kingdoms recorded the voyage from the Malay Peninsula to China, which stated "In the northeast trip, there are large twisted atolls on the rising sea, the water is medium-shallow and therer are many shoals and reefs. "*Qitou*" is the ancient Chinese term for reefs and shoals. "*Zhanghai*" is the earliest name for the SCS in ancient China. "*Zhanghaiqitou*" refers to the islands and reefs in the Nanhai Zhudao. It can be seen that at least in the Eastern Han Dynasty, China discovered and named the SCS.

During the Song Dynasty, the Nanhai Zhudao began to be referred to by specialized names such as "*Changsha*" (long sand cays) and "*Shitang*" (rocks). "*Changsha*" is also known as "*Qianlishitang*" (thousand-li rocks) and "*Wanlishitang*" (ten thousand-li rocks). "*Changsha*" is also known as "*Qianlichangsha*" (thousand-li sand cays), "*Wanlichangsha*" (ten thousand-li sand cays) and "*Wanlichangdi*" (ten thousand-li sand cays). Among them, "*Shitang*" mostly refers to the Nansha Qundao, while "*Changsha*" mostly refers to the Xisha Qundao. At the same time, the Song Dynasty included the Nanhai Zhudao in the scope of "Qiong Management," that is, "*Qianlichangsha*" and "*Wanlishitang*" belonged to the jurisdiction of Qiongzhou of the Guangnan Xilu at that time; thus, it can be seen that the Nanhai Zhudao had already begun to be incorporated into the map of China.[13]

During the Ming and Qing dynasties, the Chinese Government continued to include the Nanhai Zhudao in the map of China and placed them under the jurisdiction of Wanzhou, Qiongzhou Prefecture of Guangdong Province, exercising effective jurisdiction. In addition, from the Song Dynasty onward, the Nanhai Zhudao and their adjacent waters became an important area for naval patrols. For example, after Emperor Taizu of the Song Dynasty pacified Liu Chang of the Southern Han Dynasty in 971 AD, a patrol navy was established, and the patrol area included the Xisha Qundao. Thereafter, the Ming and Qing dynasties regarded the Nanhai Zhudao and their adjacent waters as their jurisdictional areas, and it became a customary practice for Chinese patrol navies to patrol and defend the sea and exercise jurisdiction. One of the tasks of Zheng He's seven expeditions in the early years of the Ming Dynasty was to patrol the Nanhai Zhudao, which is the declaration of sovereignty in the sense of international law.[14]

---

[13] See Guoqiang, Li. 2011. The formation of China's Sovereignty over the South China Sea Islands and the origin of the South China Sea issue, *Qiu Shi* 15.

[14] See Hailin, Zheng. China's territorial rights over the islands in the South China Sea cannot be provoked, http://www.pacificjournal.com.cn/CN/news/news152.shtml, accessed June 26, 2011.

In addition, Chinese fishermen have been operating in the Xisha Qundao and Nasha Qundao since the Ming and Qing dynasties, and in the "*Geng Lu Bu*" (Manual of Sea Routes) and "Nautical Charts" preserved by the fishermen of Hainan, the common place names of the Xisha Qundao and Nasha Qundao have been recorded in 34 and 75 places, with detailed records of the sea routes and directions for each place. These records show that China's fishermen are very familiar with the Nansha Qundao and establish the historical fact that they have continued to operate and develop the Nansha Qundao.[15]

From the late Qing Dynasty onward, the Chinese Government has inherited the traditional view of the maritime boundaries of the SCS, on the one hand, resisting foreign intrusion and safeguarding its sovereign rights and interests, including the recovery of the Nanhai Zhudao invaded by Japan after the Second World War and the dispatch of warships and officials to bring the SCS under the jurisdiction of Guangdong Province. At the time, the neighboring countries did not raise any objection to this exercise of sovereignty. On the other hand, it is even more noteworthy that successive Chinese governments named, approved, and announced the Nanhai Zhudao three times in 1935, 1947, and 1983, making China's sovereignty over the Nanhai Zhudao more solid.

On September 4, 1958, after the founding of New China, the Chinese Government published the Declaration of the Government of the PRC on China's Territorial Sea, in which it declared that the breadth of China's territorial sea is 12 nautical miles and that this provision applies to all territories of China, including the mainland and its offshore islands, Taiwan and the various affiliated islands including Diaoyu Dao, Penghu Qundao, Dongsha Qundao, Xisha Qundao, Nansha Qundao and other islands that belong to the PRC. In this regard, on September 14, 1958, the Prime Minister of the Government of Vietnam, Pham Van Dong, sent a letter to the Premier of China, Zhou Enlai, in which he stated on behalf of the Government of the Democratic Republic of Vietnam that "recognizes and supports the declaration dated 4th September, 1958 of the of the government of the People's Republic of China fixing the width of the Chinese territorial sea, and will give instructions to its State bodies to respect the 12-mile width of the territorial waters of China in all their relations in the maritime field with China."[16] This letter indicates that Vietnam recognizes that the Xisha Qundao and Nansha Qundao belong to China.

In the case of the Philippines, prior to the 1970s, no legal documents relating to the Philippines (including the U.S.–Spain Treaty of Paris in 1898, the U.S.–Spain Treaty of Washington in 1900, the U.S.–Philippine Treaty of General Relations in 1946, Republic Act No. 3046 of 17 June 1961: An Act to Define the Baselines of the Territorial Sea of the Philippines, and the Philippines Act 5446 of September 18, 1968), in the regulations on its territorial scope, mentioned that the Nansha Islands belong to the Philippines. After the 1970s, the Philippines began to modify

[15] See Liangfu, Zhang. 2006. Problems of maritime delimitation disputes between China and its neighbors. Beijing: Ocean Press. pp. 68–70.

[16] See People's Daily, September 22, 1958, cited in Liangfu, Zhang. 2006. *Problems of maritime delimitation disputes between China and neighboring countries*. Beijing: Ocean Press. pp. 78–80.

its territorial scope or issue new documents on its territorial scope in order to occupy the Nansha Qundao.[17]

In addition, the Law of the PRC on the Territorial Sea and the Contiguous Zone, which was enacted and put into effect on February 25, 1992, reiterates China's sovereignty over the Nanhai Zhudao. For example, Article 2(2) stipulates that the territorial land includes the mainland and its offshore islands, Taiwan and the various affiliated islands including Diaoyu Dao, Penghu Qundao, Dongsha Qundao, Xisha Qundao, Nansha Qundao and other islands that belong to the PRC.

Therefore, China's claim to the Nanhai Zhudao is consistent, and China has indisputable sovereignty over the Nanhai Zhudao, which is consistent with the territorial requirements of international law.

5.1.2.2 The Argument that Some ASEAN Countries Have Sovereignty Over the Nansha Qundao is Invalid

Vietnam and the Philippines are ASEAN countries that have illegally seized the largest number of Nanhai Zhudao. Thus, their claims over the Nanhai Zhudao (Nansha Qundao) will be analyzed.

(1) Analysis of Vietnam's claim to sovereignty over the Nanhai Zhudao. Among the countries surrounding the SCS, Vietnam is the only country that claims sovereignty over the Xisha Qundao and the entire Nansha Qundao. The basis for Vietnam's claims is as follows:

First, historical "occupation." Vietnam claims to be the first country in history to occupy, organize, control, and explore the Nansha Qundao. This is done by first renaming China's Xisha Qundao and Nansha Qundao as the "Hoang Sa" and "Truong Sa" archipelagos and referring to the historical records on the Hoang Sa and Truong Sa archipelagos as those of China's Xisha Qundao and Nansha Qundao, thus becoming the "first occupying country."[18] In fact, Hoang Sa and Truong Sa in Vietnam's historical atlases are some islands and beaches in Vietnam's coastal waters, which have nothing to do with the Xisha Qundao and Nansha Qundao.[19] This practice of changing the name of the islands does not alter China's sovereignty over them.

Second, Vietnam claims to have inherited sovereignty over the Nansha Qundao as the successor to France. However, France did not own the Nansha Qundao after the Second World War, and there are no documents confirming the transfer between France and Vietnam. According to France, the Nansha

---

[17] See Liangfu, Zhang. 2006. Problems of maritime delimitation disputes between china and its neighbors. Beijing: Ocean Press. pp. 80–81.

[18] See Jinming, Li. 2011. The origin and status quo of territorial disputes in the South China Sea, *World Knowledge* 12, cited in Xinhua Monthly, July 2011, p. 67.

[19] See Zhenhua, Han, ed. 1998. *Compilation of historical materials on the islands in the South China Sea.* Shanghai: Oriental Publishing House. pp. 15–22.

Qundao were not handed over to Vietnam, which was later granted independence. Meanwhile, because North Vietnam, which recognized China's sovereignty over the Xisha Qundao and Nansha Qundao, took over South Vietnam, and the current Government of Vietnam succeeded North Vietnam rather than South Vietnam, according to the principle of "estoppel," Vietnam must insist the original recognition.[20] In other words, Vietnam's claim to sovereignty over the Xisha Qundao and Nansha Qundao is untenable.

(2) Analysis of the Philippines' claim to sovereignty over the Nanhai Zhudao. The Philippine claim to some of the maritime features in the Nansha Qundao is based on Philippine Presidential Decree No. 1596 of June 11, 1978: first, that the Nansha Qundao are vital to the security and economic lifeblood of the Philippines; second, that the Philippines is closest to the Nansha Qundao; and third, that the Nansha Qundao do not legally belong to any country and are *terra nullius*, and that if there is a claim of sovereignty made by any other country, such claims have been nullified by waiver.[21]

None of the above arguments can be justified. First, the Philippines could not arbitrarily claim sovereignty over the territory of other countries on the basis of security and economic interests. Moreover, it cannot challenge the territorial sovereignty of other countries despite its strong demand for energy resources to sustain its social development. To do otherwise would confuse the issue of international territorial ownership, which would seriously undermine international order. Second, proximity is not a reasonable justification for acquiring territory under international law. Finally, the Nansha Qundao are not *terra nullius*. After the Second World War, the Chinese Government recovered its sovereignty over the Nansha Qundao from Japan and strengthened its jurisdiction, including stationing a naval force on Taiping Dao, which it had never abandoned.[22] Therefore, the Philippines' claim to some of the Nansha Qundao is untenable and does not change the historical fact that they belong to China.

Thus, the claims of some ASEAN countries over the Nanhai Zhudao (including occupation, succession, proximity, and abandonment) do not change the historical facts and legal basis of China's long-established sovereignty. Of the many historical and legal bases, the most important is the dotted line announced by China in the SCS.

[20] See Jinming, Li. 2011. The origin and status quo of territorial disputes in the South China Sea, *World Knowledge* 12, cited in Xinhua Monthly, July 2011, p. 67.

[21] See Jinming, Li. 2003. *South China Sea disputes and international law of the sea*. Beijing: Ocean Press. pp. 83–88.

[22] After the Second World War, the Chinese Government recovered the Nanhai Zhudao occupied by Japan. On September 2, 1946, the Chinese Government issued a decree on the recovery of the Xisha Qundao and Nansha Qundao. After consultation among the Ministry of the Interior, Ministry of Foreign Affairs, and Ministry of Defense, it sent out reception personnel, mainly naval personnel, to successfully take over the Xisha Qundao and Nansha Qundao, and to erect stone monuments, such as "Taiping Dao," "Taiping Dao of the Nansha Qundao," "Nanwei Dao," and "Xiyue Dao" to reaffirm China's sovereignty over the islands. For the above, see Guoqiang, Li. 2011. The formation of China's sovereignty over the South China Sea islands and the origin of the South China Sea issue, *Qiu Shi* 15.

The following is an analysis of the formation and background of China's dotted line in the SCS.

5.1.2.3 Formation and Background of the Dotted Line in the SCS

One of the ways that successive Chinese governments have strengthened the management of the Nanhai Zhudao is to name and mark them on maps after investigation and exploration. There are two most representative actions, including the "Nan Hai Zhu Dao Xin Jiu Ming Cheng Dui Zhao Biao" (Comparison Table on the Old and New Names of the Nanhai Zhudao), officially published by the Chinese government on December 1, 1947, with a total of 159 collective and individual names of islands and reefs and the "Nan Hai Zhu Dao Wei Zhi Tu" (Location Map of the Nanhai Zhudao), officially published by the Ministry of the Interior of the Chinese Government on February 1948, indicating the names of all the maritime features, with a U-shaped dotted line formally delineated to include the Dongsha Qundao, Xisha Qundao, Zhongsha Qundao, and Nansha Qundao. The southernmost Zengmu Ansha is clearly located at approximately 4° north latitude. This U-shaped dotted line is not coherent and is divided into 11 sections.[23] Thus, the dotted line in the SCS is formed.

In the author's view, the background of the dotted line in the SCS includes the following aspects:

First, it was forced by foreign invasion. In 1933, French warships invaded the nine small islands in the Nansha Qundao, resulting in a major shock to the Chinese people. The government believed that the maintenance of sovereignty over the Nanhai Zhudao was urgent. On December 21, 1934, China's Committee for the Examination for the Land and Sea Maps, which was composed of representatives of the Ministry of the Interior, Ministry of Foreign Affairs, Ministry of Education, Ministry of the Navy, General Staff Headquarters, Mongolian and Tibetan Affairs Commission and other institutions, held its 25th meeting. The government reviewed and approved Chinese and English names of maritime features in the SCS and published "Nan Hai Zhu Dao Xin Jiu Ming Cheng Dui Zhao Biao" (Comparison Table on the Old and New Names of the Nanhai Zhudao). This is the first "quasi-standardized" naming of the Nanhai Zhudao by the Chinese government, officially dividing the Nanhai Zhudao into four parts: Dongsha Qundao, Xisha Qundao, Zhongsha Qundao (then named Nansha Qundao) and Nansha Qundao (then named Tuansha Qundao or Shanhu Qundao). In the table, 132 names of islands, shoals, submerged reefs, banks and cays are listed. In April 1935, the Committee for the Examination for the Land and Sea Maps published the "Zhong Guo Nan Hai Ge Dao Yu Tu" (Map of the Nanhai Zhudao of China). This is an official map of the SCS special project published by the Chinese Government, which depicts the SCS islands in details and the southernmost end of the SCS is

[23] See Kuen Chen, Fu. *Sovereignty and deposits in the South China Sea—history and law*. Taipei: Youth Publishing. pp. 192–202; Kuen Chen, Fu. 1995. *Study on the legal status of the South (China) Sea*. Taipei: Taipei 123 Information Publishing. pp. 2–3; Jinming, Li. 2003. *South China Sea disputes and international law of the sea*. Beijing: Ocean Press. pp. 50–52.

plotted at Zengmu Ansha about 4°north latitude. On December 1, 1947, the Ministry of the Interior of the Chinese Government re-established the names of the Dongsha Qundao, Xisha Qundao, Zhongsha Qundao, and Nansha Qundao and their affiliated islands, shoals, submerged reefs, banks and cays. It formally published "Nan Hai Zhu Dao Xin Jiu Ming Cheng Dui Zhao Biao" (Comparison Table on the Old and New Names of the SCS Islands), of which there were 3 in the Dongsha Qundao, 33 in the Xisha Qundao, 29 in the Zhongsha Qundao, and 102 in the Nansha Qundao, for a total of 167 islands, shoals, submerged reefs, banks, and cays. It also marked the eleven dotted lines on the chart, which constituted a U-shaped dotted line. In February 1948, the Ministry of the Interior of the Chinese Government published the "Zhong Hua Min Guo Xing Zheng Qu Yu Tu" (Map of the Administrative Districts of the Republic of China) with the "Nan Hai Zhu Dao Wei Zhi Tu" (Location Map of the SCS Islands).[24]

In other words, the U-shaped line in the SCS took shape when France invaded nine islands of Nansha Qundao. It took shape as a precautionary action after the war against Japan when France once again occupied the Shanhu Dao of the Xisha Qundao and some maritime features of the Nansha Qundao and when the Philippines attempted to "merge the archipelagos into the scope of national defense". The purpose of these precautionary measures was to safeguard the territorial sovereignty of the Chinese Government over the Nanhai Zhudao and to publicize the areas under its jurisdiction. That is, the purpose of the Chinese Government's announcement of the U-shaped line in the SCS was to establish China's sovereignty and jurisdiction over the Xisha Qundao and Nansha Qundao.[25]

Second, the situation of the oceans and seas is a matter of record. On September 28, 1945, the U.S. issued the Truman Proclamation, aiming to establish exclusive resource protection zones and acquire the benefits of the continental shelf.[26] Latin American countries have adopted a more radical policy of adopting 200-nautical-mile EEZs. Against this backdrop, the Chinese Government has adopted a moderate policy, announcing a U-shaped line in the form of "the median line" in an attempt to separate the rights and interests of other SCS neighboring countries from those of China in the sea and safeguard China's own "historic interests" in the SCS.[27] The Chinese Government's act of drawing a U-shaped line is not a maritime enclosure

[24] See Guoqiang, Li. 2011. The formation of China's sovereignty over the South China Sea islands and the Origin of the South China Sea issue, *Qiu Shi* 15. It should be noted that, regarding the number of islands in the South China Sea announced by the Chinese Government on December 1, 1947, Professor Li Guoqiang's number (167) is different from Professor Fu Kuen Chen's (159). As it is impossible to determine the true number, the discrepancy is duly noted.

[25] See Jinming, Li. 2011. 2011. Review of domestic and international studies on the legal status of the dotted line in the South China Sea, *Southeast Asian Affairs* 2: 59; See also Jinming, Li. 2003. *South China Sea disputes and international law of the sea*, Beijing: Ocean Press. pp. 52–53.

[26] For the contents of the Truman Proclamation, see Department of International Law of Peking University Law School, ed. 1974. *Law of the sea materials compilation.* Beijing: People's Publishing House. pp. 386–387.

[27] Kuen Chen, Fu. 1995. *Study on the legal status of the South (China) Sea.* Taipei: Taipei 123 Information Publishing. pp. 43–44.

movement influenced by the Truman Proclamation, nor does it intend to expand the scope of its claims in the sea.[28] Instead, it accelerates the pace of the Chinese Government's announcement of U-shaped lines in the SCS under the influence of the Truman Proclamation to safeguard the territorial sovereignty and jurisdictional boundaries of the Nanhai Zhudao, to ensure China's historic rights and declare them to the international community.

What has been the role and effect of China's drawing of the dotted line in the SCS? To answer this question, it is necessary to analyze the nature of the dotted line and the legal status of the waters within the line.

5.1.3 *Nature of the Dotted Line in the SCS and the Legal Status of the Waters Within the Line*

The U-shaped line in the SCS was inherited by the PRC after the Government of the Republic of China published it in December 1947, basically following the previous map. In 1953, two sections within the Beibu Gulf were removed with the approval of Premier Zhou Enlai, and all maps of China published since then have included the nine dotted line.[29] In view of the importance of the U-shaped line in the SCS disputes, it is necessary to examine the U-shaped line and the legal status of the waters within the line.

5.1.3.1 The Nature of the Dotted Line or the U-shaped Line in the SCS

As mentioned above, there are various views in the international community on the meaning of the U-shaped line in the SCS, mainly of the following four doctrines: the theory of historic rights, the theory of historic waters, the theory of the maritime boundary line, and the theory of the islands ownership line.[30] Among these doctrines, some emphasize that the status of the waters within the U-shaped line is based on China's historic interests or rights in the SCS, for instance, the theories of historic rights or waters line, while others emphasize the legal status of the U-shaped line

---

[28] Jinming, Li. 2011. 2011. Review of domestic and international studies on the legal status of the dotted line in the South China Sea, *Southeast Asian Affairs* 2: 59.

[29] See Keyuan, Zou. Some legal reflections on the U-shaped lines in the South China Sea, in *Proceedings of the South China Sea Issue Seminar*, Zhong Tianxiang, Han Jia, Ren Huaifeng, Ren., eds. 2002. Haikou: Hainan Institute for South China Sea Studies. pp. 27–28. cited in Senan, Xu. 2000. The connotation of the dotted national boundary line in the South China Sea, in *Selected papers of the 21st Century South China Sea issue and prospects seminar*, ed, Hainan Institute for South China Sea Studies. Haikou: Hainan Institute for South China Sea Studies. p. 83.

[30] For the international community's debate and views on the U-shaped line in the South China Sea, see Jinming, Li. 2011. 2011. Review of domestic and international studies on the legal status of the dotted line in the South China Sea, *Southeast Asian Affairs* 2: 54–62.

itself, such as the theories of maritime boundary line or the islands ownership line, and on this basis, they explain the nature of the dotted line.

In fact, the U-shaped line in the SCS and the legal status and attributes of the waters within the line are two different yet closely related issues. Generally, as mentioned above, the legal status and attributes of the waters within the U-shaped line in the SCS can be determined only after sovereignty, especially over the maritime features of the Nansha Qundao, has been established, as "the land dominates the sea" is the basic principle of the international law of the sea.

Both the theories of the historic rights and historic waters line emphasize the special attributes of the U-shaped line in the SCS, in particular historic rights, including fishing rights, navigational rights, and surveying rights, which are important for China to obtain the greatest benefits based on the U-shaped line. These rights should not be given up, but there are deficiencies in these doctrines with regard to proving that China has effectively exercised or continues to exercise its exclusive rights in the waters within the U-shaped line. Although the international community does not have a clear definition of historic rights and waters, most scholars believe that since historic rights are related to territorial acquisition under international law, the following three elements must be present: effective jurisdiction, long-standing jurisdiction, and acquiescence of other states. That is, the coastal State must have exercised its sovereignty over the maritime area in a clear, effective, and continuous manner for more than a particular period of time with the acquiescence of the international community.[31]

That is, the claim to "historic waters" based on historic rights must, at the very least, be based on the fact that there has been effective and uninterrupted jurisdiction over the maritime area in question. In this regard, China's case may not be ripe for recognition by the international community.

First, from the time China drew the U-shaped line to the present, the exercise of sovereignty by the Chinese mainland and Chinese Taiwan has been confined to the waters surrounding the islands under their respective effective control, but not over the waters within the U-shaped line.

Second, as mentioned above, Chinese Taiwan's executive branch declared in its Policy Guidelines for the South China Sea on April 13, 1993, that "The South China Sea area within the historic water limit is the maritime area under the jurisdiction

[31] See Bouchez, L. H. 1964. *The regime of bays in international law*. Hague: Maritime Nijhoff. p. 281. Kaye, Stuart B. 2004. Territorial sea baselines along ice-covered coasts: International practice and limits of the law of the sea, *Ocean Development & International Law* 1: 90. Cikuan, Yu. 2001. The legal status of the U-shaped lines from the perspective of the international law of the sea, in *Proceedings of the South China Sea Issue Seminar*, Zhong Tianxiang, Han Jia, Ren Huaifeng, eds. Haikou: Hainan Institute for South China Sea Studies. pp. 427–439. Furthermore, for historic waters based on historic rights, the following elements must be present: first, the coastal State must publicly claim that the body of water is within its sovereign jurisdiction and exercise its sovereignty; second, the coastal State must exercise its sovereignty effectively over a long period of time; and third, the exercise of sovereignty must be peaceful and continuous, and must be known and acquiesced to by foreign states. See Kuen Chen, Fu. 2004. *Study on the law of the sea*. Xiamen: Xiamen University Press, pp. 326–328.

of China." On February 10, 1999, in the table of the first batch of baselines, territorial waters, and adjacent outer boundaries, Chinese Taiwan's authority in relevant documents announced that, "All the maritime features of the Nansha Qundao within the traditional U-shaped line are Chinese territory. Furthermore, the baselines of the territorial sea are delineated by the normal baseline and the mixed baseline method of straight and normal baselines. The names of the relevant baselines, geographic coordinates and nautical charts are announced in a separate announcement." However, the issue of whether the waters within the U-line are historic waters is not specifically addressed. At the same time, although Article 14 of the June 1998 Law of the PRC on the Exclusive Economic Zone and the Continental Shelf stipulates that "the provisions of this Law shall not affect the historic rights enjoyed by China," no specific clarification has been made.

Third, in all the Conferences on the Law of the Sea, China never made any declaration about the waters within the U-shaped line. Meanwhile, Hasjim Djalal, the former Indonesian Ambassador to Germany, and Ben Ahmed Hamzah, the leader of the Malaysian Maritime Affairs Association, have questioned and objected to the legal status of the U-shaped line at the SCS conferences after China's claim was made. Therefore, as for the "time element" that constitutes "historical rights", it is too short and opposed by neighboring countries, and does not meet the "implied consent" requirement of third countries.[32]

Since the boundary constituting the territory of a State is exclusive, and China has never treated the waters within the U-shaped line as state territory, nor has it ever protested against freedom of navigation of foreign vessels in the waters within the U-shaped line, the theory of the maritime boundary line cannot be established. Therefore, for the legal status of the U-shaped line in the SCS, the more easily accepted one is the theory of the island's ownership line, that is, the most basic nature or legal status of the U-shaped line in the SCS is the islands ownership line. In other words, all islands, shoals, submerged reefs, banks and cays in the SCS belong to China. The theory of the island's ownership line for the U-shaped line in the SCS is consistent with the original intention of the Ministry of the Interior of the Chinese Government in deciding to mark the U-shaped line. It is also the consistent position of the Chinese Government after the establishment of the New China, as well as with the relevant institutional norms of the law of the sea.[33]

Thus, with regard to the dotted line of the SCS, China cannot claim the historic waters line, the historic rights line, or the maritime boundary line. From the legal meaning and policy system standpoint, it is more appropriate to claim the islands ownership line. However, the problem is that the islands ownership line does not satisfy China's historic rights and jurisdiction over the Nanhai Zhudao, and in particular, it does not reflect China's traditional rights in the Nanhai Zhudao, especially the Nansha Qundao. Neither does it reflect, nor claim relevant maritime zones from

[32] Jingfen, Wei. 2008. *The law of the sea.* Taipei: Taipei Wu-Nan Book Inc. pp. 331–332.

[33] Nanlai, Liu. 2002. The legal status of the U-shaped lines from the perspective of the international law of the sea, in *Proceedings of the South China Sea Issue Seminar*, Zhong Tianxiang, Han Jia, Ren Huaifeng, eds. Haikou: Hainan Institute for South China Sea Studies. p. 56.

the territory such as Zengmu Ansha. Therefore, in the author's opinion, the nature of the dotted line in the SCS should be the line of islands ownership and resource jurisdiction. Its basic meaning is as follows: first, all islands, shoals, submerged reefs, banks and cays within the dotted line belong to China; second, China may choose to use straight baselines to delineate the archipelagic waters of some of the Nansha Qundao, but within the archipelagic waters there should be no obstacle to the right of transit passage of other countries; third, China enjoys sovereign rights over the natural resources of the waters superjacent to the seabed and of the seabed and its subsoil, within the Nansha Qundao. As for the scope of the sea area, it should be determined according to the law of the sea regime and the waters based on historic rights to reflect jurisdiction over resources; and fourth, in the maritime areas beyond China's internal waters, other countries continue to enjoy freedom of navigation, overflight, and the laying of submarine cables and pipelines, as well as other internationally lawful uses of the sea related to these freedoms.[34] This characterization of the dotted line in the SCS is specifically reflected in the legal status and attributes of the waters within this line.

5.1.3.2 Legal Status and Attributes of the Waters Within the Dotted Line or U-shaped Line in the SCS

Because most of the regimes in the UNCLOS have become customary international law, it is more reasonable to characterize the legal status and attributes of the waters within the U-shaped line in the SCS in relation to the regime of maritime zones in the Convention. This is also in line with the requirement that China, as a State party to the Convention, should comply with the norms of the Convention.

First, the waters within the line are not internal waters. This is because the Chinese Government has never indicated that the waters within the line are internal waters, and objected to the freedom of navigation of vessels of other countries in the waters within the line.

Second, the waters within the line are not territorial sea. Paragraph 1 of the Declaration of the Government of the PRC on China's Territorial Sea states that the breadth of the territorial sea of the PRC is 12 nautical miles. This provision applies to all territories of the PRC, including the Chinese mainland and its offshore islands, Taiwan and the various affiliated islands, the Penghu Qundao, the Dongsha Qundao, the Xisha Qundao, the Zhongsha Qundao, the Nansha Qundao and other islands belonging to China. Paragraph 2 states that the baselines of territorial sea of China's mainland and its offshore islands are straight lines joining the base points on the mainland shore and the islands along the outer edge of the coast and the waters extending 12 nautical miles from the baseline are China's territorial sea. At the same time, Article 3(1) of Law of the PRC on the Territorial Sea and the Contiguous Zone stipulates that "The

[34] Zhonghai, Zhou. 2001. On "historic title" in the law of the sea," in *Selected Papers on Chinese and Foreign Research on the South China Sea* (2001), Zhong Tianxiang, Han Jia, Yunshan, Su Yan, eds. Haikou: Hainan Center for South China Sea Studies. pp. 120–121.

extent of the PRC's territorial sea measures 12 nautical miles from the baseline of the territorial sea." Only the belt of water within 12 nautical miles from the baselines of the Nanhai Zhudao within the U-shaped line is China's territorial sea. Other vast waters within the U-shaped line are not territorial sea.

Finally, the waters within the line are not the high seas. If the waters within the U-shaped line, except for the 12-nautical-mile-wide territorial sea surrounding maritime features, were the high seas, there would have been no need for the Chinese Government to draw the U-shaped line in the "Nan Hai Zhu Dao Wei Zhi Tu" (Location Map of the SCS Islands) in 1947. As the purpose of the publication of the U-shaped line was to establish China's sovereignty and jurisdiction over the Nanhai Zhudao, the waters inside the U-shaped line must be different from those outside the line, and it cannot be the high seas. Even though, according to paragraph 1 of the Declaration of the Government of the PRC on China's Territorial Sea, there may be a small number of high seas in the SCS.

In the author's view, regarding the legal status and attributes of the waters within the dotted or U-shaped line, the territorial sea, contiguous zone, and exclusive economic zone can be determined based on the line of the islands ownership and in accordance with the system regulated by the Convention. Then, China's historic rights or elements over the Nanhai Zhudao can be considered to determine the legal status and attributes of the remaining waters within the U-shaped line. In other words, part of the waters within the dotted line is determined on the basis of China's historic rights over the Nanhai Zhudao and is a special type with historic rights. Therefore, there are two types of waters within the dotted line with different natures depending on their origin, which do not contradict each other and can exist in parallel.

The first category comprises waters under the law of the sea, established under the Convention, including the territorial sea, the contiguous zone, and the EEZ. In light of the special characteristics of the Nanhai Zhudao, which contains most of the islands, shoals, submerged reefs, banks, and cays. Thus, it is challenging for China to implement the regime of archipelagic waters by delineating two or three areas of archipelagic waters with straight baselines in the Nansha Qundao. This is because, according to Article 46 of the regime of archipelagic State of the UNCLOS, the term "archipelago" means "a group of islands, including parts of islands, interconnecting waters and other natural features which are so closely interrelated that such islands, waters and other natural features form an intrinsic geographical, economic and political entity, or which historically have been regarded as such." Therefore, China must prove the elements constituting archipelagic waters. However, the Declaration of the Government of the PRC on the Baselines of the Territorial Sea of the PRC (May 15, 1996), which declared straight joining lines as the baselines of the territorial sea in the Xisha Qundao, provides the basis for China to continue utilizing straight baselines in the Nansha Qundao.[35]

---

[35] For example, Article 3(2) of China's Law on the Territorial Sea and the Contiguous Zone stipulates that the PRC's baseline of the territorial sea is designated with the method of straight baselines, formed by joining the various base points with straight lines; The Government of the PRC will announce the remaining baselines of the territorial sea of the PRC at another time.

The archipelagic regime of the UNCLOS, in particular Article 47(1), seems to preclude the applicability of straight or archipelagic baselines to "mid-ocean archipelagos" that do not belong to "archipelagic States."[36] However, there is a legal theory that the same legal system should be applied to the same object, that is, whether they are "mid-ocean archipelagos" of "archipelagic States" or "mid-ocean archipelagos" of "non-archipelagic States," the same legal system should be applied. As they form an inseparable part of the territory of a state, they have the same political, economic, and security status and role. At the same time, the UNCLOS does not contain clear provisions on how the baselines of "mid-ocean archipelagos" of "non-archipelagic States should be delimited.

In addition, from the specific legal regime of the law of the sea and the practice of ocean legislation of various countries, it is clear that countries will make the most advantageous and feasible decisions regarding their special circumstances and to safeguard their maritime interests to the greatest extent possible. Therefore, it is feasible for China to apply the regime of archipelagic waters to part of the Nansha Qundao on the basis of the archipelagic baselines. Other countries have also applied this regime, for example, the Galapagos Islands for Ecuador, the Faeroe Islands for Denmark, the Svalbard Islands for Norway, the Andaman and Nicobar Islands and Lakshadweep Islands for India, and Micronesia.[37] As long as China continues to adhere to this position, it can apply the archipelagic waters regime to parts of the Nansha Qundao.

The second category is special waters based on historic rights. After establishing the first category under the UNCLOS, China can claim special waters in the remaining area based on historic rights. The main basis for this argument in domestic law for China's claim to the remaining waters of the SCS as special waters is Article 14 of the Law of on the Exclusive Economic Zone and the Continental Shelf and Article 2 of the Marine Environment Protection Law.[38]

China enjoys a variety of priority rights in these special waters that reflect its jurisdiction over the resources within the dotted line, including priority rights for exploring, exploiting, conserving and managing the natural resources; protecting and preserving the environment; engaging in scientific research; regulating navigation and aviation, even regulating the relevant navigational activities of neighboring countries. The Chinese Government's failure to regulate certain rights (for example, the right to regulate navigation and aviation) in the waters within the dotted line is a point of contention.

Thus, the nature of the U-shaped line in the SCS and the legal status of the waters within the line are directly related to maintaining and ensuring China's sovereignty in the SCS, especially in the Nansha Qundao. In order to maximize China's interests

---

[36] Article 47(1) of the UNCLOS provides that "An archipelagic State may draw straight archipelagic baselines joining the outermost points of the outermost islands and drying reefs of the archipelago."

[37] See Jingfen, Wei. 2008. *The law of the sea.* Taipei: Taipei Wu-Nan Book Inc. pp. 336–338.

[38] For example, Article 2 of China's Marine Environment Protection Law (1999) provides that the Law applies to China's internal waters, territorial sea, contiguous zone, continental shelf, the EEZ, and other maritime areas under China's jurisdiction.

in the Nanhai Zhudao, it poses a huge challenge to the diplomatic wisdom of the Chinese government and people. It is also an important topic that our scholars should continue to work together to study and solve.[39]

5.2 Attributes and Status of the Maritime Features of the Nanhai Zhudao

In the *SCS* Arbitration, the harsh, or even erroneous, rulings of the Arbitral Tribunal on the maritime features (islands, rocks, etc.) had an important effect on the resolution of the SCS issue. For this reason, the legal elements of islands and rocks are analyzed in the context of the regime of islands of the UNCLOS.

5.2.1 Origins of the Problem

Prior to the SCS Arbitration, the issue of the status of islands and rocks arose from the fact that, on November 12, 2008, the Government of Japan issued a submission on the outer continental shelf that based its claim on the Oki-no-Tori (Oki-no Tori-shima) as the base point, with the maritime zone of approximately 740,000 square kilometers.[40] Japan's practice of treating the rock of Oki-no-Tori (Oki-no Tori-shima) as an island in its outer continental shelf submission has created concern and dissatisfaction among the international community. China and the Republic of Korea put forward their own national positions on the rock of Oki-no-Tori (Oki-no Tori-shima) issue in written statements to the UN Secretary-General, declaring that the rock of Oki-no-Tori (Oki-no Tori-shima) is a rock, not an island, and that it is not possible to use it as a base from which to claim the continental shelf or the outer continental shelf. Furthermore, the CLCS does not have the authority to consider the information relating to the outer continental shelf using the rock of Oki-no-Tori (Oki-no Tori-shima) as a base point[41] As a result, disputes over the qualification and legal status of the rock of Oki-no-Tori (Oki-no Tori-shima) have arisen. These disputes involve the regime of islands of

[39] For details on the legal status of the U-shaped line in the South China Sea, see Kuen Chen, Fu. 1995. *A study of the legal status of the South China Sea.* Taipei: Taipei 123 Information Publishing. pp. 201–210.

[40] For more details on Japan's outer continental shelf submission, see Yongming, Jin. 2009. The contents of Japan's submission on the extended continental shelf and China's position, *China Oceans Law Review* 1: pp. 28–39.

[41] The Permanent Mission of China to the UN submitted a written statement to the Secretary-General on February 6, 2009, in response to Japan's submission concerning the rock of Oki-no-Tori, see https://www.un.org/depts/los/clcs_new/submissions_files/jpn08/chn_6feb09_e.pdf, accessed March 12, 2009. The Republic of Korea submitted a written statement with the same content as the Chinese Government's statement on February 27, 2009, in response to the issue, see https://www.un.org/depts/los/clcs_new/submissions_files/jpn08/kor_27feb09.pdf, accessed March 12, 2009.

the law of the sea. The reason for the above-mentioned disputes is that the regime of islands is the product of compromise and the fuzziness of related terms on the constitutive elements of rocks. Therefore, there are differences in understanding and different interpretations of the constitutive elements and legal status of islands and rocks.

Japan's submission on the outer continental shelf, which claims the EEZ and continental shelf based on the rock of Oki-no-Tori (Oki-no Tori-shima), seeks to utilize the international community's diverse interpretations of the regime of islands, namely, that, in Japan's view, rocks should not satisfy the constituent elements of islands. Japan's rationale is that Article 121(3) of the UNCLOS is a provision only for rocks, not islands. Thus, rocks, as they are not islands, should not be subject to the elements of paragraph 1. Japan's position is that paragraphs 1 and 3 of Article 121 of the UNCLOS are independent, but this view contradicts the view of the majority of the international community.

The law of the sea refers primarily to the UNCLOS, the treaty that comprehensively regulates ocean issues. The regime of islands is provided for in Article 121 of the UNCLOS.[42] Paragraph 1 provides that "An island is a naturally formed area of land, surrounded by water, which is above water at high tide." Paragraph 2 provides that, "Except as provided for in paragraph 3, the territorial sea, the contiguous zone, the exclusive economic zone and the continental shelf of an island are determined in accordance with the provisions of this Convention applicable to other land territory." Paragraph 3 provides that "Rocks which cannot sustain human habitation or economic life of their own shall have no exclusive economic zone or continental shelf."

As can be seen from Japan's position on the rock of Oki-no-Tori (Oki-no Tori-shima) issue, the controversy within the international community over the regime of islands relates to the following matters: first, differences in knowledge and understanding of the structure of Article 121 of the UNCLOS, which regulates the regime of islands, that is, whether paragraphs 1–3 of Article 121 should be understood in their entirety or independently of each other; second, differences in interpretations of the terms related to the elements constituting rocks in Article 121(3).

In sum, the above-mentioned differences stem from divergent understandings of the provisions of the regime of the islands and the ambiguity of the terminology relating to the constituent elements of rocks.

[42] For an analysis of the South China Sea Arbitration case on the determination of the island element and Article 121(3) of the regime of islands, see Michael Shengti, Gau. 2018. On the questionable interpretation of Article 121 (3) of UNCLOS in the Award ofthe South China Sea Arbitration, *Pacific Journal* 12(1): 24–34.

5.2.2 *Integrity and Independence of the Regime of Islands in the Law of the Sea*

Japan's understanding of the terms of the regime of islands (the separation theory) is contrary to the majority view (the integrity theory) of the international community. From the structure of the provisions on the regime of islands mentioned above paragraphs 1–3 of Article 121 of the UNCLOS are provisions on the regime of islands. Specifically, Paragraph 1 refers to islands in a broad sense, that is, the UNCLOS provides for a broad concept of islands. Paragraph 2 is a provision on islands in the general sense, that is, islands with the same status as land territories may claim the corresponding maritime zones. Paragraph 3, which deals with rocks, is not a provision directly derived from the concept of rocks, rather, it is derived from the perspective of their effectiveness, that is, rocks capable of sustaining human habitation or economic life of their own can, like islands, claim the EEZ and continental shelf. Thus, there are two kinds of rocks: those that can claim the EEZ and continental shelf and those that cannot. Simultaneously paragraph 3 is a constraint on paragraph 2, in the sense that not all rocks can claim the EEZ and continental shelf in the same way as islands can, as established in paragraph 2.

Paragraphs 1–3 of Article 121 of the UNCLOS have different characteristics and constitute the entirety of the regime of islands. The main reason for the vagueness of Article 121(3) of the UNCLOS is that a uniform definition of rocks is not possible. This is evidenced by the contentious elements of the regime of islands at the Third UN Conference on the Law of the Sea, where the UNCLOS was discussed.

At the Third UN Conference on the Law of the Sea (1973–1982), the controversial elements of the regime of islands comprised the following views. The first was the "classification" group, which advocated that islands should be categorized on the basis of certain criteria and that different legal statuses should be accorded to each type. The reason for this is that the acquisition of the 200-nautical-mile EEZ and other vast areas of the sea by small islands that are not habitable or economically viable would seriously impact the free use of the oceans and limit the scope of the Area based on the common heritage of mankind. Therefore, some countries advocated that islands should be categorized as islands and rocks based on a wide range of criteria, such as the shape and size of islands and the size of the population. The second was the "unification" group, which advocated that no specific criteria should be established for islands and that all islands should be given a unified status. While the former group aims to classify islands according to whether or not they have an EEZ and continental shelf, the latter aims to recognize that all islands have an EEZ and continental shelf.[43]

As a result of these negotiations, the definition of islands in the UNCLOS (Art. 121(1)) does not provide relevant elements or criteria. Article 121 is the product of

---

[43] See [Japanese] Kagami, Yasuhiko. 2006. The United Nations Convention on the Law of the Sea as a method for sustainable development: A discussion of Article 121(3), in *Report on the Study of the Regeneration of Okinotorishima (2005)*, Japan Ocean Policy Research Foundation, ed. pp. 102–103.

a compromise between the two groups mentioned above, reflecting the international community indirectly adopting both groups of thoughts. That is, the regime of islands can be described as a product of reconciliation between two opposed views, as reflected by paragraphs 1 and 3.

It is difficult for the UNCLOS to define rocks in the context of the regime of islands because rocks must consider their own natural (geological and topographical formations and patterns), social, historical, cultural, and economic attributes. The concept of rocks also takes into account the interests of all countries, and balancing these attributes and interests is indeed a very difficult thing. Therefore, the UNCLOS avoided the practice of making provisions directly as concepts and only defined some rocks from the perspective of effectiveness. However, the ambiguity of these provisions is the origin of the controversies that have arisen in practice.

It is generally believed that the rocks in Article 121(3) of the UNCLOS should be a kind of island in paragraph 1, that is, the rocks in paragraph 3 are regarded as a special form of island. This view is generally recognized by academics.[44] In other words, Article 121 of the UNCLOS as a whole is a provision on the regime of islands, the rocks in paragraph 3 are exceptional islands but are called rocks. Thus, the rocks in paragraph 3 should meet the elements of an island stipulated in paragraph 1, that is, an island is a naturally formed area of land, surrounded by water, which is above water at high tide. Otherwise, the rocks should not have the EEZ and continental shelf. Such a textual interpretation of Article 121 of the UNCLOS is subject to divergent opinions. This is exactly where the controversy between Japan, China, and Korea over the status of the rock of Oki-no-Tori (Oki-no Tori-shima) has arisen. For example, the representative of the Government of Japan, in response to a question on the rock of Oki-no-Tori (Oki-no Tori-shima) at the Construction Committee of the House of Representatives held on April 16, 1999, pointed out that the rock of Oki-no-Tori (Oki-no Tori-shima) fulfills the conditions of an island under Article 121(1) of the UNCLOS, and that it is not a rock but an island. The representative also pointed out that Article 121(3) is not a provision on islands but on rocks. Furthermore, there is no definition of rocks in the UNCLOS, even from the point of view of state practice, this article does not constitute a basis on which the EEZ and continental shelf cannot be possessed in respect of a particular geography.[45] The Government of Japan continues to hold this position, from which it can be seen that paragraphs 1 and 3 of Article 121 of the UNCLOS are treated and understood separately. Such an understanding is the essential origin of the disagreement in the international community and is contrary to the viewpoint derived from the textual

[44] See [Japanese] Hayashi, Moritaka. 2008. *The shaping and issues of the modern law of the sea.* Tokyo: Shinzansha Publishing. p. 187. See also Fusillo, M. S. 1978–79. The legal regime of uninhabited "rocks" lacking an economic life of their own, *Italian Yearbook of International Law* 4: 51; Anderson, D. H. 1997. British accession to the UN Convention on the Law of the Sea, *International & Comparative Law Quarterly* 46: 761; Charney, J. 1999. Rocks that cannot sustain human habitation, *American Journal of International Law* 93: 864.

[45] See Official website of the House of Representatives of Japan, http://www.shugiin.go.jp/index.nsf/htm/index_kaigiroku.htm, accessed December 16, 2009.

interpretation of the regime of islands and to the legislative purpose of the regime of islands of the UNCLOS.

Paragraphs 1–3 of Article 121 of the UNCLOS are to be treated as a whole, and paragraph 3, in particular, is a constraint on paragraph 2. Therefore, Japan's attempt to separate paragraphs 1 and 3 and to ignore the role of paragraph 3 is not acceptable to the international community.

5.2.3 Connotation Analysis of Relevant Terms Concerning Constitutive Elements of Islands and Rocks

Because the regime of islands of the UNCLOS does not positively define the concept of rocks, some States have taken advantage of the ambiguity to exercise their rights under the UNCLOS, as in the case of Japan's position and practice with regard to the rock of Oki-no-Tori (Oki-no Tori-shima) in its submission on the outer continental shelf.

Because Article 121(1) and (3) of the UNCLOS are dealt with as a whole, how can one determine whether an island or a rock? To determine the legal status of an island or a rock, it is necessary to define the legal elements that constitute a rock. The key is to define the meaning of the terms used to determine rocks, that is, to define what is a rock, what are the specific contents of human habitation or economic life of its own, what is a naturally formed area of land, and so on, so as to determine whether it is an island or a rock.

5.2.3.1 The Concept and Problems of Rocks

As mentioned above, although elements such as the size and the number of the population are not considered in the definition of islands in Article 121(3) of the UNCLOS, and rocks are mostly considered to be treated as special forms of islands, the issue of the size of islands has indirectly survived in the UNCLOS. Meanwhile, at the Third UN Conference on the Law of the Sea, there was a proposal to utilize the criteria of size of an island and geologically solid characteristics to differentiate between islands and rocks. However, given that even large islands consisting of geologically solid rocky material may be recognized as rocks and not have EEZs and continental shelves. On the contrary, small islands formed mainly of earth and sand may be treated as islands, which would lead to unfair results. Thus, on the grounds that the identification is not based on the geological formation process, the terms of rocks are finally retained in the provisions of the Convention without adding any other elements.[46] Paragraph 3, which stipulates that rocks that do not satisfy

[46] See [Japanese] Kuribayashi, Tadao. 1994. The regime of islands, in Studies on the Domestic Legal System on the Occasion of the Conclusion of the New Convention on the Law of the Sea, Internal Materials. Oceanographic Society of Japan, ed. pp. 107–126.

the requirements of economic life, etc., cannot be granted an EEZ or continental shelf, partly reflects the views of these countries. Therefore, rocks in the legal sense within the regime of islands of the UNCLOS are generally defined independently of their size and geological characteristics, and even sandcays, atolls, etc., are mostly considered to be rocks, which should be subject to the element of being above water at high tide. If a rock is only above the water at low tide and is submerged at high tide, it is recognized as a low-tide elevation. "Where a low-tide elevation is situated wholly or partly at a distance not exceeding the breadth of the territorial sea from the mainland or an island, the low-water line on that elevation may be used as the baseline for measuring the breadth of the territorial sea." Otherwise, the low-tide elevation does not have a territorial sea of its own.[47]

In addition, there is no record of the definition of rocks and no discussion of it at the Third UN Conference on the Law of the Sea, so there is no reference to the definition of rocks in the UNCLOS.[48] For this reason, the definition of rocks is subject to state practice.

In state practice, there are some states treating isolated features far offshore as islands and creating EEZs without regard to their geological characteristics. For example, the Venezuelan island of Abes, located in the Caribbean Sea, consists of sand and reefs and is about 600 m long and about 30 m wide at its narrowest point; the volcanic island of Jan Mayen, with an area of about 373 square kilometers, is located in Norway near England and Scotland; the French-occupied Clipperton Island, about 670 nautical miles off the coast of Mexico and located in the Pacific Ocean, is made up of coral reefs and volcanic rocks, and has an area of about 1.6 square kilometers. These countries have set up EEZs around these islands.[49] In contrast, some countries have not established EEZs on rocks that are apparently composed only of rocky blocks. For example, Mexico has not established the EEZ around the rock of Alijos, which is located in the northern Revillagigedo Archipelago[50]; according to the Fishery Waters Act in 1976, the UK has established fishery waters around the Rockall (with an area of about 624 square meters), which is located about 200 nautical miles off the coast of England. As part of the fishery sea area, this practice was opposed by Denmark, Finland, and other countries because they considered that these so-called islands were rocks and could not claim the EEZ (fishery waters). For this reason, the

[47] For example, Article 13(1) of the Convention provides that "1. Where a low-tide elevation is situated wholly or partly at a distance not exceeding the breadth of the territorial sea from the mainland or an island, the low-water line on that elevation may be used as the baseline for measuring the breadth of the territorial sea. 2. Where a low-tide elevation is wholly situated at a distance exceeding the breadth of the territorial sea from the mainland or an island, it has no territorial sea of its own."

[48] [Japanese] Kuribayashi, Tadao. 2007. The island system and the legal status of Okinotorishima, in *Report on the Study of the Maintenance and Regeneration of Okinotorishima*, ed, Japan Foundation for Marine Policy Studies. pp. 64–65.

[49] [Japanese] Hayashi, Moritaka. 2008. *The shaping and issues of the modern law of the sea*, Tokyo: Shinzansha Publishing. pp. 190–191.

[50] [Japanese] Kagami, Yasuhiko. 2006. The United Nations Convention on the Law of the Sea as a method for sustainable development: A discussion of Article 121(3), in *Report on the Study of the Regeneration of Okinotorishima (2005)*, ed, Japan Ocean Policy Research Foundation. p. 115.

UK made the following declaration when it acceded to the UNCLOS in 1997: The Rockall could not be a valid basis for determining the boundary of the UK's fishery waters under Article 121(3) of the UNCLOS, and its limits had to be reconsidered. Because then, the UK has amended the Fisheries Waters Act in 1976 to fully satisfy the elements of Article 121 of the UNCLOS.[51]

Thus, even in state practice, there are different opinions and practices regarding the status and role of rocks, and a unified approach has not yet been formed. The identification of rocks and islands continues to be subject to state practice and the supplementation of new international rules, including the modification of the regime of islands of the UNCLOS and adding content of the definition of rocks.

5.2.3.2 The Relationship and Connotation of Maintenance of Human Habitation or Economic Life

Given Article 121(3) of the UNCLOS, the following issues should be clarified with regard to its interpretation or identification:

First, the relationship between human habitation and economic life. Article 121(3) of the UNCLOS contains two elements, "human habitation" and "economic life," which are connected by "or," meaning that as long as one element is met, the rock cannot claim the EEZ and continental shelf. In other words, as long as one element is met, the rock will be treated as an island in general. In contrast, there is also the view that the aforementioned two elements should be considered together (that they should be considered as a whole, cannot be separated, and must be satisfied at the same time). Some scholars advocate that the requirement that there must be a community of people utilizing the ocean space should be added to be able to claim the EEZ and continental shelf.[52] These views, however, which strictly interpret Article 121(3) of the UNCLOS, are in the minority. It should be added that when this article was being drafted at the Third UN Conference on the Law of the Sea, a Danish proposal to use the word "and" was quickly rejected during the negotiations, and the word "or" was used as the term for discussion and utilization.[53] Therefore, the negotiations on the formulation of the UNCLOS also proved that the relationship between human habitation and economic life should be considered separately, rather than as the same element. This view was also supported by the Conciliation Commission between Ireland and Norway in the case concerning the Delimitation of the Continental Shelf in respect of Jan Mayen Island in 1981. The case was summarized as follows: there was no settled population on Jan Mayen, there were only a few dozen persons on the island for meteorological observations and as a permanent base under the jurisdiction

[51] See Anderson, D. H. 1997. British accession to the UN Convention on the Law of the Sea, *International & Comparative Law Quarterly* 46: 778–779.

[52] See Van Dyke, J., J. Morgan, J. Gurish. 1988. The exclusive economic zone of the Northwestern Hawaiian Islands: When do uninhabited islands generate an EEZ? *San Diego Law Review* 25: 437–438.

[53] See Charney, J. 1999. Rocks that cannot sustain human habitation, *American Journal of International Law* 93: 868.

of the Ministry of Defense, and there were no economic activities on the island. In its report and recommendations of 1981, the Conciliation Commission rejected the claims of Ireland (which considered the island to be a rock) and found that Jan Mayen was subject to the application of Article 121(1) and (2) of the UNCLOS which was being drafted at the time and had an EEZ and a continental shelf.[54]

Second, regarding the meaning of human habitation. From the literal understanding of the provisions of the Convention, it can be considered that "human habitation" is not limited to the current situation. If materials that can sustain human habitation even in the future can be provided, Article 121(3) of the Convention cannot be applied, and exclusive economic zones and continental shelves can be claimed, but the premise is that evidence of the possibility of human habitation now or in the future must be provided.[55]

As mentioned above, scholars who argue that the two elements of Article 121(3) of the UNCLOS should be taken as a whole, consider that in order to meet the requirements for human habitation, there must be a certain size and organized community on or near the rocks. This view is based on the fact that such a community is indispensable for the continuation of economic life. If the two elements of Article 121(3) of the UNCLOS are regarded as separate views as a general statement, there is also a certain degree of irrationality.[56] From a practical point of view, the Conciliation Commission considered that Jan Mayen did not fall within the category of rocks under Article 121(3) but the Commission did not make a specific determination as to whether it fulfilled the element of "human habitation." The Clipperton Island case is another one related to human habitation. This is an isolated French-occupied island approximately 670 nautical miles off the coast of Mexico that was inhabited from 1892 to 1917 by a few plant-gatherers who lived on externally supplied food and water.[57] For this reason, in 1978, while the UNCLOS draft was under consideration, France established an EEZ around the island. At the same time, France, believing that the island did not meet the requirements for sustaining economic life, built coastguard facilities (a radar base and a base for marine scientific surveys) and stationed military personnel and a number of scientists on the island.[58]

These cases illustrate that, in theory and practice, there is uncertainty about the elements of human habitation that require continued attention.

---

[54] See Conciliation Commission on the Continental Shelf between Iceland and Jan Mayan: Report and Recommendations to the Governments of Iceland and Norway. 1981. *International Legal Materials* 20: 803–804.

[55] See Kwiatkowska, B., A. H. A. Soons. 1990. Entitlement to maritime areas of rocks which cannot sustain human habitation or economic life of their own, *Netherlands Yearbook of International Law* 21: 160, 163, and 166.

[56] See [Japanese] Hayashi, Moritaka. 2008. *The shaping and issues of the modern law of the sea.* Tokyo: Shinzansha Publishing. pp. 193–194.

[57] See [Japanese] Yamamoto, Sōji. 1997. *Law of the Sea.* Tokyo: Sanseido. pp. 96–98.

[58] See [Japanese] Kagami, Yasuhiko. 2006. The United Nations Convention on the Law of the Sea as a method for sustainable development: A discussion of Article 121(3), in *Report on the Study of the Regeneration of Okinotorishima (2005)*, ed, Japan Ocean Policy Research Foundation. p. 114.

Third, the meaning of economic life. That is, what is meant by economic life that cannot sustain itself? Economic life naturally includes the exploitation of natural resources and other productive activities. Activities such as lighthouses and other navigational support facilities that contribute to maritime transportation, fishery activities, and recreational industries are generally considered to be part of "economic activities." Meanwhile, depending on the geographical location, there are cases where the bases of commercial satellites are utilized for economic activities.[59]

However, unmanned lighthouses and communication facilities can be installed even on very small rocks. Some scholars have argued that their presence is not enough to satisfy the elements of economic life but that the elements of commercial or productive activities must also be satisfied.[60] Even though weather observation and communication facilities are not generally commercial activities, if their activities and data are publicized through the Internet, for example, they may become widely used, and economic activities or elements of economic life may emerge or be present. In this sense, it would be difficult to distinguish them from "economic life" in current society.

Another issue is that of the maintenance and utilization of unmanned facilities and structures (or buildings) on rocks for economic purposes through remote control. With developments in science and technology, this type of maintenance and utilization may increase in the future, and it has been argued that these activities should be included in "economic life."[61]

Moreover, some scholars have suggested that the establishment of marine protected areas and nature reserves in the vicinity of rocks satisfies the element of "economic life."[62] In this regard, the author believes that although the above measures can generate various economic benefits, such as increasing fish stocks, expanding income from ecotourism, developing and selling coral products, and reducing the health effects of pollution, there is no doubt that these activities will ultimately satisfy the element of "economic life." In state practice, there have been cases where small maritime features have been designated as nature reserves or specially protected areas, such as Abes Island in Venezuela and the Hawaiian Islands in the northwestern part of the U.S. However, if specific activities such as those mentioned above (the development and sale of coral products, ecotourism, etc.) are not recognized as economic activities, the mere establishment of nature reserves or specially protected areas cannot directly and automatically be linked to "economic life" as stipulated in Article 121(3). Therefore, activities such as the establishment

[59] See Brown, E. D. 1994. *The International Law of the Sea, Vol. I*. Aldershot: Dartmouth Publishing. p. 150; Charney, J. 1999. Rocks that cannot sustain human habitation, *American Journal International Law* 93: 871.

[60] See [Japanese] Hayashi, Moritaka. 2008. *The shaping and issues of the modern law of the sea*. Tokyo: Shinzansha. p. 195.

[61] See Kwiatkowska, B., A. H. A Soons. 1990. Entitlement to maritime areas of rocks which cannot sustain human habitation or economic life of their own, *Netherlands Yearbook of International Law* 21: 164–146.

[62] See [Japanese] Hayashi, Moritaka. 2008. *The shaping and issues of the modern law of the sea*. Tokyo: Shinzansha. p. 195.

of nature reserves or marine protected areas should be judged on a case-by-case basis, including the practices of the majority of states, to develop a consensus in the international community that these activities satisfy the criteria for "economic life." In the present circumstances, however, such a consensus remains difficult to achieve.

In addition, a view was expressed that the "economic life" of a rock should not be limited to economic activities on the land itself but should also include economic activities within its territorial sea. As even a rock that cannot sustain its own economic life should have the territorial sea, activities such as fisheries conservation, management activities, and mineral resources exploitation are *ipso facto* part of the "economic life" provided for in Article 121(3). Conversely, economic activities outside the territorial sea of rock do not fall within the "economic life" mentioned in the article.

Most states today have established EEZs and continental shelves on uninhabited islands far from their coasts by enacting domestic laws and are now engaged in activities to exploit oil and other mineral and biological resources in their vicinity (not in their territorial waters, but mainly in their EEZs and continental shelves).[63]

Finally, there is the question of the temporal scope of "unsustainability." As noted above, the meaning of "unsustainable" in Article 121(3) of the UNCLOS encompasses not only the present state of affairs but also those in the future. This view has been confirmed in practice, albeit only to a certain extent. For example, on the uninhabited Norwegian island of Abel, which covers an area of approximately 13.2 square kilometers, hunting polar bears is prohibited by the Government. The Norwegian Supreme Court stated in 1996 that a large amount of hunting could be maintained if not prohibited on the island, and for that reason, ruled that the island was not a rock but rather an island for the purposes of Article 121(3) of the UNCLOS.[64]

Fourth, the meaning of "of their own" in the context of economic life of their own. The meaning of "of their own" in Article 121 (3) of the Convention regarding "economic life of its own" is uncertain whether it refers to activities that are only dependent on the resources of the rocks to maintain themselves, or whether it includes maintaining their own economic life through external support. During the drafting of the provision, there were suggestions of the need for self-sufficiency, some scholars emphasized the need for a stable and organized community but pointed out that self-sufficiency was not entirely necessary.[65]

If the rock itself includes its territorial waters and has economic value, such as fishery resources, oil, and gas, tourism resources, and power generation resources such as wind and seawater temperature differences, and if the rock has suitable conditions as a satellite base, it can also generate economic value. Therefore, if the development and utilization of these resources are successful, as long as necessary

[63] See [Japanese] Hayashi, Moritaka. 2008. *The shaping and issues of the modern law of the sea*. Tokyo: Shinzansha. p. 196.

[64] Oude Elferink, A. 2000. Is it either necessary or possible to clarify the provision on rocks of Article 121 (3) of the Law of the Sea Convention? in *Borderlands under Stress*, eds, M. A Pratt, J. A. Brown, Hague: Kluwer Law International. p. 392.

[65] See [Japanese] Hayashi, Moritaka. 2008. *The shaping and issues of the modern law of the sea*. Tokyo: Shinzansha. p. 197.

items are purchased from outside, their economic activities can be supported, thus fully maintaining economic life.

The crux is what level of external support can be considered as the economic life of "their own". It is well-known that, even in some areas of the mainland, if there were no external support, it would be nearly impossible to maintain economic activities in modern society. Thus, it is unreasonable and unjustified to require an isolated island to satisfy these requirements of self-sufficient economic activities. Thus, what form and degree of support is reasonable? The international community does not have clear criteria for this. Generally speaking, when relying on external support, the greater the external dependence of a rock, the more difficult it will be to develop and sustain its own activities. However, this is not an absolute rule, as the situation may change significantly with an increase in the variety of activities possible and further developments in science and technology, which may change the general viewpoint mentioned above. Therefore, the degree of dependence on external support and the mode of support can only be judged by considering the country's future practices and in the light of various circumstances.

5.2.3.3 Meaning of a Naturally Formed Area of Land

Article 121(1) of the UNCLOS provides that an island is "a naturally formed area of land, surrounded by water, which is above water at high tide." As rocks in Article 121(3) are classified as a type of island, the elements of an island should also apply. That is, rocks should also be naturally formed area of land. What does a naturally formed area of land mean? As we all know, constructions such as lighthouses and platforms built on low-tide elevations are artificial installations or structures. It is obvious that they are not naturally formed. Therefore, it is not possible to establish the territorial sea around them.[66]

From the content of this article, it is not clear what is meant by a naturally formed area of land. That is, it is unclear whether it is concerned with the material that forms or expands the land or if it seeks to exclude the engagement (or participation) of human activities in the process of formation. There are two interpretations of this among the international community.[67] To facilitate clarifications, the author will refer to them as the two-element and one-element theories.

The two-element theory argues that a naturally formed area of land should emphasize the natural properties of the formative materials and process.

Meanwhile, the one-element theory is divided into two categories, emphasizing the material elements theory and the process elements theory. According to theorists of the material elements, if natural materials such as coral reefs, soil, and sand are used to fill in the low-tide elevation and create land that is a naturally formed area of land, the natural formation element is considered to have been met. However, theorists of

---

[66] See Articles 60 and 80 of the UNCLOS.

[67] [Japanese] Yamamoto, Sōji. 1997. *Law of the sea*. Tokyo: Sanseido. pp. 83–85; O'Connell, D. P. 1982. *The International Law of the Sea. Vol. I*. Oxford: Clarendon Press. p. 196.

the process elements argue that the formed area of land based on the aforementioned materials cannot be treated as a new island. Those who hold this view do not answer whether they completely exclude artificial intervention or agree that it can still be considered a naturally formed area of land because artificial intervention promotes natural processes in the land area. For example, if a small area of dry land emerges naturally and is kept dry by artificial means, or if a rock submerged in the water at full tide is kept dry by artificial means and is kept above the water, at this time, it cannot be said that they are completely unnaturally formed land areas, of course, it cannot be said that they are completely naturally formed land areas.

Therefore, the international community has not developed a uniform interpretation of what constitutes a naturally formed area of land.

5.2.4 *Some Suggestions to Improve the Regime of Islands*

As can be seen from the above analysis, the international community has different interpretations of and disputes over the regime of islands of the UNCLOS (Article 121), with a focus on the status of islands and rocks. However, the international community generally agrees that Article 121(1)–(3) of the UNCLOS should be recognized and understood as a whole, which is in line with the development of the regime of islands and the purpose of the formulation of the regime of islands in the UNCLOS. Even so, there continues to be ambiguity in the terminology, especially in Article 121(3).

To enable the international community to harmonize its knowledge and understanding of Article 121 of the UNCLOS, consideration needs to be given to amending and improving the regime on islands, including a definition of rocks. The amendment of Article 312 of the UNCLOS, however, requires consensus, which cannot be achieved overnight.[68] In accordance with Article 313, which provides for amendments through the simplified procedure, if a state proposes to amend the UNCLOS by means of the simplified procedure such as a written communication addressed to the UN Secretary-General, the proposal shall be deemed not to have been adopted if a state objects to the proposed amendment or to the proposal for adoption of the amendment using the simplified procedure.[69] Therefore, it would be rather difficult to improve the Convention's regime of islands.

---

[68] For example, Article 312 of the UNCLOS provides that, "After the expiry of a period of 10 years from the date of entry into force of this Convention, a State Party may, by written communication addressed to the Secretary-General of the United Nations, propose specific amendments to this Convention, other than those relating to activities in the Area, and request the convening of a conference to consider such proposed amendments. The Secretary-General shall circulate such communication to all States Parties. If, within 12 months from the date of the circulation of the communication, not less than one half of the States Parties reply favorably to the request, the Secretary-General shall convene the conference."

[69] For example, Article 313 of the UNCLOS provides that "A State Party may, by written communication addressed to the Secretary-General of the United Nations, propose an amendment to this

In the absence of any modification of the Convention's regime of islands or a unified consensus among the international community on the status of islands and rocks, the relevant terms of the regime of islands should be strictly interpreted to avoid expansions of interpretations that would jeopardize the regime of the high seas and of the Area. This is in line with the original intention and purpose of the regime of islands established by the Convention, especially the main purpose of paragraph 3, which is to deny the right of certain rocks to enjoy EEZs and continental shelves, so as not to lose the restrictive meaning of paragraph 2. This is also reflected in Article 300 of the UNCLOS, which requires states to fulfill their obligations in good faith and refrain from abusing their rights.[70] The so-called strict interpretation of rocks is mainly reflected in the following aspects:

(1) Rocks are a special form of island that must be naturally formed areas of land emphasizing the natural properties of the constituent materials and processes.
(2) Rocks must be capable of sustaining human habitation for a significant period of time.
(3) The resources required by the rocks to sustain an economic life of their own should be limited to those produced by the rocks themselves and should not include resources imported from within their territorial waters or from outside, as this may lead to a tendency toward abuse of that right.
(4) The exploitation of the resources of the rocks must be consistent with economic principles and the protection of the marine environment. This is because some states will try to exploit the resources of the rocks to make them compatible with the elements of "economic life" without respecting the general principles of economic exploitation and polluting the marine environment in contravention of the obligations of states to protect and preserve the marine environment.

From the above analysis, Japan's position and approach to the rock of Oki-no-Tori (Oki-no Tori-shima) issue cannot be recognized by the international community, and its attempts to expand the area of the sea and acquire more marine resources cannot be accepted. The major insurmountable problems of the rock of Oki-no-Tori (Oki-no Tori-shima) issue are as follows.

First, claiming the EEZ and continental shelf based on the rock of Oki-no-Tori violates the principle of equity. This is because the area of the EEZ (approximately 420,000 square kilometers) claimed on the basis of the rock of Oki-no-Tori (Oki-no Tori-shima) far exceeds the actual area of the rock of Oki-no-Tori (Oki-no Tori-shima) and seriously jeopardizes the interests of other countries with regard to, *inter*

Convention, other than an amendment relating to activities in the Area, to be adopted by the simplified procedure set forth in this article without convening a conference. If, within a period of 12 months from the date of the circulation of the communication, a State Party objects to the proposed amendment or to the proposal for its adoption by the simplified procedure, the amendment shall be considered rejected."

[70] For example, Article 300 of the UNCLOS provides that "States Parties shall fulfil in good faith the obligations assumed under this Convention and shall exercise the rights, jurisdiction and freedoms recognized in this Convention in a manner which would not constitute an abuse of right."

alia, navigational and surveying activities in this area, and undermines the regime of the Area in a manner that is grossly contrary to the principle of equity.

Second, the artificial processing of the rock of the Oki-no-Tori (Oki-no Tori-shima) fortification fails to meet the requirements of a naturally formed area of land. Although the Government of Japan has invested heavily in strengthening the protection of the rock of Oki-no-Tori (Oki-no Tori-shima) including the construction of titanium nets and dykes to prevent it from sinking underwater, the introduction of such artificial methods does not change the fact that it is not a naturally formed area of land. In other words, the rock of Oki-no-Tori (Oki-no Tori-shima) remains a rock and cannot become an island.[71]

Third, Japan's actions have damaged and polluted the marine environment. Japan has attempted to cultivate suitable conditions for the growth of corals by investigating the living environment in the waters around the rock of Oki-no-Tori (Oki-no Tori-shima) and attempting to construct islands using coral fragments and foraminiferal shells to satisfy the requirements for economic life. Such acts of cultivating and propagating corals are detrimental to the marine environment and cause pollution. Article 192 of the UNCLOS stipulates that states have the obligation to protect and preserve the marine environment. "Pollution of the marine environment" is defined in Article 1(1) of the UNCLOS as "the introduction by man, directly or indirectly, of substances or energy into the marine environment, including estuaries, which results or is likely to result in such deleterious effects as harm to living resources and marine life, hazards to human health, hindrance to marine activities, including fishing and other legitimate uses of the sea, impairment of quality for use of sea water and reduction of amenities."

5.3 The Impact of the SCS Arbitration on the Law of the Sea

The SCS has an important geopolitical and strategic position due to its spatial location and geographical endowment, making the region significant in international trade. Notably, the *SCS* Arbitration was unilaterally filed by the Philippines on January 22, 2013, under Articles 286 and 287 and Annex VII of the UNCLOS. The Arbitral Tribunal ignored the position of the Chinese Government (nonacceptance and nonrecognition), continued the arbitration proceedings, and issued the ruling on jurisdiction and admissibility on October 29, 2015, and the final award on July 12, 2016. These have all attracted great attention from the international community.

The author argues that the Philippines ignored the Chinese Government's opposition and unilaterally filed the *SCS* Arbitration. The Arbitral Tribunal pushed forward the arbitration process by taking advantage of its duties and competencies as well as

[71] For Japan's specific policies and measures against Okinotori, see Yongming, Jin. 2010. Japan's policies and measures against okinotori and our countermeasures suggestions, *Shanghai Law Studies* 3: 22–27.

the institutional weaknesses of the UNCLOS system. Exceeding and expanding its own jurisdiction, the Arbitral Tribunal issued a flawed and illegal award regarding the facts and application of the law, making the SCS issue more complicated and difficult to settle. Furthermore, the award does not promote the development of the law of the sea, rendering the system chaotic, damaged, and under siege. It poses a major challenge to the international ocean order, severely undermining the basic functions of international arbitration institutions.

5.3.1 The SCS Arbitration Cannot Resolve the SCS Disputes

Dispute resolution is a basic function of international adjudication or arbitration. The entire submission by the Philippines contains neither disputes concerning the interpretation or application of the UNCLOS nor real disputes between China and the Philippines. Thus, the SCS disputes, including core and incidental disputes between China and the Philippines, cannot be fundamentally solved.

The core disputes between China and the Philippines in the SCS are territorial disputes over some maritime features in the Nansha Qundao and the ensuing sea delimitation. According to Article 288 of the UNCLOS and China's optional exceptions declaration to the UN Secretary-General in August 2006, however, in the case of no special agreement between two states, the Arbitral Tribunal has no jurisdiction over these disputes, i.e., no competence to resolve core disputes in the SCS.

Do the matters submitted to arbitration by the Philippines, therefore, constitute real disputes between China and the Philippines? Can the Arbitral Tribunal's award resolve the incidental disputes between China and the Philippines in the SCS?

In light of the Chinese government's position paper on matter of jurisdiction in SCS Arbitration initiated by the Philippines (hereinafter referred to as "China's Position Paper"), the Philippines' 15 claims can be primarily summarized into three categories.[72] First, China's assertion of the "historic rights" to the waters, sea-bed and subsoil within the "nine-dash line" (i.e., China's dotted line in the SCS) beyond the limits of its entitlements under the Convention is inconsistent with the Convention Second, China's claim to entitlements of 200 nautical miles and more, based on certain rocks, low-tide elevations and submerged features in the SCS, is inconsistent with the Convention. Third, China's assertion and exercise of rights in the SCS have unlawfully interfered with the sovereign rights, jurisdiction, and rights and freedom of navigation that the Philippines enjoys and exercises under the Convention.[73]

---

[72] See Position Paper of the Government of the People's Republic of China on the matter of jurisdiction in the South China Sea Arbitration initiated by the Republic of the Philippines, http://www.gov.cn/xinwen/2014-12/07/content_2787663.htm (Accessed on December 8, 2014).

[73] See China's Position Paper, para. 8.

5.3.1.1 There is no Dispute Over the Status and Nature of Maritime Features in the Nansha Qundao

Regarding the maritime features in the Nansha Qundao, the Arbitral Tribunal holds that human habitation is not a transient residence but requires the residence of a stable community of people. However, in the Nansha Qundao, there is no indication that a stable community of people ever developed on these islands. The Arbitral Tribunal declared that all high-tide features in the Nansha Qundao (including Taiping Dao, Zhongye Dao, Xiyue Dao, Nanwei Dao, Nanzi Dao, and Beizi Dao) cannot sustain human habitation or economic life of their own and, therefore, that they are rocks within the meaning of Article 121(3) of the UNCLOS and unable to generate an EEZ or continental shelf.[74]

Although the Arbitral Tribunal has jurisdiction over the interpretation or application of the UNCLOS, it does not own the legislative function. Nevertheless, the Arbitration Tribunal adopted a strict interpretation of the regime of islands, constituting a new kind of legislation and, thus, exceeding its own jurisdiction and rendering the arbitral award illegal and invalid. Accordingly, such a strict interpretation of the regime of islands by the Arbitral Tribunal is not accepted by the international community and subsequent cases. It does not have a positive impact on the development of the law of the sea and, in fact, challenges the system and authority thereof.[75]

In fact, before deciding these matters, the Arbitral Tribunal should first determine territorial sovereignty over relevant maritime features and complete the delimitation of relevant maritime zones. Without determining the ownership of sovereignty over relevant maritime features, the Philippines requires that China's maritime entitlements in the SCS must be determined by provisions of the UNCLOS. By submitting a series of arbitration requests, the Philippines violated general international law and international judicial practice in the settlement of international maritime disputes. The Arbitral Tribunal's ruling on any submissions made by the Philippines must determine, directly or indirectly, the sovereignty over relevant maritime features

[74] See In the Matter of the South China Sea Arbitration before an Arbitral Tribunal Constituted under Annex VII to the 1982 United Nations Convention on the Law of the Sea between the Republic of the Philippines and the People's Republic of China Award, July 12, 2016. pp. 252–260, paras. 618, 621, 625, and 646.

[75] The Arbitration Tribunal's strict interpretation of the regime of islands is reflected in the following ways. First, to "sustain" means to provide that which is necessary to keep humans alive and healthy over a continuous period of time, according to a set standard. Second, in connection with economic life, to "sustain" means to provide that which is necessary not only to commence but also to continue an activity over a period of time in a way that remains viable. Third, the presence of a small number of persons does not constitute permanent or habitual residence and does not equate to habitation. Rather, sustained human habitation would require that the feature be able to support, maintain, and provide food, water, and shelter to humans and enable them to reside there permanently or habitually over an extended period of time. Fourth, for economic activity to constitute the economic life of a feature, the resources on which the economic activity revolves must be local and not imported. See *In the Matter of the South China Sea Arbitration before an Arbitral Tribunal Constituted under Annex VII to the 1982 UNCLOS between the Republic of the Philippines and the People's Republic of China Award*, July 12, 2016. pp. 252–260, paras. 487, 489–490, and 500.

involved in this case and other maritime features in the SCS. Simultaneously, this ruling will generate maritime delimitation in practice. The Chinese Government, therefore, argues that the Arbitral Tribunal clearly has no jurisdiction over this case.[76] Additionally, even if the Arbitral Tribunal has issued the award, it cannot settle the core disputes in the SCS.

In the meantime, in terms of the structure of the Convention's regime of islands, paragraph 1 to paragraph 3 of Article 121 are all provisions on the regime of islands, as follows: Paragraph 1 points to islands in a broad sense; that is, the UNCLOS stipulates a broad concept of islands. Paragraph 2 concerns the rules of the island in a general sense. Paragraph 3 is about rocks that are not defined directly from the concept of rocks but from the perspective of their effect, meaning, like islands, rocks that can sustain human habitation or economic life of their own can claim the EEZ and continental shelf. Rocks have two categories: those that can claim the EEZ and continental shelf and those that cannot. At the same time, Paragraph 3 is a restriction on paragraph 2 and essentially states that not all rocks can claim the EEZ and continental shelf. Paragraphs 1–3 of Article 121 in the UNCLOS clearly have different features and constitute an integral entirety of the regime of islands. The main reason for the vagueness of paragraph 3 under Article 121 is the lack of a unified definition of rocks, including human habitation and economic life of their own, which can be proved by different opinions on the regime of islands in the discussion of the UNCLOS in the Third United Nations Conference on the Law of the Sea.[77]

In view of the complexity of the regime of islands and the diversity of the types of islands and rocks, both the ICJ and the ITLOS have avoided the issue of determining the legal status and nature of maritime features.[78] Although the Arbitral Tribunal has jurisdiction over the interpretation or application of the UNCLOS, China has not thus far ascertained or clarified the nature of each maritime feature at issue and claims maritime entitlements based on the archipelago as a unit. For example, on May 7, 2009, the Permanent Mission of China to the UN submitted a note verbale to the UN Secretary-General with reference to the Joint Submission by Malaysia and Vietnam and individual Submission by Vietnam to the CLCS concerning the outer limits of the continental shelf beyond 200 nautical miles. China stated its position as follows: China has indisputable sovereignty over the Nanhai Zhudao and the adjacent waters and enjoys sovereign rights and jurisdiction over the relevant waters and the seabed

[76] See China's Position Paper, paras. 26–29.

[77] See Yongming, Jin. 2010. Analysis of the legal elements of islands and reefs—from the perspective of the Okinotoro problem, *Political Science and Law* 12: 100–101. See also *In the Matter of the South China Sea Arbitration before an Arbitral Tribunal Constituted under Annex VII to the 1982 UNCLOS between the Republic of the Philippines and the People's Republic of China Award*, 2016. pp. 252–260, paras. 522, 540–551.

[78] See Keyuan, Zou. 2015. The impact of artificial islands on territorial disputes over the South China Sea: A dilemma for international law, *Asia-Pacific Security and Maritime Study* 3: 10.

and subsoil thereof. China's position is widely known by the international community.[79] The legal status of maritime features in the Nansha Qundao, especially those occupied by China, therefore, is not the real dispute between China and the Philippines. A dispute refers to a disagreement on the point of law or fact, a conflict of legal views or interests between two parties, that is, two parties' competing arguments.[80] As far as the legal status or nature of the maritime features in the Nansha Qundao, especially those occupied by China, they are not real disputes and, therefore, cannot be submitted for arbitration because China has neither clarified their nature and legal status nor claimed corresponding maritime zones and entitlements on the basis of individual maritime features.

5.3.1.2 Submissions for Arbitration Fall Within Subject Matter Excluded by the Declaration Filed by China and Thus Are Non-Arbitrable

One of the features of the Convention's system (the UNCLOS, its nine annexes, and two implementation agreements) is a comprehensive, systematic dispute settlement mechanism. This mechanism not only eliminated the defects of separately stipulating the dispute settlement mechanism in four Geneva Conventions on the Law of the Sea in 1958 but also established a specific dispute settlement body, ITLOS. Meanwhile, distinct methods of settlement are provided for different disputes,[81] a key point being that States shall settle any dispute between them by peaceful means. The UNCLOS respects agreed-upon peaceful dispute settlement mechanisms and endows party the right to choose the methods in accordance with the principle of national sovereign equality.[82] Its main characteristics are as follows:

First, there are various and different provisions in terms of types of disputes. General maritime disputes shall be governed by Articles 279 to 299 under Part XV. International seabed disputes shall be handled by Section 5 of Part XV (Articles 186 to 191). Disputes relating to marine scientific research shall be handled by Section 6

---

[79] See The note verbale Addressed to the Secretary-General of the United Nations by China concerning Relevant Countries' Application for Outer Continental Shelf and Preliminary Information. 2011. Research Group of the China Institute for Marine Affairs of the State Oceanic Administration. *Research Report of Marine Development of China*. Beijing: Ocean Press. 2011. pp. 593–598.

[80] See PCIJ, Series A, No.2, p. 11. For details of the Judgment of the *Right of Passage over Indian Territory* of International Court of Justice, see ICJ Reports of 1960, p. 34. For details of the Judgment of *El Salvador v. Honduras concerning the Land, Island and Maritime Frontier Dispute*, see ICJ Reports of 1992, p. 555, para. 326.

[81] Collier, John., Vaughan Lowe. 2000. *The Settlement of Disputes in International Law*. Oxford: Oxford University Press. p. 84.

[82] Carnegie, A. R. 1979. The Law of the Sea Tribunal, *International and Comparative Law Quarterly* 28(4): 669–684.

(Article 264) of Part XIII. Part XV includes different provisions based on the dispute's distinct nature.[83]

Second, the UNCLOS has provided for both optional and compulsory procedures. Optional procedures are based on methods provided in Article 33 of the UN Charter (Article 297). Parties thus have an obligation to settle disputes by peaceful means and shall seek a solution by the means indicated in Article 33(1) of the UN Charter. If the state parties to a dispute have agreed to resolve their dispute through an agreement (regional or bilateral), such agreement shall prevail. Meanwhile, compulsory procedures under Part XV apply only where no settlement has been reached by recourse to peaceful means chosen by the parties, and the agreement does not exclude any further procedure (Article 280, Article 281(1)); that is, if the state parties continue diplomatic negotiations or consultations, compulsory procedures cannot be applied. Simultaneously, if any party initiates compulsory arbitration procedures, it shall submit evidence to prove that the dispute cannot be resolved by peaceful means prescribed in the agreement.[84]

Third, there are restrictions on the application of compulsory procedures. Although the UNCLOS provides multiple means of such procedures, their fundamental basis relies on optional declarations of state parties to the dispute and limits the compulsory jurisdiction of an international court or tribunal (Articles 297–298). Thus, many defensive provisions in Part XV exclude the application of compulsory procedures, meaning it is not a thorough system of compulsory dispute settlement.[85]

To this end, on August 25, 2006, China submitted a written declaration to the UN Secretary-General in accordance with Article 298 of the UNCLOS, which stated that China does not accept any of the procedures provided for in Section 2 of Part XV of the UNCLOS with respect to all the categories of disputes referred to in paragraph 1 (a) (b) and (c) of Article 298 of the UNCLOS (namely, disputes concerning sea boundary delimitation, territorial sovereignty, military activities, etc.).[86]

The exclusionary declaration made by China on August 25, 2006, once filed, automatically came into effect. When there are disputes over exclusionary matters, other states shall not unilaterally submit relevant disputes against China to compulsory dispute settlement procedures without China's consent.

Regarding the dispute over whether the jurisdiction contains exclusionary matters, Article 288(1) under the UNCLOS provides that a court or tribunal referred to in Article 287 shall have jurisdiction over any dispute concerning the interpretation or application of this UNCLOS. Paragraph 4 stipulates that, in the event of a dispute as to whether a court or tribunal has jurisdiction, the matter shall be settled by that court or tribunal.

---

[83] See [Japanese] Hayashi, Moritaka, Yukio Shimada, and Mamoru Koga. 2016. *International Law of the Sea (2nd edition)*. Tokyo: Yushindo. p. 175.

[84] See [Japanese] Hayashi, Moritaka, Yukio Shimada, and Mamoru Koga. 2016. *International Law of the Sea (2nd edition)*. Tokyo: Yushindo. p. 176.

[85] See [Japanese] Hayashi, Moritaka, Yukio Shimada, and Mamoru Koga. 2016. *International Law of the Sea (2nd edition)*. Tokyo: Yushindo. p. 176.

[86] Exclusionary Declaration Submitted by China, according to Article 298 of the United Convention on the Law of the Sea. 2007. *China Ocean Law Review* 1: 178.

Consequently, the Arbitral Tribunal declared that "the dispute relating to sea boundary" delimitation excluded by China should be narrowly interpreted, merely including matters related to the sea boundary delimitation itself. As for exclusionary disputes, China argues that "the dispute relating to sea boundary delimitation" should be interpreted broadly, including all matters or elements concerning sea boundary delimitation. This is because maritime delimitation is an integral, systematic project involving the basis of entitlements, the effect of maritime features, and principles and methods of delimitation, as well as relevant circumstances that must be considered to achieve an equitable solution. The Philippines fragmented the maritime delimitation dispute between China and the Philippines into various issues and submitted them to arbitration, undermining the integrity and indivisibility of maritime delimitation and violating the principle that maritime delimitation should be based on international law stipulated in Article 38 of the ICJ Statute and must "consider all relevant circumstances" that will directly affect the equitable settlement of the delimitation between China and the Philippines.[87]

If a dispute arises over the interpretation of exclusionary matters, it is determined by the Arbitral Tribunal, but such a decision is conditioned on the self-satisfaction of arbitrators. Additionally, the UNCLOS system is seriously flawed in the fact-finding and application of law as well as how to ensure the rights of a non-appearing party[88] because it has no reasonable or feasible remedial measures.[89] That is, even if a state makes an exclusionary declaration, it is the Arbitral Tribunal that determines whether these disputes are arbitrable. This will give rise to the unpredictability of exclusionary disputes, impact the right of states to choose peaceful means of their own choice, impair national sovereignty, and destroy the Convention's dispute settlement mechanism, thus encroaching upon the integrity and authority of the Convention's system.

Although the Philippines contends that submissions for arbitration are not disputes covered by China's 2006 declaration, because China disagrees with this determination, the Philippines should first resolve the issue with China before deciding whether it can be submitted to arbitration. Should the Philippines' rationale be followed, any state may unilaterally initiate compulsory arbitration proceedings by asserting that a

---

[87] See China's Position Paper, para. 67. For example, Article 74(1) of the Convention provides that "The delimitation of the exclusive economic zone between States with opposite or adjacent coasts shall be effected by agreement on the basis of international law, as referred to in Article 38 of the Statute of the International Court of Justice, in order to achieve an equitable solution."

[88] Article 9 of the Annex VII in the Convention provides that "If one of the parties to the dispute does not appear before the arbitral tribunal or fails to defend its case, the other party may request the tribunal to continue the proceedings and to make its award. Absence of a party or failure of a party to defend its case shall not constitute a bar to the proceedings. Before making its award, the arbitral tribunal must satisfy itself not only that it has jurisdiction over the dispute but also that the claim is well founded in fact and law."

[89] For instance, Article 12(1) under Annex VII provides that "Any controversy which may arise between the parties to the dispute as regards the interpretation or manner of implementation of the award may be submitted by either party for decision to the arbitral tribunal which made the award. For this purpose, any vacancy in the tribunal shall be filled in the manner provided for in the original appointments of the members of the tribunal."

dispute is not exempted by the exclusionary declaration of another state, rendering Article 299 of the UNCLOS meaningless.[90] Accordingly, the exclusionary declaration made by a state in accordance with Article 298 of the UNCLOS will be uncertain and worthless, undermining states' confidence in the UNCLOS system and the effectiveness of the UNCLOS in maintaining ocean order.

5.3.2 *The SCS Arbitration Affects the Integrity of the Law of the Sea System*

In the case that neither China nor the Philippines, as State parties to the UNCLOS, makes a written declaration choosing one of the procedures outlined in Article 287 of the UNCLOS, notwithstanding Articles 286 and 287 and Article 1 of Annex VII of the UNCLOS, the Philippines has the right to unilaterally initiate arbitration, for which multiple requirements must be met. Pursuant to Article 286, Article 287, and Annex VII of the UNCLOS, the Philippines alleged to seek a "peaceful and permanent solution to settle" their bilateral disputes. In terms of its form, the arbitration filed by the Philippines meets the above requirements. That is, the unilateral initiation of arbitration for the Philippines does not need consent from other State parties, and the Philippines is qualified as a claimant to initiate arbitration. However, it is undeniable that filing an arbitration must satisfy multiple preconditions, especially exhausting solutions stipulated in the relevant agreements and the obligations to exchange views, as well as fulfilling the burden of proof that cannot be solved by the aforementioned methods. These preconditions are the admissibility of arbitration and the fundamental requirements of the Convention's system.

5.3.2.1 Neither of the Parties Has Exhausted Its Obligations to Seek Settlement of the Dispute by a Peaceful Means Through Negotiation

Article 281 of the UNCLOS provides that if the States parties to a dispute concerning the interpretation or application of this UNCLOS have agreed to seek settlement of the dispute peacefully by choosing their own means, the procedures provided for apply only where no settlement has been reached by recourse to such means and the agreement between the parties does not exclude any further procedure. Article 286 of

[90] See China's Position Paper, para. 73. Paragraph 1 of Article 299 under the Convention provides that a dispute excluded under Article 297 or by a declaration made under Article 298 from the dispute settlement procedures provided for in Section 2 may be submitted to such procedures only by agreement of all parties to the dispute. The function of applying Articles 297 and 298 of the Convention prevents states from unilaterally submitting disputes to procedures in the Convention without prejudice to the rights of all parties to such procedures through agreement. See Merills, J. G. 2013. *International dispute settlement (Fifth edition)*, trans, Han Xiuli, Li Yanyu, et al. Beijing: Law Press. p. 221.

the UNCLOS provides that, subject to Section 3, any dispute over the interpretation or application of this UNCLOS shall, where no settlement has been reached by recourse to Section 1, be submitted at the request of any party to the dispute to the court or tribunal having jurisdiction.

Agreements between China and the Philippines consist of a series of Sino-Philippine joint statements and documents, as well as other regional documents. The question is whether the two countries have exhausted the solutions stipulated in the agreements and excluded compulsory arbitration procedures. China and the Philippines have long held a consensus that the final settlement of the dispute in the SCS will be reached through friendly negotiations.

This consensus is reflected in several joint statements, including the Joint Statement between the People's Republic of China and the Republic of the Philippines concerning Consultations on the South China Sea and on Other Areas of Cooperation, issued on August 10, 1995. The statement points out that both sides "agreed to abide by" the principle that "disputes shall be settled in a peaceful and friendly manner through consultations on the basis of equality and mutual respect," "a gradual and progressive process of cooperation shall be adopted with a view to eventually negotiating a settlement of the bilateral disputes," and "disputes shall be settled by the countries directly concerned without prejudice to the freedom of navigation in the South China Sea." The Joint Statement of the China-Philippines Experts Group Meeting on Confidence-Building Measures, issued on March 23, 1999, states that the two sides reiterated their commitment to "the understanding to continue to work for a settlement of their difference through friendly consultations," "the two sides believe that the channels of consultations between China and the Philippines are unobstructed," and "they have agreed that the dispute should be peacefully settled through consultation." The Joint Statement between the Government of the People's Republic of China and the Government of the Republic of the Philippines on the Framework of Bilateral Cooperation in the Twenty-First Century, issued on May 16, 2000, states that "The two sides commit themselves to the maintenance of peace and stability in the South China Sea. They agree to promote a peaceful settlement of disputes through bilateral friendly consultations and negotiations in accordance with universally-recognized principles of international law, including the 1982 United Nations Convention on the Law of the Sea. They reaffirm their adherence to the 1995 joint statement between the two countries on the South China Sea." The Joint Press Statement of the Third China-Philippines Experts Group Meeting on Confidence-Building Measures, dated April 4, 2001, states, "The two sides noted that the bilateral consultation mechanism to explore ways of cooperation in the South China Sea has been effective. The series of understanding and consensus reached by the two sides have played a constructive role in the maintenance of the sound development of China-Philippines relations and peace and stability of the South China Sea area."

In the meantime, the above-mentioned cases of consensus between China and the Philippines on resolving relevant disputes through negotiation have also been confirmed in multilateral cooperation documents. For example, paragraph 4 of the DOC, signed on November 4, 2002, states that "The Parties undertake to exercise self-restraint in the conduct of activities that would complicate or escalate disputes and affect peace and stability including, among others, refraining from action of inhabiting on the presently uninhabited islands, reefs, shoals, cays, and other features and to handle their differences in a constructive manner." On September 3, 2004, the two sides issued the Joint Press Statement between the Government of the People's Republic of China and the Government of the Republic of the Philippines, stating that "they agreed that the early and vigorous implementation of the 2002 ASEAN-China Declaration on the Conduct of Parties in the South China Sea will pave the way for the transformation of the South China Sea into an area of cooperation." The Joint Statement between the People's Republic of China and the Republic of Philippines, issued on September 1, 2011, stated: "They reiterated the commitment to settling their disputes in the South China Sea through negotiations and reaffirmed their commitments to respect and abide by the Declaration on the Conduct of Parties in the South China Sea signed by China and the ASEAN member countries in 2002."

The term "agree" is therefore used to settle relevant disputes through negotiation in the Sino-Philippine bilateral documents, which is significant. Meanwhile, the term "undertake" used in the DOC indicates the obligation of agreeing to accept negotiations, which, therefore, has binding force upon both states. In other words, although the DOC is a political document, its provisions are legally binding, such as paragraph 4. That is, both sides are legally bound to resolve territorial and jurisdictional disputes between the two states through friendly consultations and negotiations. Meanwhile, these bilateral documents between China and the Philippines and the DOC do not explicitly refer to "excluding other procedures of dispute settlement," just as stated by the Arbitral Tribunal in the *Southern Bluefin Tuna* case, "the absence of an express exclusion of any procedure ... is not decisive."[91]

Additionally, regarding significant issues, such as territorial sovereignty and maritime rights and interests, China has always insisted on resolving disputes through negotiations and has gained certain achievements.[92] This position was made clear to the international community, including the Philippines.

In other words, regarding all disputes between China and the Philippines in the SCS, including submissions for arbitration from the Philippines, the only means of settlement as agreed by the two sides in the agreement is negotiation, excluding other procedures of dispute settlement and rendering compulsory arbitration inapplicable.[93]

---

[91] See China's Position Paper, paras. 38–41.

[92] Since the 1960s, China has resolved land boundary disputes with 12 of its 14 neighbors through negotiations and consultations, delimiting and demarcating approximately 20,000 kilometers in length of land boundaries in the process, accounting for over 90% of the total length of China's land boundaries. Additionally, China and Vietnam have delimited the maritime boundary in the Beibu Gulf through negotiation and consultation (i.e., China–Vietnam Agreement on the Delimitation in Beibu Gulf, and China–Vietnam Agreement on Fisheries, entered into force on August 30, 2014). See the Director General of the Department of Boundary and Ocean Affairs of the MFA Ouyang Yujing Gives Interview to Chinese and Foreign Media on South China Sea Issue, http://www.fmprc.gov.cn/web/wjbxw_673019/t1361270.shtml, accessed May 8, 2016.

[93] Under international law, regardless of the designation or form of the above-mentioned instruments, as long as they intend to create rights and obligations for the parties, these rights and obligations are binding. See China Position Paper, para. 38.

5.3.2.2 Neither State Has Exhausted the Obligation to Exchange Their Views to Settle Their Disputes Through Negotiation

Article 283 of the UNCLOS provides that when a dispute arises between States concerning the interpretation or application of this UNCLOS, the parties shall proceed expeditiously to an exchange of views regarding its settlement by negotiation or other peaceful means. The parties shall also proceed expeditiously to an exchange of views where a procedure for the settlement of such a dispute has been terminated without a settlement or where a settlement has been reached and the circumstances require consultation regarding the manner of implementing the settlement.

The Philippines claims that the two countries have been involved in exchanges of views since 1995 regarding the subject matter of the Philippines' claims for arbitration without reaching a settlement and that it is justified in believing that it is meaningless to continue the negotiations and the Philippines has the right to initiate arbitration. However, the truth is that the two countries have never engaged in negotiations over the subject matter of the arbitration. In contrast, the exchange of views between China and the Philippines on relevant disputes is mainly in response to emergencies in the disputed areas, focusing on measures to prevent conflicts, reduce friction, stabilize the situation, and promote cooperation. Even based on the evidence submitted by the Philippines, these exchanges are far from constituting negotiations.[94]

Among the methods of peaceful settlement of international disputes, negotiation means that the parties to the dispute coordinate their claims directly through diplomatic means and seek ways to resolve the dispute; this is a general and the most primitive way of handling disputes.[95] In other words, negotiation is a basic way to deal with various kinds of international disputes, being a way to resolve disputes and a strategy to prevent disputes.[96]

According to the ICJ's judgment in the *Delimitation of the Maritime Boundary in the Gulf of Maine Area* between Canada and the U.S., issued October 12, 1984, the parties to the dispute have "the duty to negotiate with a view to reaching an agreement and do so in good faith, with a genuine intention to achieve a positive result."[97] In the *North Sea Continental Shelf* case (February 20, 1969), the ICJ pointed out that "The parties are under an obligation to enter into negotiations with a view to arriving at an agreement, and not merely to go through a formal process of negotiation as a sort of prior condition for the automatic application of a certain method of delimitation in the absence of agreement; they are under an obligation so to conduct themselves that the negotiations are meaningful, which will not be the case when either of them insists

---

[94] See China's Position Paper, paras.45 and 47.

[95] See [Japanese] Tabada, Shigejiro. 1995. *New Notes on International Law (Volume II)*. Tokyo: Toshindo. p.70.

[96] See Merills, J. G. 2013. *International dispute settlement (Fifth edition)*, trans, Han Xiuli, Li Yanyu, et al. Beijing: Law Press. pp. 2–3.

[97] See ICJ, *Case Concerning Delimitation of the Maritime Boundary in the Gulf of Maire Area (Canada v. United States of America)*, Judgment of October 12, 1984, ICJ Reports 1984, para. 87; Szu-Shen, Ho., Wang Kuan-Hsiung, eds. 2012. *The East China Sea and South China Sea disputes and peace prospect*. Taipei: The Prospect Foundation. p.165.

upon its own position without contemplating any modification of it."[98] Essentially, parties to the dispute should abide by the obligations of good faith and make positive efforts to reach an agreement in the negotiation process.

At the same time, in accordance with international law and judicial practice, a general exchange of views without the purpose of dispute settlement does not constitute negotiation. For example, on April 1, 2011, the ICJ in the *Georgia v. Russia* case declared that "negotiations entail more than the plain opposition of legal views or interests between two parties, or the existence of a series of accusations and rebuttals, or even the exchange of claims and directly opposed counter-claims." In the same case, the ICJ went on to say, "As such, the concept of 'negotiations' differs from the concept of 'dispute' and requires—at the very least—a genuine attempt by one of the disputing parties to engage in discussions with the other disputing party, with a view to resolving the dispute" and concluded that "[t]he subject-matter of the negotiations must relate to the subject-matter of the dispute which, in turn, must concern the substantive obligations contained in the treaty in question."[99]

The obligation to exchange views through negotiations in a dispute settlement was also confirmed by a resolution of the UNGA on December 8, 1998. The UNGA Resolution on the Principles and Guidelines for International Negotiations provides for the principles and various obligations for states to negotiate, including the following: "Negotiations should be conducted in good faith;" "States should adhere to the mutually agreed framework for conducting negotiations;" "States should endeavor to maintain a constructive atmosphere during negotiations and to refrain from any conduct that might undermine the negotiations and their progress;" "States should facilitate the pursuit or conclusion of negotiations by remaining focused throughout on the main objectives of the negotiations;" and "States should make their best efforts to continue to work toward a mutually acceptable and just solution in the event of an impasse in negotiations."[100]

Additionally, as mentioned above, on September 1, 2011, China and the Philippines issued a joint statement reiterating their commitment to addressing the disputes through peaceful dialogue. Before negotiations could formally begin, however, on April 12, 2021, the Philippines sent a naval vessel to the waters of China's Huangyan Dao to seize Chinese fishing boats and fishermen. In the face of such provocations, China was forced to take measures to safeguard its sovereignty.[101] Thereafter, China once again proposed to the Philippine Government that the two sides restart the China–Philippines consultation mechanism for confidence-building measures. That proposal again fell on deaf ears. On April 26, 2012, the Philippine Department of

[98] See ICJ, North Sea Continental Shelf Case (Federal Republic of Germany v.Netherlands), ICJ Reports 1969, p. 47; Szu-Shen, Ho., Wang Kuan-Hsiung, eds. 2012. *The East China Sea and South China Sea disputes and peace prospect*. Taipei: The Prospect Foundation. p. 265.

[99] See China's Position Paper, para. 46.

[100] See [Japanese] Tanaka, Norio., Fumio Yakushiji, Shigeki Sakamoto. 2014. *Basic Documents of International Law*. Tokyo: Toshindo. p. 881.

[101] See State Council Information Office of The People's Republic of China. 2016. China adheres to the position of settling through negotiation the relevant disputes between China and the Philippines in the South China Sea. Beijing: People's Publishing House. p. 37.

Foreign Affairs delivered a note verbale to the Chinese Embassy in the Philippines, proposing that the issue of Huangyan Dao be referred to a third-party adjudication body for resolution and indicating no willingness to negotiate. On January 22, 2013, the Philippines unilaterally initiated the present compulsory arbitration proceedings.[102]

China and the Philippines have clearly not sufficiently exchanged their views, and the previous exchanges of views regarding the SCS issue between the two countries did not concern the subject matter of the Philippines' claim to arbitration. The Philippines, therefore, had no reason or right to unilaterally submit the disputes for arbitration.

5.3.2.3 The Arbitral Tribunal's Award on Historic Rights Damages the Integrity of the System of the Convention

China's sovereignty, sovereign rights, and jurisdiction in the SCS do not entirely rely on the UNCLOS but also count on general or customary international law, the so-called intertemporal law issues, and the relationship between historic rights and the UNCLOS. The disputes relating to the Philippines' first and second submissions concern the source and scope of their respective maritime entitlements in the SCS. The Arbitral Tribunal held that China's claims to historic rights or other sovereign rights or jurisdiction in the SCS region are contrary to the UNCLOS and without lawful effect to the extent that they exceed the limits of China's maritime entitlements under the UNCLOS. Meanwhile, the Tribunal concluded that the term "historic rights" is general in nature and can describe any rights that a State may possess, including sovereignty.[103]

First, the compatibility of historic rights with the UNCLOS must be considered. The historic rights originated from the concept of historic bays, and the ICJ raised the concept of historic waters in the *Fisheries* case between the UK and Norway on December 18, 1951. The ICJ confirmed that the sovereignty of coastal states over the waters was not limited to the gulf or to other waters adjacent to the coast.[104] The origin of historic rights is general international law and includes exclusive (titles) and nonexclusive rights (rights to use).

Despite numerous consultations by the Third UN Conference on the Law of the Sea on historic bays and historic waters, the Convention's system that was finally adopted failed to make clear and specific provisions on the definition, nature, and elements of historic bays, historic waters, and historic titles. Nevertheless, the UNCLOS refers to the historic title, historic bays, and the like in relevant articles, e.g., Articles 10,

[102] See China's Position Paper, para. 48.

[103] See *In the Matter of the South China Sea Arbitration before an Arbitral Tribunal Constituted under Annex VII to the 1982 United Nations Convention on the Law of the Sea between the Republic of the Philippines and the People's Republic of China Award*, July 12. 2016. pp. 96 and 116–117, paras. 225 and 276–278.

[104] See Yu, Jia. 2014. On the constitutive requirements for the historic rights. *Chinese Review of International Law* 2: 37–38.

15, 50, and 298. These provisions in the UNCLOS contain general or exceptional rules for historic rights without excluding them, and thus, they are compatible.

Second, historic rights are superior to all rights relating to sea waters provided in the UNCLOS. As noted above, historic rights include both exclusive and nonexclusive rights. The rights of coastal states in the maritime zones stipulated in the UNCLOS, especially those in the EEZ and continental shelf, are mainly sovereign rights and jurisdiction. The above-mentioned sovereign rights under the UNCLOS in these maritime zones are reflected in the exploration, exploitation, conservation, and management of living and non-living resources by coastal areas, as well as economic exploitation and exploration activities. The jurisdiction over the aforementioned maritime zones is reflected in the construction and use of artificial islands, installations, and structures in the coastal areas, marine science research, and the conservation and preservation of the marine environment.[105]

It is true that the UNCLOS does contain some regulations concerning historic rights, including traditional fishing rights and navigation, as demonstrated in the above provisions (e.g., Articles 10, 15, and 298). The view that the connotation of historic rights is fully absorbed by the UNCLOS, therefore, cannot be established.[106] In other words, the UNCLOS stipulates that coastal states in their maritime zones cannot be deprived of all rights contained in accordance with historic rights, for instance, the exclusive jurisdiction of coastal states over resources of the seafloor, seabed, and subsoil.

Third, China has exercised exclusive control over the Nanhai Zhudao based on its historic rights. China's historic rights in the SCS are primarily fishing and navigation rights. However, the Arbitral Tribunal erred in the fact that China had not exercised its exclusive rights in such maritime zones. In August 1956, First Secretary Donald E. Webster of the U.S. institution in Taiwan made a verbal request to China's Taiwan authorities for permission for the U.S. military personnel to conduct a geodetic survey in Huangyan Dao, Shuangzi Qunjiao, Jinghong Dao, Hongxiu Dao, and Nanwei Dao of Zhongsha Qundao, and Nansha Qundao, which China's Taiwan authorities later approved. In December 1960, the U.S. Government sent a letter to China's Taiwan authorities to "request permission be granted" for its military personnel to carry out a survey at Shuangzi Qunjiao, Jinghong Dao, and Nanwei Dao of Nansha Qundao, which was approved by China's Taiwan authorities.[107] Although China has long and consistently opposed the resource development activities of other countries within the dotted line of the SCS, it has exercised the greatest restraint in order to maintain peace there and has not taken any substantive actions to prevent them. Nonetheless, this cannot be the basis for China's failure to exercise jurisdiction over the maritime zones within the dotted line of the SCS.

---

[105] For example, Articles 56 and 77 of the Convention.

[106] See *In the Matter of the South China Sea Arbitration before an Arbitral Tribunal Constituted under Annex VII to the 1982 United Nations Convention on the Law of the Sea between the Republic of the Philippines and the People's Republic of China Award*. July 12, 2016. p. 111, paras. 261–262.

[107] See Position Paper on China's Taiwan Authority South China Sea Policy. p. 22.

However, it is undeniable that China's domestic law and relevant statements of the Chinese Government are still vague about the connotation of China's historic rights in the SCS and the scope of the claimed maritime zones based on historic rights, which must be further deepened and clarified. For example, Article 14 of the Law of the People's Republic of China on the Exclusive Economic Zone and the Continental Shelf (June 26, 1998) states: "The provisions in this Law shall not affect the historic rights that the PRC enjoys." Article 2(1) of the Marine Environmental Protection Law of the People's Republic of China (August 23, 1982) provides that "this law shall apply to the internal seas and territorial seas of the People's Republic of China and all other sea areas under the jurisdiction of the People's Republic of China." Paragraph 3 of the Statement of the Government of the People's Republic of China on China's Territorial Sovereignty and Maritime Rights and Interests in the South China Sea (July 12, 2016) states that China has territorial sovereignty and maritime rights and interests in the SCS, including the following: First, "China has sovereignty over Nanhai Zhudao, consisting of Dongsha Qundao, Xisha Qundao, Zhongsha Qundao and Nansha Qundao;" Second, "China has internal waters, territorial sea and contiguous zone, based on Nanhai Zhudao;" Third, "China has the EEZ and continental shelf, based on Nanhai Zhudao;" and Fourth, "China has historic rights in the SCS."[108]

5.3.3 *The* SCS *Arbitration is not Conductive to the Stability and Development of Ocean Order*

According to the Philippines' submission for arbitration, the purpose of the arbitration is to obliterate China's maritime claims in the SCS on the basis of historic rights. It intends to degrade the legal status and nature of China's maritime features in the Nansha Qundao, making it impossible for China to claim more maritime zones from its occupied maritime features and representing the isolating trend of maritime features. It aims to find that China's actions and activities in the Nansha Qundao and its adjacent waters infringe on the rights of the Philippines based on the UNCLOS to seek "justifications" for the Philippines to obtain more rights in the SCS. As observed by Fu Ying and Professor Wu Shicun, the crux of the *SCS* Arbitration initiated by the Philippines is to unilaterally and selectively take advantage of relevant provisions of the UNCLOS on the EEZ and other articles to advance the shift of the core traditional legal struggle in the SCS. The arbitration questions China's sovereign ownership over the Nansha Qundao, the legal status of maritime features, and the legal effect of the

[108] See Statement of the Government of the People's Republic of China on China's Territorial Sovereignty and Maritime Rights and Interests in the South China Sea, at http://world.people.com.cn/n/2016/0712/c1002-28548370.html, accessed July 12, 2016.

dotted line in the SCS to evade the essence of territorial sovereignty disputes and erode China's sovereignty over maritime features, rights, and interests.[109]

5.3.3.1 Contents of the Jurisdictional Award and Final Award by the Arbitral Tribunal

On October 29, 2015, the Arbitral Tribunal issued a ruling on jurisdiction and admissibility stating the following.[110] The Arbitral Tribunal was properly constituted in accordance with Annex VII of the UNCLOS. China's nonappearance in these proceedings does not deprive the Tribunal of jurisdiction. The Philippines' initiating this arbitration did not constitute an abuse of process. There is no indispensable third party whose absence deprives the Tribunal of jurisdiction. The DOC, the joint statements of the Parties, the Treaty of Amity and Cooperation in Southeast Asia, and the Convention on Biological Diversity do not preclude, under Articles 281 or 282 of the UNCLOS, recourse to the compulsory dispute settlement procedures available under Section 2 of Part XV of the UNCLOS. The parties have exchanged views as required by Article 283 of the UNCLOS. The Tribunal has jurisdiction to consider the Philippines' Submissions No. 3, 4, 6, 7, 10, 11, and 13. A determination of whether the Tribunal has jurisdiction to consider the Philippines' Submissions Nos. 1, 2, 5, 8, 9, 12, and 14 would involve consideration of issues that do not possess an exclusively preliminary character and, accordingly, reserves consideration of its jurisdiction to rule on Submissions Nos. 1, 2, 5, 8, 9, 12, and 14 to the merits phase. The Arbitral Tribunal directs the Philippines to clarify the content and narrow the scope of its Submission No. 15 and reserves consideration of its jurisdiction over Submission No. 15 to the merits phase. The Arbitral Tribunal reserves for further consideration and directions all issues not decided in this award.[111]

On July 12, 2016, the Arbitral Tribunal announced the final ruling of the *SCS* Arbitration.[112] The so-called final award fully favors or even exceeds the claims of the Philippines and negates China's positions and claims in the SCS, resulting in serious infringements upon China's rights and interests in the SCS. This decision lacks fairness and reasonableness and causes serious criticism and controversy. The final award of the Arbitral Tribunal contains two aspects: (1) Regarding the award on jurisdiction, the Arbitral Tribunal held that each submission of the Philippines involves the dispute concerning the UNCLOS and that it has jurisdiction and (2) regarding the award on merits, the Arbitral Tribunal finds that, beyond the extent that the UNCLOS defines

[109] See Ying, Fu and Wu Shicun. 2016. South China Sea: How we got to this stage. *China Newsweek*. p. 65.

[110] See *The Republic of the Philippines v. The People's Republic of China, Award on Jurisdiction and Admissibility*. October 29, 2015.

[111] See *The Republic of the Philippines v. The People's Republic of China, Award on Jurisdiction and Admissibility*. October 29, 2015. p. 149, para. 413.

[112] See *In the Matter of the South China Sea Arbitration before an Arbitral Tribunal Constituted under Annex VII to the 1982 United Nations Convention on the Law of the Sea between the Republic of the Philippines and the People's Republic of China Award*. July 12, 2016.

as the scope of maritime entitlements, China does not have the legal basis of historic rights to be entitled to marine resources within the nine-dash line (namely, the dotted line). Second, the Arbitral Tribunal found that none of the maritime features that are above water at high tide in the Nansha Qundao (including Taiping Dao, Zhongye Dao, Xiyue Dao, Nanwei Dao, Beizi Dao, and Nanzi Dao) generate entitlements to an EEZ or continental shelf and that these features are legally rocks. Meanwhile, the Arbitral Tribunal held that the UNCLOS does not stipulate that a series of islands like the Nansha Qundao can generate maritime entitlements as a whole. Third, the Arbitral Tribunal found that China interfered with the Philippines' oil exploration in the Liyue Tan, intended to prevent Philippine fishing vessels from fishing in its EEZ, failed to prevent fishermen from Chinese flagged vessels from engaging in and even protected their fishing in the Philippines' EEZ surrounding Meiji Jiao and Ren'ai Jiao, and constructed artificial islands, installations, and structures on Meiji Jiao without the permission of the Philippines, which infringed on the sovereign rights of the Philippines over its EEZ and continental shelf. The Arbitral Tribunal stated that in the sea waters adjacent to Huangyan Dao, China unlawfully prevented Philippine fishermen from engaging in traditional fishing. With respect to the protection and preservation of the marine environment, the Arbitral Tribunal found that China's land reclamation and construction of artificial islands, installations, and structures have damaged the marine environment and that China failed to fulfill its obligations to prevent fishermen from Chinese flagged vessels from fishing in a manner that is destructive of the environment and harvesting of endangered species. Fourth, the Philippines requested the tribunal to rule that certain acts by China, especially since the commencement of the arbitration, have unlawfully aggravated and extended the dispute by conducting dredging, artificial island-building, and construction activities. With respect to this submission, the Arbitral Tribunal found that China has breached its obligation, in general, not to allow any step of any kind to be taken that might aggravate or extend the dispute during such time as dispute resolution proceedings were ongoing.[113]

5.3.3.2 The Award of the Arbitral Tribunal Damages the Arbitration Institution and Has no Binding Force upon China

According to the provisions of the Convention's system, even if China does not appear before the Arbitral Tribunal, the final ruling is binding upon China. For example, Article 9 of Annex VII of the UNCLOS provides that, "If one of the parties to the dispute does not appear before the Arbitral Tribunal or fails to defend its case, the other party may request the tribunal to continue the proceedings and to make its award. The absence of a party or failure of a party to defend its case shall not constitute a

[113] See *In the Matter of the South China Sea Arbitration before an Arbitral Tribunal Constituted under Annex VII to the 1982 United Nations Convention on the Law of the Sea between the Republic of the Philippines and the People's Republic of China Award*. July 12, 2016. pp. 471–477, para. 1203.

bar to the proceedings. Before making its award, the Arbitral Tribunal must satisfy itself not only that it has jurisdiction over the dispute but also that the claim is well founded in fact and law." Article 11 of Annex VII states that, "The award shall be final and without appeal unless the parties to the dispute have agreed in advance to an appellate procedure. It shall be complied with by the parties to the dispute." Article 12 of Annex VII stipulates that, "Any controversy which may arise between the parties to the dispute as regards the interpretation or manner of implementation of the award may be submitted by either party for decision to the Arbitral Tribunal which made the award. For this purpose, any vacancy in the tribunal shall be filled in the manner provided for in the original appointments of the members of the tribunal. Any such controversy may be submitted to another court or tribunal under Article 287 by agreement of all the parties to the dispute." Article 296 of the UNCLOS provides that, "any decision rendered by a court or tribunal having jurisdiction under Section 2 (compulsory procedures entailing binding decisions) shall be final and complied with by all the parties to the dispute."

China has, however, consistently maintained its position of non-acceptance, non-participation, and non-recognition and the award made by the Arbitral Tribunal obviously has no effect on the settlement of disputes in the SCS or on the development of the law of the sea. China argues that because the award of the Arbitral Tribunal is not recognized by China, it cannot be enforced.

In general, international judicial or arbitral institutions have the following three functions: dispute resolution, legal interpretation or application, and promoting the legal order.[114] If the SCS Arbitration award is evaluated in light of those three aspects, the following conclusions can be drawn:

First, the Arbitral Tribunal cannot resolve the core disputes between China and the Philippines (territorial sovereignty over Nansha Qundao and maritime delimitation disputes) because it has no jurisdiction over these disputes. At the same time, because the Philippines' submissions for arbitration do not represent real disputes between the two sides, it has no role to play in "resolving disputes and settling differences" without recognition from China, and its award has no enforcement effects. In other words, the so-called award made by the Arbitral Tribunal cannot perform the function of dispute settlement.

Second, regarding the function of legal interpretation or application, because of China's nonappearance without formal defense, the Arbitral Tribunal cannot comprehensively clarify and collect facts to satisfy itself in fact-finding and the application of laws, rendering it impossible to make an accurate judgment. In particular, the Arbitral Tribunal expands and goes beyond its jurisdiction, including identification of the legal status of Taiping Dao, the result of delimitation in disguise, stringent interpretation of the regime of islands, and other salient issues. These are beyond the

---

[114] See [Japanese] Tamada, Dai. 2012. On Effectiveness of International Judgement. Tokyo: Yuhikaku Publishing. p. 148.

scope of the function of legal interpretation and application of the Arbitral Tribunal and, thus, have no legal effect.[115]

Finally, regarding the function of promoting legal order, although the Arbitral Tribunal's award is only binding upon the parties to the case, international cases play a role in improving legal systems in the development of international law, including the law of the sea. In the *SCS* Arbitration, the Arbitral Tribunal adopted stringent legislation on the regime of islands, determined the nonexistence of islands in the Nansha Qundao, rejected the legality of China's historic rights in the SCS, and so on. Thus, it is highly doubtful whether it can be invoked by subsequent and similar judicial decisions and national practice in the international community. The Arbitral Tribunal's award is ineffective in promoting international law, including the law of the sea, or maintaining ocean order, including the SCS. Thus, this award does not promote legal order.[116]

Given Articles 59 and 60 of the ICJ Statute, combined with Article 11 of Annex VII and Article 296 of the UNCLOS, the force of *res judicata* of a court's judgment or award is merely confined to the parties to the dispute and the case at hand and is not binding upon a third party in principle, according to the principle of *stare decisis*. However, if a judgment or award of an international court or tribunal involves confirming the existence of customary international law, the validity of relevant multilateral treaties and the interpretation of their provisions are binding on third parties.[117]

In terms of Article 296 of the UNCLOS, "that which is binding force is definitive" and "what has been finally decided by a tribunal is binding upon the parties." However, the limitation of the aforementioned principle of the binding force is that such principle "applies only where there is identity of … the question at issue."[118] The sameness of the question at issue is mainly reflected in three aspects: the parties,

[115] In general, the main reasons for the invalidity of court decisions or arbitral awards are as follows: the invalidity of the agreement, being beyond the jurisdiction, lacking grounds for adjudication, corrupt arbitrators, and serious violation of basic procedural rules. See [Japanese] Tamada, Dai. 2012. *On Effectiveness of International Judgement*. Tokyo: Yuhikaku Publishing. p. 55. The correcting procedure for errors of the court judgment is the revision (re-trial) procedure, and the elements for exercising this revision are the misrecognition of facts in the original judgment and the discovery of new facts. The specific requirements are set out in Article 61 of the ICJ Statute. In accordance with Article 12 of Annex VII of the UNCLOS, "any controversy that may arise as regards the interpretation or manner of implementation of the award may be submitted for decision to the arbitral tribunal that made the award."

[116] For example, Article 38(1)(4) of the ICJ Statute provides that "Subject to the provisions of Article 59, judicial decisions and the teachings of the most qualified publicists of the various nations are subsidiary means for the determination of rules of law." Under Article 60, "The judgment is final and without appeal."

[117] [Japanese] Shugihara, Takane. 1996. *The Regime of International Court of Justice*. Tokyo: Yuhikaku Publishing. p. 341, pp. 344–348.

[118] Michael Sheng-ti, Gau. 2015. The Sino-Philippine Arbitration on the South China Sea disputes: Ineffectiveness of the award, inadmissibility of the claims, and lack of jurisdiction, with special reference to the legal arguments made by the Philippines in the hearing on 7–13 July 2015, *China Oceans Law Review* 2, pp. 12–13.

submissions, and reasons are all the same.[119] In light of the above-mentioned analysis, it can be seen that the issues in question between China and the Philippines are not the same, and the award of the Arbitral Tribunal obviously has no such effect. Meanwhile, the Arbitral Tribunal's lack of objective and comprehensive fact-finding and the application of laws, the absence of identification norms and remedial mechanisms in the UNCLOS, and the inability to ensure the rights and interests of nonparticipants are also reasons for China's nonacceptance of this award.

5.3.3.3 Adverse Impacts of the SCS Arbitration Award

As mentioned above, the SCS Arbitration unilaterally filed by the Philippines has an adverse impact on the Convention's system and the SCS dispute itself. It will not help develop the law of the sea; in contrast, it will have an overwhelmingly negative effect, including the following.

First, it gravely damages the authority and integrity of the Convention's system by impairing its legislative purposes and objectives, prejudicing the right of the state to choose dispute settlement means of their own choice, especially the unpredictability of jurisdiction over the subject matter excluded by states in an exclusionary declaration, and undermining states' confidence in the UNCLOS system. The award has also created controversy in determining the relationship between historic rights and the UNCLOS and in defining islands in the international community.

Second, it affects the original function of postponing disputes through bilateral and multilateral instruments among countries. The Arbitral Tribunal narrowly interprets a bilateral or multilateral "agreement" as a "legal agreement," namely, the Arbitral Tribunal holds that member States of the DOC do not intend this document to become a legally binding agreement involving the settlement of disputes. Instead, it constitutes a consensus that this declaration is a political document of willingness. This reduces the willingness of countries to adopt the political method to reach a consensus, blocking the promotion and implementation of confidence measures between states. Thus, the settlement of disputes in the SCS is more difficult.[120]

Third, if the "right" in the final award of the Arbitral Tribunal cannot be satisfied, the Philippines and other countries are bound to have varying reactions to the enforcement of the award to pressure China to comply with it. To this end, they may request China to obey the final award in international organizations, including the UNSC and the UNGA, leaving China in a serious political and diplomatic predicament, impairing its international image and weakening its diplomatic relations.

Fourth, other states may follow the Philippines by constantly initiating arbitration or judicial procedures against China over the SCS and ECS issues, stabilizing its own

---

[119] [Japanese] Tamada, Dai. 2012. *On Effectiveness of International Judgement*. Tokyo: Yuhikaku Publishing. p. 39.

[120] See *In the Matter of the South China Sea Arbitration before an Arbitral Tribunal Constituted under Annex VII to the 1982 United Nations Convention on the Law of the Sea between the Republic of the Philippines and the People's Republic of China Award*. July 12, 2016. pp. 82–88, paras. 212–226.

maritime rights and interests, yet damaging the ocean order, complicating relevant disputes, and encroaching upon national sovereignty and interests.

Fifth, some states, especially the U.S., may increase their actions and activities in the SCS based on the final ruling, including the implementation of the Freedom of Navigation Programs, individually or in association with other countries (1 + X), therefore increasing the threat to China's security in the SCS and making it more difficult to respond to it. This will lead to a continuing dilemma over the proper legal response and may end in an arms race.

Sixth, the Arbitral Tribunal exceeds its jurisdiction by determining that the Meiji Jiao, Ren'ai Jiao, and Liyue Tan are located in the EEZ of the Philippines, which constitutes, in effect, an illegal award of maritime delimitation. Such a ruling prejudices China's rights and interests in the Nanhai Zhudao, reduces the scope of China's jurisdictional maritime zones, increases the difficulty of law enforcement in China, and impairs the operational scope and interests of Chinese fishermen. There may even be future illegal requests to dismantle construction projects and facilities, causing greater disorder in the SCS.

5.3.4 Some Thoughts

China's basic position on the SCS Arbitration unilaterally filed by the Philippines is one of non-acceptance, non-participation, and non-recognition. On February 19, 2013, China rejected and returned the Philippines' note verbale and the attached Notification and Statement of Claim. China's "non-participation" means that the Chinese Government does not participate in any procedures of the arbitration, including all formal activities such as not appointing arbitrators, not submitting written submissions or memorials, not participating in the hearing, and departing wholesale from the Arbitral Tribunal. The upshot of "non-recognition," regardless of the final outcome decided by the Arbitral Tribunal, is that China will not accept, recognize, or implement the award. To this end, China will not discuss the SCS issue with any state on the basis of the award, nor will it accept any requests and propositions raised by any state, institution, or individual regarding the arbitral award. The above-mentioned policies and positions of the Chinese Government are consistent and will not be changed in the future.

The *SCS* Arbitration is the first relating to maritime disputes that have been passively dealt with since China ratified and acceded to the UNCLOS. China will likely encounter similar cases in the future. The *SCS* Arbitration maliciously filed by the Philippines has enabled arbitrators to take advantage of institutional weaknesses of the Convention's system to exceed its jurisdiction and to issue a so-called award, especially under circumstances of flawed fact-finding and application of laws. The award neither resolves a dispute nor plays a role of "settling differences." On the contrary, it complicates the SCS situation, undermines the integrity and authority of the Convention's system, and deprives state parties of the UNCLOS of their right to seek dispute settlement by their own choice, undermining the principles and systems of international law established since Second World War and harming the rights and interests of China as a victory state in the Nanhai Zhudao. The Chinese Government's position of "non-acceptance, non-participation, and non-recognition" is based on international law and has the purpose of safeguarding the authority, respect, and integrity of the UNCLOS.

Ultimately, China should view the *SCS* Arbitration as an opportunity to not only systematically study the dispute settlement mechanism of the UNCLOS but also to raise views and suggestions to amend and improve the UNCLOS to further strengthen and improve the Convention's system. At the same time, China should promote the ocean system and mechanism and establish ocean strategic objectives, including formulating and implementing the (basic) law of the sea and revising and improving the departmental laws and regulations of the ocean sector to promote the strategic process of maritime country in China and safeguard national maritime rights and interests. This is undoubtedly China's undertaking and obligation. It is also its modern calling and requirement.

5.4 FONPs in the Adjacent Waters of the Nansha Qundao

Freedom of navigation in the SCS is generally safe, but there are some security risks. For example, according to the 2016 Reports on Acts of Piracy and Armed Robbery Against Ships published by the International Maritime Organization (IMO) on March 30, 2017, between 1985 and 2016, incidents of piracy and armed robbery against ships in the SCS increased from 3 (1985) to 68 (2016) per year. The most during this period was in 2003 (152 incidents), followed by 2013 (142 incidents). Of these, 90 incidents took place in 2012, 93 incidents in 2014, 81 incidents in 2015, and 68 incidents in 2016. During the 2013–2016 period, incidents of piracy and armed robbery against ships in the SCS decreased, with the security situation in the SCS (region) considered to be relatively safe currently.[121]

However, since the Philippines unilaterally initiated the *SCS* Arbitration on January 22, 2013, the U.S., to show its support for the final award, has repeatedly dispatched warships to the territorial and adjacent waters of China's Xisha Qundao without authorization, engaging in the so-called FON. These actions have seriously threatened China's sovereignty and security interests in the SCS, triggering confrontations between China and the U.S. in the region over FON activities, especially in the Xisha Qundao and Nansha Qundao, and has posed a risk of security accidents in the region due to ship–aircraft clashes.

The U.S. FONP was proposed by the Carter Administration in 1979 and has been implemented since 1983 to challenge "excessive maritime claims" that have been unilaterally recognized by the U.S. under the law of the sea around the world (including customary international law, the 1958 Geneva UNCLOS on the Law of

[121] See Reports on Acts of Piracy and Armed Robbery Against Ships Annual Report-2016. March 30, 2017. MSC.4/Circ.245. p.16.

the Sea, and the UNCLOS) to uphold FON and security of the oceans, especially in the high seas.[122]

The FON activities of U.S. warships enter the territorial waters of the Xisha Qundao and the surrounding waters of the Nansha Qundao without permission from the Chinese Government, which undermines China's territorial sovereignty and security interests in the SCS. These activities violate the Declaration of the Government of the People's Republic of China on the Territorial Sea, the Law of the People's Republic of China on the Territorial Sea, and the Contiguous Zone. and are likely to cause security conflicts and endanger the implementation and effectiveness of agreements between the military departments of China and the U.S. Thus, the Chinese Government has vigorously opposed and protested these actions. The U.S.' actions are not only detrimental to the stability of the SCS region but also jeopardize the dispute resolution process in the region.

Given the importance of the SCS, especially the waters around the Nansha Qundao, in terms of freedom of navigation and security, this paper analyzes the nature and impact of the FON operations implemented by the U.S. in the SCS, to explore the effects of China–the U.S. cooperation on freedom of navigation and security in the SCS and maintain the regional security order.

5.4.1 Examples of the U.S. Warships Entering the Waters of Nanhai Zhudao in the SCS Without Authorization and China's Attitudes

Between October 2015 and April 2019, U.S. warships entered the territorial waters of China's Xisha Qundao, Zhongsha Qundao, and the waters surrounding the Nansha Qundao (adjacent and near-shore waters) to engage in FON operations without the permission of the Chinese Government. Based on media reports, China's MFA and the MND (the Southern Theater Command) have issued statements on the cases, mainly on the following 15 incidents.

---

[122] According to the 2016 FONP implementation report released by the U.S. DOD in March 2017, 22 countries were challenged. The U.S. identified "excessive maritime claims" for reasons including "excessive straight baselines," "prior authorization for warships to pass through territorial waters," and "historic gulf claims." See Yann-huei, Song. 2018. The July 2016 Arbitral Award, interpretation of Article 121(3) of the UNCLOS, and state practices: the case of the United States, in *South China Sea Commentary* (*Vol. II*), ed. Wu Shicun, 4. Beijing: World Affairs Press. The 22 claimant states being challenged include U.S. allies, such as Japan, the Philippines, South Korea, and Thailand, and U.S. non-allies, such as China, Brazil, India, Indonesia, Malaysia, and Vietnam. For an analysis and critique of FON activities by the U.S., see Yinan, Bao. 2019. The "Voice of America" for the Sino-US "maritime legal debate": Analysis and commentary on "freedom of navigation with Chinese characteristics" in the free sea: The American fight for freedom of navigation, *Chinese Review of International Law* 2(2): 3–10.

(1) On October 27, 2015, the U.S. warship USS Lassen entered the 12-nautical-mile Zhubi Jiao in the Nansha Qundao to exercise FON.[123] (2) On January 30, 2016, the U.S. guided-missile destroyer USS Wilbur entered the territorial waters of China's Xisha Qundao without permission, implementing the innocent passage regime. (3) On May 10, 2016, the U.S. Navy destroyer USS Lawrence illegally entered the waters adjacent to relevant islands of China's Nansha Qundao without China's permission.[124] (3) On May 10, 2016, the U.S. Navy's USS Lawrence, a destroyer of the U.S. Navy, illegally entered the waters adjacent to relevant maritime features of China's Nansha Qundao without China's permission to carry out FON activities.[125] (4) On October 21, 2016, the U.S. naval vessel Decatur entered the territorial waters of China's Xisha Qundao without authorization to carry out FON activities.[126] (5) On May 25, 2017, the U.S. Navy's USS Dewey entered the adjacent waters of the relevant maritime features of the Nansha Qundao without the permission of the Chinese Government to carry out FON activities.[127] (6) On July 2, 2017, the U.S. Navy's guided-missile destroyer USS Statham entered the territorial waters of the Xisha Qundao without authorization to conduct FON activities.[128] (7)

[123] See Foreign Ministry Spokesperson Lu Kang's remarks on USS Lassen's entry into waters near relevant islands and reefs of China's Nansha Islands, https://www.gov.cn/xinwen/2015-10/27/content_2954649.htm, accessed October 28, 2015; See Defense Ministry Spokesperson Yang Yujun's remarks on entry of the U.S. warship into adjacent waters of relevant islands and reefs in China's Nansha Qundao, http://www.xinhuanet.com/mil/2015-10/27/c_1116957522.htm, accessed October 28, 2015.

[124] See Foreign Ministry Spokesperson Hua Chunying's remarks on the U.S. Navy vessel's entry into territorial waters of Zhongjian Dao of China's Xisha Islands, http://www.xinhuanet.com/politics/2016-01/30/c_128687144.htm, accessed January 31, 2016; Defense Ministry Spokesperson Yang Yujun's Remarks on U.S. Warship's unauthorized entry into territorial waters of Xisha Qundao, https://www.gov.cn/xinwen/2016-05/11/content_5072078.htm, accessed January 31, 2016.

[125] Foreign Ministry Spokesperson Lu Kang's Regular Press Conference, see http://www.mfprc.gov.cn/web/fyrbt_673021/t1361960.shtml, accessed May 11, 2016; Defense Ministry Spokesperson Yang Yujun's remarks on entry of the U.S. warship into adjacent waters of China's relevant maritime features in the Nansha Qundao, see https://www.gov.cn/xinwen/2016-05/11/content_5072078.htm, accessed May 11, 2016.

[126] Foreign Ministry Spokesperson Hua Chunying's remarks on the U.S. warship's entry into Chinese territorial waters off Xisha Islands, see https://www.mfa.gov.cn/fyrbt_673021/dhdw_673027/201610/t20161022_5434409.shtml, accessed October 22, 2016; Defense Ministry Spokesperson Wu Qian's remarks on unauthorized entry of the U.S. warship into territorial waters of Xisha Qundao, see https://www.gov.cn/xinwen/2018-10/02/content_5327613.htm, accessed October 22, 2016.

[127] Foreign Ministry Spokesperson Lu Kang's Regular Press Conference, see http://nagasaki.china-consulate.gov.cn/chn/fyrth/201705/t20170526_4577662.htm, accessed May 28, 2017; Ministry of National Defense identifies, checks and warns away the U.S. warships, see http://military.people.com.cn/n1/2017/0525/c1011-29300161.html, accessed May 25, 2017.

[128] Foreign Ministry Spokesperson Lu Kang's remarks on the U.S. Missile Detroyer Stethem trespassing China's territorial waters off Xisha Islands, see https://www.mfa.gov.cn/web//gjhdq_676201/gj_676203/bmz_679954/1206_680528/fyrygth_680536/201707/t20170702_9361514.shtml, accessed July 3, 2017; Defense Ministry Spokesperson Wu Qian's remarks on unauthorized entry of the U.S. warship into territorial waters of Xisha Qundao, see http://military.people.com.cn/n1/2017/0703/c1011-29380131.html, accessed July 3, 2017.

On August 10, 2017, the guided-missile destroyer USS McCain entered the waters adjacent to maritime features of China's Nansha Qundao without authorization. The Chinese guided-missile frigates Huaibei and Fushun took immediate action, identified and verified the U.S. ship, and warned and drove it away.[129] (8) On October 10, 2017, the US Navy's USS Chafee missile destroyer entered the territorial waters of China's Xisha Qundao without authorization and carried out the so-called FON operation. The Chinese Navy's missile destroyer Huangshan, as well as two J-11B fighter jets and one Z-8 helicopter, responded urgently, warned and drove the U.S. ship away.[130] (9) On January 17, 2018, the U.S. Navy's guided-missile destroyer USS Hopper entered within 12 nautical miles of China's Huangyan Dao without permission from the Chinese Government. The Chinese Navy's guided-missile destroyer Huangshan took immediate action, identified and verified the U.S. ship, warned and drove it away.[131] (10) On March 23, 2018, the U.S. Navy's guided-missile destroyer USS Mastin entered the waters adjacent to the relevant maritime features in the SCS without permission from the Chinese Government. The Chinese naval vessels 570 and 524 took immediate action, identified and verified the U.S. ship, and warned and drove it away in accordance with the law.[132] (11) On May 27, 2018, the U.S Navy's warships USS Higgins and USS Antietam entered the territorial waters of China's Xisha Qundao without permission from the Chinese Government. The Chinese Navy identified and verified the U.S. warships, warned and drove them away in accordance with the law.[133] (12) On September 30, 2018, the U.S. Navy's USS Decatur, a destroyer, entered the waters near the Nansha Qundao without the permission of the

---

[129] Foreign Ministry Spokesperson Geng Shuang's remarks on the US Warship's unauthorized entry into the neighboring waters of relevant islands and reefs of China's Nansha Qundao, see https://www.mfa.gov.cn/web/fyrbt_673021/dhdw_673027/201708/t20170810_5434608.shtml, accessed August 11, 2017; Ministry of National Defense Spokesperson Wu Qian's remarks on the US Warship's unauthorized entry into the neighboring waters of relevant islands and reefs of China's Nansha Qundao, see http://www.xinhuanet.com/politics/2017-08/11/c_1121468109.htm, accessed August 11, 2017.

[130] Foreign Ministry Spokesperson Hua Chunying's Regular Press Conference," see http://www1.fmprc.gov.cn/gjhdq_676201/gj_676203/oz_678770/1206_679810/fyrygth_679818/201710/t20171011_5415346.shtml, accessed October 11, 2017; Ministry of National Defense Spokesperson's remarks on unauthorized entry of the U.S. warship into territorial waters of Xisha Qundao, see http://www.scio.gov.cn/xwfb/bwxwfb/gbwfbh/gfb/202207/t20220715_203635.html, accessed October 11, 2017.

[131] Foreign Ministry Spokesperson Lu Kang's Remarks, see http://www.fmprc.gov.cn/web/fyrbt_673021/t1527156.shtml, accessed January 20, 2018; Defense Ministry Spokesperson Wu Qian's remarks on unauthorized entry of the U.S. warship into neighboring waters of China's Huangyan Island, see http://www.mod.gov.cn/gfbw/xwfyr/fyrth/4802824.html, accessed January 20, 2018.

[132] Foreign Ministry Spokesperson Hua Chunying's remarks on the U.S. Ship's entry into neighboring waters of China's islands and reefs in the South China Sea, https://www.gov.cn/xinwen/2018-03/23/content_5277179.htm, accessed March 24, 2018; Ministry of National Defense Spokesperson Ren Guoqiang's remarks on the U.S. Ship's entry into the neighboring waters of China's islands and reefs in the South China Sea, https://www.gov.cn/xinwen/2018-03/24/content_5277001.htm, accessed March 23, 2018.

[133] Foreign Ministry Spokesperson Lu Kang's Remarks on unauthorized entry of the U.S. warship into territorial waters of Xisha Qundao, see https://www.gov.cn/xinwen/2018-05/27/content_5294105.htm, accessed May 28, 2018; Ministry of National Defense Spokesperson Wu Qian's Q&A

Chinese Government. The Chinese Navy identified and verified the ship, warned and drove it away in accordance with the law.[134] (13) On November 26, 2018, the U.S. Navy's guided-missile cruiser USS Chancellorsville entered the territorial waters of China's Xisha Qundao without permission. China dispatched warships and military aircraft, identified and verified the ship, warned and drove it away in accordance with the law. The Chinese Government also lodged serious representations to the U.S.[135] (14) On January 7, 2019, the U.S. Navy's USS McCampbell entered the territorial waters of the Xisha Qundao without permission. The Chinese PLA's Southern Theater of Operations organized sea and air forces to monitor the situation, conducted identification and verification operations, and warned and drove it away. At the same time, China lodged serious representations to the U.S.[136] (15) On February 11, 2019, the U.S. Navy's warships USS Spruance and USS Preble entered the waters adjacent to Ren'ai Jiao and Meiji Jiao in the Nansha Qundao without permission. The Chinese Navy identified and verified the U.S. ships, and warned and drove them away in accordance with the law.[137]

In terms of the scope of unauthorized entry of these U.S. warships into the maritime areas under China's jurisdiction, the main areas are the territorial waters of the Xisha Qundao and the surrounding waters of the Nansha Qundao (adjacent and near-shore waters). They conducted "FON operations" on the basis of the so-called unilaterally

---

on unauthorized entry of the U.S. warship into territorial waters of Xisha Qundao, see https://www.gov.cn/xinwen/2018-05/27/content_5294104.htm, accessed May 28, 2018. In addition, on August 31, 2018, the British dockyard transport shi Poseidon's Son illegally entered the territorial waters of China's Xisha Qundao without the permission of the Chinese government. The Chinese military sent ships and aircraft to verify and identify the British ship in accordance with the law and regulations, warned and drove it away, and made solemn representations to the British side. Ministry of National Defense Spokesperson Ren Guoqiang's remarks on unauthorized entry of the U.S. warship into territorial waters of Xisha Qundao, see http://www.mod.gov.cn/topnews/2018-09/06/content_4824306.htm, accessed September 6, 2018; Foreign Ministry Spokesperson Hua Chunying's Regular Press Conference, see http://new.fmprc.gov.cn/web/fyrbt_673021/jzhsl_673025/201809/t20180906_5416590.shtml, accessed September 6, 2018.

[134] Foreign Ministry Spokesperson Hua Chunyin's remarks on the U.S. warship's unauthorized entry into the neighboring waters of relevant islands and reefs of China's Nansha Qundao, see https://www.gov.cn/xinwen/2018-10/02/content_5327611.htm, accessed October 2, 2018; Defense Ministry Spokesperson Wu Qian's remarks on the U.S. Ship's entry into the neighboring waters of China's islands and reefs in the South China Sea, see http://www.mod.gov.cn/topnews/2018-10/02/content_4826058.htm, accessed October 2, 2018.

[135] Foreign Ministry Spokesperson Geng Shuang's Regular Press Conference, see https://www.mfa.gov.cn/nanhai/chn/fyrbt/201811/t20181130_8522962.htm, accessed November 30, 2018.

[136] Southern Theater of Operations Spokesperson's remarks on the U.S. Missile Detroyer Stethem trespassing China's territorial waters off Xisha Islands, see http://www.mod.gov.cn/topnews/2019-01/07/content_4833825.htm, accessed January 8, 2019; Foreign Ministry Spokesperson Lu Kang's Regular Press Conference, see http://www.fmprc.gov.cn/web/fyrbt_673021/t1627554.shtml, accessed January 8, 2019.

[137] Southern Theater of Operations Spokesperson's remarks on the warship trespassing the neighboring waters of relevant islands and reefs of China's Nansha Qundao, See http://www.mod.gov.cn/topnews/2019-02/11/content_4836053.htm, accessed on February 12, 2019; Foreign Ministry Spokesperson Hua Chunying's Regular Press Conference, see http://www.fmprc.gov.cn/web/fyrbt_673021/t1636893.shtml, accessed February 12, 2019.

recognized "excessive maritime claims" and the final award of the *SCS* Arbitration, challenging China's sovereignty and security interests in the SCS.[138] The Chinese Government, especially the MND (Southern Theater of Operations), issued a special timely discussion, and sent Chinese warships to identify, verify, and warn the U.S. ships away, pointing out that the U.S. behavior is likely to cause accidents at sea and in the air. China firmly opposes such provocative activities and calls on the U.S. to cease them, as they violate China's domestic and international laws. Such unilateral acts can easily lead to the militarization of the region, are not conducive to resolving the issues in the SCS, and are detrimental to China–the U.S. relations, including mutual military trust. Finally, they affect the legal order of the sea.

5.4.2 Legal Issues Involved in the U.S. FONP

Regarding the unauthorized entry of U.S. warships into territorial waters of the Xisha Qundao and the adjacent waters of the Nansha Qundao to conduct so-called FONP, it is necessary to examine legal issues involved, in particular, the status of maritime areas in which they operated and the nature of their operations. The scope of the U.S. warships' FONP shows that the main areas involved are territorial waters of the Xisha Qundao (seven times) and waters surrounding relevant maritime features of the Nansha Qundao (seven times in the adjacent and offshore waters). The U.S. FONPs are mainly related to the innocent passage regime of territorial waters and the status of waters surrounding relevant maritime features of the Nansha Qundao.

5.4.2.1 Regime of Innocent Passage in the Territorial Sea

According to Article 2 of the UNCLOS, the territorial sea is the sea area that the sovereignty of a coastal State extends, beyond its land territory and internal waters; This sovereignty extends to the air space over the territorial sea as well as to its bed and subsoil. In other words, the coastal State has full rights (legislative, administrative, and judicial jurisdiction) over its territorial sea because it is a natural and indivisible appendage of the coastal State, that is, it adopts the view that the territorial sea is the "theory of territory." This theory means that the territorial sea is an extension of the land territory of the coastal State, over which the coastal State has exclusive jurisdiction.[139]

---

[138] On the theory of "excessive maritime claims" and the evolution of "freedom of navigation," see Yinan, Bao. 2017. The U.S. "Excessive Maritime Claims": A Critical Analysis, *China International Studies* 5: 106–128.

[139] See O'Connell, D. P. 1971. The juridical nature of the territorial sea, *British Yearbook of International Law* 45: 381. The view that the territorial sea is "territorial" is reflected in Articles 1–2 of the Convention on the Territorial Sea and the Contiguous Zone (1958). At the same time, the effect of the territorial sea being a natural extension of, and an inseparable appendage to, the land territory is that the territorial sea alone cannot be ceded to another state. See [Japanese] Hayashi,

The exception to the regime of the territorial sea is the right of innocent passage of foreign ships, including warships. The legal basis for this is, first, Article 17 of the UNCLOS, which provides that, "Subject to this Convention, ships of all States, whether coastal or land-locked, enjoy the right of innocent passage through the territorial sea;" and second, Article 30, which provides that "If any warship does not comply with the laws and regulations of the coastal State concerning passage through the territorial sea and disregards any request for compliance therewith which is made to it, the coastal State may require it to leave the territorial sea immediately."

Nevertheless, the regime of innocent passage of warships in the territorial sea is ambiguous in theory and has different approaches in practice. This is because the modern law of the sea (in statutory law or treaties, this system consists of the 1958 Geneva UNCLOS on the Law of the Sea and the 1982 UNCLOS) substantively cedes the criterion of "innocent" to the coastal state, leading to different state practices. On a procedural level, the controversy over the innocent passage of warships in the territorial sea centers on the "doctrine of prior notification" (the "doctrine of prior authorization") and the "doctrine of freedom use."[140] In other words, most developing countries insist on the "doctrine of prior notification" to ensure that the rights and interests of the coastal State in the territorial sea, especially its security interests, are not infringed upon,[141] whereas ocean powers insist on the "doctrine of freedom use" to expand the space and freedom of movement of weaponry, including warships, in the territorial sea of other countries, to conduct FON operations.[142]

5.4.2.2 Elements of Passage and Innocent Passage

(1) Elements of passage. Article 18(1) of the UNCLOS provides that "Passage means navigation through the territorial sea for the purpose of: (a) traversing that sea without entering internal waters or calling at a roadstead or port facility outside internal waters; or (b) proceeding to or from internal waters or a call at such roadstead or port facility." Article 18(2) of the UNCLOS provides that "Passage shall be continuous and expeditious. However, passage includes stopping

Moritaka, Yukio Shimada, and Mamoru Koga. 2016. *International Law of the Sea (2nd edition)*. Tokyo: Yushindo. p. 18.

[140] See Yongming, Jin. 2016. On the regime of innocent passage in the territorial sea, *Chinese Review of International Law* 2: 66–68.

[141] More than 40 states have imposed procedural (prior authorization or notification) restrictions on the innocent passage of warships in their territorial sea. See Roach, J. Ashley., Smith, Robert W. 2012. *Excessive Maritime Claims (3rd Edition)*, Hague: Maritinus Nijhoff Publishers. pp. 250–251, 258–259. The legal basis for these states' domestic legal restrictions on innocent passage of warships in the territorial sea is Article 310 of the UNCLOS, which intends to harmonize the state's domestic laws and regulations with the provisions of the Convention.

[142] For the restrictive regulations and declarations made by developing countries and maritime countries on the innocent passage of warships in the territorial sea based on domestic laws or Article 310 of the UNCLOS, see Xinjun, Zhang. 2017. New progress of the U.S. freedom of navigation program in the South China Sea: "De-regulation" or "rebalancing," in ed. Wu Shicun, *South China Sea Review Vol. 1*, 49–53. Nanjing: Nanjing University Press.

and anchoring, but only in so far as the same are incidental to ordinary navigation or are rendered necessary by force majeure or distress or for the purpose of rendering assistance to persons, ships or aircraft in danger or distress."

(2) Elements of innocent passage. Article 19(1) of the UNCLOS provides that "Passage is innocent so long as it is not prejudicial to the peace, good order or security of the coastal State. Such passage shall take place in conformity with this Convention and with other rules of international law." Article 19(2) of the UNCLOS stipulates that, "Passage of a foreign ship shall be considered to be prejudicial to the peace, good order or security of the coastal State if in the territorial sea it engages in any of the following activities."

From the content and structure of Articles 18 and 19 of the UNCLOS, if "passage" does not meet the requirements set out in Article 18, it can be judged by the acts stipulated in Article 19. That is to say, the UNCLOS has adopted the method of separating the requirements of "passing" and "innocent passage" into legislation and regulations (separability), which distinguishes it from the overall provisions of Article 14 (2) and (4) of the Convention on the Territorial Sea and the Contiguous Zone in the Geneva Convention on the Law of the Sea, which include the requirement of "innocent passage" for "passing."[143]

As for the relationship between Article 19 (1) and (2) of the UNCLOS, there are two views in the academic community. The first is the enumeration theory. It is of the view that Article 19(2) regulates the classification of ships based on their actions or status. It is only a list of Article 19(1). Whether their actions are harmful should be judged in conjunction with Article 19(2). The second is the non-enumeration theory. It does not require the coastal State to provide evidence. It is a "presumption" provision designed based on the action or status standards of the ship, not a complete enumeration of Article 19(1). The legal effect of these views is that, if the "passage" of foreign ships is not a harmful act under Article 19(2), or may be considered not a harmful act under 19(1), the coastal State can still have jurisdiction over the "passage" of these ships by stipulating the conditions for the use of the territorial sea, because Article 21 of the UNCLOS gives coastal States the right to regulate eight types of actions.[144]

(3) Foreign warships should comply with the regulations on innocent passage in the territorial sea. As mentioned above, regarding the innocent passage of foreign warships in the territorial sea, there is a procedural dichotomy between the "doctrine of freedom use" and the "doctrine of prior notification" in the international community. However, there is no contradiction in the fact that the innocent passage of foreign warships in the territorial sea should, at a minimum, be subject to the laws and regulations of the coastal State on an innocent passage

[143] For example, Article 14(2) of the Convention on the Territorial Sea and the Contiguous Zone provides "Passage means navigation through the territorial sea for the purpose either of traversing that sea without entering internal waters, or of proceeding to internal waters, or of making for the high seas from internal waters." Article 14(4) provides that, "Passage is innocent so long as it is not prejudicial to the peace, good order or security of the coastal State. Such passage shall take place in conformity with these articles and with other rules of international law."

[144] See [Japanese] Yamamoto, Sōji. 1997. *Law of the sea*. Tokyo: Sanseido. pp. 125–127.

in the territorial sea, which has become a rule of customary international law and must be observed by all States.[145] The legal basis for this is Article 30 of the UNCLOS. The specific requirements are as follows: first, compliance with the laws enacted by the coastal State, e.g., Articles 25 and 21(1), of the UNCLOS; second, compliance with the navigation in the sea lanes designated or regulated by the coastal State, e.g., Article 22 of the UNCLOS; third, measures to be taken for infringement of the laws of the coastal State, e.g., Article 30 of the UNCLOS.

5.4.2.3 Ambiguity in the Terminology of the Waters Adjacent to the Maritime Features of the Nansha Qundao and Inshore Waters

As mentioned above, in response to the incident of the U.S. warship USS Larson (October 27, 2015), Foreign Ministry Spokesperson's remarks on USS Lassen's entry into waters near relevant islands and reefs of China's Nansha Qundao, Defense Ministry Spokesperson's remarks on entry of the U.S. warship into adjacent waters of relevant islands and reefs in China's Nansha Qundao and in subsequent statements or talks, the terms "adjacent waters" and "offshore waters" were involved. In this context, then, what kind of status do the "adjacent waters" and "offshore waters" of the Nansha Qundao have under the modern law of the sea system, i.e., the legal status of the adjacent waters and offshore waters of the Nansha Qundao.

(1) Classification of maritime areas in the modern law of the sea system. The law of the sea is an important part of international law, and its sources of law naturally include treaties (statutory law), international customs, the general principles of law, judicial decisions, and the teachings of the most highly qualified publicists of the various nations.[146] For this reason, the modern law of the sea system can be divided into two types: the narrow sense and the broad sense. Broadly speaking, it refers to the modern system of the law of the sea (codified law), customary international law, and all regulations and regimes relating to oceans and seas, including resolutions and regimes adopted by international organizations such

[145] The U.S. refused to sign the UNCLOS based on its provisions related to the deep seabed mining regime, which were "irreparably flawed"; the Reagan Administration emphasized that the U.S. supported the rest of the UNCLOS and would support ratification of the dissenting provisions of Part XI (including a lack of certainty in awarding mining contracts and unaffordable economic requirements) if they could be amended. See Sohn, Louis B., et al. 2014. *The law of the sea in a nutshell (2nd ed.),* (trans. Fu Kuen Chen, et al). Shanghai: Shanghai Jiao Tong University Press. p. 192. However, with the enactment of the Part XI Implementing Agreement, this argument that Part 11 is not satisfied has been largely eliminated. The Clinton Administration intended to accede to the UNCLOS and was supported by officials and scholars from the Departments of State, Defense, and Commerce, but the U.S. Senate Committee on Foreign Affairs had not ratified accession to the UNCLOS due to misinterpretations of the provisions of the Convention by Conservative members of the Senate Committee on Foreign Affairs. See [Japanese] Hayashi, Moritaka, Yukio Shimada, and Mamoru Koga. 2016. *International Law of the Sea (2nd edition).* Tokyo: Yushindo. pp. 124–125.

[146] See Article 38 of the Statute of the ICJ.

as the IMO. In a narrow sense, it refers to the two major systems of the law of the sea (the modern law of the sea system), namely, the 1958 Geneva Convention on the Law of the Sea system and the 1982 UNCLOS system. For the sake of analysis, this paper adopts the narrow definition of the modern law of the sea system.

Under the 1958 Geneva Convention on the Law of the Sea system, the maritime area is divided into areas beyond the territorial sea, i.e., the high seas, in a so-called "dualistic" structure. For example, Article 1 of the Convention on the High Seas stipulates that "The term 'high seas' means all parts of the sea that are not included in the territorial sea or in the internal waters of a State." Article 24(1) of the Convention on the Territorial Sea and the Contiguous Zone stipulates that "In a zone of the high seas contiguous to its territorial sea, the coastal State may exercise the control necessary to: (a) Prevent infringement of its customs, fiscal, immigration or sanitary regulations within its territory or territorial sea; (b) Punish infringement of the above regulations committed within its territory or territorial sea."

(2) Relationship between the 1958 Geneva Convention on the Law of the Sea and the 1982 Convention system. Article 311(1) of the UNCLOS provides that "This Convention shall prevail, as between States Parties, over the Geneva Conventions on the Law of the Sea of 29 April 1958." It should be noted that although the U.S. is not a member of the UNCLOS, the regime of the territorial sea and the regime of the EEZ has become customary international law. Therefore, the U.S. is also subject to the relevant regimes regulated by the UNCLOS.

According to the 1982 Convention, the maritime areas are divided into territorial sea, archipelagic waters, EEZ/continental shelf, high seas, the Area, etc., that is, the so-called "plurality" structure.[147]

(3) The ambiguity of the nature of the adjacent waters and offshore waters. It can be seen that maritime areas in which the so-called FONP carried out by the U.S. warships surrounding the Nansha Qundao (the waters surrounding the Nansha Qundao occupied by China) are referred to by the MFA and the MND as the adjacent waters and offshore waters. They are not maritime areas with a lawful status in a narrow sense of the modern law of the sea system and are not the proprietary terminology under the modern law of the sea system.

At the same time, in response to the joint submission made by Malaysia and Vietnam on the outer continental shelf (May 6, 2009) and the separate submission made by Vietnam on the outer continental shelf (May 7, 2009), the Government of China, in its note verbale to the UN Secretary-General of May 7, 2009 (with the map of the dotted line) pointed out that "China has indisputable sovereignty over the islands in the South China Sea and the adjacent waters, and enjoys sovereign rights and jurisdiction over the relevant waters as well as the seabed and subsoil

[147] The UNCLOS system refers primarily to the preamble, text, and nine annexes. Article 318 of the UNCLOS provides that, "The Annexes form an integral part of this Convention and, unless expressly provided otherwise, a reference to this Convention or to one of its Parts includes a reference to the Annexes relating thereto."

thereof. The above position is consistently held by the Chinese Government, and is widely known by the international community." Here, too, the nature and extent of the waters adjacent to the Nanhai Zhudao and the relevant waters are uncertain.[148] From the supplementary note verbale submitted by the Chinese Government to the UN Secretary-General on April 14, 2011, it is clear that the waters adjacent to the Nanhai Zhudao, especially the Nansha Qundao, refer to the territorial sea, while the relevant waters mainly refer to the EEZ and the continental shelf. This is because the supplementary note verbale points out that, in accordance with the relevant provisions of the UNCLOS, the Law of China on the Territorial Sea and the Contiguous Zone in 1992 and the Law of China on the Exclusive Economic Zone and the Continental Shelf in 1998, China's Nansha Qundao have the territorial sea, an EEZ, and a continental shelf.[149]

In addition, the Statement of the Government of the People's Republic of China on China's Territorial Sovereignty and Maritime Rights and Interests in the SCS (July 12, 2016) states that, "China has territorial sovereignty and maritime rights and interests in the South China Sea, including, inter alia: (1) China has sovereignty over Nanhai Zhudao, consisting of Dongsha Qundao, Xisha Qundao, Zhongsha Qundao and Nansha Qundao; (2) China has internal waters, territorial sea and contiguous zone, based on Nanhai Zhudao; (3) China has exclusive economic zone and continental shelf, based on Nanhai Zhudao; (4) China has historic rights in the South China Sea."[150] In addition to the territorial sea, contiguous zone, EEZ, and continental shelf under the UNCLOS, China has historical rights in the SCS. However, its connotation is not only unclear, but also vague for the sea area based on it. In other words, the nature and specific connotation of "historic rights" are still unclear, as stipulated in Article 14 of the Law on the Exclusive Economic Zone and Continental Shelf.[151]

Because the locations of the so-called FONP carried out by the U.S. warships in the adjacent waters and offshore waters of the Nansha Qundao are not, in the strict sense of the term, waters under the modern law of the sea system, what is their nature and status? It is necessary to analyze the connotation of the Convention's system to define the true status and role of the adjacent waters and offshore waters of the Nansha Qundao.

[148] From the perspective of the "adjacent waters" referring to the term of "sovereignty," the "adjacent waters" here mainly refer to territorial sea; From the perspective of the "relevant waters" referring to the term of "sovereign rights and jurisdiction," the "relevant waters" here mainly refer to the EEZ and continental shelf. See Yongming, Jin. 2015. Maritime Silk Road and issues over South China Sea, *The Journal of South China Sea Studies* 4: 1–2.

[149] See http://www.un.org/depts/los/clcs_new/submissions_files/vnm37_09/chn_2011_re-phl.pdf, accessed May 5, 2011.

[150] See http://world.people.com.cn/n1/2016/0712/c1002-28548370.html, accessed July 12, 2016.

[151] Article 14 of the Law of China on the Exclusive Economic Zone and the Continental Shelf provides that "The provisions of this Act shall not affect the historical rights of the People's Republic of China."

5.4.3 Development Stage of the System of the UNCLOS and Its Application

5.4.3.1 Development Stage of the System of the UNCLOS

It is generally recognized that the Convention's system, which is the core element of the modern law of the sea system, has gone through two stages of development.[152] During the first stage, that is, the stage of its adoption, the Convention's system consisted mainly of a preamble, a main text, and nine annexes. The Part XI Implementing Agreement and the Straddling Fish Stocks Implementing Agreement were also adopted. These are complementary to and complete the UNCLOS system, and they constitute the second phase of the UNCLOS system. For example, Article 2(1) of the Part XI Implementing Agreement provides that, "The provisions of this Agreement and Part XI shall be interpreted and applied together as a single instrument. In the event of any inconsistency between this Agreement and Part XI, the provisions of this Agreement shall prevail." Article 4 of the Straddling Fish Stocks Implementing Agreement provides that, "Nothing in this Agreement shall prejudice the rights, jurisdiction andduties of States under the Convention. This Agreement shall be interpreted andapplied in the context of and in a manner consistent with the Convention."

This legislative model of supplementing and completing the relevant original norms by means of an "implementing agreement" outside the UNCLOS avoids the difficulty of amending it by means of an "amendment conference" (Article 312) and the "simplified procedure" (Article 313), and is consistent with Articles 30 and 59 of the VCLT. For this reason, the relevant provisions of the Part XI Implementing Agreement and the Straddling Fish Stocks Implementing Agreement are reasonable and compatible with the UNCLOS, that is, the two implementing agreements are an important part of the UNCLOS system and constitute the second stage of its development.[153]

---

[152] If the elements of the UNGA resolution of June 19, 2015 (A/RES/69/292) to develop an legally binding instrument on the conservation and sustainable use of marine biodiversity in areas beyond national jurisdiction were incorporated and the elements of the Consultative Process for the launching of the Intergovernmental Meeting from September 2018 were included, the UNCLOS would be in its third stage of development. Given that this new agreement is now at the stage of consideration and discussion, it has not been included and remains categorized according to the two stages of development. For the issue of marine biodiversity in areas beyond national jurisdiction, see Yongming, Jin. 2018. Issues relating to the conservation and sustainable use of marine biological diversity beyond areas of national jurisdiction, *Journal of Social Science* 9(1): 12–21.

[153] The Part XI Implementation Agreement is primarily aimed at improving the regulation of deep-sea prospecting, particularly in the areas of finance and technology transfer, with a view to increasing the universality of the UNCLOS; meanwhile, the Straddling Fish Stock Agreement is primarily aimed at addressing overfishing of living resources on the high seas, particularly straddling fish stocks.

5.4.3.2 Principles and Effects of the Convention's System in Determining the Various Types of Maritime Areas

The extent of maritime areas in the UNCLOS is determined by the principles of land dominance over the sea and of proximity (e.g., 12-nautical-mile territorial sea, 24-nautical-mile contiguous zone, and 200-nautical-mile EEZ and continental shelf). The "principle of land dominance over the sea" originated in the *North Sea Continental Shelf* case (1969) and was confirmed in the *Aegean Sea Continental Shelf* case (1978) and the *Black Sea Delimitation* case (2009). The "principle of distance," which determines the extent of maritime areas, was established in the UNCLOS.[154] Thus, the "principle of distance" can be changed according to changes in the content of treaty provisions. In determining the extent of maritime areas, the "principle of land dominance over the sea" therefore plays a dominant role supplemented by the "principle of distance." On this basis, there are four categories to define the extent of maritime areas within the UNCLOS.

(1) Maritime areas requiring a proclamation or declaration by the State, including territorial sea, archipelagic waters, EEZs, maritime security zones, marine development zones, and marine protected areas.[155]
(2) Maritime zones that do not require a national declaration or proclamation, for example, the continental shelf within 200 nautical miles. Article 77(3) of the UNCLOS provides that "The rights of the coastal State over the continental shelf do not depend on occupation, effective or notional, or on any express proclamation."
(3) Maritime zones (mining areas) requiring recommendations or approvals from international bodies (CLCS or ISA). For example, Article 76(8) of the UNCLOS provides that, "Information on the limits of the continental shelf beyond 200 nautical miles from the baselines from which the breadth of the territorial sea is measured shall be submitted by the coastal State to the CLCS set up under Annex II on the basis of equitable geographical representation. The Commission shall make recommendations to coastal States on matters related to the establishment of the outer limits of their continental shelf. The limits of the shelf established by a coastal State on the basis of these recommendations shall be final and binding."
(4) Potential jurisdictional maritime zones. Although the coastal State may not have announced the baselines of the territorial sea, according to the modern law of the sea system, especially the UNCLOS and domestic law, the coastal State has potential jurisdiction over a certain range of maritime zones. The legal status of the waters around the Nansha Qundao where the U.S. warships conducted FONP fall within this type of waters; that is, according to domestic law, China has potential jurisdiction over a certain range of waters around the Nansha

[154] For example, Articles 3, 33(2), 57, 76(1) and (5) of the Convention.

[155] Contents relating to maritime safety zones, for example, Articles 25(3), 52(2), 60 (4)-(5) of the Convention. Relating to marine development zones, for example, Article 246(6). Relating to marine protected areas, for example, Articles 211 (6) and 234.

Qundao. For example, Article 2 of the Marine Environmental Protection Law of the People's Republic of China (adopted in 1982, amended in 1999, 2013, and 2016) provides that this Law shall apply to the internal waters, territorial seas, contiguous zones, exclusive economic zones, and continental shelves of the PRC and all other sea areas under the jurisdiction of the PRC. Meanwhile, Article 2 of the Fisheries Law of the People's Republic of China (adopted in 1986, amended in 2000 and 2004) stipulates that all productive activities of fisheries, such as aquaculture and catching or harvesting of aquatic animals and plants in the inland waters, tidal flats and territorial waters" of the PRC, or in other sea areas under the jurisdiction of the PRC, must be conducted in accordance with this Law. Article 14 of the Law of the People's Republic of China on the Exclusive Economic Zone and the Continental Shelf stipulates that the provisions of this Law shall not affect the historical rights of the People's Republic of China. That is, China may, in accordance with international law (including general international law), in particular, the UNCLOS, and domestic law, determine the scope of its jurisdiction in the maritime zones surrounding the Nansha Qundao to implement and regulate freedom of navigation in maritime areas of a different nature.

5.4.3.3 Basic Functions of the Various Jurisdictional Maritime Zones

The coastal State has sovereignty, sovereign rights, and jurisdiction over the identified jurisdictional maritime zones, but these rights are to be exercised, *inter alia*, with "due regard" to the rights of other States, including freedom of navigation and overflight, achieving a balance of rights between the coastal and user States. For example, Article 87(2) of the UNCLOS provides that "These freedoms shall be exercised by all States with due regard for the interests of other States in their exercise of the freedom of the high seas." The term "due regard" here refers to restrictions on the exercise of freedom of the high seas by all countries, and at the same time, "due regard" has reciprocity. In other words, "due regard" requires all countries to be aware of and consider the interests of other countries in using the high seas when exercising freedom of the high seas, and to avoid activities that interfere with the exercise of freedom of the high seas by other countries; States should avoid any possible adverse effects on the use of the high seas by nationals of other countries.[156] In fact, the development history of the law of the sea is the history of the coordination and balance between the rights of coastal States and the rights of user States, especially the freedom of navigation and overflight. In other words, the history of the law of the sea is the history of the conflict and adjustment between the jurisdiction claimed by coastal countries and the maritime freedom claimed by other countries, the individual interests of coastal countries and the general/universal interests of the international community.[157]

---

[156] See Sohn, Louis B., et al. 2014. *The law of the sea in a nutshell (2nd ed.),* (trans. Fu Kuen Chen, et al). Shanghai: Shanghai Jiao Tong University Press. p. 17.

[157] See [Japanese] Mizukami, Chiyuki. 2004. The Formation of the Freedom of the Seas (1), *Hiroshima Law Journal* 28(1): 1–2.

5.4.3.4 The Nature of the Maritime Zones in Which U.S. Warships Implements FONP

(1) The nature of the adjacent waters and offshore waters of the maritime features of the Nansha Qundao. China has indisputable sovereignty over the Nanhai Zhudao. Thus, it claims jurisdiction over the waters of the Nansha Qundao based on the principles of land dominance over the sea and of distance in the UNCLOS. However, due to various reasons, China has not yet announced the baselines of the territorial sea of the Nansha Qundao, meaning the scope of China's jurisdictional waters in the Nansha Qundao remains unclear. According to the Declaration of the Government of the PRC on China's Territorial Sea (September 4, 1958), the Law of the PRC on the Territorial Sea and the Contiguous Zone (February 25, 1992), the Decision of the Standing Committee of the NPC of the PRC on the Ratification of the UNCLOS, the Declaration of the Government of the PRC on the Baselines of China's Territorial Sea (May 15, 1996), and the relevant provisions of the Law of the PRC on the Exclusive Economic Zone and the Continental Shelf (June 26, 1998), Marine Environment Protection Law and the Fisheries Law of the PRC, China has potential jurisdiction over the waters within a certain range around the Nansha Qundao. In other words, China's jurisdictional waters within a certain range around the Nansha Qundao can be determined based on domestic law, historic rights, and the UNCLOS regime. China should have the right to regulate the so-called FONP, that is, innocent passage, that U.S. warships have conducted in the waters surrounding the Nansha Qundao, especially within 12 nautical miles.[158] The actions of U.S. warships within 12 nautical miles of the Nansha Qundao should be subject to China's laws and regulations on the regime of innocent passage of foreign warships in its territorial waters.

In other words, the maritime zones under China's jurisdiction in the Nansha Qundao can be declared by China in its capacity as a party to the UNCLOS

[158] For example, Article 1 of the Declaration of the Government of the PRC on China's Territorial Sea provides that "The breadth of the territorial sea of the People's Republic of China shall be twelve nautical miles. This provision applies to all territories of the People's Republic of China, the mainland and its offshore islands, Taiwan and the various affiliated islands including Diaoyu Dao, Penghu Qundao, Dongsha Qundao, Xisha Qundao, Nansha Qundao and other islands that belong to the People's Republic of China." Article 2 of the Law of the PRC on the Territorial Sea and the Contiguous Zone stipulates that "The People's Republic of China's territory includes the mainland and its offshore islands, Taiwan and the various affiliated islands including Diaoyu Dao, Penghu Qundao, Dongsha Qundao, Xisha Qundao, Nansha Qundao and other islands that belong to the People's Republic of China." Article 3 provides that "the breadth of the territorial sea of the People's Republic of China is 12 nautical miles from the baseline of the territorial sea." Article 3 of the Decision of the Standing Committee of the NPC of the PRC on the Ratification of the UNCLOS declares that "China reaffirms its sovereignty over the archipelagos and islands listed in Article 2 of the Law of the People's Republic of China on the Territorial Sea and the Contiguous Zone promulgated on February 25, 1992. Declaration of the Government of the People's Republic of China on the Baselines of the Territorial Sea provides that, "The Government of the People's Republic of China will announce the remaining baselines of the territorial sea of the People's Republic of China at another time."

(the territorial sea, the contiguous zone, and the EEZ) and can be claimed based on historic rights (historical special maritime areas). The former is the primary claim, and the latter is the secondary claim, which together constitute the scope of China's jurisdictional maritime areas in the Nansha Qundao.[159]

The question of whether China can claim maritime jurisdiction over the Nansha Qundao as a whole, the scope of the maritime area that can be claimed on the basis of historic rights, the special nature of historic rights, and whether they are covered by the UNCLOS, and the status and nature of the maritime features in the Nansha Qundao are other important issues that require further deliberation. These elements constitute the crux of the SCS issue, including the dotted line, the status of historic rights and their relationship with the UNCLOS, and the regime of archipelagic waters and the identification and role of maritime features (islands, rocks, low-tide elevations, etc.).[160]

(2) The U.S. warships' intention to conduct FONP in the waters surrounding the Nansha Qundao. There are multiple reasons for the so-called FON operations conducted by U.S. warships in the SCS. In terms of political security, the U.S. must fulfill its obligation to protect its allies and "ensure" the security of the international community by implementing its domestic defense budget. In terms of diplomatic objectives, the U.S. needs to fulfill its obligations, such as the SCS issue, expressed in the statements by the G7 heads of State and foreign ministers.[161] In terms of legal objectives, the U.S. must maintain the FONP in the waters around the Nansha Qundao and the surrounding waters of the Nansha Qundao, including adopting U.S. standards to curb the practice of excessive

[159] See Yongming, Jin. 2012. Nature of the dashed line and legal status of internal water areas in South China Sea, *China Legal Science* 6: 36–48.

[160] See Chinese Society of International Law. 2018. *The South China Sea Arbitration awards: A Critical Study.* Beijing: Foreign Languages Press. pp. 183–299. For a critique of the South China Sea Arbitration Tribunal's award on maritime features, see Michael Shengti, Gau. 2018. On the questionable interpretation of Article 121 (3) of UNCLOS in the Award ofthe South China Sea Arbitration, *Pacific Journal* 12(1): pp. 24–34.

[161] For example, the G7 Foreign Ministers' Declaration on Maritime Security and Safety (April 15, 2015) states tahat, "We call on all states to pursue the peaceful management or settlement of maritime disputes in accordance with international law, including through internationally recognised legal dispute settlement mechanisms, and to fully implement any decisions rendered by the relevant courts and tribunals which are binding on them. We underline the importance of coastal States refraining from unilateral actions that cause permanent physical change to the marine environment in areas pending final delimitation." The G7 Heads of State Declaration (June 8, 2015) states that, "We are committed to maintaining a rules-based order in the maritime domain based on the principles of international law, in particular as reflected in the UN Convention on the Law of the Sea. We are concerned by tensions in the East and South China Seas. We underline the importance of peaceful dispute settlement as well as free and unimpeded lawful use of the world's oceans. We strongly oppose the use of intimidation, coercion or force, as well as any unilateral actions that seek to change the status quo, such as large-scale land reclamation." See also http://www.MFA.go.jp/MFAj/ecm/ec/page4_001250.html, accessed June 10, 2015. G7 Foreign Ministers' Declaration on Maritime Security (April 11, 2016), http://www.MFA.go.jp/MFAj/files/000147443.pdf, accessed April 13, 2016. G7 Foreign Ministers' Statement on Recent Developments in Asia, http://www.MFA.go.jp/MFAj/files/000189834.pdf, accessed September 22, 2016. G7 Taormina Leaders' Communiqué (May 26–27, 2017), http://www.MFA.go.jp/MFAj/files/000260041.pdf, accessed May 28, 2017.

straight baselines, solidifying the final award of the *SCS* Arbitration, objecting to the exercise of jurisdiction over the security matters in the contiguous zone, and objecting to the need to obtain prior consent for military activities in the EEZ.[162] However, from a legal perspective, the dispute between China and the U.S. over the Nansha Qundao centers on the legal status of the maritime features occupied and constructed by China, that is, whether they are islands, rocks, or low-tide elevation.

The U.S. argues that the maritime features occupied by China in the Nansha Qundao are low-tide elevations, which, under Article 13 of the UNCLOS, does not have their own territorial sea if the distance between all of the area of the low-tide elevations and the mainland or islands exceeds the breadth of the territorial sea. The purpose of this provision is to discourage coastal States from leapfrogging from one low-tide elevation to another to claim a baseline away from the coast.[163] Meanwhile, Article 7(4) of the UNCLOS provides that, except in the case of a lighthouse or similar installation on a low-tide elevation permanently above sea level, or where the use of such an elevation as a point of departure for the establishment of a baseline is generally recognized internationally, the low-tide elevation shall not be used as a point of departure for the establishment of a straight baseline. Offshore installations and artificial islands shall not be considered harbor works (e.g., Article 11 of the UNCLOS), meaning "structures" and "installations" that are "integral parts of the land," in a sense enclosing and protecting the waters therein and " forming part of the coast."[164] For this reason, the U.S., in its capacity as protector of the interests of the international community, has been carrying out so-called FONP in the waters surrounding the Nansha Qundao to challenge China's rights and interests in the SCS and with the aim of curbing the demand for the so-called excessive maritime claims. In essence, the FON operations are not only in line with U.S. "national interests" in the SCS region but are also an opportunity and pretext for the U.S. to get involved in SCS affairs. In other words, the U.S. FONP is packaged under the international legal cloak of "safeguarding the right to

---

[162] For the U.S. position paper on China's straight baselines in the Xisha Qundao, see the U.S. Department of State's report "Limits in the Seas-Straight Baseline Claim: China" (No.117), issued on June 9, 1996. For the development process of the U.S. policy on FON, including FON in the waters surrounding the SCS maritime features, see Yongming, Jin. 2015. Maritime Silk Road and issues over South China Sea, *The Journal of South China Sea Studies* 4: 2–3. For the United States exercising the so-called FON based on "excessive maritime claims," see Yinan, Bao. 2017. The U.S. "excessive maritime claims:" A critical analysis, *China International Studies* 5: 2–3, 117.

[163] See Sohn, Louis B., et al. 2014. *The law of the sea in a nutshell (2nd ed.),* (trans. Fu Kuen Chen, et al). Shanghai: Shanghai Jiao Tong University Press. p. 64. The U.S. argues that unless China's land reclamation projects have given island status to Zhubi Jiao and others, they are merely low-tide elevations with no territorial sea *per se*, and thus do not need to exercise innocent passage. SeeXinjun, Zhang. 2017. New progress of the U.S. freedom of navigation program in the South China Sea: "De-regulation" or "rebalancing," in ed. Wu Shicun, *South China Sea Review Vol. 1,* 49–53. Nanjing: Nanjing University Press. pp. 47–48.

[164] See Sohn, Louis B., et al. 2014. *The law of the sea in a nutshell (2nd ed.)*, (trans. Fu Kuen Chen, et al). Shanghai: Shanghai Jiao Tong University Press. p. 64.

freedom of navigation," while the substantive purpose is to promote its domestic policy of safeguarding its right to "navigation."[165]

In view of the fact that China has now completed the land reclamation and construction activities in the Nansha Qundao, the U.S., to curb China's claim of jurisdictional waters and expanding its jurisdictional scope and in anticipation of the damage to the so-called freedom of navigation and overflight, has carried out so-called FON operations with the entry of warships within the 12-nautical-mile limit of relevant features of the Nansha Qundao. This is to eliminate China's claims in the SCS, especially in the Nansha Qundao, as well as their ongoing expansion.[166]

(3) The adverse effects and consequences of the trespassing of U.S. warships into the maritime areas under the jurisdiction of the Nanhai Zhudao. This is mainly reflected in the following aspects:

First, it has seriously jeopardized China's sovereignty over the Nanhai Zhudao and the security of its jurisdictional waters and challenged the legitimacy of China's laws and regulations. For example, Wu Qian, Spokesperson for the MND, made a statement on the unauthorized entry of U.S. ships into the adjacent waters of the relevant maritime features of China's Nansha Qundao (August 11, 2017), pointing out that the U.S. is provoking trouble under the guise of FON by sending military ships and aircraft to illegally

---

165 See Kuan-Hsiung, Wang. 2018. A probe into the US Navy FONOP: Collision between law and policy, *Journal of South China Sea Studies* 4(1): 71.

166 Foreign Ministry Spokesperson Hua Chunying, presiding over a regular press conference (June 30, 2015), pointed out that, "the land reclamation project of China's construction on some stationed islands and reefs of the Nansha Islands has been completed recently as scheduled. In the next stage, the Chinese side will start the building of facilities to meet relevant functional requirements. The facilities, which mainly provide various civilian services, will enable China to better perform its international obligations and responsibilities in areas such as maritime search and rescue, disaster prevention and mitigation, marine scientific research, meteorological observation, ecological environment conservation, navigation safety as well as fishery production service. Necessary military defense requirements will also be fulfilled." See also http://www.fmprc.gov.cn/mfa_chn/fyrbt_602243/t1277205.shtml, accessed July 1, 2015. In terms of infrastructure building in the SCS region, relevant personnel from the Chinese Ministry of Transport pointed out that since 2014, China has gradually increased its construction efforts, which has initially formed a civil navigation support infrastructure network in the SCS. In addition to the construction of five lighthouses on islands and reefs in the Nansha Qundao, China has also built four lamp piles in the waters of Xisha Qundao, including Jinqing Dao; set up four ship automatic identification system base stations in Yongxing Dao and other places, achieving full coverage of signals in key waters of the Xisha Islands; provided maritime safety information broadcasting services, achieving coverage of signals in the waters of Xisha Qundao and Zhongsha Qundao. Meanwhile, in improving the cruise mechanism, through inspection, the hydrological and meteorological conditions, navigation environment, ship traffic and operations, and sea pollution in the SCS have been preliminarily grasped, and various illegal actions that occur during ship navigation, berthing, and operations have been prevented and corrected. For the above, see Ministry of Transport introduces construction of 5 lighthouses on South China Sea maritime features, points out China always pursues maintenance of vessel navigation safety in the South China Sea, *People's Daily*, July 11, 2016, p. 6.

enter the adjacent waters of the maritime features of China's SCS, considered a serious threat to China's sovereignty and security interests, the lives and safety of front-line personnel on both sides, and regional peace and stability.[167] Meanwhile, Article 6(2) of the Law of the PRC on the Territorial Sea and the Contiguous Zone stipulates that "To enter the territorial sea of the People's Republic of China, foreign military ships must obtain permission from the Government of the People's Republic of China."[168] From the Chinese Government's response to the so-called FONP of the U.S. warships' unauthorized entry into the maritime features in the SCS, i.e., regardless of any provocation by the U.S., the Chinese military will take all necessary measures to safeguard the country's sovereignty and security interests. According to Article 10 of the Law of the PRC on the Territorial Sea and the Contiguous Zone, "The relevant responsible organs of the People's Republic of China shall have the right to order an immediate eviction of foreign military ships or ships owned by foreign Governments and operated for non-commercial purposes that violate the laws or regulations of the People's Republic of China while passing through the territorial sea of the People's Republic of China. Losses or damage caused shall be borne by the nations whose flag is being flown by the ship in question." In other words, according to Article 21(1) of the UNCLOS further improve the laws on innocent passage through territorial waters, as well as corresponding domestic regulations, including procedures and supervisory authorities for prior permission or notification to coastal States.

Second, the continued implementation of the so-called FONP by U.S. warships undermines the Memorandum of Understanding on the Notification of Major Military Activities and the Memorandum of Understanding on the Rules of Behavior for Safety of Air and Maritime Encounters in November 2014, as well as the subsequent annexes signed in September 2015. It is not conducive to the exchange and mutual trust between the military departments

---

[167] See also http://www.mod.gov.cn/topnews/2017-08/11/content_4788473.htm, accessed August 11, 2017.

[168] Article 6 of the Law of the PRC on the Territorial Sea and the Contiguous Zone of China, which regulates the innocent passage of foreign warships in the territorial sea of China, provides for prior authorization or approval. This is inconsistent with the statement of the Decision of the Standing Committee of the NPC of the PRC on the Ratification of the UNCLOS. Article 4 in the Decision provides that the PRC reaffirms that "the provisions of the UNCLOS relating to innocent passage through the territorial sea are without prejudice to the right of a coastal State to require, in accordance with its laws and regulations, that the passage of foreign warships through the territorial sea be subject to prior authorization or notification to that State." From the perspective of the subject who makes and interprets laws, both documents have the same status because they are all passed and decided by the Standing Committee of the NPC; from the perspective of the hierarchy of the law itself, "law" is higher than "decision;" from the perspective of the time of law making, whether the principle of "later law" being superior to "earlier law" should be followed for the same matter, then it is necessary to modify the provisions of "earlier law" and supplement the procedural content of innocent passage through territorial waters to coordinate and unify specific norms for the same matter and act according to procedures.

of the two countries.[169] For example, in the "Ministry of National Defense Spokesperson Wu Qian's Remarks on unauthorized entry of U.S. warships into the adjacent waters of the relevant maritime features of China's Nansha Qundao" (August 11, 2017), it was pointed out that the above-mentioned provocative actions by the U.S. have seriously damaged the strategic mutual trust between the two sides and created difficulties and obstacles for the development of military-to-military relations. We strongly urge the U.S. to immediately correct its mistakes and stop illegal provocations under the guise of so-called freedom of navigation. The provocative actions of the U.S. will only prompt the Chinese military to further strengthen its defense capabilities and firmly defend national sovereignty and security.[170]

Third, the so-called FONP carried out by U.S. warships in the waters surrounding the Nanhai Zhudao jeopardized the consensus and willingness reached between China and ASEAN countries, as well as between China and the Philippines, and created uncertainties and unpredictability in the resolution of the matter. For example, the Joint Statement of the Foreign Ministers of ASEAN Member States and China on the Full and Effective Implementation of the Declaration on the Conduct of Parties in the South China Sea (July 25, 2016) reaffirms the importance and role of the DOC in maintaining peace and stability in the region; they are committed to the full and effective implementation of the DOC in its entirety and working substantively towards the early adoption of a COC based on consensus.[171] Paragraph 40 of the Joint Statement of the People's Republic of China and the Republic of the Philippines (October 21, 2016) states "Both sides affirm that contentious issues are not the sum total of the China-Philippines bilateral relationship. Both sides exchange views on the importance of handling the disputes in the South China Sea in an appropriate manner. Both sides also reaffirm the importance of maintaining and promoting peace and stability, freedom of navigation in and over-flight above the South China Sea, addressing their territorial and jurisdictional disputes by peaceful means, without resorting to the threat or use of force, through friendly consultations and negotiations by sovereign states directly concerned, in accordance with universally recognized principles of international law, including the Charter of the United

---

[169] For the the Notification of Major Military Activities between the U.S. and Chinese militaries, see https://dod.defense.gov/Portals/1/Documents/pubs/141112_MemorandumOfUnderstandingOnNotification.pdf, accessed February 10, 2015. For the Rules of Behavior for Safety of Air and Maritime Encounters between the U.S. and Chinese militaries, see https://dod.defense.gov/Portals/1/Documents/pubs/141112_MemorandumOfUnderstandingRegardingRules.pdf, accessed February 10, 2015.

[170] Ministry of National Defense Spokesperson Wu Qian's Remarks on unauthorized entry of U.S. warships into the adjacent waters of the relevant maritime features of China's Nansha Qundao, see http://www.mod.gov.cn/topnews/2017-08/11/content_4788473.htm, accessed August 11, 2017.

[171] Joint Statement of the Foreign Ministers of ASEAN Member States and China on the Full and Effective Implementation of the Declaration on the Conduct of Parties in the South China Sea, see http://www.fmprc.gov.cn/web/zyxw/t1384157.shtml, accessed July 25, 2016.

Nations and the 1982 UNCLOS."[172] These are recognized in the Joint Statement of the People's Republic of China and the Republic of the Philippines (November 21, 2018) and developed. For example, paragraph 25 of the Statement states the following: "Both sides note that the situation in the South China Sea has become generally more stable as a result of joint cooperative efforts between China, the Philippines, and other ASEAN Member States. Both sides, together with ASEAN Member States, will work for the full and effective implementation of the Declaration on the Conduct of Parties in the South China Sea in its entirety. Both sides agree to maintain the positive momentum of the negotiations on the Single Draft Code of Conduct Negotiating Text, with a view towards the early adoption of an effective COC, based on consensus." In paragraph 26, it is stated that "Both sides also note the importance of confidence-building measures to increase mutual trust and confidence. In this regard, both sides affirm the importance of the Bilateral Consultation Mechanism on the South China Sea and the Joint Coast Guard Committee on Maritime Cooperation." Paragraph 27 states that "Both sides welcome the signing of the Memorandum of Understanding on Cooperation on Oil and Gas Development between the two governments, and agree to discuss maritime cooperation including maritime oil and gas exploration, sustainable use of mineral, energy and other marine resources."[173]

Fourth, if U.S. warships continue to carry out so-called FONP based on the so-called final award of the *SCS* Arbitration (July 12, 2016), the security confrontation between China and the U.S. will intensify, the SCS region will be unstable, and the U.S.–China relationship will be adversely affected. Regardless of whether the U.S. implements the so-called FONP in the territorial waters of China's Xisha Qundao or in the waters surrounding the Nansha Qundao, including the potential jurisdictional waters within 12 nautical miles, it should abide by the regime of innocent passage through the territorial waters and potential jurisdictional waters (territorial waters). Any behavior beyond innocent passage (i.e., harmful actions) constitute provocative actions that threaten the security of China's jurisdictional waters and damage its interests. Naturally, such actions will continue to meet with strong opposition and protests from the Chinese Government. For example, "The Spokesperson of MND's remarks on unauthorized entry of the U.S. warship into territorial waters of Xisha Qundao" (October 11, 2017) pointed out that, the U.S. sent warships to enter China's territorial waters once again, infringing on China's sovereignty and security interests, damaging the strategic mutual trust between the armies of China and the U.S., destroying regional peace and stability. Furthermore, such actions are prone to cause accidents, and the MND is resolutely opposed. The Chinese military will, in response to the

[172] Joint Statement of the People's Republic of China and the Republic of the Philippines, see http://www.fmprc.gov.cn/web/zyxw/t1407676.shtml, accessed October 21, 2016.

[173] Joint Statement of the People's Republic of China and the Republic of the Philippines, see http://www.fmprc.gov.cn/web/zyxw/t1615198.shtml, accessed November 21, 2018.

repeated provocations of the U.S. military, continue to strengthen its naval and air combat readiness and improve its defense capabilities to defend the country's sovereignty and security interests.[174]

5.4.4 Some Measures and Prospects for China to Maintain Its Rights and Interests in the South China Sea

The U.S. Government's dispatch of warships to carry out the so-called FONP in the waters surrounding the Nansha Qundao (the main purpose of which is to curb the "excessive" claims of the coastal States according to its own judgment) will not stop as a result of China's protests, representations, and warnings. The U.S. will still occasionally dispatch warships to the waters surrounding the Nanhai Zhudao in a "1 + X" mode without authorization based on the final ruling of the *SCS* Arbitration. To curb China's maritime activities and claims, fulfill its obligations to its allies and maintain the so-called rules of freedom of navigation, the U.S. will continue to dispatch warships to the waters surrounding the Nanhai Zhudao based on the so-called final award of the *SCS* Arbitration in the mode of "1 + X" without authorization. In this regard, to safeguard its rights and interests in the SCS, including FONP and security, China should take the following measures:

First, efforts should be made to eliminate the negative impacts of the final ruling in the *SCS* Arbitration, especially the adverse legal impacts. China should focus on refuting the non-jurisdiction and inadmissibility of the Arbitral Tribunal in this case, as well as the ineffectiveness of its use and expansion of the institutional weaknesses of the UNCLOS system, especially its erroneous rulings on factual determinations and the application of the law.[175] It should also strengthen its research on the constituent elements of the regime of islands, the possibility of applying the regime of archipelagic waters to continental States with outlying archipelagos, the relationship between historic rights and the UNCLOS, and the international judicial system, etc.

Second, China should use the existing channels of dialogue to strengthen communication and coordination with the U.S. In particular, it should implement the Memorandum of Understanding on the Notification of Major Military Activities and the Memorandum of Understanding on the Rules of Behavior for Safety of Air and Maritime Encounters and its subsequent annexes concluded by the military departments of the two countries, to jointly control maritime security in the SCS.

---

[174] Ministry of National Defense Spokesperson's remarks on unauthorized entry of the U.S. warship into territorial waters of Xisha Qundao, see http://www.mod.gov.cn/topnews/2017-10/11/content_4794392.htm, accessed October 11, 2017.

[175] Yongming, Jin. 2017. The impact and influence of the South China Sea Arbitration on the law of the sea, *Political Science and Law* 7: 105–116. For a systematic critique of the *SCS* Arbitration, see Chinese Society of International Law. 2018. *The South China Sea Arbitration awards: A Critical Study*. Beijing: Foreign Languages Press. pp. 1–446.

Third, China's legal system on the Nanhai Zhudao should be further clarified. In the Nansha Qundao, including the timely announcement of the latest location of Nansha Qundao based on the new status area after land reclamation, renaming of some Nansha Qundao, creating conditions to gradually announce the basis points and baselines of Nansha Qundao, and more importantly, the nature of the SCS dotted line and the specific connotation of historic rights should be clarified to avoid misunderstandings and misjudgments by other countries, especially the U.S. With regard to the regime of the territorial sea in the Xisha Qundao, the laws and regulations related to innocent passage should be strengthened in accordance with Article 21 of the UNCLOS. For the unauthorized and continuous entry of U.S. warships into the territorial waters of the Xisha Qundao, measures such as designating sea lanes and traffic separation systems in the territorial sea and establishing protected areas in the territorial sea to protect national security can be taken from the perspective of navigation safety and national security in accordance with Articles 22 and 25 of the Convention.

Fourth, China and the U.S. should take the lead in creating an international law forum on freedom of navigation. Based on the consensus of holding several forums on freedom of navigation and in conjunction with existing international regimes (e.g., the Guidelines for Navigation and Overflight in the Exclusive Economic Zone of September 2005 and the Principles for Building Confidence and Security in the Exclusive Economic Zones of the Asia–Pacific of October 2013), this would lead to a new agreement to implement the UNCLOS on freedom of navigation and safety of navigation, avoiding the ongoing FONP by the U.S., curbing the claims of coastal States based on their own standards, and controlling actions jeopardizing the regime of freedom of navigation.[176]

Finally, it should be emphasized that the FON and overflight pursued by the U.S., including in the SCS, is not a core interest pursued by China. As China's import and export of raw materials and commodities, as well as its socioeconomic activities, depend on the security of FON and overflight, the U.S. and China share a common and broad interest in ensuring FON and overflight; thus, this is an important area where both countries must and can cooperate.

Regarding the law of the sea norms on FON and overflight, China and the U.S. have different understandings and practices due to the ambiguous nature of the UNCLOS. Thus, only by strengthening exchanges and consultations between the two sides can these diverse understandings be overcome, contributing to developing the modern law of the sea system. This is the goal of the joint efforts by the two sides. The FON actions taken by the U.S. based on unilaterally recognized EMCs have limitations in terms of effect—other countries do not change their original legal positions and claims as a result of such actions. On the contrary, confrontations will increase, which

[176] For Guidelines for Navigation and Overflight in the Exclusive Economic Zone, see Japan Ocean Policy Research Foundation. 2006. *Ocean white paper: Japan's trends, world trends*. Tokyo: Japan Ocean Policy Research Foundation. pp. 195–197; for the Principles for Building Confidence and Security in the Exclusive Economic Zones of the Asia-Pacific, see Ocean Policy Research Foundation. 2013. *Principles for Building Confidence and Security in the Exclusive Economics Zones of the Asia-Pacific*. Tokyo: Japan Ocean Policy Research Foundation. pp. 1–12.

is not conducive to the resolution of the problem. Ruling the sea based on the law is pivotal to the understanding and sustainable practice of the modern law of the sea system, maintaining maritime security, including the SCS region, and ensuring FON and overflight in a safe and orderly manner.

Chapter 6
Objectives and Vision of China's Ocean Governance in the New Era

In the current era, a maritime community with a shared future has become an important guideline for China's ocean affairs, accelerating the construction of a strong maritime country and promoting the 21st Century Maritime Silk Road, both now and in the longer term. Thus, it is necessary to discuss the meaning, development paths, and safeguards of a maritime community with a shared future to observe and assess China's performance in ocean affairs and its ability to deal with ocean issues, that is, to examine the modernization of China's ocean governance system and capacity. In view of the relatively short period of time since a maritime community with a shared future initiative was proposed and the lack of research on the topic, it is important to analyze its meaning.[1]

6.1 Proposal and Sources of a Maritime Community with a Shared Future

President Xi Jinping, Chairman of the Central Military Commission, met with the heads of foreign delegations invited to attend a multinational naval event on the 70th anniversary of the founding of the Chinese People's Liberation Army Navy (PLAN) in Qingdao on April 23, 2019. In this meeting, based on the nature, status, and role of the ocean, the goal of building the 21st Century Maritime Silk Road, China's participation in the role of ocean governance and the contribution of its navy, and the principle of dealing with maritime disputes, he observed the need to join forces to build a maritime community with a shared future.[2] This provides a direction for

[1] See Xi Jinping collectively met with the heads of foreign delegations attending the 70th anniversary of the establishment of the navy, Xinhuanet, http://www.xinhuanet.com/politics/leaders/2019-04/23/c_1124404136.htm, accessed on April 23, 2019.
[2] *Ibid.*

Y. Jin, *Ocean Law and Policy of the People's Republic of China*,
https://doi.org/10.1007/978-981-95-3166-0_6

China to accelerate in becoming a strong maritime country, developing the twenty-first Century Maritime Silk Road, and improving the global ocean governance system, which has great value and practical significance.

President Xi Jinping's summary of the nature and characteristics of ocean space and resources reveals the dependence and importance of ocean space and resources on the development of human society. Meanwhile, with the development of marine technology and equipment and the increasing dependence of countries on ocean space and resources, countries have different interests and rights when developing and utilizing the ocean. Therefore, it is impossible to eliminate disputes between countries within the limited sea area. For these disputes, political or diplomatic methods should be given priority for communication and coordination to achieve compromise and balance, eliminate the harm caused by ocean disputes, and jointly use ocean space and resources.

When political or diplomatic methods cannot resolve maritime disputes, crisis management measures can be taken, including the establishment of crisis management systems, to enhance political mutual trust and cooperation interests, and to oppose or prohibit the use of force or the threat of force to resolve disputes. Of course, when the conditions for resolving maritime disputes are not fully mature, the mode of shelving disputes and joint development can be adopted. This approach and value orientation reflect respect for the rights and demands of all parties, take care of the concerns of all parties, and achieve the goal of common benefit, embodying the basic spirit of the global governance concept of pursuing shared growth through discussion and collaboration. A maritime community with a shared future, as envisioned by China, is consistent with current development trends, the principles of ocean governance, and the requirements to maintain marine order and extends China's long-standing ocean policy. Thus, joint efforts to build a maritime community with a shared future is an important goal and direction that must be adhered to and followed.

The concept of a maritime community with a shared future is not a situational or arbitrary proposal. It is the refinement and development of our country's concept of a harmonious world and harmonious oceans, and the application and deepening of a community of shared future for mankind in the field of the oceans, that is, the community with a shared future for the oceans has a broad and profound origin and legal basis.[3]

At the 60th anniversary of the founding of the Chinese PLAN in April 2009, China proposed building "harmonious oceans" in light of international and domestic development needs, with a view to jointly safeguard lasting peace and security in the oceans. The concept of "harmonious oceans" is the crystallization of building a "harmonious world" in the field of the oceans since President Hu Jintao proposed the "harmonious world" concept at the 60th anniversary summit of the UN on September 15, 2005, reflecting the international community's understanding of the oceans and marking China's contribution to the development of the international law of the

[3] The legal basis for "a maritime community with a shared future" is the principle of "community." See Yongming, Jin. 2021. On the theoretical regime of the maritime community with a shared future, *Journal of Ocean University of China (Social Sciences)* 1: 3–5.

sea.[4] Therefore, "a maritime community with a shared future" is the legacy and development of "harmonious oceans."

It is generally believed that the concept of a community of shared future for mankind was originally proposed at the Conference on the Diplomatic Work with Neighboring Countries held on October 24–25, 2013, in Beijing. President Xi Jinping pointed out that a community of shared future for mankind should take root in neighboring countries.[5] The idea of a community of shared future for mankind has taken shape from its articulation at the UNGA. For example, President Xi Jinping pointed out during the general debate of the 70th UNGA on September 28, 2015, that China "should renew our commitment to the purposes and principles of the UN Charter, build a new type of international relations featuring win–win cooperation, and create a community of shared future for mankind."[6] A community of shared future for mankind, embodied in President Xi Jinping's speech at the UN headquarters in Geneva on January 18, 2017, is manifested in five aspects—politics, security, economy, culture, and ecology. These elements constitute the basic system of a community of shared future for mankind.[7] The solidification and sublimation of a community of shared future for mankind is defined in the Report of the 19th National Congress of the CPC, the constitution of the PRC and the constitution of the CPC.[8]

---

[4] The concept of "harmonious oceans" proposed by China is as follows: The content of harmonious oceans includes: adhering to the leadership of the UN, establishing a fair and reasonable ocean; adhering to equal consultation, building a free and orderly ocean; adhering to treating both symptoms and root causes, building a peaceful and peaceful ocean; adhering to communication and cooperation, building a harmonious and coexisting ocean; adhering to respecting and loving the sea, and building a unified ocean. See Yongming, Jin. 2016. *Theoretical study on ocean law of China (2nd Edition)*, Shanghai: Shanghai Academy of Social Sciences Press. pp. 305–306.

[5] Jinping, Xi. 2018. Adhering to the concepts of friendship, sincerity, benefit and inclusiveness, in *On building a human community with a shared future*, 67. Beijing: Central Party Literature Press. "The goal of a community of shared future for mankind" in terms of economy, development paths, and goal orientation, appears in the White Paper "China's Peaceful Development" (September 2011). See State Council Information Office of The People's Republic of China. 2011. *China's peaceful development*. Beijing: People's Publishing House. pp. 18, 23–24. Before the Conference on the Diplomatic Work with Neighboring Countries, President Xi Jinping's speeches included phrases such as "China–Africa community with a shared future," "Asia community with a shared future," "the awareness of community with a shared future," "China–ASEAN community with a shared future," and "Asia-Pacific community with a shared future." See Xi Jinping. 2018. *On building a human community with a shared future*. Beijing: Central Party Literature Press. pp. 15–16, 29, 38, 51, 54, and 62–63.

[6] Jinping, Xi. 2018. Working together to forge a new partnership of win-win cooperation and create a community of shared future for mankind, in *On building a human community with a shared future*, 67. Beijing: Central Party Literature Press. p. 254.

[7] Jinping, Xi. 2018. Work together to build a community of shared future for mankind, in *On building a human community with a shared future*, 67. Beijing: Central Party Literature Press. pp. 416–422.

[8] For example, "We call on the people of all countries to work together to build a community of shared future for mankind, to build an open, inclusive, clean, and beautiful world that enjoys lasting peace, universal security, and common prosperity. We, the Chinese, are ready to work with the people of all other countries to build a community of shared future for mankind and create a bright tomorrow for all of us." See Jinping, Xi. 2017. *Secure a decisive victory in building a moderately prosperous society in all respects and strive for the great success of socialism with*

"Promoting the building of a community of shared future for mankind" has become an important policy and action guide for guiding the modernization of socialism with Chinese characteristics, and has also become the core content and action plan of Xi Jinping's new era of socialist diplomacy with Chinese characteristics, and has become a hot and important issue for scholars to continue to study.[9]

6.2 Objectives, Vision, and Basic Scope of a Maritime Community with a Shared Future

A maritime community with a shared future applies and deepens the concept of a community of shared future for mankind in the maritime domain. Thus, examining this system of a community of shared future for mankind, including its contents, principles, paths, and goals, is necessary to provide directions and guidance for building a maritime community with a shared future.

A community of shared future for mankind includes the following aspects: first, building "a world of lasting peace through dialogue and consultation;" second, building "a world of common security for all through joint efforts;" third, building "a world of common prosperity through win-win cooperation;" fourth, building "an open and inclusive world through exchanges and mutual learning;" and fifth, making "our world clean and beautiful by pursuing green and low-carbon development."[10]

Chinese characteristics for a new era: Report to the 19th National Congress of the Communist Party of China. Beijing: People's Publishing House. pp. 58–60.

[9] According to the CNKI (August 22, 2019), the results related to a community of shared future for mankind and international law are (1) Deming, Huang, Lu Weibin. 2015. "Awareness about human beings sharing a community of common destiny" in the context of international law, *Journal of Shanghai Administration Institute* 6. (2) Zan, Li. 2016. Doctrine of international law and ways to construct the community of common destiny for mankind, *Chinese Review of International Law* 6. (3) Baihua, Gong. 2018. The principles of extensive consultation, joint contribution, and shared benefits are the cornerstone of international law for building a community of shared future for mankind, *Oriental Law* 1. (4) Huanxin, Luo. 2018. Innovation of common community of human destiny in international law: A comparative analysis of "obligations *erga omnes*," *Chinese Review of International Law* 2. (5) Hui, Zhang. 2018. A community of shared future for mankind: The contemporary development of the social foundations theory of international law, *Social Sciences in China* 3. (6) Naigen, Zhang. 2017. Exploring the international law concept of a community with a shared future for mankind, *Chinese Yearbook of International Law (2017)*. Beijing: Law Press. (7) Hong, Xu. 2018. A community of shared future for mankind and international law, *Chinese Review of International Law* 5; (8) Naigen, Zhang. 2018. The issues of international law related to constitution revision with the community of shared future for mankind, *Gansu Social Science* 6. (9) Research Team on Community of Shared Future for Mankind International Law. 2019. Building a community of shared future for mankind via international law, *Wuhan University International Law Review* 1.

[10] Jinping, Xi. 2018. Work together to build a community of shared future for mankind, in *On building a human community with a shared future*. Beijing: Central Literature Publishing House. pp. 418–422.

These elements suggest specific ways to build a community of shared future for mankind and regulate specific directions and goals.

The principles and requirements that should be observed in building a community of shared future for mankind are as follows: first, all countries "should respect each other, discuss issues as equals, resolutely reject the Cold War mentality and power politics, and take a new approach to developing state-to-state relations with communication." In other words, they should respect the principle of sovereign equality of all countries and establishing a partnership of equal treatment, mutual consultation and understanding; second, all States "should commit to settling disputes through dialogue and resolving differences through discussion, coordinate responses to traditional and non-traditional threats, and oppose terrorism in all its forms." Namely, they should adopt the principle of using peaceful means to resolve disputes and comprehensively eliminate security threats, and creating a fair, just, and shared security pattern; third, all countries "should stick together through thick and thin, promote trade and investment liberalization and facilitation, and make economic globalization more open, inclusive, and balanced so that its benefits are shared by all." In other words, they should respect the principles of fair and open free trade and achieve common development, and seek open, innovative, inclusive, and mutually beneficial development prospects; fourth, all States "should respect the diversity of civilizations. In handling relations among civilizations, let us replace estrangement with exchange, clashes with mutual learning, and superiority with coexistence." This means that, they should abide by the principles of inclusiveness, mutual learning, and the elimination of discrimination, and promote civilized exchanges that are harmonious in diversity and inclusive; fifth, all countries "should be good friends to the environment, cooperate to tackle climate change, and protect our planet for the sake of human survival." In other words, they should abide by the principles of environmental protection and intensive use of resources, and build an ecological system that advocates natural and green development.[11]

The principles that a community of shared future for mankind should follow include those of the UN Charter and the norms of international relations because building a community of shared future for mankind must be based on and guaranteed by international law. Thus, it is fully consistent with the principle of "extensive consultation, joint contribution, and shared benefits" and must be fully implemented and enforced without any bias in favor of either principle. In other words, the construction and implementation of a community of shared future for mankind is based on international rules, which require the participation and coordination of all states and the reflection of their will. The principle of "extensive consultation, joint contribution, and shared benefits" should be reflected and implemented here, so that the established international law can play its due and sustained role.

---

[11] See Jinping, Xi. 2017. Secure a decisive victory in building a moderately prosperous society in all respects and strive for the great success of socialism with Chinese characteristics for a new era: Report to the 19th National Congress of the Communist Party of China. Beijing: People's Publishing House. pp. 58–59; Jinping, Xi. 2018. Working together to forge a new partnership of win-win cooperation and create a community of shared future for mankind, in On building a human community with a shared future, 254–258. Beijing: Central Party Literature Press.

Meanwhile, a maritime community with a shared future originated from the concept of "harmonious oceans," therefore, the values and objectives embedded in the concept of "harmonious oceans" should be followed in a maritime community with a shared future.

The concept of "harmonious oceans" is a current necessity and has a deep foundation in international law. As ocean issues are complex, sensitive, and interrelated, they require comprehensive consideration and responses.[12] A single country is obviously unable to respond to and deal with the problems of the oceans. Thus, it is necessary for international organizations, in particular the UN, to play a leading role in building a fair and reasonable system to manage the oceans. When developing and utilizing oceans, countries are bound to have various disputes due to their differing interests and positions. It is necessary to solve such disputes through consultation, where the equal status of all parties in the negotiation process is ensured, and the basic principle of international law, the sovereign equality of states, should be ensured to maintain the order of the oceans. Meanwhile, due to the relevance and complexity of ocean issues, implementing integrated management that treats the symptoms and the root causes when dealing with ocean issues is necessary. In addition, the resolution of international issues, including ocean issues, requires a combination of cooperative forces based on international law. For example, Articles 1, 2, 11, and 49 of the UN Charter, and Articles 100, 108, 117–118, 123, 197, 242, 266, 270, 273, and 287 of the UNCLOS. The principle of "the duty of States to cooperate with one another in accordance with the Charter" was recognized in the Declaration on Principles of International Law concerning Friendly Relations and Cooperation among States in accordance with the Charter of the United Nations, adopted by the UNGA on October 24, 1970. Finally, rationally developing and utilizing marine resources for the benefit of humankind requires the oceans to be protected to achieve the goals of unity between humans and nature and sustainable development.[13] The objectives of the concept of "harmonious oceans" thus provide an important basis and code of conduct for China's building of "a maritime community with a shared future," which must be fully and effectively implemented.

In this regard, the basic meaning and value of a maritime community with a shared future can be defined as follows: politically, the goal is one of non-hegemony and peaceful development. In other words, "China remains firm in pursuing an independent foreign policy of peace. We respect the right of the people of all countries to choose their own development path. We endeavor to uphold international fairness and justice, and oppose acts that impose one's will on others or interfere in the internal affairs of others as well as the practice of the strong bullying the weak." "No matter what stage of development it reaches China will never seek hegemony or engage in expansion." In terms of the security goal, China pursues "a holistic approach to

---

[12] For example, the "Preamble" to the UNCLOS points out that, the Convention is "conscious that the problems of ocean space are closely interrelated and need to be considered as a whole."

[13] Yongming, Jin. 2016. *Theoretical study on ocean law of China (2nd Edition)*, Shanghai: Shanghai Academy of Social Sciences Press. pp. 305–306; Yongming, Jin. 2018. *Research on the strategy of China's ocean power in the new era*, Beijing: Ocean Press. pp. 79–80.

national security" and "new security" (mutual trust, mutual benefit, equality and cooperation), "resolutely safeguards China's sovereignty, security, and development interests. China will never pursue development at the expense of others' interests, but nor will China ever give up its legitimate rights and interests. No one should expect us to swallow anything that undermines our interests. China pursues a national defense policy that is in nature defensive. China's development does not pose a threat to any other country."[14] Economically, China's goal is adopting "a new vision for development" (innovative, coordinated, green, and open) to develop and strengthen the marine economy, share the benefits of marine space and resources, and achieve win–win cooperation goals. Its specific external path is, by building a new type of international relations and utilizing the BRI, especially the process of building the twenty-first Century Maritime Silk Road, China will strengthen cooperation with other countries in various fields of the ocean. Its specific external path is to adhere to the overall planning of land and sea, develop and strengthen the marine economy, and achieve the goal of comprehensive marine management. Culturally, the goal is to promote the core values of socialism with Chinese characteristics, and construct an open, inclusive, and mutually beneficial marine culture, that is, to construct a new global marine cultural concept of harmony in diversity and inclusiveness. The ecological goal is to build a sustainable marine ecosystem by protecting the marine environment, achieve the goal of "harmonious oceans" advocating the unity of people and the sea, and then achieve green and sustainable development goals.

6.3 Practical Path and Guarantee for a Maritime Community with a Shared Future

To achieve the vision of a maritime community with a shared future, it is necessary to find an appropriate and feasible path for building it. Because countries have different levels of development, interests, development strategies, environments and requirements, and cultural and institutional norms, building a maritime community with a shared future, like constructing a community of shared future for mankind, requires a phased, step-by-step, and focused approach. This is also determined by the essential or legal attributes of a maritime community with a shared future.

The main body for promoting and implementing a maritime community with a shared future is humankind, which refers to all humankind, both present and future generations. This reflects that oceans are a public good and the common heritage of mankind and that the principle of intergenerational equity should be observed. The main bodies of action are states, international organizations, and other important nongovernmental organizations. The state plays a leading and central role in

[14] Jinping, Xi. 2017. Secure a decisive victory in building a moderately prosperous society in all respects and strive for the great success of socialism with Chinese characteristics for a new era: Report to the 19th National Congress of the Communist Party of China. Beijing: People's Publishing House. p. 59.

building a maritime community with a shared future because it is the main body of international law. In terms of objects, a maritime community with a shared future regulates the oceans as a whole, including all activities of human beings in developing and utilizing ocean space and resources, as well as the protection and conservation of all living and non-living resources endowed in the oceans. This reflects the holistic requirements for the effective and rational use of ocean space and resources, determined by the essential attributes of oceans (e.g., public welfare, relevance, mobility, carrying capacity, purification capacity, etc.) and the power of the oceans. It also embodies the requirements for the normative and holistic nature of the oceans to achieve the goal of sustainable utilization and development.[15] In terms of operations, the principle of extensive consultation, joint contribution, and shared benefits should be adhered to, as well as other basic principles consistent with international law. A multidimensional and multidirectional cooperative approach should be adopted to achieve the goals of common development, management, benefit, and progress.

To achieve the above goals, a maritime community with a shared future should be built through bilateral and regional agreements on the SCS and ECS, as a matter of priority, committed to a sea of peace, friendship, and cooperation. The actions and contributions of the SCS and ECS issues are the concrete path for China to build a maritime community with a shared future. This is determined by the status and role of the SCS and ECS issues in China's economic and social development and for China's construction of a strong maritime country. Therefore, the policy and dispute resolution of the SCS and ECS issues so that they do not seriously affect the overall strategic goals and development process of China, test the wisdom of the Chinese Government and people, and also correlate with China's strategic goal of becoming a strong maritime country. They also have a greater bearing on the modernization of the country's national governance system and capacity.

There are two main aspects of the SCS issue: first, the disputes over the territorial sovereignty of the maritime features of the Nansha Qundao, by extension, over the delimitation of maritime boundaries and the exploitation of resources, which are contentious issues between China and the ASEAN countries; and second, the status of the waters surrounding the Nanhai Zhudao and their freedom of navigation in the adjacent waters between China and the U.S.-led countries.[16]

---

[15] For example, the "Preamble" to the UNCLOS states that "Recognizing the desirability of establishing through this Convention, with due regard for the sovereignty of all States, a legal order for the seas and oceans which will facilitate international communication, and will promote the peaceful uses of the seas and oceans, the equitable and efficient utilization of their resources, the conservation of their living resources, and the study, protection and preservation of the marine environment."

[16] On the issue of the FONP of U.S. warships in the islands of the SCS, see Yongming, Jin. 2019. Law of the sea analysis of freedom and security of navigation in the South China Sea, in Chinese Society of International Law, *Chinese Yearbook of International Law (2018)*, 410–438. Beijing: Law Press; Bao Yinan, International law Issues concerning the unauthorized intrusions of US warships into the adjacent waters of Chinese maritime features in the South China Sea: A positivist analysis, *Pacific Journal* 6: 52–63. Documents related to freedom of navigation between the U.S. and China include the Notification of Major Military Activities between the U.S. and Chinese militaries, see https://dod.defense.gov/Portals/1/Documents/pubs/141112_MemorandumOfUnderstandingOnNotification.pdf, accessed February 10, 2015. For the Rules of Behavior for Safety of Air

The legal issues related to these disputes involve the following: the nature of the dotted line in the SCS and the legal status of the waters within the line, the nature and status of maritime features and their role in delimitation, the relationship between historic rights and the UNCLOS, the sources and specific connotations of historic rights, the possibility of applying the straight baselines of archipelagic waters to continental States outlying archipelagos, the question of whether low-tide elevations constitute territory and whether they can be occupied, the scope and interpretation of exclusionary declarations made by states under the UNCLOS, etc.[17] These legal issues must be resolved through consultation and negotiation with the relevant countries, i.e., priority is given to the use of political or diplomatic methods, while legal methods, including arbitration, have some shortcomings in cases where the relevant parties are unable to conclude an agreement or have not expressly agreed to arbitration, as demonstrated by the *SCS* Arbitration.[18] Therefore, at the bilateral level, the "dual-track approach" (i.e., disputes related to the SCS should be addressed properly through negotiations and consultations among countries directly concerned, and China and the ASEAN countries should work together to safeguard peace and stability in the SCS) is a feasible and effective method to resolve the issues based on history and international law, including the UNCLOS. This is evidenced by the concrete practice and track record between China and the Philippines.[19] At the regional level, complying with the DOC (November 4, 2002), implementing the Guidelines for the Implementation of the Declaration on the Conduct of Parties in the South China Sea (July 20, 2011), enforcing the Guidelines for Hotline Communications among Senior Officials of the Ministries of Foreign Affairs of China and ASEAN Member States in Response to Maritime Emergencies, and complying with the Joint Statement on the Application of the Code of Unplanned Encounters at Sea in the South China Sea is important, as well as following the Joint Statement of the

---

and Maritime Encounters between the U.S. and Chinese militaries, see https://dod.defense.gov/Portals/1/Documents/pubs/141112_MemorandumOfUnderstandingRegardingRules.pdf, accessed February 10, 2015.

[17] For the dotted line in the South China Sea, see Zhiguo, Gao., Jia Bingbing. 2014. *The nine-dash line in the south China sea: history, status and implications*, Beijing: Ocean Press. pp. 1–49; Kuen Chen, Fu., Cui Haoran. 2019. The U-shaped line's legal nature and historic rights of the South China Sea, *Journal of Xiamen University (Arts & Social Sciences)* 4: 66–75. For China's position and attitude toward the *SCS* Arbitration, see Chinese Society of International Law. 2018. *The South China Sea Arbitration awards: A Critical Study.* Beijing: Foreign Languages Press. pp. 1–446.

[18] Yongming, Jin. 2017. Empirical researches on non-application of legal means to territorial disputes over Nansha Qundao and reefs, *Pacific Journal* 4: 20–30; Yongming, Jin. 2017. On the Impact of the *South China Sea* Arbitration on the Law of the Sea, *Political Science and Law* 7: 105–116.

[19] For example, when Chinese President Xi Jinping met with visiting Philippine President Rodrigo Duterte in Beijing on August 29, 2019, in accordance with the Memorandum of Understanding on Cooperation on Oil and Gas Development between the two governments, the two sides announced the establishment of the Intergovernmental Joint Steering Committee and Inter-Entrepreneurial Working Group on oil and gas cooperation to push for substantial and rapid progress in joint development. China and the Philippines Announce Establishment of Intergovernmental Joint Steering Committee and Inter-Entrepreneurial Working Group on Hydrocarbon Cooperation, available at https://www.gov.cn/xinwen/2019-08/29/content_5425737.htm, accessed on August 30, 2019.

Foreign Ministers of ASEAN Member States and China on the Comprehensive and Effective Implementation of the Declaration on the Conduct of Parties in the South China Sea (July 25, 2016), which centers on the development and implementation of a COC in the SCS. The core is to formulate and implement a COC in the SCS to eliminate the shortcomings of the DOC in the SCS, to achieve the goal of normative harmonization of spatial and resource activities in the SCS region, and provide guidance for the eventual resolution of disputes in the region.[20]

There are two main areas of dispute in the ECS. The first is the dispute over the sovereignty of the Diaoyu Dao and their affiliated islands, including whether there is a consensus on "sovereignty disputes" and "shelving disputes?" The second is the dispute over resource exploitation, maritime boundary delimitation, and air and sea security arising from the dispute over territorial sovereignty over the islands. Regarding these disputes, a number of agreements have been signed between China and Japan, such as the Sino-Japanese Fisheries Agreement (signed on November 11, 1997, and entered into force on June 1, 2000), the Sino-Japanese Principled Consensus on the East China Sea Issue (June 18, 2008), Four-Point Principled Agreement on Handling and Improving Bilateral Relations between China and Japan (November 7, 2014), the Memorandum of Understanding on Maritime and Air Communication Mechanism between the Ministry of Defense of Japan and the Ministry of Defense of China (signed on May 9, 2018, and entered into force on June 8, 2018), and the Agreement on Maritime Search and Rescue Cooperation between Japan and China (signed on October 26, 2018, and entered into force on February 14, 2019). Therefore, implementing these points of consensus and considering the concerns of the other party are important aspects of stabilizing the dispute over the ECS issue and building a Sino-Japanese relationship that meets the requirements of the modern era. This will make the ECS a sea of peace, friendship, and cooperation, which is a goal that China and Japan should strive toward.[21]

---

[20] On May 18, 2019, the 17th Senior Officials' Meeting on the Implementation of the Declaration on the Conduct of Parties in the South China Sea was held in Hangzhou, China. At the meeting, the outcomes of the reading of the single draft negotiating text of the COC for the current stage were confirmed. All parties agreed to speed up the negotiations and reach the COC at an early date. The 17th Senior Officials' Meeting on the Implementation of the Declaration on the Conduct of Parties in the South China Sea (DOC) held successfully in China, see http://asean.china-mission.gov.cn/dmdt/201905/t20190520_8868700.htm, accessed May 20, 2019.

[21] During his meeting with Japanese Prime Minister Shinzo Abe in Osaka on June 27, 2019, Chinese President Xi Jinping stated that "We should jointly commit to building China-Japan relations that fit the needs of the new era to make China-Japan relations an important and positive factor for maintaining world peace and promoting common development;" "It is hoped that the Japanese side will abide by the consensus it has reached with China so far and honor the commitments it has made so far, properly handle history and other sensitive issues, and jointly safeguard peace and stability in the East China Sea." Xi Jinping meets with Prime Minster Shinzo Abe of Japan, available at http://www.xinhuanet.com/politics/leaders/2019-06/27/c_1124681266.htm, accessed on June 28, 2019. Foreign Ministry Official: Xi, Abe reach 10-point consensus to promote bilateral relations (June 27, 2019), point 8, states that "The two leaders (China and Japan) agreed to properly handle sensitive issues and manage disputes and differences constructively. The two sides will continue to promote the implementation of the principled consensus on East China Sea issues and make joint efforts to safeguard peace and stability of the East China Sea, so as to turn it into a sea of peace,

It should be noted that to ensure stability in the SCS and ECS, analyzing the existing problems through consultations on an equal footing, based on the claims and positions of all parties, and resolving them on the basis of history and international law is significant, so as to achieve the goal of "governing the sea according to the law." In other words, claiming rights on the basis of rules, using rules to utilize and maintain rights, and relying on rules to resolve disputes over rights are important foundations for guaranteeing the realization of a community of shared future in the SCS and the ECS. The rules mentioned here are mainly the rules of international law (including customary international law and statutory law) accepted by both parties, especially the law of the sea. If there are different understandings and perceptions of these rules, it is necessary to show that they are accepted by other parties before they can be applied.

To this end, China's basic position and attitude toward the issue of maritime disputes can be summarized as follows: Efforts should be made to reach an agreement through equal consultation; if an agreement cannot be reached, a system for managing crises should be established, including taking into account the other party's position and concerns, implementing a regime of sovereignty belonging to China, pursuing joint development while shelving disputes; by strengthening cooperation, especially in low-sensitive areas of the ocean (such as marine environmental protection, marine scientific research, maritime navigation and traffic safety, search and rescue, and combating transnational crime), mutual trust should be enhanced, and the foundation and conditions for the final resolution of disputes should be created to regulate the actions and activities of all parties, achieve the unity of ocean functionality and standardization, and achieve the goal of rational and effective use of ocean space and resources.[22] Therefore, the reasonable handling of the SCS and ECS issues is an

---

cooperation and friendship." See Xinhuanet, http://www.xinhuanet.com/politics/leaders/2019-06/27/c_1124681233.htm, accessed on June 28, 2009.

[22] For example, China's position and attitude towards the SCS issue and the *SCS* Arbitration mainly include: Position paper of the Government of the People's Republic of China on the matter of jurisdiction in the South China Sea Arbitration initiated by the Republic of the Philippines, see http://www.gov.cn/xinwen/2014-12/07/content_2787671.htm, accessed on December 18, 2014. Statement of the Ministry of Foreign Affairs of the People's Republic of China on settling disputes between China and the Philippines in the South China Sea through bilateral negotiation, see http://www.fmprc.gov.cn/web/zyxw/t13704.shtml, accessed on June 8, 2016. Statement of the Government of the People's Republic of China on China's territorial sovereignty and maritime rights and interests in the South China Sea, see http://world.people.com.cn/n1/2016/0712/c1002-28548370.html, accessed on July 12, 2016. See State Council Information Office of The People's Republic of China. 2016. China adheres to the position of settling through negotiation the relevant disputes between China and the Philippines in the South China Sea, in Compilation of documents on China's response to the South China Sea Arbitration, Department of Boundary and Ocean Affairs of the Ministry of Foreign Affairs of the People's Republic of China, ed. 97–124. Beijing: World Knowledge Press. The Chinese government's policy and position on oil and gas resources in the ECS: China's oil and gas exploration in the East China Sea is rightful and legitimate, https://www.mfa.gov.cn/web/ziliao_674904/1179_674909/201507/t20150724_7947598.shtml, accessed on July 29, 2015. The Chinese government's policy documents on the Diaoyu Dao issue mainly include: Statement of the Ministry of Foreign Affairs of the People's Republic of China (December 30, 1971, September 10, 2012). See China Oceanic Information Center, ed. 2012. *Diaoyu Dao-China's*

important practical step and platform for China to promote the building of a maritime community with a shared future, which is directly related to the mission and success of building a maritime community with a shared future.

6.4 Vision for a Maritime Community with a Shared Future

In accordance with the nature and characteristics of the oceans themselves, as well as the status and role of the space and resources of the oceans in economic and social development, China has proposed a policy of rationalizing the use of the oceans and solving marine issues, with the ultimate goal of building a maritime community with a shared future. This is in line with humanity's need for a marine order and with China's long-standing policy and position on the oceans, and it refines the concept of "harmonious oceans" and deepens the application of a community of shared future for mankind in the marine sphere. However, just as in the case of constructing a community of shared future for mankind, building a maritime community with a shared future requires overcoming a number of challenges and promoting cooperation in a variety of modes, including at the bilateral, regional, and international levels. In particular, it requires dealing with major issues, such as the SCS and ECS, which are important to building a maritime community with a shared future.

To solve these major problems of the oceans and to build a maritime community with a shared future, it is necessary to adopt peaceful methods to resolve issues through negotiation and dialogue, and it is important to use international rules (international law and the UNCLOS) that exist and are widely accepted by the international community. Governing the ocean according to law means actively participating in the formulation of new international ocean rules and expressing opinions, especially complying with the consensus and agreements already reached, and creating conditions and foundations for the final resolution of disputes, including the formulation of crisis management regimes to mitigate and eliminate tensions and contribute to the realization of a sea of peace, friendship, and cooperation.

To gradually advance toward building a maritime community with a shared future, it is essential to establish and utilize platforms such as the BRI. Therefore, China can use existing platforms (such as the Maritime Silk Road Fund and the China–ASEAN Investment and Cooperation Fund) and create new platforms (such as the Marine Safety Forum, the Marine Ecology Forum, the Marine Culture Forum, and the Marine Economy Forum) to build a maritime community with a shared future and to make a new and greater contribution to the sustainable use of the oceans by humankind.

In conclusion, the vision of a maritime community with a shared future is beautiful, but the process of building a maritime community with a shared future is tortuous and

inherent territory. Beijing: Ocean Press. pp. 25–30; State Council Information Office of The People's Republic of China. 2012. *White Paper on Diaoyu Dao, an inherent territory of China*. Beijing: People's Publishing House. pp. 1–16.

requires making long-term and arduous efforts, centering on securing and expanding common interests, strengthening the process of multidimensional cooperation and, in particular, rationally dealing with major maritime disputes affecting the order of the oceans, so that they do not, or have little, impact on building a maritime community with a shared future. This should be the direction of China's long-term and sustained efforts and the goal of its efforts.

Chapter 7
Opportunities for China to Maintain and Expand Ocean Rules

To follow the principles and spirit embedded in China's ocean policies (the harmonious oceans, the strategy of a strong maritime country, and the BRI), and taking into account China's own status, especially the experience and achievements made after the reform and opening-up, China should play an important role in improving and constructing international ocean rules and make contributions to the goal of ruling the sea in accordance with the law, including maintaining and expanding the rules of the sea and building a maritime community with a shared future.

7.1 China's Basic Policy and Guiding Thought for Maintaining Ocean Order

In the course of the 70th anniversary of the founding of New China, China has put forward important guidelines and policies, such as harmonious oceans, building a strong maritime country, and the BRI. How to implement these ocean policy concepts must be guaranteed by China's long-established ocean policies, including the principles of peaceful settlement of disputes ("sovereignty belongs to China, disputes can be shelved, and we can pursue joint development") and the "dual-track approach." These approaches to resolving disputes are in line with the principles of international law and the norms of international relations, as well as with current trends.

At the same time, to realize these ocean policy concepts, applying the norms of international law and international relations in dealing with ocean affairs is necessary; in particular, the foreign affairs ideology of Xi Jinping Thought on Socialism with Chinese Characteristics for a New Era should be used to guide ocean affairs and realize the goal of build a maritime community with a shared future from the perspective of a community of shared future for mankind.

Among the notable concepts in China's diplomatic thinking in the new era are development, security, amity, sincerity, friendship and interests. The goal of applying

Y. Jin, *Ocean Law and Policy of the People's Republic of China*,
https://doi.org/10.1007/978-981-95-3166-0_7

these concepts is to build a community of shared future for mankind, and the way to achieve this goal is by developing a new type of international relations and the BRI. These concepts and specific paths are fully applicable to the maritime field and are reflected in the BRI.

The BRI meets the development needs of China and the countries along the routes and the region, serves the common interests of all parties concerned, and is in line with regional and global cooperation trends. It also has great vitality. The BRI framework considers the needs of all countries, integrates the two major aspects of land and sea, and has wide coverage, strong inclusiveness, and the radiation effect of development. China has proposed the BRI to strengthen the connectivity of countries along the traditional land and sea routes and achieve mutual economic prosperity, trade complementarity, and people-to-people bonds, with a view toward jointly building interstate partnerships of mutual trust, inclusiveness, cooperation, and win-win results.[1]

"All participating countries should stick to the principles of extensive consultation, joint contribution and shared benefits when implementing the Belt and Road Initiative. Consultation means that China and other countries shall pool wisdom and share good ideas with each other to achieve desirable results, so that the development of the Initiative could accommodate the interests and concerns and reflect the wisdom and creativity of both sides. Making joint contribution means China and others need to do their best to bring into play their respective advantages, tap the potential and register major achievements from accumulated efforts in a persevering way. Sharing benefits means China and other states should make more development achievements benefit people of the all sides in a fairer way and build a community of shared interests and common destiny for China and other states."[2] In other words, extensive consultation, joint contribution and shared benefits should be implemented throughout the entire process of the development of the Belt and Road project, reflecting a rational division of labor, ensuring full play to the benefits, and assuming a shared responsibility to promote prosperity and development, with a view to achieving the goal of common progress.

Today, human beings live in a world of different cultures, races, colors, religions, and social systems; at the same time, with economic globalization, the informatization of societies, and the diversification of cultures in the international community, humanity has become a community of shared future for mankind in which everyone's interests are inseparably entwined. Therefore, building a community of shared future for mankind is practical and inevitable, in the process of which, China should insist on mutual respect and equal treatment among countries; cooperation and common development; common, comprehensive, cooperative and sustainable security; and the principles and policy of openness and inclusiveness, exchanges and mutual learning of different civilizations. These elements comprise the political, economic, security,

---

[1] Jinping, Xi. 2018. *The Belt and Road Initiative*. Beijing: Central Party Literature Press. pp. 68, 51 and 41.

[2] Jinping, Xi. 2018. *The Belt and Road Initiative*. Beijing: Central Party Literature Press. p. 35.

and cultural requirements in building a community of human destiny, are consistent with current trends, and are easily accepted by the international community.

7.2 China's Position and Role in the Formulation of International Ocean New Rules

As mentioned above, after 70 years of development of New China, China has formed a domestic ocean legal system for maritime affairs. It initially constructed the Chinese ocean legal system, which made important contributions to China's maritime endeavors. However, in the domestic maritime legal system, some elements are complicated for the international community to understand. Thus, elaborating and clarifying China's ocean policy and position is an important task. To this end, an important option is for China to actively participate in formulating new international ocean rules and expressing its views and position to enrich ocean governance.

Currently, the international community's legislation on new international rules for the oceans is dominated by the development of legally binding instruments on the conservation and sustainable use of marine biodiversity in areas beyond national jurisdiction (referred to as BBNJ issues). The major and central landmark was the adoption by the UNGA on June 9, 2015, of the Resolution on the Development of an International Legally Binding Instrument under the United Nations Convention on the Law of the Sea on the Conservation and Sustainable Use of Marine Biological Diversity in Areas Beyond National Jurisdiction (A/RES/69/292).

The Preparatory Committee established, pursuant to this resolution, and submitted a draft recommendation titled "Draft Recommendation for a Legally Binding International Instrument for the Conservation and Sustainable Use of Marine Biological Diversity" (A/AC.287/2017/PC.4/2, July 31, 2017) to the UNGA on July 20, 2017, recommending that a decision be made as soon as possible to convene an intergovernmental meeting under the auspices of the UN. To this end, on December 24, 2017, the UNGA adopted a resolution (A/RES/72/249) to convene four sessions between 2018 and the first half of 2020. The UNGA decided to convene an intergovernmental conference on the subject.[3]

A three-day organizational meeting was held in New York on April 16–18, 2018, to ensure the smooth conduct of the Intergovernmental Meeting. At this organizational meeting, Rena Lee, Singapore's Ambassador for Oceans and the Law of the Sea and Special Envoy of the Minister for Foreign Affairs, was elected Speaker. The first session was held on September 14–17, 2018, at the UN Headquarters in New York. The foundational document for the discussions of the first intergovernmental session, the President's aid to discussions (A/CONF.232/2018/3), was

---

[3] See Yongming, Jin. 2018. Issues relating to the conservation and sustainable use of marine biological diversity beyond areas of national jurisdiction, *Journal of Social Sciences* 9: 12–13.

presented by the Speaker. The purpose of this document was to steer the Conference toward preparing an advance draft of the instrument (A/CONF.232/2018/2).[4]

At this meeting, Ma Xinmin, head of the Chinese delegation and Deputy Director General of the Department of Treaty and Law of the MFA, put forward four proposals: (1) the negotiations on the BBNJ international instrument should follow the principle of consensus, during the whole process of negotiation, parties should avoid decision-making by taking votes; (2) the BBNJ international instrument should be based on the United Nations Convention on the Law of the Sea (UNCLOS). It should supplement and improve the Convention, not departing from its principles and spirit, jeopardizing the institutional framework of the Convention, or contradicting the existing international law and global, regional and sectoral mechanisms governing the ocean; (3) the BBNJ international instrument should strive to safeguard common interests and preserve the common interests of all countries, in particular, the interests of developing countries, and should also preserve the interests of the international community or the humankind as a whole, with an aim to achieving mutual benefit and win-win results, and; (4) the institutional design of BBNJ international instrument should be reasonably balanced. The new instrument should strike a rea-sonable balance between the interests of all parties and all sides to avoid favoring one over the other.[5]

The Chinese Government's position on the BBNJ issue is fully consistent with the content and spirit of the relevant resolutions adopted by the UNGA, as well as with the principles and regime enshrined in the Convention. Even more so, it is consistent with China's position on ocean affairs, and China is certain to have a role in formulating an international legal instrument on the BBNJ issue.

7.3 Some Recommendations for China to Enhance Domestic Ocean Rules

In addition to actively participating in the formulation of international and regional maritime rules to maintain the order of the oceans, China must further improve its domestic maritime rules. This is because the SOA issued the CCP Central Committee Decision Regarding Some Major Questions in Comprehensively Promoting Governance According to Law and Accelerate the Construction of the Rule of Law for the Ocean based on the Decision of the CPC Central Committee on Major Issues Pertaining to Comprehensively Promoting the Rule of Law on July 20, 2015, so as to establish the authority of the law in safeguarding the rights and interests of the oceans and promoting marine economic development. The purpose is to demonstrate the concept of the rule of law in safeguarding the interests of the people, reflect on

[4] See [Japanese] Sakamoto, Shigeki. 2018. A Redaction of the Maritime Order, *International Affairs* 674: 4.

[5] Min, Yi. Gathering Consensus to Protect High Seas Biogenetic Resources, China Ocean News, September 11, 2018, p. 4.

the rule of law, and adhere to the bottom line of the rule of law in reforming the field.[6]

In terms of China's domestic legal system for the oceans, in addition to the necessary modifications and adjustments to improve the competent institutions as a result of state institutional reforms, the laws of the sea or the basic law of the oceans, as well as the functional laws of the oceans need to be formulated and improved. This is reflected in the following areas:

First, the status of "oceans" in the national legal system should be established. China's Constitution does not contain any reference to the status of "oceans" in the national legal system; therefore, it is necessary to raise the status of the oceans and seas to enhance their continuing role. The main ways to do this are to add that "oceans" are part of natural resources and should be protected by the Constitution or define and regulate the status of oceans by enacting the "Basic Law on Ocean," clarifying the competence of sea-related institutions.

Second, the study should focus on the elements of the domestic law of the sea under challenge from other countries. As mentioned above, other countries have doubts about China's system of straight baselines in the Paracel Islands, that of procedural permission or notification for innocent passage of warships in the territorial sea, and of permission for military activities in the EEZ. For this reason, to continue drawing on the practice of other countries, China should strengthen its communications and coordination with other countries on these controversial issues and make preparations to further enrich the Convention, including the formulation of a new "implementing agreement" and the appropriate adjustment of the relevant domestic legal system, and revising it at the correct time.

Third, additional laws and regulations should be formulated on matters related to the functionality of the oceans and seas. To develop and utilize the space and resources of the ocean sustainably, it is very important to strengthen research and development of marine science and technology, which is the key to China becoming a maritime country. Marine science and technology play an important supporting role in developing and utilizing ocean space and resources, including the ocean economy. Therefore, with regard to the functionality of the oceans, China should upgrade and improve such laws as regulations to manage foreign-related marine scientific research, the formulation of the law on marine science and technology, and the law on marine safety to conduct research and implement legislation and revisions.

Fourth, the institutional mechanism for the oceans should be improved to provide guarantees. To modernize the national governance system and capacity, China has reformed its marine institutions; thus, it should seize this opportunity of this national institutional reform to coordinate and clarify the functions of sea-related management institutions (e.g., the State Oceanic Commission, the MNR, the MEE, the MARA, the GACC, and the CCG). Further, China has included the Decision of the Standing

[6] For the Decision of the Leading CPC Members' Group of the State Oceanic Administration to Comprehensively Advance Law-based Administration and Accelerate the Construction of the Rule of Law for the Ocean, see http://www.soa.gov.cn/zwgk/ga-gg/201508/t20150807_39403.html, accessed August 19, 2015.

Committee of the NPC on the Exercising of the Marine Right Safeguarding and Law Enforcement Functions and Powers by the CCG (adopted on June 22, 2018, and effective as of July 1, 2018) and further developed and improved relevant laws and regulations such as the Basic Law of the Sea and the Organization Law of the CCG. These laws and regulations are important safeguards for the construction of a strong maritime country and comprehensively managing maritime affairs.[7]

[7] Program for Deepening the Reform of the Party and State Institutions issued by the Central Committee of the Communist Party of China (Mar. 21, 2018), http://www.xinhuanet.com/politics/2018-03/21/c_1122570517.htm, accessed October 18, 2018. Decision of the Standing Committee of the 13th National People's Congress on the Exercising of the Marine Right Safeguarding and Law Enforcement Functions and Powers by the China Coast Guard, adopted on June 22, 2018, http://www.npc.gov.cn/npc/xinwen/2018-06/22/content_2056585.htm, accessed October 18, 2018.

Epilogue

This book is a synthesis of the results of the "70th Anniversary of the Founding of the PRC" research project "New China's Ocean Policy and Legal System: Review and Prospect" (2017BHB005), based on the results of the research project "New China's Ocean Policy and Legal System: Review and Prospect" (2017BHB005), and the results of the author's work on the theory of the law of the sea and ocean issues.

Considering the development of modern international law of the sea as an entry point, this book points out the principal features, content, principles, problems, and development trends of the modern law of the sea system in a narrow sense, particularly the UNCLOS system. Furthermore, it analyses the development of the legal system of the oceans in the past 70 years of New China in light of the structure of the UNCLOS system, divides it into four stages (embryonic, development, shaping, and enrichment), indicating what China has accomplished in each of these stages.

Second, it analyses New China's achievements in ocean policy, including specific measures in the formulation of comprehensive ocean policy, national ocean development plans, and the promotion of the ocean cause to the outside world. At the same time, the achievements and tasks of New China in terms of ocean management institutions and reforms are elaborated to strengthen comprehensive ocean management and enhance ocean governance capacity. Moreover, it focuses on analyzing the initiatives and effects of New China's marine endeavors, especially the background and effects of the concept of harmonious oceans, the strategic system of a strong maritime country, and the BRI initiative. In this section, the strategic system of China's maritime country (including the development process, basic path, core indicators, important features, and target positioning) and the practical path toward becoming a maritime country are systematically studied. The BRI, including its nature and mission, spatial scope, basic content, goals and vision, safeguards, and evaluation of its effects, is reviewed.

In light of the basic contents and structure of the UNCLOS and customary international law, China's domestic ocean legislation practices are described, the problems and challenges of New China's legal system for the oceans are analyzed, and recommendations for further improvement are proposed. These recommendations include the establishment of the status of "ocean" in the national legal system, such as the

Y. Jin, *Ocean Law and Policy of the People's Republic of China*,
https://doi.org/10.1007/978-981-95-3166-0

formulation of a basic law on the ocean, focusing on the elements of the domestic law of the sea that has been challenged by other countries, especially the U.S., such as the straight baseline system of the Xisha Qundao, the regime of innocent passage of foreign warships in the territorial waters, and the issue of military activities in the EEZ, as well as the supplementation, refinement and formulation of regulations related to functional matters of the oceans. For example, amending the Provisions on Administration of Foreign-related Marine Scientific Research and formulating marine science and technology and security laws. The maritime system and mechanism should be further improved to provide security, including coordinating and clarifying the duties and powers of ocean-related management agencies, such as clarifying the duty and power of the SOC, and solidifying them by law.

To echo the aforementioned issues and in response to the problems and challenges encountered in promoting China's goal of becoming a maritime country, issues related to the SCS are selected and analyzed, including the regime of innocent passage of foreign warships in the territorial waters, the nature of the SCS dotted line and the legal status of the waters within the line, the legal basis of the islands and rocks, the impact of the *SCS* Arbitration on the law of the sea, and the FONP of the U.S. warships in the waters surrounding the Nanhai Zhudao.

Finally, it is pointed out that it is necessary and reasonable for China to maintain and expand sea rules in order to maintain maritime order, ensure maritime safety, and make rational use of ocean space and resources. Meanwhile, given China's special identity and status, the goal of transforming the role and positioning should be achieved in the process of improving maritime rules, and China's role should be played. These roles and positioning with regard to maritime rules include the transformation from the follower to the maker, from the "destroyer" to the follower, from the safeguarder to the leader, from the ambiguity to the precision, from the implementer to the supervisor, the characteristic to the ordinary, from the receiver to the supplier.

To achieve this role and positioning transformation goals, the principles and spirit contained in Xi Jinping Thought on Socialism with Chinese Characteristics for a New Era, especially the new diplomatic thinking of China in the new era, should guide ocean work, including the use of new development concepts, new security concepts, new openness concepts, new governance concepts, as well as diplomatic concepts including the concept of amity, sincerity, mutual benefit, and inclusiveness, and a more balanced approach to upholding principles and pursuing interests, to build a new type of international relations, use the BRI practice platform, and make long-term and unremitting efforts to achieve the goal of governing the sea by law and comprehensive management of the ocean, and to achieve the goal of a maritime community with a shared future for mankind in the context of a community with a shared future for mankind. In particular, it is necessary to continue to deepen and increase the theoretical research on international rules for the sea and the specific practices of various countries for reference and for our use and service, so as the strategic goal of a maritime country (stage goals and ultimate goals) presents a vision of harmony and unity among the sea of people, benefiting humanity.

In addition, we would like to emphasize that we are grateful for guidance and assistance from various sources and people in this process of research and writing, especially in the analyses of the legal elements of innocent passage in the territorial sea and the terminology of the legal elements of islands and rocks, in particular from the monographs of Prof. Shigeki Sakamoto and Prof. Moritaka Hayashi. I would also like to express my gratitude to Editor Xue Yingchun of Intellectual Property Publishing House for his kind cooperation in making this book available as soon as possible. The publication of this book will further enrich the "Ad Mare" thesis. The publication of this book has been funded by the China Association of Marine Affairs and the Academy of Ocean of China, toward whom we would like to express our gratitude!

Bibliography

I. Publications in Chinese

1. Lihai Zhao. 1984. *New developments in the law of the sea.* Beijing: Peking University Press.
2. Ying-jeou Ma. 1985. *Discussing the Diaoyutai Islands and the drawing boundary of the East China Sea from the new law of the sea.* Taipei: Cheng Chung Bookstore.
3. Nanlai Liu, Keju Wang et al. 1986. *International law of the sea.* Beijing: Ocean Press.
4. Min Wei. *Law of the sea.* 1987. Beijing: Law Press.
5. Lihai Zhao. 1987. *Theory and practice of the contemporary law of the sea.* Beijing: Law Press.
6. Tieya Wang. *International law.* 1995. Beijing: Law Press.
7. Kuen Chen Fu. 1995. *A Study on the legal status of the South (China) Sea.* Taiwan: 123 Information Information Publishing.
8. Shouben Lu. 1997. *General theory of ocean management.* Beijing: Ocean Press.
9. Hailin Zheng. 1998. *A study of the history and jurisprudence of the Diaoyutai Islands (2nd edition).* Hong Kong: Ming Pao Press.
10. Hui Wu. 2002. *Studies on the International Tribunal for the Law of the Sea.* Beijing: Ocean Press.
11. Haopei Li. 2003. *Introduction to the law of treaties.* Beijing: Law Press.
12. Guoqiang Li. 2003. *South China Sea studies: History and present situation.* Harbin: Heilongjiang Education Press.
13. Hailin Zheng. 2003. *The ownership of sovereignty over Diaoyutai Islands from the perspective of history and international law.* Taiwan: Straits Academic Press.
14. Jianjun Gao. 2004. *China and the international law of the sea: Commemorating the 10th anniversary of the entry into force of the United Nations Convention on the Law of the Sea.* Beijing: Ocean Press.
15. Jianguo Xiao. 2006. *Joint development of offshore oil & gas across the international maritime boundaries.* Beijing: Ocean Press.
16. Liangfu Zhang. 2006. *Problems of maritime delimitation disputes between China and its neighbors.* Beijing: Ocean Press.
17. Deyuan Ju. 2006. *The rightful names of the Diaoyu Dao.* Beijing: Kunlun Publishing House.
18. Hailin Zheng. 2007. *A study of the history and jurisprudence of the Diaoyu Dao (updated edition).* Beijing: Zhonghua Book.
19. Hailong Ju. 2007. *Theory of geopolitical patterns of Asian sea power.* Beijing: China Social Science Press.
20. Zhiguo Gao, Zhang Haiwen. 2007. *Anthology of research on ocean state policy.* Beijing: Ocean Press.
21. Jinsen Yang. 2007. *A Brief history of the rise and fall of ocean powers.* Beijing: Ocean Press.

Y. Jin, *Ocean Law and Policy of the People's Republic of China*,
https://doi.org/10.1007/978-981-95-3166-0

22. Yongming Jin. 2008. *Study on the path of settlement of the East China Sea Issue*. Beijing: Law Press.
23. Degong Chen. 2009. *Modern international law of the sea*. Beijing: Ocean Press.
24. Wenmu Zhang. *On China's maritime power (second edition)*. 2010. Beijing: Ocean Press.
25. Exiang Wan. 2011. *Studies on the relationship between international law and domestic law*. Beijing: Peking University Press.
26. Hailin Zheng. 2011. *Diaoyutai Islands: A study in history and jurisprudence (updated edition)*. Hong Kong: Ming Pao Press.
27. Xinjun Zhang. 2011. *Legal aspects of the Sino-Japanese Disputes over the East China Sea*. Beijing: Law Press.
28. Shicun Wu. 2013. *The South China Sea dispute: Origin and development (revised edition)*. Beijing: Economic Press China.
29. Tianying Wu. 2013. *Examination of the ownership of the Diaoyu Dao before Sino-Japanese War of 1894 (updated edition)*. Beijing: China Democracy Legal System Publishing.
30. Jinsen Yang . 2014. *A brief history of the rise and fall of ocean powers (second edition)*. Beijing: Ocean Press.
31. Jingguang Li. 2014. *Foreign ocean management and law enforcement mechanism*. Beijing: Ocean Press.
32. Jianjun Gao. 2014. *Dispute settlement system under the United Nations Convention on the Law of the Sea (revised edition)*. Beijing: China University of Political Science and Law Press.
33. Yongming Jin. 2014. *Theoretical study on ocean law of China*. Shanghai: Shanghai Academy of Social Sciences Press.
34. Zhiguo Gao, Bingbing Jia. 2014. *The nine-dash line in the South China Sea: History, status, implications*. Beijing: Ocean Press.
35. Hailin Zheng. 2014. *A study of the history and jurisprudence of the Diaoyu Dao (latest update edition)*. Beijing: Ocean Press.
36. Junmin Wang. 2014. *Focus on the Diaoyu Dao: Sovereign ownership of the Diaoyu Dao and dispute resolution*. Beijing: Party School of the Central Committee of the C.P.C Press.
37. Cuibai Yang. 2015. *Legal study on China's sovereignty over the Nansha Islands*. Beijing: Commercial Press.
38. Yongming Jin. 2015. *Maritime issues review (Volume 1)*. Beijing: Central Compilation & Translation Press.
39. Jiangyong Liu. 2016. *Examination of the ownership of the Diaoyu Dao: Facts and jurisprudence*. Beijing: People's Publishing House.
40. Jianqiang Guan. 2016. *International law study on the historical problems of the Sino-Japanese War*. Beijing: Law Press.
41. Bin Xiu. 2016. *Japan marine strategy research*. Beijing: China Social Science Press.
42. Degui Lian, Jin Yongming. 2016. *Maritime strategy of Japan*. Beijing: Current Affairs Press.
43. Yongming Jin. 2016. *Theoretical study on ocean law of China (2nd Edition)*. Shanghai: Shanghai Academy of Social Sciences Press.
44. Zewei Yang. 2016. *International legal issues on joint development in the sea*. Beijing: Social Sciences Academic Press.
45. Department of Boundary and Ocean Affairs of the Ministry of Foreign Affairs of the People's Republic of China. 2016. *Compilation of documents on China's response to the South China Sea Arbitration*. Beijing: World Affairs Press.
46. Chinese Society of International Law. 2016. *Chinese Yearbook of International Law: Special issue on jurisdictional issues in the South China Sea Arbitration*. Beijing: Law Press.
47. Shicun Wu. 2016. *Selected recent cases on international law of the sea*. Beijing: China Democracy and Legal System Press.
48. Yu Jia, Zhiguo Gao. 2017. *Anthology of research on the ocean policy of China*. Beijing: Ocean Press.
49. Yingben Liu, Liang Feng. 2017. *Research on the theory and practice of a strong maritime country with Chinese characteristics*. Nanjing: Nanjing University Press.
50. Zhipeng He et al. 2017. *The Chinese theory of international law*. Beijing: Law Press.

51. Bo Hu. 2018. *China's sea power in the post Mahan era*. Beijing: Ocean Press.
52. Chinese Society of International Law. 2018. *The South China Sea Arbitration awards: A critical study*. Beijing: Foreign Languages Press.
53. Dahui Huang et al. 2018. *The ins and outs of the Diaoyu Dao dispute*. Beijing: China Democracy and Law Press.
54. Yongming Jin. 2018. *Maritime issues review (Volume 2)*. Beijing: Central Compilation and Translation Press.
55. Yue Chen, Ping Pu. 2018. *Building a community of shared future for mankind (revised edition)*. Beijing: People's University of China Press.
56. Jinping Xi. 2018. *On building a community of shared future for mankind*. Beijing: Central Literature Publishing House.
57. Jinping Xi. 2018. *The Belt and Road Initiative by Xi Jinping*. Beijing: Central Literature Publishing House.
58. Yongming Jin. 2018. *Research on China's ocean power strategy in the new era*. Beijing: Ocean Press.
59. Zhan Zhang et al. 2019. *Study on the thought of building a community of shared future for mankind*. Beijing: Current Affairs Press.
60. [Netherlands] Hugo Grotius. 2005. *The freedom of the seas or the right which belongs to the dutch to take part in the East Indian trade*. trans, Zhongfa Ma; proofread, Naigen Zhang. Shanghai: Shanghai People's Publishing House.
61. [UK] Timothy Hillier. 2005. *Principles of public international law*. trans, Bo Qu. Beijing: People's University of China Press.
62. [Australia] Victor Prescott, Clive Schofield. 2014. *The maritime political boundaries of the world (second edition)*. trans, Jilu Wu, Haiwen Zhang. Beijing: Ocean Press.
63. [U.S.] Louis B. Sohn et al. 2014. *Law of the sea: In a nutshell (second edition)*. trans, Kuen Chen Fu et al. Shanghai: Shanghai Jiao Tong University Press.
64. [UK] Malcolm N. Shaw. 2011. *International law (Sixth Edition)*. trans, Guimei Bai, Jianjun Gao, Lijiang Zhu, Yongsheng Li, Xiaohui Liang. Beijing: Peking University Press.
65. [Fiji] Satya N. Nandan. 2009. *Commentary on the 1982 United Nations Convention on the Law of the Sea*. trans, Yongke Jiao et al. Beijing: Ocean Press.
66. [Fiji] Satya N. Nandan. 2014. Shabtai Rosenne. *Commentary on the 1982 United Nations Convention on the Law of the Sea (Vol.2)*. trans, Wenzheng Lu and Bin Mao. Beijing: Ocean Press.
67. [Fiji] Satya N. Nandan. 2016. *Commentary on the 1982 United Nations Convention on the Law of the Sea (Vol. 3)*. trans, Wenzheng Lu, Bin Mao. Beijing: Ocean Press.
68. [U.S.] Myron H. Nordquist. 2018. *Commentary on the 1982 United Nations Convention on the Law of the Sea (Vol. 4)*. trans, Wenzheng Lu, Bin Mao. Beijing: Ocean Press.

II. Works in Japanese

1. Kisaburo Yokota. 1977. *The international law of the sea (Volume 1)*. Tokyo: Yuhikaku Publishing.
2. Shigeru Oda. 1969. *The international law of the sea (Volume II) (Updated edition)*. Tokyo: Yuhikaku Publishing.
3. Hideo Takabayashi. 1979. *A study of the territorial sea system (second edition)*. Tokyo: Yushindo.
4. Shigeru Oda. 1989. *Inquiring into the origins of the law of the sea*. Tokyo: Yushindo.
5. Yoshihiko Ogawa. 1989. *Theory of the law of treaties*. Tokyo: Toshindo.
6. Takane Sugihara. 1996. *The regime of International Court of Justice*. Tokyo: Yuhikaku Publishing.
7. Kanae Taijudo. 1998. *The international law of territorial ownership*. Tokyo: Toshindo.

8. Kentaro Serita. 1999. *Island possession and delimitation of the exclusive economic zone.* Tokyo: Yushindo.
9. Sōji Yamamoto. 2001. *Law of the sea.* Tokyo: Sanseido.
10. Japanese Association of International Law. 2001. *Land, space, cosmos (100 Years of Japan and International Law) (Vol. 2).* Tokyo: Sanseido.
11. Japanese Association of International Law. 2001. *Oceans (100 Years of Japan and International Law) (Vol. 3).* Tokyo: Sanshodo.
12. Shigeru Oda. 2002. *Commentary on the United Nations Convention on the Law of the Sea (Vol. 1).* Tokyo: Yuhikaku Publishing.
13. Tadao Kuribayashi. 1994. *Commentary on the United Nations Convention on the Law of the Sea (Vol. 2).* Tokyo: Yuhikaku Publishing.
14. Takabayashi Hideo. 1996. *Outcomes and issues of the United Nations Convention on the Law of the Sea.* Tokyo: Toshindo.
15. Shigeki Sakamoto. 2004. *Theory and practice of the law of treaties.* Tokyo: Toshindo.
16. Chiyuki Mizukami. 2005. *The law of the sea unfolds and the presence.* Tokyo: Yushindo.
17. Chiyuki Mizunami. 2006. *Exclusive economic zone.* Tokyo: Yushindo.
18. Yoshiro Matsui. 2006. *Cases of International Law (2nd ed.).* Tokyo: Toshindo.
19. Moritaka Hayashi. 2008. *The formation and issues of the modern law of the sea.* Tokyo: Shinzansha Publishing.
20. Sugihara Takane. 2008. *Lecture notes on international law.* Tokyo: Yuhikaku Publishing.
21. Shinya Murase, Junichi Edo. 2008. *International law on maritime delimitation.* Tokyo: Toshindo.
22. Soji Yamamoto. 2009. *The maritime security rule of law: The intersection of the law of the sea and domestic law.* Tokyo: Sanseido.
23. Dai Tamada. 2012. *On the effectiveness of international judgements.* Tokyo: Yuhikaku Publishing.
24. Yoshiro Matsui. 2014. *International law scholars' commentary on the Senkaku issue: An expansion of dispute settlement.* Tokyo: Japan Review.
25. Shunji Yanai, Shinya Murase. 2015. *The Practice of International Law.* Tokyo: Shinzansha Publishing.
26. Norio Tanaka. 2015. *The modern formation of the international law of the sea.* Tokyo: Toshindo.
27. Shigeki Sakamoto. 2015. *International straits.* Tokyo: Toshindo.
28. Moritaka Hayashi, Yukio Shimada, Mamoru Koga. 2016. *International law of the sea (2nd edition).* Tokyo: Yushindo.
29. Yoshiro Matsui, Hitoshi Tomioka, Shigeki Sakamoto, et al. 2016. *Topics in international law and the law of the sea in the 21st century.* Tokyo: Toshindo.
30. Shigeki Sakamoto. 2018. *Japan's ocean policy and the law of the sea.* Tokyo: Shinzansha Publishing.

III. Publications in English

1. Ian Brownlie. 1998. *Principles of the public international law.* Fifth edition. Oxford: Clarendon Press Oxford.
2. John Collier, Vaughan Lowe. 1999. *The settlement of disputes in international law.* Oxford: Oxford University Press.
3. R. R. Churchill, A. V. Lowe. 1999. *The law of the sea.* Third edition. Manchester: Manchester University Press.
4. Keyuan Zou. 2005. *China's marine legal system and the law of the sea.* Leiden: Martinus Nijhoff Publishers.
5. Keyuan Zou. 2005. *Law of the sea in East Asia.* London: Routledge.
6. D. Freestone, R. Barnes, D. Ong (Editors). 2006. *The law of the sea: Progress and prospect.* Oxford: Oxford University Press.

7. Sir Robert Jennings, Sir Arthur Watts (Editors). 2008. *Oppenheim's international law*. Ninth edition. Oxford: Oxford University Press.
8. Olivier Corten, Pierre Klein (Editors). 2011. *The Vienna Conventions on the Law of Treaties: A commentary*. Volume I. Volume II. Oxford: Oxford University Press.
9. James Kraska. 2011. *Maritime country and the law of the sea: Expeditionary operations in world politics*. Oxford: Oxford University Press.
10. Bardo Fassbender, Anne Peters (Editors). 2012. *The oxford handbook of the history of international law*. Oxford: Oxford University Press.
11. George K. Walker (General Editor). 2012. *Definitions for the law of the sea: Terms not defined by the 1982 Convention*. Leiden: Martinus Nijhoff Publishers.
12. Donald R Rothwell, Alex G Oude Elferink, Karen N Scott, Tim Stephens (Editors). 2015. *The oxford handbook of the law of the sea*. Oxford: Oxford University Press.
13. James C. Hsiung. 2015. *An anatomy of Sino-Japanese disputes and U.S. involvement: History & international law*. Beijing: CN Times Books.
14. Alexander Proelss (Editor). 2017. *United Nations Convention on the Law of the Sea: A Commentary*. Oxford: C. H. Beck. Hart. Nomos.
15. Gordon Houlden, Nong Hong (Editors). 2018. *Maritime order and the law in East Asia*. London: Routledge.

Further Readings

To facilitate readers' further understanding of the theory of the law of the sea and ocean issues. the authors' papers on related subjects are listed together for reference and information.

1. On the Regime of Innocent Passage in the Territorial Sea. 2016. *Chinese Review of International Law* 2. On the Regime of Innocent Passage in the Territorial Sea. 2016. *China Social Science Excellence: International Law* 8.
2. On the exclusive economic zone and the continental shelf system. 2008. *Journal of Social Sciences* 3.
3. The problem of military activities in the exclusive economic zone and state practice. 2008. *Law Science* 3.
4. Study on countermeasures to the problem of military activities in the exclusive economic zone. 2011. *Chinese Review of International Law* 4.
5. A dissection of disputes between China and the United States over military activities in exclusive economic zone by the law of the sea. 2011. *Pacific Journal* 11. A dissection of disputes between China and the United States over military activities in exclusive economic zone by the law of the sea. 2012. *Kagawa Law Journal* 32 (1).
6. Analysis of the legal elements of islands and rocks. 2010. *Political Science and Law* 12. Analysis of the legal elements of islands and rocks. 2011. *China Social Science Excellence: International Law* 3.
7. A study of juristic property of the wealth as common heritage of humankind. 2005. *Journal of Social Sciences* 3.
8. System of developing resources in international deep sea-bed. 2006. *Journal of Social Sciences* 3. System of developing resources in international deep sea-bed. 2006. *China Social Science Excellence: Introduction to the World Economy* 5.
9. Evaluation of the international seabed regime. 2007. *Chinese Yearbook of International Law (2005)*, Beijing: World Knowledge Publishing House.
10. Legal status of the international seabed area and the resource exploitation regime (1). 2004. *Hiroshima Law Journal* 28(2).
11. The legal status of the international seabed area and the resource exploitation regime (2). 2006. *Hiroshima Law Journal* 29(4).

12. A comparative study on the International Tribunal for the Law of the Sea and the International Court of Justice. 2005. *China Oceans Law Review* 1. A comparative study on the International Tribunal for the Law of the Sea and the International Court of Justice. 2004. *International and Comparative Law Review* 13, 2004.
13. A study of the organizational characteristics of the United Nations Convention on the Law of the Sea. 2011. *Oriental Law* 1.
14. On development and challenges of the law of the sea. 2015. *Southeast Asian Affairs* 3. On development and challenges of the law of the sea. 2016. *Proceedings of the Institute for World Studies of Kyoto Sangyo University* 31, Kyoto: Kyoto Sangyo University.
15. Issues relating to the conservation and sustainable use of marine biological diversity beyond areas of national jurisdiction. 2018. *Journal of Social Science* 9. Issues relating to the conservation and sustainable use of marine biological diversity beyond areas of national jurisdiction. 2019. *China Social Science Excellence: International Law* 2.
16. Delimitation dispute and development of continental shelf in East Sea. 2006. *Political Science and Law* 1.
17. On the East Sea Issue and Joint Development. 2007. *Journal of Social Science* 6. On the East Sea Issue and Joint Development. 2007. *China Social Science Excellence: International Law* 10.
18. On the East China Sea resource problems and solutions. 2008. *Hiroshima Law Journal* 31(3).
19. The latest tendency of Japanese ocean legislations and their implications on China. 2007. *Law Science* 5.
20. The connotation of the consensus of principles and development trend of the East China Sea issue between China and Japan. 2009. *Oriental Law* 2.
21. New development of Japanese ocean laws and policies. 2009. *Oriental Law* 6. New development of Japanese ocean laws and policies. 2010. *China Social Science Excellence: International Law* 5.
22. From international law to examine the illegality of Japan's arrest of Chinese fishing vessels and fishermen. 2010. *Oriental Law* 5.
23. On the nature of the issue of the East China Sea and its solution. 2010. *Pacific Journal* 11.
24. Criticism of the wrongfulness of Japan's basic opinion on the territorial rights of the Diaoyu Dao and other islands. 2011. *Journal of Yunan University (Law Edition)* 2. Criticism of the wrongfulness of Japan's basic opinion on the territorial rights of the Diaoyu Dao and other islands. 2011. *China Social Science Excellence: International Law* 7.
25. Re-refuting the error of Japan's basic opinion on the territorial rights of the Diaoyu Dao and other islands. 2012. *Oriental Law* 5.
26. Key causes of Japan's 'nationalisation' of the Diaoyu Dao: An overview of maritime strategy and the maritime legal system. 2012. *Oriental Law* 6.
27. Reasons for Japan's "nationalisation" of the Diaoyu Dao and China's Response. 2012. *Pacific Journal* 12.
28. A refutation to the mistakes in arguments of "three truths" on Diaoyu Islands proposed by Japan. 2013. *Pacific Journal* 7.
29. On wrongfulness of evidences in Senkaku Islands flyer issued by Japan. 2014. *Pacific Journal* 4. On wrongfulness of evidences in Senkaku Islands flyer issued by Japan. 2015. *China Social Science Excellence: International Law* 5.
30. Analysis on the policy of Japan's active pacifism. 2015. *International Review* 2.
31. An international law analysis of China's sovereignty over the Diaoyu Islands. 2013. *China Legal Science (English Edition)* 2. An international law analysis of China's sovereignty over the Diaoyu Islands. 2013. *Contemporary Law Review* 5.
32. A study of some questions on international law concerning the sovereignty of Diaoyu Islands. 2014. *China's Borderland History and Geography Studies* 2.
33. Analysis of China's maintenance of rights and interests in the East China Sea according to international law. 2016. *Journal of Shanghai University (Social Sciences Edition)* 4.
34. The origin and development of the China-Japan High-Level Consultation Mechanism on Maritime Affairs. 2018. *East Asia Outlook* 6.

35. A study on the mechanism for maritime and air security in the East China Sea in the new era. 2020. *Journal of Ocean University of China (Social Science)* 1.
36. On the special characteristics of the South China Sea issue and the law of the sea regime. 2011. *Oriental Law* 4. On the special characteristics of the South China Sea issue and the law of the sea regime. 2012. *China Social Science Excellence: International Law* 1.
37. On the legal disputes and steps to resolve the South China Sea issue. 2012. *Journal of Yunnan University (Law Edition)* 1.
38. On the goal orientation of resource development in the South China Sea: Functionality and normativity. 2013. *Journal of Hainan University (Humanities & Social Sciences)* 4.
39. Empirical researches on non-application of legal means to territorial disputes over Nansha Islands and Reefs. 2012. *Pacific Journal* 4. Empirical researches on non-application of legal means to territorial disputes over Nansha Islands and Reefs. 2012. *China Social Science Excellence: International Law* 9.
40. On limitation of setting dispute over South China Sea by the law of the sea. 2013. International Review 4.
41. Nature of the Dashed Line and Legal Status of Internal Water Areas in South China Sea. 2012. *China Legal Science* 6.
42. South China Sea: Politics and the innovation of the international law system. 2014. *Contemporary Law Journal* 3.
43. Maritime Silk Road and issues over South China Sea. 2015. *Journal of South China Sea Studies* 4. Maritime Silk Road and issues over South China Sea. 2016. *China Forum Quarterly (Spring)* March.
44. Possible influence of the US Warship's entry into the territorial sea of the Nansha Islands and Reefs and the countermeasures. 2015. *Journal of Hainan University (Humanities and Social Sciences)* 4.
45. The impact and influence of the South China Sea Arbitration on the law of the sea. 2017. *Political Science and Law* 7. The impact and influence of the South China Sea Arbitration on the law of the sea. 2017. *China Social Science Excellence: International Law* 9. The impact and influence of the South China Sea Arbitration on the law of the sea. 2017. *China Legal Science (English Edition)* 4. The impact and influence of the South China Sea Arbitration on the law of the sea. 2018–2019. *Waseda Law Journal* 94(1)-(2).
46. Law of the sea analysis of freedom and security of navigation in the South China Sea. 2019. *Chinese Yearbook of International Law (2018)*, Beijing: Law Press.
47. Analysis and prospect of the U.S. South China Sea policy. 2021. *People's Daily: Frontiers* 3, 2021.
48. On China's ocean policy and legal system. 2007. *Hiroshima Law Journal* 30(4).
49. The success and contribution of New China in the area of ocean law and policy. 2009. *Studies on Mao Zedong and Deng Xiaoping Theories* 12.
50. Study on China's maritime security problems and the improvement of the maritime legal system. 2010. *Kagawa Law Journal* 29(3–4).
51. Study on the current status of China's ocean issues and countermeasures. 2011. *Hiroshima Law Journal* 34(4).
52. Some opinions on China's formulation of the basic law of the sea. 2011. *Exploration and Free Views* 10.
53. Study on the strategy of the ocean security of China. 2012. Global Review 4. Study on the strategy of the ocean security of China. *China Social Science Excellence: China's Foreign Affairs* 10.
54. Some opinions on the formulation of China's ocean development strategy. 2012. *International Monitor* 4.
55. Path to a maritime power for China and the guarantee in system. 2013. *Studies on Mao Zedong and Deng Xiaoping Theories* 2.
56. On the content of China's strategy of maritime power and its legal system. *Southeast Asian Affairs* 1, 2014. On the content of China's strategy of maritime power and its legal system. 2015. *China Legal Science (English Edition)* 1. On the content of China's strategy of maritime

power and its legal system. 2015. *Proceedings of the Institute for World Studies of Kyoto Sangyo University* 30, Kyoto: Kyoto Sangyo University.

57. Cultural dimension in China's ocean policy. 2016. *Asia-Pacific Security and Maritime Affairs* 5. Cultural dimension in China's ocean policy. 2016. *China Forum Quarterly(Autumn)* October. Cultural dimension in China's ocean policy. 2017. *Hiroshima Law Journal* 40(3).
58. The essentials of the BRI and Shanghai. 2017. *China Forum Quarterly(Autumn)* October.
59. On diplomatic innovation and discourse power in building an ocean power. 2018. *Studies on Mao Zedong and Deng Xiaoping Theories* 2, 2018. On diplomatic innovation and discourse power in building an ocean power. 2018. China Forum Quarterly*(Autumn)* October. On diplomatic innovation and discourse power in building an ocean power. 2018. *Hiroshima Law Journal* 42(2).
60. Modern system of the law of the sea and China's practice. 2018. *Chinese Review of International Law* 6. Modern system of the law of the sea and China's practice. 2018. *China Legal Science (English Edition)* 6.
61. The success and contribution of new China in the area of ocean law and policy. 2019. *East Asian Outlook* 3.
62. China's strategic governance system of building a marine power in a new era. 2019. *Journal of Ocean University of China (Social Sciences)* 5.
63. On the system of the law of the sea in China and some relevant issues. 2020. *Journal of Ocean University of China (Social Sciences)* 5.
64. On the theoretical regime of the maritime community with a shared future. 2021. *Journal of Ocean University of China (Social Sciences)* 1.
65. On the implementation, impact and countermeasures/improvement of China's maritime police law. 2021. *Hiroshima Law Journal* 45(2). On the implementation, impact and countermeasures/improvement of China's maritime police law. 2021. *People's Daily: Frontiers* 22.

MIX
Papier aus verantwortungsvollen Quellen
Paper from responsible sources
FSC® C105338

If you have any concerns about our products,
you can contact us on
ProductSafety@springernature.com

In case Publisher is established outside the EU,
the EU authorized representative is:
Springer Nature Customer Service Center GmbH
Europaplatz 3, 69115 Heidelberg, Germany

Printed by Libri Plureos GmbH
in Hamburg, Germany